A CONCISE HISTORY OF JAMAICA

Kenneth Morgan's history of Jamaica is a social, economic, political and cultural assessment of the island's most important periods and themes over the past millennium. This includes the island's development before 1500, with detailed material on the Taino society; the two centuries of slavery and its aftermath between 1660 and 1860; the continuance of colonialism between 1860 and 1945; the background to Jamaican independence between 1945 and 1960; and the evolution of Jamaica as an independent nation since the early 1960s. Throughout, Morgan discusses important themes such as race, slavery, empire, poverty and colonialism, and the unbalanced social structure that existed for much of Jamaica's history – the small, overwhelmingly white elite overseeing and controlling the lives of black and brown people beneath them on the social scale. Ending with an assessment of the contemporary period, this work offers an authoritative, up-to-date history of Jamaica.

Kenneth Morgan is Professor of History at Brunel University London. An economic and social historian of the Atlantic world between 1650 and 1850, he is a fellow of the Royal Historical Society.

CAMBRIDGE CONCISE HISTORIES

Cambridge Concise Histories offer general introductions to a wide range of subjects. A series of authoritative overviews written by expert authors, these books make the histories of countries, events and topics accessible to both students and general readers.

A full list of titles in the series can be found at:
www.cambridge.org/concisehistories

A CONCISE
HISTORY OF
JAMAICA

KENNETH MORGAN
Brunel University London

CAMBRIDGE
UNIVERSITY PRESS

Shaftesbury Road, Cambridge CB2 8EA, United Kingdom

One Liberty Plaza, 20th Floor, New York, NY 10006, USA

477 Williamstown Road, Port Melbourne, VIC 3207, Australia

314–321, 3rd Floor, Plot 3, Splendor Forum, Jasola District Centre,
New Delhi – 110025, India

103 Penang Road, #05–06/07, Visioncrest Commercial, Singapore 238467

Cambridge University Press is part of Cambridge University Press & Assessment,
a department of the University of Cambridge.

We share the University's mission to contribute to society through the pursuit of
education, learning and research at the highest international levels of excellence.

www.cambridge.org
Information on this title: www.cambridge.org/9781108472258

DOI: 10.1017/9781108633765

First published 2024

Printed in the United Kingdom by TJ Books Limited, Padstow Cornwall

A catalogue record for this publication is available from the British Library.

*A Cataloging-in-Publication data record for this book is available from the Library of
Congress.*

ISBN 978-1-108-47225-8 Hardback
ISBN 978-1-108-45918-1 Paperback

*To the memory of my parents – Kenneth Albert Morgan
and Clare Frances Morgan*

CONTENTS

FIGURES

ACKNOWLEDGEMENTS

This book would have been impossible to write without the many fine publications by historians, archaeologists and sociologists of Jamaica, some of whose work is listed in the bibliography. I have also benefited from visiting Jamaica on several occasions for research and conference trips and from teaching Caribbean history for several decades to successive cohorts of students at the now-defunct West London Institute of Higher Education and Brunel University London. I would like to thank the libraries and archives noted in the references to quotations cited in the book for their willingness to let me cite from manuscripts in their possession. Most of the reading was done by using the resources of the British Library, the British Museum, Cambridge University Library, University College London Library, the Institute of Archaeology Library, University of London, and the library of Brunel University London. I am grateful for the suggestions for improvements on a draft version of the text by two anonymous referees for Cambridge University Press and to my editor at the press and her assistant, Cecilia Cancellaro and Victoria Phillips, for their expert assistance. Thanks are also due to Getty Images for permission to reproduce the images. The maps were based on material first presented in David Watts, *The West Indies: Patterns of Development, Culture and Environmental Change since 1492* (Cambridge University

Press, 1987) and Mary Turner, *Slaves and Missionaries: The Disintegration of Jamaican Slave Society, 1787–1834* (University of Illinois Press, 1982). My wife and family have offered their customary warm support during the composition of this book.

Introduction

∾

A Concise History of Jamaica attempts to provide a comprehensive overview of the most populous English-speaking nation in the Caribbean, an island that has experienced tumultuous changes from the days of its first inhabitants, the Tainos, up to its present position as an independent nation. By combining political, economic, social and cultural history, this book aims to encompass the main developments in the historical trajectory of Jamaica. This is not an easy task to accomplish in a fair and balanced way because of the sheer amount of racial prejudice and social deprivation combined with highly unequal power structures that have characterised the island's modern history. Many issues connected with Jamaica's past are contentious and rightly so, and this book will not shirk discussion of the difficult issues. As an Englishman who has visited Jamaica for research purposes on numerous occasions and who has experienced daily life in Jamaica as an outsider, my interpretation of Jamaica's historical evolution will undoubtedly have different emphases from approaches that might be taken by an insider, so to speak, but I hope that the book will offer judicious assessments that are not dominated by my British background.

Following the format of other volumes in this series, the chapters are organised to cover different chronological periods in sequence over time, but each chapter includes evaluation and analysis as well as narrative sections. The historical periods covered by the first two chapters discuss two discrete eras in Jamaica's history – the long centuries of Taino settlement before Columbus's discovery of the New World and the Spanish settlement of Jamaica that followed. Deciding where to draw the chronological lines for most of the remaining chapters, however, has been a personal choice based on careful consideration about what works well as a coherent period for investigation. The slavery era in Jamaica is the focus of the third and fourth chapters, with the dividing line between them situated in the American revolutionary era. The fourth chapter is extended beyond slave emancipation in the 1830s in order to assess the immediate aftermath of freedom for black Jamaicans. The British imposition of Crown Colony government in 1866, a major turning point in Jamaica's history, is taken as the starting point for Chapter 5, which continues through to the major changes emerging in Jamaica with a labour rebellion in the late 1930s followed by an extended franchise and the birth of modern political parties by the end of the Second World War. Chapter 6 offers a substantive discussion of modern Jamaica from 1945 until the present, a period that juxtaposes positive and negative developments.

Two main groups settled in Jamaica during the medieval centuries – the Ostionoid communities that lived there before c. AD 900 and the Meillacans who followed them from c. AD 900 to AD 1500. The earliest date for pre-colonial settlement in Jamaica is around AD 650. Chapter 1 examines the Taino culture that appeared in Jamaica sometime between the late ninth century and AD

1200: the exact date of the Taino's arrival in Jamaica is yet to be determined. Many facets of the Taino communities remain mysterious and not a single Taino chief's name has been handed down to posterity. They originally came from Hispaniola via South America, but why they migrated in such numbers over a large distance is unknown. They had an oral culture and the surviving ethnographic evidence about their presence in Jamaica is limited and fragmentary. Nevertheless, Chapter 1 shows that the Taino created a distinctive society in Jamaica, with communities organised under the leadership of a *cacique* (chief) based on hereditary descent. The Taino believed in various gods and spirits and participated in trance-like ceremonies that involved taking a hallucinogenic substance. Skilled at working in stone and wood and sustaining themselves with planted root crops and fishing, there were nearly 100 Taino communities in Jamaica by the era of Columbus. The rock art, pottery, wooden carvings and burial sites associated with the Taino are the focus of continuing archaeological research and excavation, which in the future will augment our limited knowledge of Taino settlement in Jamaica.

The Spanish era in Jamaica is the subject of Chapter 2. Christopher Columbus visited the island twice but it was not until three years after his death, in 1509, that Spain decided to establish a settlement in Jamaica. For the next century and a half, Jamaica was a minor Spanish possession in the New World. Spanish place names appeared on maps of Jamaica, the Roman Catholic Church was established on the island and Spanish governors and institutions ruled the colony. The Tainos were decimated by the Spanish occupation, but only limited numbers of settlers of Iberian descent came to Jamaica to replace them as labourers and colonists: far greater numbers of Spanish subjects migrated to Cuba, Hispaniola and the Spanish Main – the collective term for parts of the Spanish Empire in mainland America. Throughout the Spanish period in Jamaica, the population appears never to have exceeded between 1,500 and 2,000 people. Crop cultivation, the absorption of Taino techniques for food preparation and livestock imported from other Spanish Caribbean territories met internal consumption demands, but only a limited external trade was conducted. The Spanish authorities never changed the route of the treasure fleets to include a call at Jamaica and so Spanish shipping and trade in the West Indies remained tied to connections between the Spanish Main and either Hispaniola or Cuba. Many raids were made on Spanish Jamaica in the first half of the seventeenth century. Though many of these attacks had a limited impact, Oliver Cromwell's Western Design – a large military expedition – led to the successful English conquest of the island in 1655 and ended the Spanish era in Jamaica.

After conquering Jamaica, England moved swiftly to establish a permanent presence on the island. English institutions, the English legal system and governors appointed from London all emerged quickly and settlers flocked to Jamaica, intending to make far greater use of the island's potential economic resources than the Spanish had ever attempted. Chapter 3 focuses on this consolidation of English colonisation in Jamaica between the initial conquest under Cromwell and the American War of Independence. Between 1700 and 1775 Jamaica eclipsed Barbados as the most lucrative English possession in the

Caribbean. The economy of Jamaica was strongly based on the rise of sugar plantations based on imported slave labour from Africa, though Jamaica was a large enough island to develop a broader economy based on livestock rearing, internal markets and the marketing of slaves and produce to Spanish America.

Chapter 3 discusses the main facets of slavery and explains the treatment of Africans by transplanted white British people. Most slaves were imported Africans rather than native-born people because of the high rate of mortality associated with the sugar plantations. Planters preferred to import rather than breed slaves. The work regime on plantations witnessed the introduction of the gang system based on a yearly seasonal round of crop production. Slave resistance is discussed along with the significance of Maroon, or rebel, communities in Jamaica. A white elite held all positions of political and legal power even though it was by far a minority in demographic terms. White planters, merchants, plantation managers and attorneys all wanted to benefit substantially economically from living in Jamaica, with the most successful wanting to retire with their fortunes to Britain. Loyalty to the crown was a hallmark of Jamaica in the era of American independence, as whites on the island were far outnumbered by slaves, whom they feared, and the economic significance of Jamaica was such that it was unthinkable to sacrifice its presence in the British Empire.

Many elements of Jamaican life already in place before the American War of Independence continued thereafter, including the importance of sugar, slavery and British dominance of the island's affairs. But, as Chapter 4 shows, significant changes affected Jamaica in the period from the peace treaty of 1783 to the implementation of Crown Colony government in 1866. Planters, who were frequently absentee owners, faced pressure from humanitarian anti-slave trade campaigners from 1788 onwards, when parliament first discussed at length the operation of the slave trade. The eventual success of abolitionists led to the British abolition of the slave trade in 1807 and then to further troubles for the plantocracy and their associates in the years leading up to slave emancipation in 1834. Amelioration measures improved the state of the slaves in Jamaica to some extent and planters were forced to take more care over the medical care of their labourers. Gradual emancipation was the dominant ideology among abolitionists in the 1820s and early 1830s, but a swing towards immediate emancipation emerged swiftly around the time of the last major Jamaican slave revolt in 1831–2.

Slave emancipation was enacted by the British parliament in 1834. As Chapter 4 shows, this important legislation overwhelmingly favoured the white planter class and elite. Slaveholders received £20 million compensation from the British parliament for the loss of slave labour through emancipation; nothing was offered to the ex-slaves. After a short period of apprenticeship, between 1834 and 1838, during which Jamaican blacks were still tied to the plantations where they resided and compelled to work for their former owners largely without wages, a quarter century of full freedom brought gains for blacks in terms of greater autonomy over their own lives and the ability to earn wages and to cultivate their own land. Social improvements for black Jamaicans and full political rights, however, were not achieved and most Jamaicans were excluded from the franchise. The Morant Bay rebellion of 1865 saw the grievances of black Jamaicans surface in demonstrations and violence. The British government responded to this revolt by quelling the outbreak through brutal force and by implementing Crown Colony government in 1866, which eliminated the role of the Assembly in Jamaican political life.

Chapter 5 concentrates on Jamaica's development during the long period of Crown Colony government that dominated the period from 1866 to 1945. Direct rule by the British governor, supported by a Legislative Council from the mid-1880s, was characterised by a benevolent paternalism that presided over administrative and political arrangements intended to preserve social and political power for the white minority. Many ordinary Jamaicans were excluded from the electorate and it was not until the efforts of religious revivalists such as Alexander Bedward and activists such as Marcus Garvey that black Jamaicans found political messages that resonated with them. Unfortunately, Bedward's career was ended by his eccentric fanaticism and Garvey's chaotic movements undermined his calls for unity among black Jamaicans. The rise of Rastafarianism offered an alternative implicit rejection of the status quo but it never became a galvanising political force. Positive developments occurred for Jamaicans between 1866 and 1945, including improvements to public health and elementary educational provision, land reform for the peasantry, the emergence of middle-class professional occupations among brown Jamaicans and the growth of the banana industry to boost export incomes. Equally, however, there were downsides as well, especially the persistence of extensive poverty, unemployment, poor housing, congestion in the largest city, Kingston, and continuing white colonial dominance. The major labour demonstrations in 1938 brought to the surface the inequalities experienced by most Jamaicans.

The history of Jamaica since 1945, covered in Chapter 6, has witnessed major and fairly rapid changes. Crown Colony government was succeeded in 1944 by a bicameral legislature and the rapid growth of two major political parties, the People's National Party (PNP) and the Jamaica Labour Party (JLP), and by a brief period of four years (1958–62) where Jamaica participated in a West Indian Federation. As part of the process of decolonisation, Jamaica was granted independence in 1962 after which it was governed by alternating prime ministers of the two major political parties. No third political party has ever made headway in Jamaica. Since 1945 the Jamaican economy has diversified considerably, notably in the rise of the tourism sector and the rise of bauxite exports, but there are still many ways in which poverty and poor health prospects for many Jamaicans have not been overcome. Jamaica has flourished in the modern world as a centre of excellence for sport, notably athletics and cricket, as a contributor to different styles of popular music, from ska to reggae, and as a creator of artistic achievements in painting, literature and the plastic arts. However, contemporary Jamaica has experienced a considerable underside of social life in terms of drug cartels, gang violence, political corruption and economic woes, and it is difficult to project whether, in the early 2020s, these problems will be eradicated or whether they will continue as a major blot on Jamaican life.

As these statements suggest, it is not feasible to interpret Jamaica's historical trajectory as one of Whiggish progress. The optimism and positive demeanour of many Jamaicans today, the welcome they extend to visitors and the efforts of the Jamaican government to improve social and economic conditions for their people are underpinned by a legacy of racial divisions, social inequalities, urban deprivation and health problems that are a continuing challenge to the island's politicians and people. Some of these difficulties can be traced to historical problems; others are self-inflicted. The history of Jamaica is very much an uneasy mixture of positive and negative developments that continually interact without clear signs that the difficulties are likely to be overcome. This book tries to evaluate these different facets of Jamaica's history, and my hope is that it will serve multiple readerships, from the educated public to specialists in Jamaican, Caribbean and Atlantic history, and to students at all levels.

I

The Taino

~

The first inhabitants of most of the Greater Antilles, including Jamaica, Cuba, Puerto Rico and Hispaniola, were an Amerindian group known as the Taino. Any overview of Jamaica's history must necessarily begin with an assessment of these people, examining their culture, communities and impact on human settlement. This is not easy to achieve because the history of the Jamaican Tainos is only partially known to historians and archaeologists owing to limited surviving ethnographic evidence and other absences in the historical and archaeological record. Thus, the Tainos left no written documents, and many sites that would yield information about Jamaica's human habitation before the arrival of Columbus have been destroyed by modern property and infrastructural development. Archaeological information and the testimony of Spanish visitors and conquerors are less plentiful for Jamaica than for Cuba, Puerto Rico and Hispaniola. Poor genetic data (DNA) preservation in Jamaica is one consequence of a patchy archaeological record. This is complicated by the fact that modern Caribbean genomes mainly comprise evidence of European and African lines of descent rather than indigenous Caribbean ancestry.

Given the large gaps in the documentary and archaeological record, and in the biological proof relating to ancestry, it is tempting to infer Taino cultural patterns in Jamaica from evidence relating to other Caribbean islands. Some historians have followed this approach to provide flesh on the bones of what is definitely known about the Jamaican Taino. There is some justification for this viewpoint because the Jamaican Tainos shared characteristics with their counterparts in Hispaniola. Thus early maps of Jamaica by both Tomaso Porcacchi Castilione (1576) and Gerard Mercator (1606) contained inscriptions suggesting that the Taino in Jamaica had the same laws, customs and religion as the people of Cuba and Hispaniola. However, modern archaeological research has increasingly emphasised the variety within Taino cultures in the Greater Antilles. This is why Irving Rouse, an acknowledged expert on this subject, divided the Tainos into three main groups: the Eastern Taino, from the Virgin Islands to Montserrat; the Classic Taino from Puerto Rico and the Dominican Republic; and the Western Taino or sub-Taino from Jamaica, the Bahamas and most of Cuba. Each of these subdivisions had distinct characteristics as well as significant differences.

The Taino era was characterised by its self-contained nature. It is unusual in the history of Jamaica in being the one major phase of the island's history where external forces had a limited impact on internal activities. Some broad themes in the history of the Taino remain unclear. No information survives to show that the Tainos, once settled in Jamaica, had the impetus to migrate elsewhere in the Caribbean. Nor is there any evidence that the Jamaican Tainos were subject to threats or raids from outsiders. Evidence is fairly slim on connections between the Tainos of Jamaica, Cuba and Hispaniola. The broad contours of Taino life in Jamaica are sufficiently known, however, to facilitate an informed analysis even though precise chronological information is unavailable. What follows in this chapter, therefore, is a description and analysis of an insular, distinctive society in Jamaica in the pre-Columbian era.

The peopling of Jamaica began much later than in other parts of the world such as the British Isles, continental Europe, the eastern Mediterranean Basin, Africa and Australia: there is no evidence that people from the Palaeolithic, Mesolithic or Neolithic periods ever lived in Jamaica. Moreover, for 6,000 years after other parts of the Caribbean were populated by Archaic Age people, Jamaica remained uninhabited. Exactly why Jamaica was neglected as a destination for human migrants when other Caribbean islands received flows of people many centuries earlier is unknown. Thus human habitation began on Cuba and Hispaniola centuries before people lived in Jamaica. People living on those islands must have known about the existence of Jamaica, but, for whatever reasons, they chose not to settle there.

Whether there was significant communication or trade across the Caribbean Sea between Cuba, Hispaniola and Jamaica before the Taino era is unknown, but the Tainos were adept at using canoes hollowed out from tree trunks to move from one place to another. They also had larger vessels called *piraguas*, capable of holding fifty people for longer voyages. They had sufficient seafaring skills to sail in these vessels to different locations in the Greater Antilles. Those capabilities were probably picked up on South American coasts, but there is no definitive account of how the Taino came to Jamaica. One theory is that they originated in the Amazon Basin, moved to the Orinoco valley and then migrated to Guyana, Venezuela, the Lesser Antilles and eventually Jamaica and other islands in the Greater Antilles. Another hypothesis is that the Taino originated in the Andes and diffused partly into Central America and partly into the West Indies. But whether or not the Taino had South American origins, it seems that they may have come to Jamaica from Hispaniola whence they had migrated from Belize and the Yucatan peninsula before 2000 BC.

The pre-Columbian inhabitants, or Native Americans, of Jamaica used to be known as Arawaks; indeed, that designation was common in museum displays and publications until the 1970s. Few studies now refer to Arawaks in Jamaica: the preferred naming has changed to Taino. This is because it is now recognised that the Arawaks and Tainos are distinct ethnic groups, though their languages had some commonalities. The word Taino means 'men of the good' or 'noble'. Its origins are obscure. One suggestion is that the Taino used it to distinguish themselves in the eyes of the Spanish from the Caribs of the Lesser Antilles. An alternative view is that the Taino used this word to differentiate themselves from the Spanish. Whatever the case, the word 'Taino' was never used as an ethnic label by the natives of Jamaica or the Europeans who arrived there even though nowadays, as already mentioned, the Taino are regarded as a particular ethnic group.

Jamaica itself was named after the Taino word *Xaymaca*. The *ca* suffix of the island's name indicated that it was a place where the Jamai (or Yamaye) people lived. The Taino name for the island has always been retained. The

Taino named places in Jamaica, but few are known and hardly any have survived. Liguanea, which refers to the extensive plain that includes Kingston, was originally a Taino place name, deriving from the iguana which was once common in Jamaica. *Guanaboa* (meaning the fruit soursop) is another place name that survives from the Taino era. Other Taino place names still in existence when Columbus visited Jamaica in 1503–4 have now disappeared. These include the villages of Aguacadiba and Ameyro. Port Royal was called *Caguay* or *Caguaya* by the Taino. In 1774, Edward Long argued that the name was 'a corruption probably of caragua, the Indian name for the coratoe, or great aloe' found abundantly in the vicinity.

The earliest archaeological evidence for human habitation in Jamaica dates from the first half of the seventh century AD. Jamaica's first colonisers were Ostionoid people, from whom the Taino are descended. Alligator Pond in Manchester parish and Little River in St Ann parish are among the earliest sites of this culture. Ostionoid communities in Jamaica, clustered around the coast, appear to have been fairly short-lived. Around AD 900 a second wave of colonisers reached Jamaica. These were the Meillacans, whose occupation of Jamaica was of far longer duration: they were the main people living in Jamaica at the time of first contact with Europeans in the 1490s. Both the Ostionoids and the Meillacans had origins in the northeast part of South America. The migration of these people extended throughout the Greater Antilles, with a particular focus on settlement in Hispaniola.

It is likely that the Taino presence in Jamaica was originally an outgrowth of the Taino settlement on Hispaniola. Certainly, there is evidence that the

Jamaican Tainos believed their origins lay in caves in a sacred mountain in Hispaniola. The causes of the migration are unknown, but it would seem to have been propelled either by difficult circumstances in the places of the migrants' origins – overpopulation, for instance, or belligerent neighbours – or by the willingness of hunter-gatherers to paddle in canoes across the Caribbean in search of new homes. It is plausible that the migration was partly related to raids by the Caribs on existing Taino settlements.

The Taino settled in different parts of Jamaica from about AD 1200. Over twenty-three Taino settlements have been discovered in Trelawny parish in the northwest of the island. Most of these are located in the area of the Martha Brae River basin, which provided ready access to fresh water. These sites include Taino settlements in Holland Hill, Braco, Rio Bueno, Pantrepant East and New Forest. The archaeological remains of these sites include ceramics, stone artefacts, burial sites and remains from a built environment; they include more than 1,000 artefacts from the Rio Bueno site.

The Tainos had various sites in the Kingston area, notably at Bellevue, Long Mountain, Hope Tavern, Jacks Hill and Chancery Hall. These are mainly situated in hilly areas: the Tainos preferred to settle on hill tops, where they could dig postholes to support their huts. No evidence survives of Taino settlement on the fertile flat lands of Liguanea Plain. Other Taino sites were situated close to beaches and the sea in St James, St Mary and St Ann parishes. Recent archaeological investigations, in 2014–15, have concentrated on the Taino hilltop settlement of Maima, near Nueva Sevilla, St Ann's Bay, which appears to have been settled in a period designated White Marl after the type of ceramics produced (AD 950–1545). Houses here were constructed on terraces or platforms.

Much evidence about the location of Taino settlements has disappeared owing to modern building development, but continuing investigations, using Geographic Information System technologies to map and analyse data, and Global Positioning System imagery and digital maps, drawn from a satellite navigation system, to undertake ground site reconnaissance, will yield new information. Our knowledge of these sites will therefore increase in the future. However, no known skeletal remains of the Taino have been uncovered in Jamaica to permit studies of dental and skeletal morphology and DNA attributes. Detailed consideration of the Taino population is also lacking from scholarly literature. It is therefore difficult to estimate the size of the Taino population in Jamaica: it may have been as low as 20,000 but probably never exceeded 60,000. It is interesting to note, however, that Columbus, visiting Jamaica in the first decade of the sixteenth century, described the coast to be full of towns and noted that both coastal and inland regions were very populous.

Knowledge of the Taino language is limited: it will never be reconstructed on a significant scale. The Tainos did not write other than on the proto-writing of inscriptions on stone petroglyphs, which are discussed later in the chapter in the section titled Rock Art. The Taino language became extinct within a century after the Spanish came to Jamaica at the very end of the fifteenth century. Only around 200 words or phrases in the Taino language are known to exist; these are taken from Spanish and Italian sources of the fifteenth and sixteenth centuries. Some Taino words were translated into Spanish and other languages after European colonisers reached the Caribbean in the sixteenth century. They include *huracan* (hurricane), *barbakoa* (barbecue), *kanowa* (canoe), *batata* (potato) and *hamaka* (hammock – originally a fish net in the Taino language). Linguists still debate whether the Taino language was a creole language or Arawakan dialect or, alternatively, an original language. It is thought that ciboney was a dialect of the Taino language spoken in Jamaica and also in Cuba.

Jamaica's Geography

The Taino settled in the third largest island in the Caribbean (after Cuba and Hispaniola). Jamaica is 146 miles long and between twenty-one and fifty-two miles wide; it covers an area of 4,213 square miles. Situated geologically on the Caribbean Plate, stretching across the Caribbean Sea from the Central American mainland to the north of Hispaniola and to the eastern West Indian islands, Jamaica is part of the archipelago of the Greater Antilles in the northern Caribbean Sea, which also includes Cuba, Hispaniola and Puerto Rico. The whole of the Greater Antilles comprises nearly 90 per cent of the total land area of the Caribbean. Jamaica's location in the western Caribbean is 100 miles west of Haiti, 90 miles south of Cuba and 390 miles from the nearest part of the Central American mainland. There are no small offshore islands near Jamaica, but a cluster of cays lies to its southeast and southwest. Some of these uninhabited cays are sand and shingle formations, while others have mangrove covering.

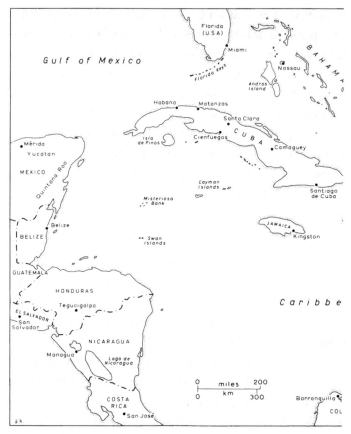

FIGURE I.I The West Indies: A locational map. Retrieved from David
Watts, *The West Indies: Patterns of Development, Culture and
Environmental Change since 1492*, 1987

Limestone and sedimentary and metamorphic rock
types abound in Jamaica, but there is no volcanic rock.
White limestone is the most common type of rock found
in Jamaica, covering most central areas, with cretaceous
rock in second place. Jamaica has a varied topography with
rugged mountains rising high over the surrounding

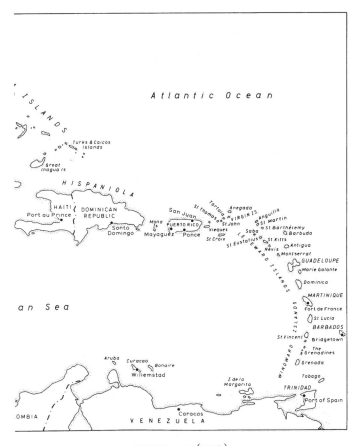

FIGURE 1.1 (cont.)

terrain. Around half of the island reaches heights greater than 1,000 feet above sea level, mainly in the island's central belt where the Blue Mountains dominate the landscape. These mountains, named after the blue shade appearing over them in the mist, spread for a length of 28 miles and a width of up to 12 miles, reaching a peak of 7,400 feet – the most elevated in the British Caribbean. The highest point of the mountains is known as Blue

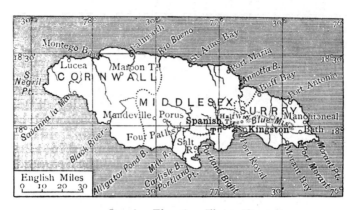

FIGURE 1.2 Jamaica: Elevation. Ilbusca/Getty Images

Mountain Peak. A steep gradient from the coastal plains leads up to the mountains. The Blue Mountains were heavily forested in the Taino era, being covered with mosses, lichen, ferns, trees and eight hundred species of endemic plants. A secondary mountain group known as the John Crow Mountains lies on a limestone plateau to the northeast of the Blue Mountains and further north lie the Dry Harbour Mountains. The west-central part of Jamaica includes many hills.

Jamaica has numerous rivers, rivulets and springs. The rivers there are mainly navigable for only short distances owing to their rapid descent from mountains to plains. Some rivers flow south (including the Rio Pedro, Plantain Garden and Yallahs Rivers), while others flow north (the Rio Grande, Martha Brae and Great Rivers). The longest river is the Rio Minho, which follows a course of fifty-eight miles from the centre of the island to Carlisle Bay on the central southern coast. Several scenic waterfalls flow down over rocks into rivers, the most spectacular being Dunn's River Falls, near Ocho Rios, now a major tourist attraction.

FIGURE I.3 Dunn's River Falls, near Ocho Rios. DEA/V. Giannella/ De Agostini/Getty Images

Cataracts and cascades deliver additional water very rapidly into rivers, especially after high levels of rainfall. Lagoons, bars, salt ponds and other sand spit formations are found around the island's coasts. One of the best-known sand spits, known since the seventeenth century as the Palisadoes spit, later connected Port Royal with the outskirts of Kingston. Jamaica has several natural harbours, including Old Harbour, Port Royal Harbour and Port Maria Harbour. Kingston Harbour, measuring ten by two miles, is the seventh largest natural harbour in the world, with deep water coming almost up to the city shoreline.

Located within the tropics, some 18° north of the Equator, a hot and humid climate predominates in Jamaica, as it does throughout the Caribbean. Temperatures range from 23°C to 32°C throughout the year, with winter temperatures just a few degrees lower than in summer. Diurnal changes in climate occur and the peaks of the mountains have temperatures somewhat lower than the coast. Sunshine is prevalent throughout the year for a daily average of 8.2 hours. Steady winds from the east predominate throughout most of the year but tropical storms and hurricanes occur periodically from July to late October, as is common throughout much of the Caribbean. Jamaica lies at the edge of the track of hurricanes, however, and only suffers a direct hit every ten or eleven years on average. Most hurricanes veer off towards Mexico or to the east of Jamaica instead. But tropical storms are more frequent, with torrential rain and winds causing serious danger to property and people. Jamaica has a trade wind season from December to April, with most winds blowing from the east.

Annual rainfall in Jamaica is heavily concentrated in May, October and November. February and March are the least rainy months. Thunderstorms in the late afternoon are commonly part of annual rainfall. The intensity of the rain can frequently lead to floods. But considerable variation exists in rainfall in different parts of Jamaica, with between 100 and 200 inches of rain falling per year on the north coast and in the Blue Mountains area and only forty inches annually elsewhere on the island. In some years, nevertheless, rainfall is much lower and droughts can occur. It is rare for Jamaica to have continuous rain throughout a particular day. The driest season is from December to April. Broadly speaking, Jamaica has a rainy windward coast, a dry leeward coast and a cool central region. The Caribbean tectonic plate is susceptible to earthquakes, though only two major ones have occurred – both of them long after the Tainos lived on the island.

Large swathes of the mountainous terrain in central Jamaica are difficult to access even today, so in the Taino era little settlement would have taken place there (though, as we will see, the caves scattered throughout the mountainous areas were sought out for important Taino religious and customary practices). Jamaica is mainly covered by a karst landscape formed from the dissolution of soluble rocks, in which most drainage was situated underground. Deep gullies intersect the mountainous parts of Jamaica. Caves and sink holes are common among the typical karst landscape in the Cockpit Country in the centre of the island. The coastal plain is either flat or gently undulating savanna land. This is particularly true of the alluvial southwestern plains. At the eastern end of Jamaica and along the north coast, however, a narrow lowland fringe predominates. Few high headlands or sea cliffs are found in Jamaica.

During the Taino era, Jamaica was heavily forested with a mixture of wet and dry limestone forests, riparian woodland and rainforest. Much of this land was wilderness before the Taino arrived. Before the arrival of Columbus, Jamaica had several distinct landscape characteristics. The southern plains were arid, with a dry forest and a ground cover of shrubs and scrub. Wet limestone forest was common on many plateaux in central Jamaica, while wetter plains areas had lignum vitae, one of the world's hardest woods, and cotton trees. Some areas had mangrove or marshy swamps. Lush vegetation, abundant flora and fauna and a varied array of insects, birds, reptiles, fish and animals were native to Jamaica before human habitation. Jamaica has over 200 species of birds, 100 different types of butterfly, many land crabs, snakes and crocodiles, but few indigenous mammals. Jamaica has a total flora of about 4,000 plants.

Community Structure

Taino people, for the most part, lived communally and peacefully: there is little evidence to indicate that they had the war-like attributes of the Caribs in the Lesser Antilles. However, James Knight's *History of Jamaica* (1746) referred to 'Warrs and intestine Divisions, which some-times hap[pe]ned among them', suggesting that the Tainos' peaceful mode of living was sometimes punctu-ated by conflict. No modern academic studies have explored this matter beyond Knight's remark. Hierarchical social divisions were an essential part of Taino settlements. The Tainos lived in tribes or chief-doms under the leadership of a chief or *cacique*, usually a man but sometimes a woman, who wielded great power. These chiefs had control over labour, material goods and sometimes tribute. Numerous chiefs were part of Taino Jamaica, and the level of their authority varied.

Simple and more complex chiefdoms existed in Jamaica. Individual communities were sometimes part of a confederation of villages bound together by communal rules. Though village layouts have not been investigated for Jamaica, it is thought that the island had around 150 Taino settlements; these were divided into provinces ruled by *caciques*. In his eighteenth-century history of Jamaica, James Knight noted that 'the Island was divided, in the time of the Native Indians, into twelve provinces . . . and they were Governed by their Respective chiefs, who were called Caciques, to whom they were very Submissive: but three of them had Superiority over the rest'.

Each community was divided into two broad hierarchical classes of people, one with a higher status than the other. An upper-class section of the community known as *nitainos*, including chiefs and warriors, ruled over a lower class referred to as *naborias*, who undertook most of the food gathering. We do not know whether the *naborias* comprised all of the labouring population or just certain subgroups. There is no evidence that the *naborias* included slaves or servile persons. Status among the elite Taino was underpinned by matrilineal descent, and *caciques* were often chosen by women. Thus name, property and status were inherited from a mother or grandmother. This means that a *cacique* was descended from his mother's brother, while his successor would be his sister's son. The line of *caciques* was therefore based on hereditary descent. It was considered a great honour for a woman to become a *cacique*'s wife.

Caciques stood out from the rest of the Taino population in two other respects. One was that they practised polygamy, took wives from other Taino communities and used the liaisons to solidify their power with neighbouring chiefs. The other was that they dressed elaborately in a manner appropriate to their standing by wearing fine clothing and jewellery, and possessed the most precious wooden and stone artefacts that formed an essential part of their system of beliefs. *Caciques* presided over meetings by sitting on ceremonial seats known as *duhos*. These were low seats or wooden stools, usually with four feet and an elaborately carved back. Ornately decorated with shell and gold laminate, *duhos* were prestigious artefacts in Taino communities that acted as a symbol for the power of the *caciques*. The *duho* should be regarded as an anthropomorphic being. *Caciques* sitting on them were, according to Taino beliefs, sitting not just on an object of furniture but on a sentient being with a soul (known as a *zemi*). The *caciques*, accorded deference for their role in a hierarchical system, often wore headdresses with gold and feathers. They customarily entrusted their children to the care of priests, who instructed them about their ancestors.

The *caciques* organised religious ceremonies known as *areytos* to unite their communities in a village's central plaza to celebrate marriages and births, to mourn the dead and to mark major staging posts in the annual calendar. Feasting, drinking, music and dancing occurred at these elaborate ceremonies that lasted for several hours. Taino history and beliefs were represented on these occasions to instruct and remind the community of their values and traditions. Thus the histories of the *caciques*, their ancestors and their communities were celebrated at these lengthy ceremonies that brought together entire village communities as well as attracting interested outside observers.

Caciques played an important leadership role in everyday life. They controlled the production of subsistence and craft goods by allocating particular tasks to individuals and groups, gathering food from them, and redistributing food among their communities. Some *caciques* were wealthy women who gathered craft items that could be used for gifts or exchanges, but most of these chiefs were men. They often possessed great canoes as a symbol of their leadership position in communities. *Caciques* were respected as leaders in death as much as in life. When they died, their bodies were cut open and dried over a fire for preservation. The *caciques* were deified in death and entered a spirit realm alongside their ancestors. The souls of dead *caciques* resided in trees chosen by the Taino communities as sites of reverence. An image or *zemi* was carved from the trees and placed in a special hut to be worshipped by villagers and protected by the *caciques*.

The Tainos built houses from wood rather than stone; they did not use mud or wattle. A special rectangular house known as a *bohio* was situated at the heart of a village or *Yucayeque*, comprising thatched structures arranged around a central plaza or *batey*. Ordinary circular dwellings, known as *caneys*, were constructed from a wall of canes driven into the ground in the form of a circle. They were tied with *lianas*, which were filaments from large trees. The huts or houses were covered with straw or long grass; they contained few items of furniture. People slept on cotton hammocks (an invention of the Tainos) or mats made from banana leaves rather than on beds. Besides houses, Taino villages also had storerooms, platforms and work huts.

Taino people had dark golden-brown skin and black hair. They practised face and body piercing and tattoos, and painted their faces and bodies in red, white or black using pigments obtained from plants and coloured clays. In common with other people from the Antilles and South America, they did not wear much clothing, though they adorned parts of their bodies with palm fronds, coloured cotton capes and ornaments made from shell and gold. Men and female virgins were naked apart from a small cotton belt. Married women wore small woven cotton skirts. *Caciques* and shamans donned fine vestments at ceremonies, with tropical bird feathers. During ceremonies, the Taino frequently played a ball game in the plazas similar to one also documented for Hispaniola, though no ceremonial ball courts have been excavated in Jamaica. The Taino also had musical instruments such as drums, wooden rattles and maracas made from gourds to enliven proceedings.

James Knight's *The Natural, Moral, and Political History of Jamaica* ... (1742) described the Taino as

of a Dun Colour. They were not so tall, as Europeans, but Robust, Active, and well proportioned. The Men were beardless, and all went naked, Women, as well as the Men, except those that had Husbands. ... Their heads were broad and flat; and their nostrils very large, not Naturally but made so, when they were Infants of about a Week old, by Squeezing or Pressing hard, with one hand behind the head, and the other on the face. They had long black hair, which hung down their Shoulders, and in general had very bad teeth.

Peter Martyr, an Italian historian and courtier in the service of Spain, never visited the Caribbean but considered, on the basis of information purveyed to him, the Jamaican Tainos to be 'of quicker wytte then in the other islandes, and more expert artificers and warrelyke men'. Taino men painted their faces with bright colours before any armed conflict in an attempt to frighten their enemies.

The Taino and the Natural Environment

The Taino were agricultural people who cultivated various crops in Jamaica, as well as gathering fruit from trees and fish from rivers and the sea. Their ancestors were already seasoned agriculturists when they arrived in

Jamaica with various plants and knowledge of numerous cultivation techniques. The plants and crops they brought with them originated from tropical lowlands east of the Andes. Taino agriculture mainly used a system of cultivation known as *conuco*. This involved clearing wooded areas and making enough space for crop production in fields. The soil was worked into large, loose mounds arranged in a way to facilitate drainage and sustained cropping. As in medieval England, some of the cultivated soil was left fallow in some years to recover its fertility. *Conucos* were usually three feet high, nine feet in circumference, and arranged in rows. Root crops were planted in the *conucos* with wooden hoes. After *conucos* had been constructed, they could be maintained relatively easily by planting, weeding and harvesting.

The variety of Taino food resources indicates that they had a nutritious diet, with a healthy mixture of fats, proteins and carbohydrates. They planted yams, sweet potatoes, corn, arrowroot and different types of squashes. The Taino ate peanuts, chilli peppers and coney (i.e. rodents); they also hunted birds and reptiles. Many fruits were consumed, including hog plum, guava, prickly pears, pineapple, papaya, bananas and golden apples. The seeds of these fruits were dispersed in a variety of ways. The Taino were skilled fishermen, using nets, hooks made of bone and shell, and canoes to gather fish and marine molluscs. They ate conch, oysters and crabs. These were gathered from the seashore and from mangrove marshes. Among the fish consumed were snapper, bass, parrot fish and grouper. During the Taino era, pigs, goats, cattle and sheep were absent from Jamaica. The lack of these large animals meant that roasting meat was uncommon. For the most part, therefore, the Taino diet was based on fish, vegetables and fruit. The foods they ate were available throughout the year without a strong need for storage or preservation.

The Taino gathered food on a daily subsistence basis, paying close attention to seasonal availability. It seems that men cleared the land and planted crops while women undertook the gathering of fruit and seeds. Stone grinders and pestles were used to reduce corn to meal and cassava to flour. Griddles, which have been found in caves and middens (rubbish heaps), were the main means of cooking, with charcoal as the fuel source, for cassava, sweet potatoes and other crops. The griddles were usually thick flat platters made out of clay. Boiling and baking rather than frying appears to have been the main means of preparing hot food by the Taino. Consumption of edible fruit along with cooked meat, fish and vegetables appears to have been carried out in a sustainable way.

The foodstuff most frequently consumed by the Taino was cassava (or manioc), a widely grown root crop in Jamaica which was an important source of carbohydrates. Such was the significance of this crop to the Taino that the name of their supreme deity *Yucahú* means 'spirit of cassava'. Grown widely in tropical climates, cassava provided the main everyday nourishment in Taino communities. It was planted in the heaped garden beds of the *conucos*, placed several feet apart from one another. Cassava is bitter and unhealthy to eat when raw, but when cooked it is a versatile foodstuff with a high calorific value. The pulp of the cassava bread was baked on clay griddles, while the boiled juice was used as flavouring when cooking.

Tapioca was the starchy liquid produced from cassava. Cassava bread, also known as bammie, is still prepared on a daily basis in Jamaica. It has the advantage over wheaten bread of staying fresh for weeks.

Wood and various fibres were a significant part of Taino material culture. The Taino used bottle gourds as containers and as floats for fish nets. Containers were obtained from the calabash tree. Wild plantain leaves were used for thatch. Women wove baskets and garments out of feathers, fibre and other natural perishable materials. The baskets could be made of either wicker or banana leaves. Nearly all of the evidence for this has disappeared from trace: only one cotton belt, with beadwork, has survived from the Taino era in Jamaica. Woodcarving became one of the main practical and aesthetic achievements of the Taino's artisan practice. Lignum vitae, a heavy hardwood with an olive green colour, was used for woodworking. Other woods were cut and shaped to make canoes and spears. Wooden paddles were carved from large trees to facilitate the use of canoes. Cotton was cultivated to make hammocks and fishing nets. Stone mortars and pestles were used for grinding food ingredients.

The Taino also made use of stone axes, petaloid adzes, flint scrapers, chisels and handstones formed like pestles. Taino women developed pottery skills with clays, crushed shells and vegetable fibres to make cups, bowls, plates and jars. Some of these artefacts from the Taino era have been found at different Jamaican sites. Taino people made axe heads as cutting tools from river stones. These were sculpted into a petaloid or peardrop shape in various sizes. Axe heads were used for cutting food, but because of their widespread practical use they could also be gifts or items of exchange. Many petaloid axes from the Taino era have been excavated in Jamaica. They were made from a variety of rock types, greenstone being the most favoured. The locations where axes have been found are often situated quite far from where the rock specimens could have originated, suggesting that the Taino engaged in domestic trade in Jamaica.

The Taino were highly skilled in using gastropod shells to make attractive objects that could be worn. Their advanced artisan skills involved the use of incision marks and carvings on the surface of shells to convey their ideas visually. The Taino exhibited technological ingenuity in using different kinds of stones, picks, wood and twine for their 'shellsmithing'. Awls and sanding stones were used regularly by the Taino as shell tools. To extract the snails that inhabited conches, craftsmen buried the shell in an ant hill as a non-corrosive way of cleaning the shell. They then removed the spire and outer whorl of the shell in order to expose the columella encasing. Small elliptical stones were inserted with twine to hang the decorated shell around a person's neck as an ornament. It is thought that women predominated among the shellsmiths. Many questions about how the Taino practised their shellsmith techniques still require answers. We do not know whether they had construction workshops, whether this activity was confined to a specific location on a site, how many of the ornaments were worn, and whether the decorative shells were distributed to particular groups.

Mythology and Religion

The Taino believed in a sacred cosmos that was closely connected to the landscape features of the world such as the sky and the earth but also linked to an unseen lower world. The Taino were pantheists who explained the origins of humanity and the natural world by deploying creation stories that connected people to deities and to the afterlife. The supernatural and the natural world were inextricably intertwined in Taino cosmology, which was underpinned by a belief in non-linear sacred time. Animism lay at the heart of Taino beliefs. Spiritual significance for these indigenous people resided in all sorts of places, seen and unseen – in flora and fauna, rocks, caves, animals, inanimate objects and human beings. The Taino believed strongly in ancestor worship: deceased relatives were honoured in ritual ceremonies in which various Taino deities would be invoked. Each of the Taino deities had names. They included *Guabanex*, who controlled wind and water; *Guaca*, the guardian spirit of the living; and *Maroio*, a rain and wind god.

A shaman or *behique* served as a ritual specialist in Taino communities to hear and understand instructions from plants, rocks and animals. *Behiques* and *caciques* both carried carved figures known as *zemis*, which were effectively village idols. These artefacts were usually made out of wood, clay or stone, but they could be formed out of shells and human bones. *Zemis* could be petroglyphs carved on rocks or stalagmites in caves or pictographs found as tattoos or on pottery. The supreme god *Yucahú* was represented by a three-pointed *zemi*, usually placed in a *conuco* to increase the yield of cassava.

A few *zemis* have been discovered. The first two were found in 1792 on Carpenter's Mountain, Manchester parish. Three others were located in the 1990s in an almost inaccessible cave near Aboukir in the Dry Harbour Mountains in St Ann parish. They comprised a spoon, a large staff and a pelican-shaped figure that appear to have belonged together for the purposes of the worship and ritual use of the *cohoba*. They are now housed at Jamaica's National Gallery in Kingston. All have been carbon-dated and predate the arrival of Columbus in Jamaica by at least a century. Believed to have numerous powers, these carved artefacts were sacred objects that incorporated idols and spirits. They could be invoked to cure the sick, control the weather, predict the future, assist women in childbirth, to bring rain, to extract revenge or to give advice in war and peace. They enabled the Taino to commune with their ancestors.

Zemis could represent male or female figures. They incorporated formal deities such as *Yúcahu*, mentioned above, and his mother *Atabey*, goddess of human fertility, or other minor deities. These had a rank order, from the most important down to the least significant. *Zemis* were also thought to have magical powers that helped the Taino to reach the goals incorporated in myths. Many rituals of Taino society in Jamaica were linked to the attributes associated with *zemis*, all of whom had names. The Taino communicated with them through food offerings, prayer and ceremonial rituals. *Zemis* were kept in special shrines placed apart from Taino houses.

Though the Taino had no place for formal worship, at ceremonies *zemis* were placed on *duhos* next to the *cacique* to indicate the connection between the spirit world and leadership in Taino society. The importance attached to *duhos* was such that they were invariably hidden from sight when not in use, and sometimes stored in caves. The only preserved *duho* in the National Gallery of Jamaica is a hollowed-out wooden carved ceremonial seat found in a cave in St Catherine parish in the 1990s. Shaped like a wooden hammock, it could hold the reclining body of a *cacique*. Topped by a *zemi* head that originally had inlays for eyes, ears and mouth, with one ear inlay still in position, it has humanised feet at its base. Etched arms can be seen in the body of the seat. This carving has been carbon-dated from AD 1000 to 1170.

Zemis pervaded other aspects of Taino life. They were thought to honour guests with their favour and were displayed at important gatherings where the Taino played *bateye*, a ritualised ball game, or at meetings where important transactions – exchanging wealth or consolidating alliances – were undertaken. *Zemis* were also kept as fetishes in Taino homes. There is virtually no European testimony about the role of *zemis* in Jamaican Taino society. But Spanish evidence from Hispaniola suggests that most Taino people would possess *zemis* with the bones of deceased parents and other relatives. *Caciques* spoke to these spirits and gave them the names of their fathers or other ancestors. This was almost a form of idolatry. *Caciques* were buried in wooden *zemis* carved out of trees; these held ancestral spirits and this form of burial was intended to lead to rebirth. The interment of *caciques* was conducted with great respect, with men and women singing over the grave for a fortnight and recounting his or her life, work and actions.

Caciques and *behiques* communed with ancestral spirits by taking *cohoba* powder, a very strong hallucinogenic substance made from the ground seeds of a mimosa-like tree. This was usually inhaled as part of a religious ceremony conducted either at the *cacique*'s *bohio*, usually situated at a distance from a town, or at other venues associated with deities and supernatural significance. Sacred objects were usually assembled for these ceremonies. Extensive preparations were made for the *cohoba* ceremony. The *caciques* fasted and eschewed bodily pleasures for several days beforehand. They dressed elaborately for the ceremony in ornate regalia, wearing capes and jewellery. It was common practice for *caciques* to vomit to cleanse their stomach before the ceremony began. The souls of the *caciques* rather than ordinary Tainos were deified in this process. There was a distinction between the soul in earthly life, which was called *Goenz*, and the soul of the departed, known as *Opea*.

Religious ceremonies followed an established pattern. Before the *cohoba* ceremony, the shaman purged himself with a vomiting stick. This was necessary to remove any undigested food from the stomach. Sometimes a stone tongue compressor was placed at the back of the throat to facilitate this process. Then the *cohoba* powder was prepared carefully. Ground from the seeds of native trees, the powder was mixed with crushed shell and tobacco and placed above a *zemi* on a wooden platform. Carved spoons were made to ladle the powder, which was lit and the smoke was inhaled through the nostrils using a forked nose pipe known as a *tabaco*. This was made from wood, pottery, bird bones or manatee. The powder had a psychedelic effect, inducing trances that could continue for several hours. This was the first use of drugs in Jamaica to produce a heightened sense of consciousness. *Behiques* used the trances induced by the *cohoba* powder to contact the spirits for help in healing the sick. They chanted with the patient while seeking to make contact with spirits. Often this ritual, effectively a séance, was conducted among a select few individuals. Some Taino stone sculptures depict shamans inhaling the powder.

Rock Art

The Taino practised rock art either in caves or on sites near rivers or the sea. Caves were places from which human beings originated according to Taino mythology; the sun and moon were also born there. Caves also served as burial chambers and as places where the *caciques* could store *zemis* and other sacred objects. Subterranean human activities were therefore important in Taino culture for their contact with the spirit world. The remoteness of caves underscored the mystery of contacts with the hidden great beyond. Unsurprisingly, therefore, one of the principle means of artistic expression for the Tainos lay in rock art, often buried deep in narrow caves. Examples can be found in Jamaica and other islands where Tainos settled. Most recently, rock paintings attributed to Taino culture in the fourteenth century have been found on the tiny uninhabited island of Mona, situated midway between Puerto Rico and the Dominican Republic.

Ostionoid and Meillacan people were linked to rock art, but it is difficult to date their sites or paintings. Half of the known rock art sites in Jamaica are situated on the south coast where the dry climate has helped to ensure their preservation. Pictographs depicted birds, tree frogs, turtles, fish and reptiles. These paintings are usually found on the ceilings or walls of caves, which were sights of socio-cultural and iconographic significance accessed only by the *caciques* and the *behiques*. Pictographs were created by the application of coloured pigments to cave walls. Sometimes bat excrement, which had absorbed natural minerals coloured yellow, red and brown from cave floors, was used for these paintings. On other occasions, charcoal was applied. The artists dipped their fingers in the bat guano or charcoal and dragged them across the cave walls. They drew systematic, carefully wrought designs with finger incisions that depicted people and spirits. Sometimes pictographs were created in stages, with fading imagery being touched up.

Petroglyphs were rock carvings incised into stalagmites, boulders and rocks at the entrance to caves; they frequently have anthropomorphic, zoomorphic and abstract motifs. The painted outlines of ancestral spirits appear on many petroglyphs. These carvings represented symbols that underpinned the daily life, religious beliefs, and social and political organisation of the Tainos. They appear to have reflected polytheistic beliefs, but archaeologists have found it difficult to unravel their precise meaning. Petroglyphs often have faces with eyes and mouths. Incised geometric designs are common. The positioning of these dyed or painted images in or near caves reflected the Tainos' cosmological view that caves, or ossuaries, were suitable repositories for the dead and for inscribing markers to the spirit world of their ancestors.

One Jamaican site with a large concentration of surviving Taino cave art is Mountain River Cave, located near Cudjoe's Hill, in St Catherine parish, to the northwest of Spanish Town. Fairly inaccessible today in a thickly wooded area, this cave has 148 identifiable pictographs on its ceiling and four or five petroglyphs. The pictographs comprise a combination of zoomorphic figures (including frogs, birds, turtles, iguanas and flamingos) and anthropomorphic figures (dancing figures, squatting figures, standing figures with a weapon in one hand, and a man with ceremonial costume and headgear). The figures may include representations of *caciques*. They appear to have been painted with a bituminous black compound. The paintings were not undertaken with any attempt to tell a story through a mural; instead, they seem to be individually painted figures. Precise dating of these artefacts is virtually impossible, but they have a relative date range of between AD 1000 and AD 1450. There is no evidence of human material culture in the vicinity. It was probably the case therefore that *caciques* and shamans visited the cave to perform their religious ceremonies, and artists painted the figures, in a location remote from Taino communities.

Pottery and Wooden Carvings

Extensive remains of pottery and wooden carvings have been found in Jamaica that originated in the Taino era. Clay pots, mortars and pestles, bowls, effigy vessels and *buréns* (cassava vessels) are among the objects produced by pottery. Decorative motifs were common. Three incised design elements were common on the pottery made by the

Tainos: continuous line, dashed line and punctate motifs. Apart from pottery, the Taino were expert carvers. The Taino carved stones into three points; the two points at the end of the stone represented a human or an animal, often with a grotesque face, and hunched legs that archaeologists refer to as frogs' legs. Women played the leading role in making Taino pottery, joining strips of wet clay in circular patterns, hand modelling the clay, and then using fingers and pointed tools to incise details. The finished dry pottery was fired in large, open pits in the ground. Taino potters had a good knowledge of local clays. They used crushed shell, vegetable fibres, sand or ash to temper the clay before firing. The pottery was usually burnished by using pebbles.

Pottery remains are found either in caves or in open-air sites where middens remain. Most of the pottery produced on the island between AD 650 and AD 900 was called redware. Thereafter a thicker pottery called white marl was produced. Redware sites are mainly situated next to sandy beaches, but the locations are relatively few in number and the deposits shallow. Sixteen open-air sites with redware pottery have been reported for Jamaica, but only three have been excavated. Open-air redware sites include Calabash Bay and Sandy Bank on the south coast and Little River and Cardiff Hall Beach on the north coast. White marl sites are common throughout much of Jamaica, especially in St Ann, St Mary and Clarendon parishes.

Wooden carvings have been recovered from caves in Jamaica, where they had probably been placed as ritual deposits needed for ceremonies. The relative dryness of the atmosphere in caves has helped to preserve these objects. They were carved with stone and shell tools on a very hard wood such as lignum vitae. Iconographic details can often be discerned on these wooden carvings, but their ritual and symbolic meaning is hard to assess. Many carvings include spectral figures or skulls that may represent human beings or animals; they are a reminder of the foreboding of death that played an important religious and cultural role in Taino life.

The earliest published depiction of a Taino wooden image is shown in a cartouche on a map of the West Indies dated 1752 by Captain John Henry Schroeter, a plantation surveyor who had served as a captain of the garrison at Fort Balcarres in Trelawny parish. Two wooden *zemis* were found near an estate in Jamaica some time before 1757. In 1792 three wooden carved objects were found in a cave near Carpenter's Mountain, Vere parish, as mentioned before; these were presented to the British Museum in 1799. Since then, only nine Taino carvings have been found in Jamaica, including those referred to above at the National Gallery of Jamaica.

The best-known wooden carving to survive from the Taino era is the 'birdman' sculpture, a seemingly unique wooden idol that has no parallel among wooden artefacts found elsewhere in Caribbean islands where the Taino settled. The 'birdman' sculpture has an avian head of a long-billed bird, and arms and legs outstretched from a human body. The legs on this carving have bands, which appear to represent cotton bandages. This anthropomorphic carving, one of the three objects found in 1792 mentioned above, has been interpreted in several ways. One argument is that the bird is a depiction of the Jamaican crow. Another interpretation is that the 'birdman' sculpture is a mixture of the animal and human world, specifically resembling the mythic woodpecker who created the first reproductive woman and a symbol of masculine potency (owing to its bare teeth, erect penis and testes). Whether one of these 'readings' of the iconography of the 'birdman' sculpture is accurate cannot be proven in our present state of knowledge.

Burials

Since 2016, archaeological investigations have been conducted into burial sites at White Marl, situated eight miles west of Kingston. This was a large village lying in an important area for social networks near Kingston Harbour, Spanish Town and the Rio Cobre and French rivers. White Marl was the first Jamaican site to reveal evidence of house structures as well as human burials in middens. Our knowledge of burials in precolonial Jamaica is scanty. Initial investigations at White Marl leave many questions unanswered about the limited, fragmentary remains found. Radiocarbon dating indicates that the three bodies located point to a long occupation of the site over about four centuries (AD 1221–1641). The analysis of these bodies suggests that burials occurred in small oval-shaped pits without a large number of grave goods, and, through estimating carbon isotope values from tooth enamel, that a plant diet predominated among these people comprising arrowroot, palm fruit, maize and wild beans.

The Taino Village at Maima

The most significant archaeological investigations dealing with the Taino era in Jamaica have been undertaken on the north coast. Columbus came across the Taino village of Maima in 1503–4, situated on a hillside overlooking the coastal plain of St Ann's Bay. Archaeological investigations were carried out there in 2014 and 2015, though previous work on this site had been undertaken periodically from the 1940s onwards. The site is now part of Seville Heritage Park. The expert archaeological view is that the Taino village of Maima was created as part of the Meillacan migration to Jamaica beginning around AD 950–1000. It is thought that the terraces on this hilltop settlement were part of a Meillacan settlement pattern brought to Jamaica. Excavations show that the Taino at Maima constructed terraces and platforms on the hillside filled with mixed clay, marl and limestone aggregate. Excavations have identified postholes, indicating that house structures had been built on these foundations. These were of a fairly small size, suggesting that the Taino had a nuclear family structure rather than an extended family residential pattern. White marl ceramic bowls have been recovered from the site along with petaloid adzes, handstones, flat-surface cobbles, vessels with geometric incisions, and four anthropomorphic or zoomorphic pieces that may represent *zemis*. Faunal remains indicate that fish and shellfish from a nearby reef were the main source of protein at this site. Hutia, large cavy-like rodents, were also raised or hunted.

2

Spanish Jamaica, 1509–1655

~

Taino society in Jamaica had been undisturbed by outsiders for centuries until the 1490s when Spanish voyagers
led by the Genoese-born navigator Christopher
Columbus arrived. Columbus had gained the financial
backing of Spanish monarchs for expeditions across the
Atlantic to discover territories of potential value for the
Spanish Empire. The voyages were intended to find
a western oceanic route to Cathay and the Indies, and
thereby to lands to conquer, possess and exploit. By the
late fifteenth century, Spain had forged a strong nation
state that had overcome many centuries of Islamic domin-
ation. Roman Catholicism was closely entwined with
nationalism in Spain. Spanish monarchs believed that
God supported their desire to increase their power
through conquest. The Spanish had witnessed the success
of the Portuguese in their maritime forays into the
Atlantic and Indian oceans during the fifteenth century,
and wanted to emulate the maritime endeavours of their
fellow Iberians.

Initial Spanish forays to the Caribbean were undertaken
between 1492 and 1503, a period when Columbus undertook four voyages to West Indian waters. These were
expeditions made under the auspices of Ferdinand and
Isabella, the husband and wife who were monarchs of
Aragon and Castile. Isabella undertook most of the

FIGURE 2.1 Christopher Columbus. JPA1999/Getty Images

negotiations with Columbus, who persuaded his Spanish sponsors he could administer any land he found for Spain in addition to 10 per cent of the proceeds arising from the discovery. On his first voyage, Columbus reached Guanahani in the Bahamas and heard about the location of Jamaica from indigenous people he came across in Cuba. On the second and fourth voyages, he reached Jamaica as well as other West Indian islands. Only a few days were spent in Jamaica on the second voyage as there was no intention to remain there. Columbus had a much longer sojourn in Jamaica on his fourth voyage in 1502–3.

Columbus's first landfall in Jamaica involved an altercation with the Taino. On 5 May 1494, after sailing from Hispaniola to explore the southern Cuban coast, Columbus heard there was gold in Jamaica and therefore directed his three caravels to sail south. The vessels

45

anchored off what they later called Santa Gloria, near St Ann's Bay, situated midway along Jamaica's northern coast. Difficulties arose immediately. The Spanish cleric Andrés Bernáldez, writing in Madrid from information supplied by Columbus, described the first meeting between Columbus and the Tainos:

As soon as the Admiral arrived off the coast of Jamaica, there immediately came out against him quite seventy canoes, all full of people with darts as weapons. They advanced a league out to sea, with warlike shouts and in battle array. And the admiral with his three caravels and his people paid no attention to them and continued to steer towards the shore, and when they saw this, they became alarmed and turned in flight. The admiral made use of his interpreter, so that one of those canoes was reassured and came to him with its crew. He gave them clothes and many other things which they held in great regard, and accorded them permission to depart.

Two canoes carrying Taino men threw spears at the Spanish, but these had little impact. An immediate retaliation came from Spanish crossbow shafts that injured six or seven people. The tension calmed down, however, and the next-day encounters between the Taino and the Spanish sailors were friendlier. The Taino offered food to their intruders, and invited them to stay. Columbus quickly moved along the north coast, stopping briefly at Rio Bueno and the site of Montego Bay. He sailed north to resume his exploration of Cuban shores but later returned to Jamaica's western and southern coasts, where Tainos greeted him cordially. His ships sailed to Morant Point and then headed east to Santo Domingo in Hispaniola, a distance of 400 miles.

Jamaica made a positive impression on Columbus. The island was 'the most lovely that eyes have seen … it is beyond measure prosperous, so that even on the seashore, as well as inland, every part is filled with villages'. Columbus's son Ferdinand wrote that his father found Jamaica 'so green and smiling, abounding in food and densely populated, that he thought it unsurpassed'. Columbus also left positive impressions of the Tainos: 'they traded with us and gave us everything we had, with good will … They are very gentle and without knowledge of what is evil; nor do they murder or steal. Your highness may believe that in all the world there can be no better people.' Bernáldez, who travelled with Columbus, described the entourage and retinue of the *cacique* who met Columbus, and their facial and body painting, the ornaments and beads they wore, and the musical instruments they played. Columbus's reward for his voyage was for Ferdinand and Isabella to confer ownership of Jamaica to him. There is no evidence, however, that this meant anything other than a nominal reward.

Favourable impressions of Jamaica and its people were subject to a more critical account nine years later, when Columbus struggled to find shelter in Jamaica for damaged ships on his fourth and final voyage in Caribbean waters. Columbus's caravel had lost three anchors in tempestuous weather when they limped into a safe location on Jamaica's north shore. The men on board the ships were exhausted owing to persistent stormy conditions. In June 1503 Columbus's caravel anchored at Puerto Seco (Discovery Bay), but finding neither water nor friendly Tainos they moved on to St Ann's Bay.

47

Attempts to repair the ships proved difficult, so much so that Columbus and his crew of 150 men remained there for a year before they were rescued and able to leave for Santo Domingo and Spain. Relations with the Tainos were strained on this visit because the local people found the daily necessity to feed so many intruders for a prolonged period was a burden. Columbus, however, was able to secure their help.

A group of Tainos told Columbus that gold and mines were available in Jamaica. Some of his men searched the island for gold, making their way through the mountainous interior, but without finding precious metal deposits. It became clear that a rescue mission was needed. Eventually, Columbus's secretary, Captain Diego Méndez, was sent from Jamaica with a small company of men to seek help in Hispaniola. He became acquainted with Ameyro, a *cacique*, and acquired a large dugout canoe from him by offering a brass helmet, shirt and frock. Méndez recruited a Spaniard and six Taino paddlers to assist him. Failing to leave Jamaica on their first attempt because of choppy seas, Méndez and his company set out for a second time in another canoe with an armed escort of seventy men to see them leave Jamaican waters. Méndez eventually reached Hispaniola, but the military leader and governor, Nicolás de Ovando, established there since 1502, refused to help. Ovando was not friendly with Columbus, and was concerned that his own authority in the Caribbean would be overshadowed by that of the Genoese navigator. In these circumstances, Méndez was forced to hire a boat and seek supplies to effect a rescue himself. This involved going to Santo Domingo to load the boat with provisions.

48

While marooned in Jamaica, Columbus contended with an increasingly dissatisfied crew. He wrote to the Spanish Crown to express despair at his situation, noting his ill health from arthritis and the prevalence of sickness amongst his men. 'The Indians have abandoned us', he wrote to the Spanish monarchs, and 'the governor of Santo Domingo, Obando [i.e. Ovando], has sent rather to see if I am dead, than to succor us, or carry me alive hence'. It must have occurred to Columbus that he might not escape from Jamaica. On 2 January 1504, a group of rebels led by Francisco Portas and his brother announced their defiance on the deck of Columbus's ship. They captured dugout canoes and took stores before paddling eastwards to leave Jamaica. Columbus drummed up support from the Tainos to quell the revolt but the rebels regrouped and planned to stage a second mutiny. A skirmish led by rebels on 20 May 1504 was put down and the Portas brothers were captured. Méndez's rescue ship arrived on 28 June 1504, one year and four days after Columbus and his crew had reached Jamaica. Columbus and 100 men who had survived from his expedition left for Hispaniola. Columbus then spent two years trying to secure the inheritance of his son Diego, which included possession of Jamaica.

A Spanish Colony

Columbus's experience of Jamaica was mixed. On the one hand, he had seen the richness of the land and the fine harbours for shipping. After initially hostile encounters with the Tainos, he had established cordial relations with them while retaining an iron glove through having

49

superior Spanish weaponry. On the other hand, his year spent marooned in Jamaica on his final voyage to the Caribbean must have led him to conclude that Jamaica was an isolated backwater that held little significance for Spanish exploration and conquest in the New World. After Columbus returned to Spain, Ferdinand and Isabella displayed no immediate enthusiasm for pursuing further connections with Jamaica: they were far more interested in forging links with Cuba, Hispaniola and the Central and South American mainland, which they referred to as Terra Firma.

Ferdinand and Isabella took back control of Jamaica from Columbus. However, his son and heir Diego Columbus (sometimes rendered Colón) successfully challenged the Spanish Crown to recognise the rights given to his father. In 1508, two years after Columbus's death, Ferdinand and Isabella returned Jamaica to the viceroy, Diego, who had succeeded to his father's titles on 20 May 1506. Three years later, Diego, holding the position of governor of the Indies and based in Santo Domingo, ordered the formal conquest and occupation of Jamaica. The Spanish monarchs decided to allow two generals, Alonzo de Ojeda and Diego de Nicuesa, who held governorships on the Spanish Main, to use Jamaica as a provision base for their military forays into Central America. Fearing that he would lose control of the island, in late 1509 or early 1510, Diego Columbus despatched Juan de Esquivel to become governor of Jamaica without the knowledge of King Ferdinand II of Aragon (who was also Ferdinand V of Castile). Esquivel arrived on 9 December 1509 and Jamaica became part of the Vice Royalty of New Spain.

Esquivel's arrival was the beginning of a permanent Spanish presence in the island and the start of official Spanish governance of what was originally known as the colony of Santiago. Settlers soon followed Esquivel to Jamaica. He remained there until his death in 1515. Ferdinand had lost confidence in him before then because Esquivel failed to find gold in Jamaica and only made limited attempts to extract resources from the island that could benefit the Spanish. In 1512–13 King Ferdinand named Pedro de Mazuelo as the factor (and later treasurer and future governor) for Jamaica and Diego Columbus, still the nominal ruler of Jamaica, selected Francisco de Garay, his uncle by marriage, as successor to Esquivel. Garay arrived in Jamaica in 1515.

The Spanish soon used the term 'Jamaica' for the island rather than the Taino name 'Xaymaca'. The modern form – Jamaica – appeared on Peter Martyr's chart of the West Indies, engraved in wood in 1512. For the next century-and-a-half, Jamaica was governed by Spanish officials. Spanish institutions and the Roman Catholic Church also made their imprint on Jamaica. And from the start of their government of Jamaica, the Spanish ensured they controlled the social and political life of the island. This involved, as we will see, a determined crushing of Taino opposition to Spanish rule.

Spanish place names gradually appeared all over the island. This continued throughout the period of Spanish rule in Jamaica. The main settlement was called Sevilla Nueva, where Columbus had been marooned for over a year. Other Jamaican towns with Spanish names were Villa de la Vega (Spanish Town) and Melilla (taken from a town on the Barbary Coast under Spanish rule) along with those still used in Jamaica – Ocho Rios, Rio Bueno, Port Antonio and Santa Cruz. Rivers such as the Rio Cobre and Rio Minho were also derived from the Spanish language. Columbus's name, curiously, was not replicated as a place name in Jamaica. Most Spanish place names did not survive the end of Spanish rule in Jamaica in 1655 but were replaced mainly by British terms.

Spanish Jamaica, however, never really flourished in social, economic and political terms. It was always a backwater, a minor part of the Spanish presence in the New World. Without its initial acquisition for Spain by Columbus after his sojourn in Jamaica and the tussle with his son over an inheritance that included controlling the island, it is likely that the Spanish would have bypassed Jamaica altogether. This was not because Jamaica lacked agricultural or commercial potential; it was more to do with Spanish priorities for trade, colonisation and settlement with the Spanish Main. King Ferdinand had hoped that gold would be found in Jamaica, but it was clear as early as 1512 that this was not the case. This hastened the Spanish exploitation of Jamaica for its food resources and finished products which could be despatched to Cuba and the Spanish Main. Garay, the second governor of the island, assured Ferdinand of the abundant produce in Jamaica and stated that 'the colonization of Terra Firma will not cease because of a shortage of supplies' from the island.

By 1534 Jamaica was a Spanish royal colony. But two years later the Spanish crown granted Jamaica to Columbus's descendants as part of a lawsuit settlement. Specifically, Jamaica and its civil and criminal jurisdiction became the fiefdom of Admiral Luis Colón y Alvarez de

Toledo, the grandson of Columbus, who became Marquis of Jamaica until 1572. Thereafter Jamaica was ruled by an absentee noble family. Spain allocated far more resources into its possessions elsewhere in the Caribbean – notably Hispaniola, Santo Domingo and Cuba – and colonised Central and South America far more extensively during the sixteenth century than Jamaica. If gold had been found in Jamaica in significant quantities, the Spanish would no doubt have assigned it a greater priority in their colonising endeavours. But few samples of alluvial gold were discovered there compared with the gold located in Hispaniola. Copper deposits were found in Jamaica, but these were no substitute for the failure to unearth glittering precious metals. Despite the fact that Jamaica was almost an afterthought for Spain in its heady years of overseas expansion, however, significant changes occurred there in the sixteenth and seventeenth centuries that left a distinctive Spanish legacy.

Governors

Spanish Jamaica was ruled by governors appointed by the Crown or selected by the Columbus family rather than locally set up. There were no life or hereditary governorships. Jamaica's governor was responsible for reporting the state of the island to the Audiencia of Santo Domingo. Appointments usually lasted for four or six years at an annual salary of 2,500 ducats. There was a frequent turnover of postholders: between 1510 and 1660 there were forty-seven governors of Jamaica. Some held full authority, but others were either temporary substitutes for those officially appointed or were sent to Jamaica as auditors of accounts.

53

The governor held the title of Captain General. His powers were judicial and administrative, including oversight of military defence. He had unlimited power, appointing all officeholders, including the treasurer, aldermen, comptrollers and public notaries. Strong leaders who held this position – probably a minority of all such governors – imposed their will and authority on Jamaica's inhabitants. Little support came from the Spanish crown, especially during the many years that the island's governorship was held by the Columbus family. Thus during the sixteenth century, relatively few officials were despatched to Jamaica from either Spain or Hispaniola.

In the early days of Spanish settlement in Jamaica, leaders who failed to keep good order were soon removed. Captains Perea and Camargo, sent to Jamaica by Diego Columbus between 1512 and 1514, were relieved of their positions after they failed to quell riots. The governors and their superior officers had committed so many abuses by 1533 that the Spanish king sent a leading lawyer, Don Gil Gonzales de Avila, to Jamaica to inspect the accounts of all Jamaican officers and to seize the estates of those found guilty of misdemeanours and then to replace these office holders. On his arrival in Jamaica, he convened a council, comprising the magistrates and main inhabitants of the island, and presented the charges against the governor, Manuel de Rojas. This resulted in release of several imprisoned planters whose confiscated estates were restored to them and the appointment of a new governor.

Governors who made their mark in Jamaica eventually left the island for perceived better prospects elsewhere. Garay, the first governor of Jamaica appointed by the king, lived in Jamaica from 1514 to 1523. He established ranches and farms settled by Spaniards in order to supply provisions to the governor and his military followers based at Castilla del Oro on the Spanish Main. Garay established the town of Oristán on Jamaica's southwest coast. But Garay left his post to venture to Mexico, where he died. His Jamaican properties were dispersed and his son lodged a claim in 1532 to inherit his father's estate. This led to continuing legal disputes that were not resolved until the 1640s. Among the more effective governors was Don Fernando Melgarejo de Córdoba (1596–1606), who established Jamaica's first coastal defences and guarded the island's west coast against pirate attacks. He also made laws and created a Registry, a record office and tariffs.

Some governors proved controversial, and were accused of corruption. This could be carried out by trading with Spain's enemies, by appropriating scarce labour to themselves, and by nepotism that promoted their own family members to positions of control and influence. At the turn of the seventeenth century, Governor Melgarejo de Córdoba was blamed for appropriating to himself the merchandise and African slaves brought to the island. He was alleged to have reserved 14,000 pesos to himself to bribe the incoming governor. Colonists also reported that he sold gunpowder to passing ships of all nationalities wherever he could make a profit. Another controversial governor was Francisco Terril, who exercised absolute power and refused to leave office in 1628 after his successor Jeronimo de Salcedo had already been appointed. Troops from Cuba took four years to force Terril out of office and wrest him from Jamaica.

Decimation of the Tainos

Jamaica's Taino population was rapidly decimated under Spanish rule. This followed the pattern already established in Hispaniola under the Spanish occupation where destruction of the Tainos occurred between 1494 and 1508 through warfare, harsh treatment and the despatch of captives to Spain. Governor Ovando eliminated the *caciques* in Hispaniola and redistributed the remaining Tainos to the crown or to *encomenderos*, the holders of crown land who were granted a monopoly on the labour of heathens. In 1515 Mazuelo, writing from Jamaica, informed the king of Spain that 'the Indians [i.e. Taino] have been very mistreated by the settlers of the island, who beat them and burn them and otherwise abuse them, to such an extent that if they continue unpunished, there will be no Indians two years from now'. Mazuelo tried to rectify this maltreatment of Tainos by putting two inspectors in charge of ensuring the natives received better treatment.

Subjugation of the Tainos to Spanish authority also accounted for loss of life through violence in Jamaica. Harsh treatment of the Tainos began as soon as the Spanish settled in Jamaica. Henry Barham, in his unpublished early eighteenth-century history of Jamaica, noted that the Spanish 'committed barbarous murders destroying many thousands of the Indians'. The first governor, Juan de Esquivel, forced the *caciques* into submission soon after he arrived on the island in 1510. The Taino were frequently treated brutally by the Spanish intruders. Many of their leaders were killed, though some *caciques* and their followers escaped capture and punishment by fleeing to mountainous areas in central Jamaica. The decimation of the Taino population was such that it was reported only 200 of the natives survived in Jamaica by the early years of the 1530s. Some had died through outbreaks of pestilential disease; others had been carried to mainland Spanish America to assist the Spaniards in their conquests there; but many had also died after experiencing dreadful conditions in mines where the Spanish forced them to search for gold. James Knight argued that these 'wretches were so harassed and distressed, that life was become Burthensome and painfull, which made them neglect the necessary means of preservation'.

Ferdinand II of Aragon issued a decree in 1513 that laid the basis for the *encomienda* land settlement system in Spanish America. Esquivel, who had captured Jamaica and had founded Sevilla Nueva, adopted this system in 1515, whereby Taino communities and their lands were assigned to Spanish settlers. He soon altered these arrangements to introduce the *repartimiento de Indias* labour system. This subjugated the Taino to Spanish authority and to work on the Crown's estates. The system enabled Spanish colonists to use Taino labour for a limited period of time. A Spanish royal decree sought to limit the harshness with which the natives could be treated, but this appears to have been largely ignored during Esquivel's brief governorship. The Taino were worked hard under this system, and put under pressure to provide maximum yields from agricultural work and ranching. Surplus cereals produced were exported to supply settlements on the Spanish Main. Mazuelo warned the Spanish monarchy as early as 1515 that ill-treatment of the Tainos, along with the spread of diseases, would lead rapidly to their disappearance, but this was ignored. A small number of Tainos were exported by the Spanish to their other Caribbean territories such as Hispaniola and Cuba. The spread of diseases was the most devastating cause of death for the natives. Europeans arrived in the Caribbean with a range of infections to which the Taino and other natives were not immune. This was part of what Alfred W. Crosby referred to as 'the Columbian exchange', the movement to and fro across the Atlantic of biological organisms ushered in by the European discovery of the New World. Virtually no inoculation or known cure existed for many diseases that were fatal when caught in a severe form. There was a long list of such diseases: chickenpox, scarlet fever, bubonic plague, measles, influenza, malaria, typhoid fever, diphtheria, dengue fever, dysentery, whooping cough and, probably most prevalent and fatal of all, smallpox. Extensive spread of smallpox in Hispaniola in late 1518 wiped out a third of the population.

Smallpox spread rapidly in Puerto Rico, Jamaica and other islands in the Greater Antilles. As was the case elsewhere in the Americas in the sixteenth and seventeenth centuries, its swift spread led to a demographic catastrophe among the native population. This proved much more problematic for Jamaica than for other colonies, whether English or Spanish, in North and South America in the sixteenth and seventeenth centuries. For whereas mainland America always attracted waves of settlers who became 'beneficiaries of catastrophe', Jamaica as a backwater never attracted a large influx of people while it remained under Spanish jurisdiction.

Decimation of the Tainos through disease and their harsh treatment as labourers curtailed their potential contributions to building up Spanish Jamaica. This was already apparent during the governorship of Garay, who was responsible for assigning Tainos to specific Spanish settlers. In 1521 Charles I, who had succeeded Ferdinand as king of Spain, wanted the Tainos to be treated well, but their numbers continued to decline. By the end of the 1530s, there was a need to import alternative sources of labour – something that, as explained below, was only achieved fitfully. In the late sixteenth century, Governor Melgarejo attempted to bring together the remaining Tainos on a reservation in an effort to stop Spanish exploitation of the Tainos. His plan was to offer the Tainos an option to settle on a site of their own choice so that they could live independently and manage their own affairs. Unfortunately, this scheme never materialised because Spanish colonists thought their cattle ranches would be ruined by natives leaving to form a self-sufficient settlement. Melgarejo wrote to King Philip III about the situation but no such Taino town came into existence. By 1600 there were very few Tainos left in Jamaica apart from those hiding in the forests of the Blue Mountains.

Population

All components of Jamaica's population during the Spanish era – whether natives, settlers, or African slaves – were relatively small. No accurate figures are available for the sixteenth century. An abbot estimated in 1611, however, that there were 1,610 people in Jamaica, including 523 Spanish, 173 Spanish children, 107 free blacks, 74

Taino, 558 slaves and 75 'foreigners'. Spanish residents in Jamaica were often closely related by marriage. Population levels appeared to remain static. By 1655, at the time of the English conquest, the population of Jamaica was about 1,500. This included some Portuguese Jewish families who had migrated there.

The lack of demographic growth resulted from plummeting numbers of natives and a failure to recruit sufficient colonisers or labourers from overseas. As early as 1515, the Spanish in Jamaica realised that they would struggle to support more than sixty settlers in the island's two main towns. This was partly the result of a lack of support from indigenous people for, as explained above, the Taino population was effectively decimated during the sixteenth century by sickness and ill-treatment. The Spanish never made up for this deficiency, however, by encouraging their own people to settle in Jamaica or providing sufficient manual labour through the shipment of Africans via the transatlantic slave trade to the western Caribbean. The relatively thin population of Jamaica under Spanish rule meant that settlements were scattered and much land remained unoccupied.

Esquivel brought only sixty Spanish settlers with him to Jamaica in 1509/10. About half left the island in the first couple of years. The rest mainly either set up ranches on the plains of what under English rule became the parishes of Clarendon, St Elizabeth, Westmoreland and St Thomas in the east, or they lived in urban centres. No large-scale flow of settlers to Jamaica followed these early arrivals. After Cortez's discovery of gold in Mexico in 1519 and riches found in Peru, the Spanish lost interest in encouraging their people to settle in Jamaica rather than in Terra Firma. Restless Spaniards in Jamaica soon migrated elsewhere. New Spanish settlements in Central America, such as Honduras and Guatemala, attracted more Spaniards than Jamaica, as did thriving settlements in Cuba, Santo Domingo and Hispaniola. As the convoy system (the *Flota de Indias*) despatching ships from Cadiz to the Americas always sailed via Havana, Cuba, avoiding a route to Jamaica, few new shipments of Spanish colonists arrived on the island. In 1521 the Spanish king waived customs duties on the household and personal goods of all Spaniards who settled in Jamaica, but this attempt to boost migration failed. In 1583 the king received reports that many Spaniards were abandoning their settlements and leaving Jamaica for locations on the Spanish Main.

Unlike other Spanish colonies in the New World, Portuguese settlers arrived in Jamaica in the sixteenth and early seventeenth centuries. In 1636 the immigration of thirty Portuguese families to Jamaica was licensed. In 1650 a report by the Spanish governor of Jamaica stated that 'the greater part of the inhabitants are Portuguese and have come by way of Angola'. The Portuguese influx appears to have operated smoothly, partly because Jamaica was underpopulated and partly because the Columbus family had married into the Portuguese nobility. Some of these newcomers came from Portuguese settlements in West Africa, while others were from Jewish families that had converted to Christianity in Portugal. The requirement that they had altered their faiths was important because people with Jewish ancestry were forbidden from leaving the Iberian peninsula for the Americas.

The sixteenth century witnessed the beginnings of a flourishing Atlantic slave trade in which Africans were forced to migrate from different West African regions to a life of hard manual labour mainly on New World plantations. However, the supply of African slaves to Jamaica was very modest, as the population estimates cited above from 1611 suggest. It appears that the Spanish were initially circumspect about introducing African slaves to Jamaica, but they turned to this option, albeit at first on a small scale, after it became clear that not enough Spaniards would settle in Jamaica. In 1523 the Spanish Crown ordered 300 enslaved Africans to be taken to Jamaica. A few years later another 700 African captives were required. Whether either or both of these shipments of slaves reached Jamaica in the numbers indicated is unknown. In the early seventeenth century, ships leaving the Portuguese settlement of Angola delivered sick slaves to Jamaica instead of taking them on to their intended landings at Porto Bello or Cartagena on the Spanish Main. These slaves were put to various types of manual work in building towns, growing and milling sugar, clearing wooded areas, hunting cattle and building fortifications.

Some slaves brought to sixteenth-century Jamaica were Coromantines from the Gold Coast. Most of these Africans were probably imported illegally because the Spanish Crown refused to grant licences or *asientos* for slave importations to Jamaica. The illegal shipments of slaves to Jamaica were irregular: in many years there appear to have been none. In addition, the Spanish colonists in Jamaica probably lacked substantial amounts of capital to purchase large batches of newly imported Africans. Not all of the slaves came directly from Africa. Some were loaded on vessels from Spain after they had been taken there from Portuguese settlements in West Central Africa. Whatever their provenance, the total size of the slave population in Jamaica was small compared with the later huge numbers of enslaved Africans who were imported to Jamaica after the English settlement of the island. The maximum size of Jamaica's slave population before 1655 was about 1,000.

Economic Activities

In theory, Jamaica should have attracted settlers under Spanish rule. It had a fairly benign climate, without excessive rain or drought; its soil had much fertility; and there was only one major mountain range where agricultural production was difficult to establish. However, the economic development of Spanish Jamaica was constrained by low population levels: there were neither enough colonists nor Tainos nor African slaves to establish a prosperous colony. Spain itself did not have the financial resources to exploit Jamaica's commercial possibilities by sponsoring migration there on a significant scale. But in any case conquistadors expected natives to undertake manual work in colonies, and, without sufficient Tainos to provide the necessary labour, this was never going to occur on a widespread basis. During the Spanish period in Jamaica, therefore, much of the land remained uninhabited and uncultivated.

The Spanish settlement in Jamaica began with a search for gold. There was a strong hope that such precious metal could be found as the Spanish had located gold supplies in Puerto Rico a few years earlier. Unfortunately for the

Spanish, however, no alluvial supplies of gold were found in Jamaica after the Tainos had helped early colonists to undertake extensive searches among the mountains and streams of the island. King Ferdinand eventually gave orders for a cessation of the search for gold, with an emphasis instead on agricultural production. The failure to find gold, with only some deposits of copper found instead, was a bitter blow to the Spanish. Within a few years, however, Spanish settlers had located gold in Cuba, and this was a major reason why Spain thereafter concentrated more on the settlement of Cuba rather than Jamaica.

After gold was not found in Jamaica, the economy focused on the cultivation of yucca, maize, pimento, sweet potatoes, cotton and other textiles along with meat, hides, lard and tallow gained from cattle ranching. Cassava bread, capable of being preserved for many months, was widely eaten. Stem cuttings of yucca and sweet potatoes, planted in *conuco* mounds, provided starch for dietary demands. The Spaniards incorporated Taino methods of food preparation into their everyday subsistence habits. Cane sugar was introduced by the Spanish from Hispaniola, where it was already flourishing. Spanish settlers introduced garden vegetables, citrus fruits such as limes, lemons and oranges, yams, pigeon peas (i.e. lentils), plantains and pawpaw from Europe, Africa and mainland America, but there was less agricultural innovation than in other Spanish Caribbean islands.

Cattle, pigs and goats were introduced from other Spanish West Indian islands. This was a marked change from the Taino era in Jamaica, where few large animals were found. Pigs produced large quantities of lard, and were hunted and killed for cooking jerk pork. Cows and bulls were mainly kept for their hides rather than for their meat. In 1583 a letter written to the king by the abbot of Jamaica, Francisco Marques de Villalobos, noted that

[l]arge and small stock are raised in abundance. This is on the south side. As it is flatter than the north it is stocked with domestic cattle. On the north, as it is a broken and mountainous country wild cattle are bread [sic] and there is a great quantity of pigs, so much so that very often the smaller ones are caught by hand.

In 1611 the abbot of Jamaica noted that the Spanish colonists spent nearly the whole year in 'killing cows and bulls only to get the hides and the fat, leaving the meat wasted'. The roaming and trampling of livestock eventually destroyed the *conucos*. Subsistence agriculture found it difficult to survive herds of animals foraging. There were few feral dogs in Jamaica to prey on livestock.

Crops and livestock had important ancillary uses. Manioc was made from yucca. Leather tanning was one by-product of rearing cattle. Salt was obtained from coastal *salinas*. The Spanish introduced bananas, oranges and lemons to Jamaica along with sugar cane and, probably, arrowroot. Many economic activities associated with the Tainos continued. Cassava bread was prepared. Edible roots such as yams and sweet potatoes continued to form a central part of dietary intake. Shirts, hammocks and cotton clothes were manufactured. The smallholdings (*conucos*) of the Tainos gradually gave way to cattle farms, pens and pasture. Spanish settlers adapted Taino skills in woodworking and masonry to build houses and towns.

Jamaica had rich natural resources even though it had no precious metals. With only a limited population, more than sufficient meat, vegetables and fruit were available in

Jamaica to meet subsistence needs. Descriptions of Jamaica under Spanish rule suggest that it was a fertile island, favoured with many plants, herbs and trees along with pumpkins, linseed, artichokes and tamarinds. Some droughts in the early part of the sixteenth century hampered crop cultivation, but these temporary difficulties were overcome. Different woods included mahogany, cedar and red ebony. In general, the southern flatter half of Jamaica bred animals for the farm and field while the more rugged northern half had plenty of pigs. Goats and sheep also roamed on pastureland, feeding on local roots, herbs and berries. The inhabitants of Spanish Jamaica bought and sold goods with copper maravedis pieces (known as *cuartos*). These were minted in Santo Domingo. It was reported in 1644 that 16,000 pieces of copper coin were being used annually in Jamaica.

Though the economic activities were sufficient to meet internal demand for food and clothing in Spanish Jamaica, external economic activities were limited. The main underlying reason for the underdevelopment of foreign trade lay in the relatively few ships – probably only three or four per year – that called at Jamaica before the English takeover in 1655. In December 1638, for instance, the governor of Santo Domingo stated that only one ship had sailed to Jamaica and no ship had returned in the past two-and-a-half years. Jamaica was an island that could provide shelter to ships needing to anchor in bad weather and its fine array of harbours could have received much more shipping than was the case. But the organisation of Spanish shipping in the Atlantic and the Caribbean was always undertaken in a way that eschewed much contact with Jamaica. Spain sent out galleons in a fleet on fixed routes that did not deviate from year to year. On maps it looked as though Jamaica lay directly in the path of the Spanish treasure fleet sailing from Vera Cruz in New Spain to Seville via either Santo Domingo or Havana, but the reality was different. After 1632, for example, galleons sailing with silver shuttled between Cartagena and Havana, but although they sometimes had Jamaica in sight, they never diverted their route to stop there. Havana was the port where Spanish ships made a rendezvous in the western Caribbean rather than any of Jamaica's harbours.

Jamaica did export products during its Spanish era, but it usually had to despatch commodities via transient vessels to neighbouring islands such as Santa Maria, la Yaguana and Cuba rather than to the Spanish Main. Nevertheless, there were annual shipments of cassava to Cartagena, where oil, wine, vinegar and manufactured goods were purchased to take back to Jamaica, and livestock and lard were exported to Cuba and Central America. But Spanish trade regulations stipulated that all trade to and from Jamaica had to be undertaken in Spanish ships. Thus there was no possibility of smaller vessels being constructed in Jamaica (where good wood for shipbuilding was available) to establish intra-Caribbean shipping routes.

Despite limited economic activities in Spanish Jamaica, the relatively sparse population in the period 1510–1655 were creative in their use of food resources. As David Buisseret has put it, Spanish Jamaica showed 'the promise of an immensely varied economy, based on remarkable natural resources'. But the emphasis is definitely on promise rather than achievement. By the last years of the Spanish occupation of Jamaica, the island's economic

VIEW IN JAMAICA.

FIGURE 2.2 A View in Jamaica. Duncan 1890/Getty Images

potential had not been realised. This was well summed up by a visiting Englishman Henry Whistler. In his journal of 1654–5, he noted that there was plenty of good land for planting crops in Jamaica, and an abundance of cattle, hogs, wild fowl and fish. Currently the island was 'poor, but it may be made one of the richest spots in the world; the Spaniard doth call it the Garden of the Indies, but this I will say, the gardeners have been very bad, for here is very little more than that which groweth naturally'.

Urban Centres

The Spanish established urban centres in different parts of Jamaica. The Royal Laws of the Indies, emanating from Spain, stipulated that new towns should be located inland to prevent pirate raids on coastal urban settlements. The first Spanish communities were Villa Diego and Melilla, established in 1508. In the following year, Sevilla la Nueva (New Seville), situated at St Ann's Bay on Jamaica's north coast, was built as the capital. The government and civil authority of Jamaica was based there. Shortly afterwards Oristan was laid out as a subsidiary town on the south coast. This was mainly used as a provision and trading centre for commerce with mainland America. Oristan was a short-lived urban centre, however, for it was moved under Garay's governorship to the vicinity of Bluefields. Melilla, situated to the east of New Seville near today's Port Maria, was constructed as another smaller town to accommodate *haciendas* (ranches). Other towns established in Jamaica by the Spaniards were St Ann, La Villa and the ranches of Mayman. In 1534 the capital was moved from Sevilla la Nueva to Santiago de la Vega (Spanish Town), which was much further south. The transfer of the capital was necessary because the swampy lowland areas and creeks surrounding New Seville had led to insects spreading diseases among the settler population. A contemporary description of Jamaica from 1582 stated that this was then the only populated town on the island.

Esquivel began the building of New Seville. Construction was largely carried out in brick and mortar by the local Tainos. The work continued under Garay after Esquivel's death in 1512. At the centre of the settlement, a governor's fortified mansion was constructed. It was probably a two-storey structure. A stone church was begun but seems to have not been completed. New Seville also had some houses and two water-powered sugar mills (*ingenious*) that were commonly used in sugar production.

During Garay's period at New Seville, one mill produced 125 tons of sugar per year. In 1519 Garay moved the original settlement at New Seville from its swampy location to a healthier, hillier location less than a quarter of a mile away.

New Seville was a tiny settlement. It was reported in 1534 that only eighty Spanish settlers lived there. At least half of them had been affected by the spread of pestilence and disease. Mazuelo, as royal factor and treasurer, advised the Spanish king that it would be beneficial to move the capital further south from New Seville. He met the town's inhabitants to explain that the new location of the capital – Santiago de la Vega – would have a healthier climate and sufficient land to cultivate. Mazuelo had an ulterior motive for choosing the new location of the capital: he owned a nearby sugar mill and would be better able to supervise its operations if he lived on the spot. The removal was agreed and the exodus from New Seville took place in 1534. Today the town of St Ann's Bay lies just to the east of the Spanish settlement at New Seville.

The site for Spanish Town was situated on a plain near the River Cobre at the junction of a main north–south route and east–west trail. It was located about seven miles from Kingston's harbour in an inland setting out of reach of possible pirate attacks. Spanish Town was intended to be an administrative and agricultural centre. Streets were laid out on a grid pattern. The houses, according to Edward Long's observations in 1774, were sturdily constructed with a mixture of hardwood, mortar and wattling, and designed to withstand the climatic vagaries of the Caribbean. Several squares were constructed, including one with the governor's house. A municipal council chamber was built along with a wooden court house. There were also religious buildings and modestly constructed houses. There were no fortifications. Surrounded by the extensive plain of Vere, Spanish Town's environs had some of the best fertile land suitable for sugar production. During the sixteenth century, Spanish Town was a small, compact town: by the 1590s it only had about 160 households. Its layout comprised about a mile in length and a quarter of a mile in breadth.

Religion

The institutions of the Roman Catholic Church soon spread to Jamaica after the Spanish conquest. This marked the coming of Christianity to the island, with the Pope in Rome exercising ultimate spiritual authority. Insufficient funds were available from Spain to support a grand establishment such as a cathedral church in Jamaica. Instead, a Franciscan house and abbacy were created there by Pope Leo X. The latter was established by 1515. During the early Spanish era, the abbacy was hardly a flourishing institution: the first four appointed abbots did not take up residence in Jamaica. The first appointment to the post was King Ferdinand's chaplain Sancho de Matienço, canon of the cathedral at Seville. He collected rents, emoluments and profits from his appointment but never left Spain to take up residence in Jamaica. Thus he served as abbot of Jamaica by proxy. The chronicler Peter Martyr was proposed by the King of Spain and Holy Roman Emperor Charles V as abbot of Jamaica, but he had not visited the island by the time of his death in 1526.

71

Such a modest outpost of Roman Catholicism in a Spanish colony was too limited in its presence to stand alone without religious support – nominal in most respects – from a superior see. Until 1547 the abbacy in Jamaica was dependent on the archbishopric of Seville. In 1574, however, Jamaica was transferred to the bishopric of Santiago de Cuba. From 1537 onwards the descendants of Columbus oversaw the appointment of abbots and other religious officers. Jamaica's abbacy was funded by tithes. These proved difficult to collect and each abbot complained about the paucity of tithes collected by his predecessor. Some tithes were collected in Jamaica's most valuable asset, hides, but others involved cash accruals. The average tithe collected in the sixteenth century was the relatively small annual sum of 400 pesos. This was insufficient money to support a bishopric in Jamaica.

The abbot of Jamaica dressed in a manner appropriate to his role as a prelate, but his role was limited in terms of what he was authorised to do. As Morales Padron has explained, the Jamaican abbot 'wore a mitre, carried a pastoral staff and enjoyed episcopal authority ... but he could not confer or administer confirmation, ordain priests, or consecrate the Holy Oil'. Abbots in Jamaica were assisted by some chaplains, but relatively few clergymen ever lived in Spanish Jamaica.

Spanish Jamaica had other institutions connected to the Catholic Church including several churches, a mission, two hermitages dedicated to St Lucy and St Barbara, and two monasteries associated with the Franciscan and Dominican orders. None of the buildings survive. Mass was celebrated on feast days and saints' days, observed with a similar ritual to European practice. Since the number of churches was limited, missionaries travelled to the *haciendas* where mass was celebrated. King Ferdinand, who believed Esquivel had been lax in carrying out Christian conversion among the Tainos, despatched ten Franciscan missionaries to Jamaica as early as 1512. Under the *Patronato Real* system, in which the state played an active role in the administration and support of the Roman Catholic Church, Spain was committed to propagation of the Christian faith in the Indies. The king's swift action to try to convert Tainos to Catholicism in the first few years of Spanish settlement in Jamaica indicated that he took this religious imperative seriously.

The Spanish were theoretically in favour of saving the souls of the Tainos through spreading the Christian gospels. Efforts were made under Governor Garay to convert and catechise Taino *caciques* and their followers to Christianity. Garay referred to this system as *requerimiento* (requirement). Some of this proselytising effort was carried out by Franciscan friars. How successful this proved to be is unknown, but Garay was informed by a circumspect King Ferdinand that it would be difficult, owing to the language barrier and need to allow time for catechism to be carried out properly, for strong foundations of Catholicism to be embedded in the native population. Tainos could be influenced to accept Christian rites while they remained in contact with the Spanish, but they frequently returned to *zemi* worship when left alone.

African slaves who converted to Christianity and acknowledged the supremacy of the Spanish sovereignty and the Pope could receive the sacraments and be married. Owing to language problems, however, it is uncertain whether many slaves complied with these conditions. Evidence survives showing that slaves often lived in concubinage. Some abbots turned a blind eye to such liaisons and paid little attention to moral doctrine. But others thought their office gave them the obligation of safeguarding the moral order and so they summoned those suspected of living without the legal sanction of marriage, questioned both parties, and then persuaded them to undertake a Christian marriage ceremony to maintain their union.

Attacks on Jamaica

From time to time, raids were made on Jamaica's shores by English, French or Dutch ships while the Spanish controlled the island. The island's defences were rudimentary, with many parts of the coast left undefended. In 1554 French pirates attacked New Seville and destroyed all of its wooden houses. Jamaica had few effective fortifications. Abbot Don Francisco Marquez de Villalobos advised the Spanish king in 1582 that if enemies attacked Jamaica, 'this would mean total destruction of her surroundings and great harm to the Armadas and Fleets of thy Majesty'. Alonzo Miranda, who became governor in 1607, informed the Spanish king that Jamaica was frequently attacked by enemy corsairs. He also pointed out that the scattered settlers throughout the island were mainly poor and found it difficult to arm themselves at their own expense for protection against invaders. Other colonial officials and settlers warned the Spanish authorities of the need for greater defence of Jamaica's coastline against enemy intruders, but the calls fell upon deaf ears.

The Spanish government provided neither funds nor personnel to improve Jamaica's defences. Neither the Columbus family nor the Spanish settlers found the resources to build defensive fortifications. Only one working fort was in place in Jamaica by 1600. King Philip IV sent Juan Bautista Antonelli, a leading military engineer, to the Caribbean to investigate the need for better Spanish fortifications for its territorial possessions, but the Cuban governor detained him to address his island's defence needs and he therefore did not give full attention to Jamaica. Letters from Spanish officials to the king in 1638 pointed out that Jamaica would be easily overrun if invaded and, once that happened, it would be very difficult to recapture the island for Spain. Despite these admonitions, however, the Spanish authorities continued to neglect Jamaica's defence. By the time of the English takeover of the island in 1655, the last time a large Caribbean island was successfully invaded, Jamaica's defences had barely improved from those in place in the late sixteenth century.

Despite the lack of fortifications, however, there were fighting men available. By 1597 there were four military companies. In 1651 the Jamaican militia comprised 500 men in six infantry companies; they had 300 firearms but some were in poor condition. There were insufficient men to augment the militia's strength. In 1597 and 1643 English raids, by Sir Anthony Shirley and Captain William Jackson, captured Spanish Town and held it to ransom. In 1603, by contrast, Spanish Town was attacked by an English flotilla under the pirate captain Christopher Newport, but this was successfully repelled by the militia. By 1640 pirates were regularly marauding in Jamaica's waters and able to mount attacks on a largely unprotected coastline, while France had a base at Tortuga, a pirate's haven off the north coast of Hispaniola, and had sent a representative to establish its claims on Hispaniola. It was not inconceivable that France, an enemy of Spain in the Thirty Years' War, would invade Spanish possessions in the western Caribbean, including Jamaica.

It would prove impossible to defend Jamaica against a large invading force, however, and when this occurred in 1655, in an English assault, the Spanish soon capitulated. Much of Spanish Jamaica – its language, architecture, agricultural organisation – was destroyed in the aftermath of the English takeover. Though Spanish place names have left their mark on modern Jamaica, including Rio Nuevo, Rio Magno, Rio Bueno, Port Antonio, Rio Cobre, Rio Grande, Port Esquivel, Mount Diablo, Savanna-la-Mar, Negril and Montego Bay, the English invaders soon provided their own names for Jamaica's landscape features and settlements, a process that continued apace thereafter.

3

Creating an English Jamaica, 1655–1775

~

On 10 May 1655, an English fleet arrived in Kingston harbour from Hispaniola. Comprising a naval force and an army under the joint command of General Robert Venables and Admiral William Penn, about 9,000 troops were landed under protective covering fire. They easily breached the weak Spanish defences, manned by between 400 and 600 men, and marched to occupy Santiago de la Vega, the chief Spanish settlement on the island. This sudden, unexpected military action – the first time Spanish Jamaica had been invaded by a large force – was an outgrowth of Oliver Cromwell's Western Design, an ambitious plan of British imperial expansion. Cromwell had led a series of military successes during the English Civil War in the 1640s. He had defeated Ireland and Scotland, and was the victor in the First Anglo-Dutch naval war (1652–4). These successes spurred him to further military endeavours. As Lord Protector of the English Commonwealth in the aftermath of the English Civil War, Cromwell had been advised that Spanish military protection of its main bases in the western Caribbean was vulnerable to attack. He wanted to seize territory there to increase the English claim to West Indian islands. There was further motivation from a Puritan-inspired attack on the wealth of Spanish Papists. The Western Design was the first time that the English state had sponsored a military and imperial initiative and had stationed a naval squadron in the tropics.

England had already settled small islands in the eastern Caribbean, including Barbados, St Kitts, Nevis and Antigua, and had begun to make profits from trade and sugar cultivation at those locations. Now the time was ripe, so Cromwell thought, to advance England's exploitation of the West Indies. He and his secretary of state, John Thurloe, had decided by the summer of 1654 that a military and naval attack should be launched against Spanish Jamaica to establish a strong English presence in the Spanish-dominated western Caribbean. The Western Design set out with 60 ships and 4,000 soldiers and added another dozen vessels and 5,000 soldiers in Barbados and a smaller number in St Kitts. Its naval commanders ended up attacking Jamaica after the expedition was first repulsed from taking Santo Domingo, the centre of Spanish administration and trade in Hispaniola. This failed attempt to conquer Hispaniola was marked by logistical blunders and dehydration, hunger and poor health among the English troops. Neither Venables nor Penn wanted to return home without evidence of the successful prosecution of their expedition. Concerned about their military reputations after the failed bombardment of Hispaniola, they decided to attack the easier target of Jamaica.

Venables allowed the Spanish in Jamaica a week to offer their surrender. During that time, many Spanish settlers quit the island for Cuba with their possessions and set their livestock and slaves free. Others hid their 'treasure which they could not carry with them, yt they buried in the bowels of the Earth, and in caves'. The formal surrender occurred on 17 May 1655. The Spanish were allowed to leave Jamaica with clothing and provisions. Non-Catholics prepared to accept English rule were allowed to remain. Venables, Penn and most of their troops left Jamaica for England, leaving Vice Admiral William Goodson there in charge of twelve naval ships. On 28 November 1655, Cromwell issued a proclamation which designated Port Royal as the new capital city of Jamaica. He stated that England was at war with Spain and that 'we will maintain Jamaica, send reinforcement after reinforcement to it; we will try yet for the Spanish Plate fleets . . . and have no peace with Spain'.

The English invasion was a miserable experience for the troops. They found it difficult to gather food, and there appeared to be no loot to appropriate as a consolation. By January 1656, two leading English army officers reported that many soldiers were 'sick and weak, the best and soundest much abated of their strength and vigor'. Faced with starvation, the soldiers were assigned to cultivating the land for four hours a day in addition to their garrison duties. Serious bouts of disease broke out. Dysentery and death decimated over 100 officers and thousands of English troops. An English army major reported that 'many of them that were alive, walked like ghosts or dead men, who, as I went through the town [i.e. Spanish Town], lay groaning and crying out, bread for the Lords' sake. The truth is, when I set foot first on land, I saw nothing but symptoms of necessity and desolation.' In the first year of the conquest of Jamaica, 5,000 out of the 7,000 soldiers died.

Wanting godly Englishmen to conquer Jamaica, Cromwell issued a proclamation from Whitehall to encourage people to colonise there. This did happen, but over a longer time period and in a less glorious way than the Lord Protector envisaged. It was not at all clear that Jamaica would be preserved as a useful acquisition for England. Cromwell was displeased at the failure to take Hispaniola, to say the least: this was the sort of military defeat he could not countenance. In addition, he viewed the botched Western Design as an example of God's displeasure with him and with England as a nation. He imprisoned Venables and Penn in the Tower of London for dereliction of their duties, though they were later released.

The English forces left in Jamaica began constructing Passage Fort to defend Kingston harbour. Fears were rife among the English invaders that Spain would direct military resources from its fleet, or raise troops in Spanish Caribbean territories, to regain the island. Don Cristolbal de Ysassi, the last Spanish governor of Jamaica, attempted to win back Jamaica from the English with the aid of Spanish-speaking enslaved people and free blacks of African descent. In the summer of 1657 he attacked the island with these forces raised in Cuba, and established a fortified foothold at Rio Nuevo on the northern coast. Acting English governor Colonel Edward D'Oyley attacked him with the support of 750 well-trained troops, and inflicted a crushing victory on the Spanish at the Battle of Rio Nuevo in June 1658. Ysassi escaped to Cuba.

Some remaining slaves joined the Spanish forces, but many withdrew to the mountains in the island's interior. They became the first 'Maroon' communities in Jamaica; in other words, they were slave runaways who maintained their freedom. Today there is a popular belief in Jamaica that the Maroons were descended not just from slaves but from the island's original inhabitants, the Taino. Specialists disagree over the connection between Tainos and Maroons: some historians argue that some remaining Tainos intermingled with escaped African slaves in the seventeenth century, while others believe the Maroons had a purely African ancestry. Genetic data gathered for the Accompong Town Maroons indicates that their ancestry extended beyond African roots to encompass non-African peoples. However, though indigenous American ancestry can be found among these Maroons, at present it can only be argued that some members of this community potentially originated from Taino ancestors.

The pacification of Jamaica under D'Oyley was protracted owing to continuing resistance from Maroons and Spaniards still on the island. Intermittent guerrilla warfare continued in the late 1650s and early 1660s. The Spanish gained additional support from troops recruited in Mexico. The English soldiers remaining on the island had difficulties supporting themselves while engaged in weeding out Spanish resistance. Despite reinforcements, the English garrison in Jamaica had fallen to 2,200 by 1660. In 1657 it was claimed that 'as yet Jamaica looks like a great garrison' that appeared to be 'rather as an Army than a Collonie'. Thus the English conquest of Jamaica proved difficult to finalise.

English forces took control of Jamaica by quelling protests. They hunted out remaining Spanish colonists in the wooded areas of Jamaica by clandestine attacks after nightfall. Patrolling of bush areas proved very effective. In addition, English naval ships were positioned along the immediate sea passages to Jamaica, providing additional military support to prevent Spanish attempts to regain

Jamaica. By 1660 the last Spanish forces were driven out of Jamaica, near Ocho Rios, after their food supplies and weapons diminished and the English occupying forces were aided by goods smuggled to them by the governor of Santiago de Cuba. Rumours spread to Spanish settlements in the western Caribbean that England was planning a further invasion force to consolidate its hold on Jamaica. To counteract this fear, Spain relied on officials throughout its possessions to take action to restore Jamaica to Spanish rule. However, governors, traders and mariners in those islands were reluctant to support that objective because an English presence in Jamaica would be of greater benefit in the future to their own colonial ports. Officials charged with supplying additional troops from New Spain to reconquer Jamaica only supplied relatively small numbers of men; using the rest of their military resources to defend port cities in the Spanish Caribbean against external attack was a higher priority for them.

When the English monarchy was restored in 1660, it was uncertain whether Jamaica would be retained because it had been a Cromwellian acquisition and therefore regarded by some in royalist circles as tainted. In addition, the Spanish Crown had offered hospitality to the exiled Stuarts during the Interregnum. A number of London's West India merchants, however, persuaded Charles II to retain Jamaica as a royal colony after both Spain and France had failed to support royalist aims in the peace treaty they signed with Cromwell's son Richard in 1659. In Jamaica, the military occupiers set about improving the island's defences much more rapidly than had ever occurred under the Spanish settlement in Jamaica. Batteries were erected around the harbour, defences were installed to protect Spanish Town, and Fort Cromwell (swiftly renamed Fort Charles) was built at Port Royal as a bulwark against enemy raids. Martial government prevailed at first in Jamaica, but it was replaced by civil administration in 1664 when Sir Thomas Modyford was appointed royal governor. He was the first important English official in Jamaica to attempt to turn a Cromwellian military outpost into a colony of settlement loyal to the Crown.

For the rest of the seventeenth century, the English set about claiming Jamaica as their own. English institutions were transferred rapidly to Jamaica. Land grants were offered to settlers. In the early 1660s thirty-acre headrights (legal land grants for fulfilling certain conditions) were offered to each settler with thirty additional acres allocated to each household member, including servants. King Charles II announced that the offspring of white settlers in Jamaica would have the full status of English subjects. Contemporary English colonists spun narratives that the Taino had disappeared from Jamaica altogether, and that Spanish brutality accounted for their erasure. Spanish place names and houses remained on the island, but by the time of the Glorious Revolution in 1689 the English had begun to consolidate their imprint on Jamaica to such an extent – in terms of politics, religion, economic affairs and language – that the island was well on the way to becoming an important English colonial settlement.

Buccaneers and Privateers

In the early years of English settlement in Jamaica, buccaneering was a prime way of generating profitable economic activity from raiding Spanish vessels trading in precious metals with Mexico and Peru. Taking their name from the French word *boucanier*, itself derived from the *boucan*, the place where strips of meat were dried and smoked, the buccaneers were sea rovers throughout the Caribbean who preyed predominantly on Spanish fleets but sometimes also on French and Dutch ships. Buccaneering was a rumbustious, sometimes violent affair, operating in both peacetime and wartime. Buccaneers were drawn from deserters from the navy, sailors captured from merchant vessels, impoverished former indentured servants, and logwood cutters from the Bays of Campeche and Honduras. Plenty of riches were there for the taking, as the Spanish treasure ships annually sailed from Central America across the Caribbean Sea en route for Spain while French and Dutch trading ships plied routes between numerous Caribbean islands. The Spanish, French and Dutch provided little naval protection for their vessels in Caribbean waters, which emboldened buccaneers in their search for booty. Pirate ships also searched for enemy vessels and their cargoes, but it is unlikely that a permanent population of pirates existed in the Caribbean until at least the 1670s.

Jamaica became an important base for buccaneers in the quarter century after England gained hold of the island. In 1657 D'Oyley invited buccaneers living on Tortuga, a well-known pirates' nest, to settle in Jamaica where they provided an additional bulwark against Spanish raids. Henry Barham, in his unpublished 1722 history of Jamaica, stated that 'there is a Great Deal of Difference between a Privateer & a Buccaneer or Freebooter' for 'the first hath Commissions Granted by a Royall Government: the Latter Acts without any legall Commission or

FIGURE 3.1 Pirates boarding a Spanish vessel in the Caribbean.
Culture Club/Hulton Archive/Getty Images

Authority from any Government but their own and therefore are no better than Pyrates'. However, to contradict these distinctions, in the 1660s and 1670s the illegal depredations of the buccaneers were accepted by several Jamaican governors who shrewdly calculated that legitimising such activities by referring to them as privateers could be valuable for economic progress in Jamaica.

Privateering vessels were privately owned ships authorised by the state to support a war effort. These ships should be seen as distinct from pirate vessels, which were illegal marauders. Privateering provided employment for seafaring men; offered victualling opportunities for merchants; served as a way of defending English possessions against Spanish incursions; and enabled lucrative prize cargoes to be brought back to Jamaica. Possibly as many men were engaged in privateering from Jamaica in the 1660s as were involved in other activities on shore. Port Royal, situated on a narrow, elongated peninsula on the south of the island, became the buccaneers' and privateers' main haven in Jamaica.

Privateers mainly attacked Spanish ships but they also raided towns and settlements on the southern coasts of Cuba and Hispaniola, the two most important Spanish settlements in the Caribbean. Such privateering activity enabled the English to consolidate their hold over Jamaica. It also helped to strengthen English sovereignty in Jamaica and to develop bases to pursue illegal trade with Spanish America. Edward Long in *The History of Jamaica* (1774) praised the bravery of the buccaneers and privateers, arguing that they helped to solidify English control in Jamaica in the late 1650s and 1660s when the Spanish tried to drive out their conquerors from the island. When the English 'had possessed themselves of Jamaica' they 'betook themselves to privateering, with no other design at first, than, by a continual annoyance of their coasts and the capture of their trading vessels, to force them into a peace, which was not likely to be obtained by any other means. This business proved successful to them beyond their utmost expectation; and brought this island into so much esteem at home, that copious supplies of provision, arms, and other necessaries, were instantly sent.'

Some early English commanders and governors of Jamaica fully supported privateering depredations against Spanish ships. D'Oyley, the first commander appointed after England seized Jamaica, led several raids on the Spanish before 1661. The privateering vessels he led operated under the patronage of the navy. Modyford, deputy governor of Jamaica between 1664 and 1671, was an even greater supporter of privateers. He initially tried to conduct peaceful relations with the Spanish in the Caribbean, but this led numerous buccaneers to desert Port Royal for French-held Hispaniola and Tortuga as a base. Plummeting economic activity at Port Royal was the result. Modyford realised he should change his policy towards the privateers, a stance given greater urgency by the Anglo-Dutch war of 1665–7 in which the Dutch allied with the French against England. Modyford now courted the buccaneers to undertake raids on England's enemies in the Caribbean. They left from Jamaica to take the Dutch island of St Eustatius in July 1665. Another group of buccaneers from Jamaica seized Tobago in 1666. In that year and 1670, Modyford declared private war on the Spanish and backed privateering raids against Spanish commerce. He was recalled to England in 1671 by Charles II because he had licensed privateers to intercept Spanish ships without royal assent.

Modyford's support for buccaneering involved support for famous raids undertaken by Henry Morgan, a Welsh privateer already based in Jamaica by the early 1660s. In 1667 Modyford issued him with a letter of marque or licence to attack Spanish ships and commerce. Morgan was involved in a series of enterprising raids over the next few years. In 1667 he successfully attacked Puerto Principe (now Camagüey) in Cuba, killing the governor and pillaging properties. In the same year he sacked the fortified town of Porto Bello in Panama, he and his men acquiring 250,000 pieces of eight in the process. In 1668

FIGURE 3.2 Henry Morgan. Science Photo Library/Getty Images

Morgan and his associates plundered towns in Venezuela and attacked a Spanish squadron. In 1671 he arrived on the Isthmus of Panama with 2,000 men and proceeded to take Panama City on its Pacific coast. This involved a difficult assault against Spanish infantry and cavalry, but the buccaneers ransacked and captured the city after Spanish guards on the ramparts fled their positions. Morgan's sack of Panama was followed by a return to Port Royal to find that England and Spain had already signed a peace treaty in Madrid in 1670. Under this accord, Spain acknowledged England's right to her Caribbean island possessions. Morgan argued he did not know about the peace when he attacked Panama: the Spanish government was not convinced by this explanation. Morgan was arrested and ordered back to London, but on arrival there in 1672 he received a hero's welcome from Charles II and the government. Morgan was knighted by the king, and returned to Jamaica in 1675 to serve as lieutenant governor. Jamaican governors in the 1670s took different sides in relation to the buccaneers. Sir Thomas Lynch, who served as lieutenant governor between 1671 and 1674, was a large landholder who supported the growth of plantations in Jamaica. To secure this aim, he tried to minimise unruly activity by offering buccaneers an amnesty to hand back property to rightful owners and to remove themselves from land on which they were squatting. Nevertheless, Lynch found it difficult to fulfil his anti-buccaneering policy. 'This cursed trade has been so long followed', he lamented in 1672, 'that like weeds or Hidras they spring up as fast as we can cut them down'. Lynch was appalled to be in post when Morgan returned to Jamaica as lieutenant governor, noting in a letter to the secretary of state his surprise at who 'ever thought it possible his Majesty should send the Admirall of the Pryvateers to governe this island'. Morgan remained on good terms with the buccaneers in Jamaica and elsewhere in the Caribbean, encouraging those operating from Tortuga to bring their wares to Port Royal for sale. Lynch's successor Lord John Vaughan, lieutenant governor between 1675 and 1678, did not favour the buccaneers, but he was followed in post between 1678 and 1680 by the Earl of Carlisle, who tolerated privateers.

Attitudes towards the buccaneers hardened in Jamaica in the early 1680s. Now the English government and merchants and planters in Jamaica cracked down on buccaneers because of the disruption they caused to the lines of trade with the island. Jamaica's

Council passed anti-pirate legislation in 1681. Two years later a Jamaica Act consolidated the attack on privateers. Trials were held at Port Royal in which buccaneers were convicted for illegal activities. For the English government and Jamaica's leading politicians and planters, buccaneering activity had now become a serious hindrance to the development of a settled economy based on legitimate trade and sugar cultivation. The concern to provide safety on the sea lanes followed by British merchant vessels in the West India trade began to trump the depredations of privateers on the Spanish treasure fleet. Privateers challenged this attempted clampdown on their operations by taking revenge on English ships. But the buccaneers succumbed to what was now an unfriendly environment for them in the Caribbean by transferring their raids to the Indian and Pacific oceans. The symbolic demise of the buccaneers in Jamaica came with the earthquake that destroyed Port Royal in 1692.

English Institutions

Unlike the Spanish, who had only a bare form of government and administration in Jamaica, the English transplanted institutions for the governance of Jamaica immediately after the restoration of the monarchy in 1660. Under Charles II, Jamaica was put under a civil government ruled by a governor, who was the head of an administration that included a Council and a House of Assembly. The governor had the independent right to grant all militia commissions. His privy seal was used for confirming orders of

Council, orders for surveying land, warrants and civil and military commissions. The Council's most senior member was a president, who was in charge of Jamaica's government during periods when governors died or were yet to take up their posts. In one period when no lieutenant governor was in post in Jamaica (1734–8), the president of the Council was in control of political affairs on the island. Twelve councillors, appointed by the monarch, supported the governor; they inspected the revenue, oversaw the governance of the island and passed laws. They formed an upper house of a legislature, modelled on English parliamentary practice, that included a lower house of assembly comprising members of parishes elected by freeholders. Jamaica's politicians controlled the militia, which defended the island from external depredations. The militias were divided into regiments, each of which had headquarters in different parts of Jamaica, with a parade ground and a place for storing gunpowder.

The entirely white Jamaican Assembly was dominated by the planter class. It held its first meeting at Spanish Town on 20 January 1664. There were originally twenty members, but the Assembly doubled its numbers within a few decades. By 1774 there were forty-three members. An income of more than £300 per annum or property worth more than £3,000 was required to become an assemblyman. Members were entitled to freedom of speech and freedom from arrest except for treasonable or felonious acts or breach of the peace. The Assembly elected a speaker from its own members. Bills were initiated and drafted by the Assembly before passing to the Council for a second reading and to the governor for his assent. Governors had the right to veto bills. If a bill passed the scrutiny of the Assembly, the Council and governor, it was sent to Britain for royal approval or disallowal.

The Assembly convened infrequently in the 1660s, but sat more regularly by the 1670s. Revenue owed to the Crown in Jamaica, including quitrents, fines and imposts, was collected by a receiver-general supported by several administrative and financial officials. The governors and Assembly of Jamaica in the late seventeenth century frequently quarrelled, however, especially over the appropriation of revenue. Governors found, despite their executive position, that they constantly had to apply to the Assembly for funds. They had no powers of appointment to the Assembly, which could therefore oppose a governor's wishes. In such situations, governors sought, often successfully, to gain the support of the Council when they were at odds with the Assembly, which occurred frequently.

In the 1670s and 1680s the Colonial Office tried to dictate the drafting of laws by the governor and Council of Jamaica, but this was not imposed. The Jamaican Assembly, however, did pass a twenty-year revenue act in 1683. The Crown battled with the Jamaican Assembly throughout the late seventeenth century. The broad issues at stake were the tussle between imperial government and local autonomy and competing priorities: the English government was mainly interested in the Assembly's role in raising taxes while the Assembly focused largely on protecting local rights and interests. The Crown insisted that Jamaica was a conquered colony and, as such, the imperial government could decide what rights it chose to bestow on Jamaica. The English attorney-general oversaw the introduction of a bill that proposed that governors were never to call assemblies without the monarch's permission. These political difficulties led to frequent fraught relations between the governor, the Council and the Assembly in Jamaica.

The Glorious Revolution of 1689, which saw the Protestant William of Orange take over with his English wife Mary as joint monarchs in England and Scotland after the departure of the Catholic James II, occurred at an awkward time for Jamaica. Governor Albemarle, who had been unpopular with a good many absentee merchants and planters in Britain, had died in October 1688, leaving squabbling factions among Jamaica's planter class. His supporters ruled by martial law until May 1689 when the anti-Albemarle planters took over. Political tension lessened in Jamaica during the 1690s after the large sugar planter Sir William Beeston became governor of Jamaica. He assumed full control of the island's government and persuaded the crown that Jamaica needed full naval support and protection against French sugar competition and possible invasion during the War of the League of Augsburg (1688–97).

The lengthiest tenure of a governor was that of Edward Trelawny between 1738 and 1752. This coincided with a turbulent period in Jamaica's history. Trelawny oversaw a successful peace treaty with the Maroons in 1739. Under its terms, the Maroons were allowed to hunt without interference within three miles of plantations. In return, they agreed to aid the governor in the event of Jamaica being externally attacked in wartime and to return runaway slaves to their owners. But not all of Trelawny's tenure was handled so calmly and decisively. His relations with the navy were more fraught, especially focusing on his aversion to the practice of pressing men into naval service during wartime favoured by successive admirals on the Jamaica station. In July 1742 animosity between Trelawny and Admiral Sir Chaloner Ogle led to a loud public quarrel, with much screaming and shouting before the pair was parted by servants. Trelawny was concerned about the serious imbalance in numbers between the modest number of white settlers in Jamaica and the large slave population. He hoped an influx of settlers to re-balance the numerical racial divide would occur after the Maroon agitation had been quelled, but this never occurred. Trelawny also contended with continual sniping between factions in the Council and Assembly, but his attempts at impartiality failed to defuse this internal unrest.

England established a wide-ranging court system in Jamaica based on the common law. The most important court was the Supreme or Grand Court, which handled both civil and criminal cases. It met three or five times per year in Spanish Town. The executive judicial officer, overseeing all of Jamaica's courts, was the provost marshal general. The chief magistrate or *custos rotulorum* was in charge of quarterly sessions dealing with criminal cases. Institutions of English local government were replicated in Jamaica. By 1677 fifteen parishes had been created; another five were added later. The parishes were the main seat of local government, presided over by the *custos rotulorum*, who was supported by vestrymen elected by local freeholders. In 1758, the parishes were incorporated into counties based on English precedents. The counties were Cornwall in the west, Middlesex in the middle, and

94

Surrey in the east. At this juncture, new assize courts were established for Cornwall and Surrey; the Grand Court was then limited to Middlesex for most cases.

To stamp their imprint on Jamaica as an important colonial possession and to eradicate the previous occupation of the island by the Spanish, English and, later, British place names were rapidly introduced in Jamaica in the later seventeenth century. These were mainly derived from England and Scotland, with only a sprinkling of names derived from Wales and Ireland. Existing place names supplied by the Taino or the Spanish were eradicated with only a few exceptions. The widespread introduction of English place names suited both the dominant political and social role of English planters in Jamaica and the deployment of English local government; it also reflected enmity towards Catholic Spain. In short, to name places was to possess; and the English takeover of Jamaica was very much designed to display English mastery and command in a colonial territory.

The White Population

From the English conquest of Jamaica in 1655, a white minority held power in Jamaica until the twentieth century. A pyramid of Jamaica's social structure would therefore show a small peak containing the white population underpinned by a fairly slender group of free blacks nestling upon a broad base of slaves, who easily comprised a majority of the population. Clear demarcation lines lay between each of these three demographic groups. A minority of slaves could join the free black population by manumission or by purchase of their freedom. Free blacks, it goes without saying, had a higher social status than the enslaved. But free blacks were considered inferior, in race and by status, by the white population, whether poor, of middling income or rich. One major consequence was that they did not achieve full subject status even after they had been manumitted.

Mixed-race liaisons were frowned upon but did occur. A person of mixed race, however, was never regarded by whites as having the same status as a free white person. Moreover, white women who engaged in mixed-race personal liaisons could ruin their personal reputations. Notions of blood ancestry justified hereditary enslavement and precluded mixed-race people from claiming the full liberties and rights of British subjects. Free people of colour in Jamaica were excluded from English common law birthright by the early eighteenth century. Whites in Jamaica tried to prevent freed men and women from civic participation, fearing that this would taint the white immigrants' desire for a Europeanised Jamaica. Turning their backs on freed people, however, encouraged free people of colour to ally more with slaves than whites.

Cromwell attributed the successful English conquest of Jamaica to God's Providence. To consolidate the victory over the Spanish, in 1655 he issued a proclamation to encourage all those who wished to emigrate to Jamaica. In *By the Protector: A Proclamation Giving Encouragement to such as shall transplant themselves to Jamaica* (1655), he set down a series of orders to benefit all who professed the Protestant religion who took up this opportunity within two years after 29 September 1656. 'Whereas, by the good providence of God', Cromwell proclaimed, 'our fleet in their late expedition into America, have possessed themselves of a certain island called Jamaica, spacious in its extent, commodious in its harbours and rivers within itself, healthful by its situation, fertile in the nature of the soil, well stored with horses and other cattle, and generally fit to be planted and improved, to the advantage, honour and interest of this nation'. This was a clear statement of the intent for England to take over Jamaica as a new colony.

Cromwell's plans for the settlement of Jamaica included granting every male aged over twelve some twenty acres of land and ten acres for every other male or female. They were entitled to hold this land in perpetuity, to pay no rent for seven years, and thereafter to pay a penny per acre. These emigrants would be accorded full legal protection as English subjects after they settled in Jamaica. Cromwell's proclamation also guaranteed that settlers would not 'without their own consent, be drawn out into the Wars, unlesse it be in case of Invasion, or Rebellion, or for the defence of the Island'. A later proclamation of December 1661, issued after Charles II became monarch, offered thirty acres of land to anyone over twelve years old who applied for land within the next two years and then settled in Jamaica within six months of the application. In religion the restored monarchy favoured the Church of England in Jamaica but offered toleration to all Protestants.

Jamaica's white population initially grew modestly. About 12,000 Englishmen arrived in Jamaica between 1655 and 1661. Some must have died or left after the island was conquered from the Spanish because by 1670 Jamaica's white population was fewer than 8,000. This rose to around 12,000 people by 1680, but twenty years later the total had declined to 7,000. Significant increase did not follow. By 1752, around 10,000 white settlers lived in Jamaica. Thus in the century before 1774 Jamaica's white population grew by less than fifty people per year. This slow growth of the white population was not what the English founders of Jamaica had envisaged. In the late seventeenth century, the intention was that Jamaica would be a European outpost in the Caribbean, a fully fledged white settler society. A significant flow of migrants from the British Isles to Jamaica supported this goal, but they were insufficient to sustain the number of white settlers over time.

Many early English migrants to Jamaica in the late seventeenth century were indentured servants. These were mainly single, young, predominantly male adults aged between sixteen and thirty who emigrated to Jamaica – and to the English colonies in the Americas – by taking out an indenture, a written document that pledged they would allow a master to purchase their labour for set number of years on arrival. The contracts were normally for periods of five to seven years after which the servants would become free workers. People who signed these indentures did so because they wished to forge a new life across the Atlantic in a British colony but needed ship owners to pay for their ocean crossing and masters to provide them with work, clothes, food and lodging.

Indentured servants were poor white people, some-times drawn from the margins of society. They had found it difficult to find employment in England, and hoped for better prospects in Jamaica. These servants were useful for their skills and for their help to planters in controlling slaves and providing a rudimentary defence force. A Jamaica act of 1681 for Regulating Servants prescribed the legal framework for the conduct and supervision of these workers. Under this legislation, disputes between servants and their masters or mistresses were to be assessed by two justices of the peace. Arrangements were also laid down under this act for servants' terms of services and for suitable punishments for misdemeanours. However, indentured servants never migrated to Jamaica in sufficient numbers. In 1679 the Earl of Carlisle estimated that Jamaica had 20 per cent fewer of these workers than it required. The supply of indentured servants began to decline by 1700 and it never recovered; instead, slaves became the main labour force for Jamaica's agricultural enterprises.

Underpinning this slow growth of the white population in Jamaica were two main factors. First, a relatively modest influx of immigrants occurred between 1700 and 1776, with a decline in particular of indentured servant migrants. Second, Jamaica's white population experienced significant mortality and low rates of self-sustained growth during the eighteenth century. The death rate among white people in Kingston was high. In a rural parish such as St Andrew, deaths outstripped births in most years recorded in the parish register between the 1670s and 1740s. Few marriages in eighteenth-century Jamaica produced children because of extensive mortality among the white population. Most widows or widowers never remarried. By 1776 Jamaica had a proportionately smaller native-born population than any of the thirteen

British North American colonies; it had failed to produce a sustainable settler society.

The relatively modest size of Jamaica's white population reflected a persistent disinclination to settle in Jamaica permanently. Several factors contributed to this situation. British and Irish settlers had reservations about living in a hot, tropical climate; they disliked the prevalence of mosquitoes; they were worried about exposure to devastating tropical storms and hurricanes; they knew about the possibility of earthquakes. 'If this island were not troubled with great thunders and lightnings, hurricanes, and earthquakes; and if the air was not at once violently hot, damp, and extremely unwholesome in most parts', observers noted in 1757, 'the fertility and beauty of this country would make it as desirable a situation for pleasure, as it is for the profits, which in spite of these disadvantages draw hither such a number of people'. But perhaps more influential in damming a white immigrant stream to Jamaica were three other factors: the disease and mortality patterns associated with Jamaica, the increasing numerical dominance of the slave population, and cultural attitudes that produced many sojourners and settlers who had no intention of remaining permanently in Jamaica.

Widespread diseases affecting the non-immune white population in eighteenth-century Jamaica included malaria and yellow fever. Family formation was fragile, with high child mortality rates. Around a quarter of the children baptised in Jamaica were born to unmarried parents. Between 1666 and the mid-eighteenth century, only 39 per cent of marriages in St Andrew parish left surviving children and just 38 per cent of the children produced by those marriages survived into adulthood. The annual death rate among the white population of Kingston in the second quarter of the eighteenth century amounted to 20 per cent. Yellow fever and malaria spread by mosquitoes in swamps adjoining Kingston were major contributors to the mortality rate. These diseases dramatically affected the health of non-immune whites whereas Africans carried immunities to these diseases. As Richard S. Dunn saliently observed, 'it was impossible to think of the sugar islands as home when they were such a demographic disaster area'.

As whites died off literally like flies, continuing influxes of enslaved Africans boosted the size of the black population. Thus Jamaica's slave population increased from 514 in 1661 to 40,000 in 1698 to 74,525 in 1730 and to 165,500 in 1775. White people in Jamaica, though they controlled slaves, lived in fear of black reprisals against their dominance; they also felt uncomfortable and disliked living as a racial minority in Jamaica. Though absenteeism among the white population c. 1750 was not as prevalent as was once thought, many whites in Jamaica lived there as sojourners, maintaining emotional and family ties with Britain and wanting to retire there after making their money in Jamaica. Michael Craton characterised these people as 'reluctant creoles'.

Most of those expecting to make a fortune in Jamaica were planters, attorneys or traders. Professional men, such as doctors and lawyers, could make a good living in Jamaica, but they most likely had more modest ambitions for wealth creation. Beneath these occupations were much poorer white people. Probably around three-quarters of the whites living in Jamaica before the American

Revolution were not planters or merchants but craftsmen, overseers and bookkeepers, many of whom died intestate. Married white women often found themselves in a precarious financial position if their husbands died first, as tended to be the case, for Jamaican men often favoured children and friends over wives in their wills. The economic status of white women was dealt a harsh blow in 1775 when the Assembly restricted women's inheritance by passing a law to prevent the division of land and property through dower rights.

Most economy activity in English Jamaica lay in the hands of men, whether in terms of overseas trade, internal exchange or plantation management. But while there was a masculine dominance in economic matters, it was not exclusively the case. As Christine Walker has pithily stated in relation to Jamaica, 'Atlantic slavery was never the sole concern of white men acting in isolation'. Nearly 80 per cent of white women in English Jamaica held property and 10 per cent of slave owners were women. The island's white women relied on inheriting enslaved people as a form of moveable wealth; they bought enslaved children as companions for their children and grandchildren; and they were involved in complex kinship ties involving legitimate and illegitimate children of free and enslaved African descent. Thus the slave-sugar economy of Jamaica was maintained through full participation by both men and women.

The Slave Trade

When the English invaded Jamaica, colonies were regarded as markets for manufactured goods and sources of raw materials for the mother country; they absorbed labour and capital and were a source of profits for Britain. Jamaica developed rapidly under English rule to become a colony that soon began to make gains from agricultural development and trade. Though never a monoculture, English Jamaica based its economic activities around sugar cane production on plantations owned and managed by English men and women. Investors sought to make good returns from sugar cultivation. To do so, they organised agricultural plantations to maximise output: this was the most efficient way of achieving gains from abundant land. Sugar became the major agricultural crop and export of Jamaica and other Caribbean islands, catering to an important shift in consumption habits amongst western Europeans in the seventeenth and eighteenth centuries that led to a sweeter diet. Sugar required a tropical or semi-tropical climate, plenty of land, access to water and a large workforce capable of undertaking the arduous tasks associated with planting and harvesting this crop. The main financial rewards from sugar production came from exports to Europe, with most sugar despatched to a protected market in England. Sugar could be imported at prices that invariably generated good profits as it was a staple crop with a high price elasticity of demand.

During the sixteenth century, Portugal's Atlantic Islands and Spanish American plantations had shown that an extensive European market existed for sugar as a sweetener for food and beverages. The English had already followed suit by developing plantations before 1650 in the Lesser Antilles, notably in Barbados and the Leeward Islands. The labour force for these rural enterprises comprised enslaved Africans brought to Jamaica via the transatlantic slave trade. In 1662 there were about 400 slaves in Jamaica, but the arrival of enslaved Africans increased this to 9,504 by 1673. Most of them arrived during the period when the governor of Jamaica was Sir Thomas Modyford, who promoted the acquisition of slaves to exploit Jamaica's land and agricultural resources.

In the first instance, plantation owners tried other sources of labour for plantation work before they turned to slavery on a significant scale. But each option proved unworkable over the long term. Native populations such as the Caribs or, in the Jamaican case, Tainos had been all but wiped out by disease and violence. Planters claimed that free wage labour was unviable because it would prove too expensive. Indentured servants shipped from England for periods of up to seven years were tried as plantation workers. But they were only a short-term stop-gap solution to labour shortage: they seeped out of the plantation labour force at the end of their terms of service, their numbers fluctuated according to economic conditions in England, and they could not be forced, under English law, to be permanent contract workers. By the 1690s relatively few indentured servants were referred to in Jamaica's inventories.

The solution to the labour shortage was found in the exploitation of enslaved Africans. They were available in large numbers from West Africa and fellow Africans colluded with English ship captains to sell them into the slave trade. If the British and other Europeans were the main perpetrators of the slave trade, then many in West Africa were the enablers. The Portuguese and Spanish had been tapping parts of coastal West Africa for slaves for over a century, and English traders now followed suit. The English viewed Africans as heathens, as culturally inferior, and as people who had no protection from English laws. Racial prejudice underpinned these views. Though it was not the extreme version of racism that prevailed in later centuries, it is difficult to conceive of the slave trade being pursued without a strong racial element. Thus if one were to ask the counterfactual question whether the English would have enslaved Africans if they were white people, the answer must be negative. It is worth remembering that no indentured servant was ever a black person and no slave was ever a white man or woman.

Economic considerations were of course important; and it was the English and other Europeans who possessed the motivation and capital to conduct a transatlantic slave trade. An African slave labour force had the attraction for investors of being permanently unfree, with any children born into slavery, which was a system of continuous forced labour. Such slaves had already been successfully imported as the labour force for plantations in Barbados and other English West Indian islands before Cromwell conquered Jamaica. Thus they were the logical and pre-ferred option to undertake sugar cultivation and, indeed, much of the other manual work associated with Jamaica's economic activities. Without the coerced labour under-taken by slaves, the large-scale production of staple agri-cultural crops for export would never have met European demand for tropical groceries.

Charles II's reign inaugurated an era in which a Protestant English Atlantic empire took shape with slavery and the slave trade lying at the heart of English commercial policy. Africans were brought under forced conditions to Jamaica in ships provided by English mer-chants. The Company of Royal Adventurers operated a fairly modest English slave trade from 1660 to 1672. Its successor the Royal African Company, operating from headquarters in London, supplied most of the slaves to Jamaica for the remainder of the seventeenth century. This joint-stock organisation had a royal monopoly to pursue the slave trade. In theory this gave it a monopoly over English slave-trading activities, but in practice its trade was supplemented by private interlopers. After the Royal African Company's monopoly was rescinded by parliament in 1698, the English slave trade was opened to private merchants. That is how it continued to operate until the British slave trade was abolished by act of parliament in 1807. London, Bristol and Liverpool merchant firms dominated the British slave trade to American markets, notably Jamaica, during the eighteenth century. The diminution of the Royal African Company's role in the slave trade, already very much in evidence by the mid-1720s, provided scope for the emergence of a merchant class in Kingston that liaised closely with private British merchants over the delivery and sale of slaves.

The slave trade was necessary for the continuing development of plantations owing to high levels of mortality among the enslaved. When blacks died, a new supply of slaves was imported from Africa regularly. John Taylor, an Englishman who spent time in Jamaica, observed in 1687 that the slave trade was already an important means through which Jamaica created wealth for the planter class. 'The Royall Company of Merchants and African Company have settled a factory here', he noted, 'and bring abundance of Negroa (506) slaves hither daily, which they sell to the planters for ye sugar, indigo, coco, etc., and give them six months' credit to pay the same, by which means the island is much enrich't and plantations are improved to admiration'. The Jamaican slaveholder Cary Helyar succinctly emphasised the importance of the slave trade as early as 1671: 'The more Negroes the greater income.'

Jamaica had the largest demand for slaves of any British colony in the Americas. In 1680, 23 per cent of blacks living in the British Empire lived in Jamaica. That proportion increased to 26 per cent by the mid-eighteenth century. The numerical increase is even more noticeable. Despite continuing high mortality, between 1700 and 1750 Jamaica's slave population more than doubled, to nearly 120,000 slaves, and multiplied a further two and a half times to more than 300,000 slaves by the end of the century. African in-migration was a central feature of Jamaican life. Between 1655 and 1808, 3,432 known voyages from Africa shipped 915,204 Africans to Jamaica. Of these slaves, just over three-quarters (701,046) were retained in the island. Adding a further 168,165 Africans who died or disembarked en route to Jamaica, a total of 1,083,369 Africans were intended for the island. The size of this trade increased greatly over time, the annual number retained growing from fewer than 3,000 in the 1710s to more than 12,000 in the 1790s. Thus over the course of the eighteenth century Jamaica's social structure became increasingly Africanised.

In many years, Jamaica's African imports exceeded the demand for enslaved labour. Those who were surplus to requirements were re-exported mainly to Spanish American markets such as Cartagena, Porto Bello and Panama on the Spanish Main and to Cuba. Already by 1677, a Spanish agent was stationed in Jamaica. He worked on behalf of the *asiento* (licence) agreement whereby the Spanish licensed the supply of slaves to its colonies to another nation. The Royal African Company was involved in this trade to a modest extent in the last quarter of the seventeenth century. The award of the *asiento* to Britain between 1714 and 1739 provided a larger role for the Royal African Company and private traders to provide slaves via Jamaica for Spanish markets. Many of these captives were carried under the auspices of the London-based South Sea Company. Re-exports of slaves from Jamaica continued after the *asiento* had ceased: between 1741 and 1790, 62,600 Africans were exported from Jamaica to foreign markets.

Enormous slave imports were needed in Jamaica to counteract the demographic instability of the slave regime in which deaths always outnumbered births and female fertility was exceptionally low, in no small part on account of the brutal work regimen on sugar plantations. Africans suffered from a range of mortal diseases, poor diet, malnutrition, closely packed poor housing, inadequate sanitation, and brutal, coercive treatment. Some 575,000 new labourers were needed in the eighteenth century to increase the slave population by about 250,000. The result was a slave population that remained mostly African. Slave owners always preferred, to use their own vocabulary, to buy rather than breed while the slave trade continued, but after the abolition of the trade in 1807 they were obliged to concentrate more on promoting ameliorative measures to encourage natural reproduction.

Jamaican slaves came in sizable numbers from every slave-trading region of Africa, except the southeast. Four regions – the Bight of Biafra, the Gold Coast, West

Central Africa and the Bight of Benin – accounted for 90 per cent of slaves, with the Bight of Biafra and the Gold Coast together contributing nearly two-thirds of Jamaican slaves. Heterogeneity of ethnic origins was a conspicuous feature of African migration to Jamaica. The structure of the slave trade to Jamaica meant that slave owners could seldom pick and choose among different ethnicities. Slave traders dealing with Jamaica gathered slaves from a wide variety of areas. In twelve five-year periods, no single region provided as many as 40 per cent of all slave arrivals. Slaves who survived the disorienting rigours of the Middle Passage – the Atlantic ship crossing from Africa to America – often arrived in a weakened condition in Jamaica. Some suffered from smallpox; others had contracted yaws; still others were in a debilitated state. After arrival, it was common for Africans to be cooped up in yards attached to Kingston merchants' warehouses before they were sold to planters.

The constant flow of the slave trade to Jamaica and the centrality of a slave labour force to an island dominated by sugar plantations ensured that, from about the 1680s onwards, the population of the island was dominated by powerless black Africans. By 1788 almost 90 per cent of Jamaica's population was enslaved. A fairly small number of blacks were free as a result of manumission, but their numbers did not increase absolutely and relative to slaves until the early nineteenth century. By the outbreak of the American War of Independence, the thousands of enslaved Africans in Jamaica were dominated socially and politically by a small white minority amongst whom an elite category of planters held the reins of power and control.

Sugar Plantations and the Sugar Trade

Sugar plantations increasingly dominated Jamaica's cultivable landscape under English rule. Already established in Barbados and the Leeward Islands by 1650, sugar estates were soon established in Jamaica after the island was conquered from the Spanish. This involved extensive work over many years to clear away Jamaica's hardwood forest and other woodland areas to provide land for sugar cultivation. Plantations were large-scale agricultural enterprises that encompassed anything between 150 and 500 acres. They were mainly situated on relatively flat land suitable for cultivating sugar cane, and were usually near to rivers. A large workforce of enslaved Africans was necessary to operate these plantations. Planting and growing sugar cane was an arduous process based on a seasonal and yearly crop cycle. Holes or trenches were dug for planting old canes, which sprouted in about two months. The fields were then weeded and fertilised and new plants positioned in places where sprouting had failed. After fourteen months the canes, which could grow to heights well above a tall person, were harvested mainly by slaves working with hand implements. The cut canes were taken on carts to a sugar mill located on the property where they were ground and the boiled, distilled juice was dried to make sugar. The residue of the distillation process comprised molasses, which was further treated to make rum. English equipment was needed in the sugar mills and specialist skilled workers – millwrights, carpenters, boilers – were trained from the slave workforce to undertake the production of semi-refined sugar.

FIGURE 3.3 Sugar cane cutting. Bildagentur/Universal Images
Group/Getty Images

Cane sugar, the main product of Jamaica's plantations
and slave workforce, became a mainstay of British direct
trade with Jamaica and the rest of the Caribbean from
the late seventeenth century onwards. Merchants in
London, Liverpool, Bristol and, after about 1750,
Glasgow regularly sent out ships with manufactured
goods to Jamaica and loaded up sugar for the return
voyages. This was an important form of British overseas
trade, as sugar became the most valuable imported product into England between about 1660 and 1820, when it
was superseded in value by raw cotton supplies entering
British ports from the southern United States. The
importance of sugar lay in the strong consumer demand
in England for a sweetener in beverages and an ingredi-
ent in cooking desserts. Its consumption marked an

important change in people's diets. As its supply increased, its price level declined and so, by the early eighteenth century, it was purchased by people throughout the entire spectrum of English society from the aristocracy and gentry down to the labouring poor.

Under the Navigation Acts passed between 1651 and 1696, the sugar trade had to be shipped back directly from Jamaica and other English Caribbean islands to English ports in English ships. The policies of mercantilism, put into practice by the Navigation Acts, were based around the increase of the mother country's wealth through the profits generated from the raw materials supplied by the colonies. The operation of those acts required customs duties to be paid on sugar imports. Given the sheer value of sugar as a consumer product, this was highly beneficial for the state's coffers. Mercantilist restrictions on the full refining of sugar in the Caribbean – a protective policy for English manufacturers – meant that the semi-refined muscovado sugar dominating the English sugar trade was further processed in sugar refineries situated near the river- and harbour-side in English ports. The operation of the Navigation Acts also meant that foreign sugar imports were effectively non-competitive with the product of English plantations owing to high import tariffs imposed on the produce of continental European colonies. The sugar trade with Jamaica mainly operated on a commission basis whereby planters provided sugar from their plantations and merchants in English ports charged a 2½ per cent commission on sugar sales. Merchants were able to sell sugar to consumers living not just in English port cities but throughout a wide hinterland.

Merchants, Planters and Wealth

British merchants and planters had the financial wherewithal to exploit Jamaica's agricultural potential. These businessmen were correct in thinking that Jamaica could provide substantial profits for their investments. Though there was always the spectre of debt and bankruptcy hanging over those who miscalculated their commercial and landed portfolios, shrewd operators could generate handsome returns from shipping, trade and plantations. Sugar production based on enslaved labour helped to make Jamaica the wealthiest colony in the British Empire. An anonymous report dated 1675 noted that Jamaica had seventy sugar works in operation and another forty in 'a great state of forwardness'. John Taylor, writing in 1687, had emphasised the comfortable position of the wealthy planter who 'lives here in full enjoyment of ease and plenty, having what 'ere his heart can wish to enjoy'. Notwithstanding problems, Jamaica and the other Caribbean islands produced substantial wealth for many planters for 'there are no parts of the world, in which great estates are made in so short a time ... the produce of a few good seasons will provide against the ill effects of the worst; as the planter is sure of a speedy and profitable market for his produce, which has a readier sale than perhaps any other commodity in the world'.

Substantial economic growth occurred in Jamaica during the mid-eighteenth century: between 1740 and 1776, the total number of plantations increased by 45 per cent and spread to include coffee as well as sugar estates, and the total value of Jamaica's exports rose from £650,000 to £2.4 million per annum. In 1745 a well-informed contemporary estimate reckoned that Jamaica's total trade was worth £1.5 million, making it the wealthiest colony in Britain's Atlantic empire. In 1774 Jamaica's private physical wealth amounted to £28 million. British West Indian merchant-planters regarded Jamaican and other Caribbean plantations as the means to providing a fortune. In the 1750s the Bristol merchant Henry Bright contrasted the prospects of Jamaica compared with those at Bristol: 'Jamaica is the only place to gett money as great fortunes are made there, and scarce livelihood can be got here at any business.'

Because of the potential economic returns to be gained from slavery, sugar and the slave trade, merchants and planters were mobile and established transatlantic networks. Merchants often spent time in Jamaica early in their careers. They served as factors and agents of their principals or, more informally, went to Jamaica to visit family members already trading there. Many Jamaican planters were also mobile, dividing their time between Jamaica and Britain. Geographical mobility helped to build up commercial and social connections and to give British merchants and planters first-hand knowledge of the business scene in Jamaica and the shipping and commerce of the Atlantic world. British merchants trading with Jamaica operated individually or in partnerships. Slave trade partnerships were arranged on an ad hoc basis, with new arrangements for each voyage. Merchants involved in the sugar trade were more inclined to establish family businesses that could be continued from one generation to another. Jamaican planters came from varied social backgrounds but acquired their real estate as a means of social and geographical mobility.

Some had aristocratic or gentry origins from their British landholdings. Some were merchants who made sufficient money to become merchant-planters. Others were parvenus who expected that money and land would be the path to gentility and social status.

Some planters overstretched their credit portfolios, misjudged their plantation investments and became mired in debt, but evidence from inventories indicates that the majority of planters were economically successful before the American Revolution. British Caribbean plantation agriculture had returns of over 10 per cent on capital in the half century before 1776, a very acceptable rate of profit on any business, whether considered historically or by today's standards. Slave ownership was widespread in Jamaica. Between 1725 and 1784 three-quarters of inventoried estates contained slaves. The ownership had a high concentration ratio: 5 per cent of the inventoried slaveholders accounted for 49 per cent of the slaves.

By the 1720s, but not before, large plantations of over 150 acres had become common in Jamaica. This meant that such landholdings increasingly became the destination for the thousands of Africans imported to Jamaica. It also 'led to the development of an elite planter class with wealth and influence unprecedented for the eighteenth-century British Atlantic'. Newcomers could penetrate the upper echelons of Jamaican planter society for three intertwined reasons. First, extensive mortality among Jamaica's white population meant that properties came up for sale regularly. Second, white immigrants working as overseers, managers and attorneys could earn sufficient wages to accumulate savings to purchase plantations. Third, opportunities to amass wealth from the slave trade and trade with Spanish America offered merchants and factors the opportunity to raise capital for plantation investment.

The importance of family connections and inheritance to Jamaican planters can be seen in the careers of Edward Long (1734–1813) and Bryan Edwards (1743–1800), who became the most important contemporary historians of the British Caribbean in the eighteenth century. Long came from a family associated with Jamaica from the 1660s. His grandfather Samuel had been speaker of the Jamaican Assembly and his father, Samuel, born in Jamaica, was a member of the Council and owner of Lucky Valley sugar plantation, a rich property in Clarendon parish. Long married the heiress of Thomas Beckford of Jamaica, and became a member of the Jamaican Assembly for St Ann parish in 1761, 1765 and 1766. He was briefly speaker of the Assembly in 1768 and left Jamaica the following year to become an absentee planter in England. Edwards was sent as a young man to Jamaica to live with his wealthy uncle, Zachary Bayly. Edwards became a member of the Jamaican Assembly in 1765 and played an important role in the island's political life. Apart from a five-year spell in the 1780s, he lived in Jamaica until returning to England permanently as an absentee planter. Zachary Bayly, a wealthy planter and planter attorney, bequeathed him two Jamaican sugar plantations. He inherited two further plantations and a cattle pen from a friend, Benjamin Hume. He owned around 1,500 slaves by the time of the American War of Independence. After returning to England, Edwards settled near Southampton and became MP for Grampound, Cornwall, in 1796.

Increasingly, planters became absentees. By 1775 around 40 per cent of the sugar plantations in Jamaica were owned by absentees and minors. Absentees were overwhelmingly the wealthier planters who had made sufficient fortunes to enable them to retire home and manage their estates from across the Atlantic by delegating management tasks to attorneys (usually responsible for several plantations) or managers (normally controlling one estate). Most planters and merchants were never fully attached to the Caribbean: they continued to regard Britain as their home. Whites in Jamaica and elsewhere in the Caribbean disliked the lack of social amenities: there were relatively few theatres, parks, gardens, assembly rooms and other centres of leisure for the middling classes. The climate was hot and deemed intolerable for long stays in the Caribbean. Whites were wary of potential tropical disasters such as earthquakes and hurricanes. They also disliked living in an island where they were heavily outnumbered by the enslaved even though such people were essential for their economic livelihoods.

Plantations and Slavery

Sugar plantations were usually found on flat land, though some were in hillier locations. Most land on a sugar estate was given over to cane cultivation but there were also factory works. These included a boiling house, a curing house, and sometimes an adjacent rum distillery where molasses drained off from the cane was made. The initial processing of sugar took place on plantations because cane needed to be cut when it reached maturity and then processed within a few hours before the juice became sour.

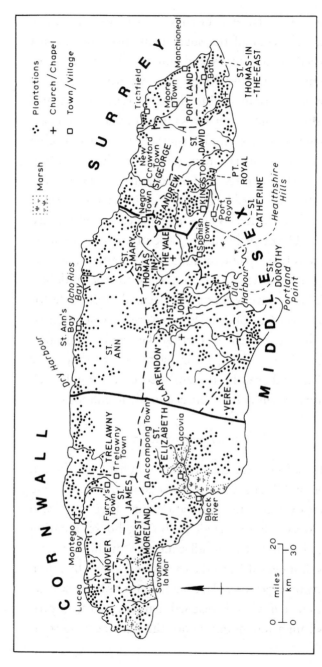

FIGURE 3.4 Estates and towns in Jamaica, 1774. Retrieved from David Watts, *The West Indies: Patterns of Development, Culture and Environmental Change since 1492* (Cambridge: Cambridge University Press, 1987)

118

Sugar-growing was not the totality of agricultural produce grown on plantations. Usually outlying parts of estates had provision grounds, where slaves cultivated their own food crops during their limited leisure time. Many sugar properties were situated next to livestock pens containing cattle and mules. Integrated plantations, with the agricultural and manufacturing capacity referred to above, were adopted in Jamaica between about 1680 and 1720. In the thirty-five years before 1775, sugar plantations were established on the north side of Jamaica in a belt situated inland about ten miles from the sea from Hanover to St Mary parishes. Jamaica had 57 sugar works in 1670 and 775 in 1774. Sugar output increased from 5,000 tons in 1700 to 40,000 tons in 1774. Guinea grass was introduced on many plantations from about 1740 onwards to provide grazing or fodder for livestock in pens.

The seasonal cycle of work began in the autumn with the planting of new sugar cane. The crop took about fifteen months to grow. The cane harvest began after the Christmas holiday, and was mainly carried out in the usually dry weather from January to March, though it took until June to be completed. During the sugar harvest, a full workforce was needed to deal with the crop so that the cane was gathered, transferred to the sugar factory and processed for shipment back to Britain. Slaves worked from dawn to dusk on six days a week, with only a couple of daily meal breaks. The sugar mainly grown in Jamaica was coarse brown muscovado. Owing to British mercantilist restrictions, sugar could only be semi-refined in the West Indies. This was undertaken in mills attached to plantations. The final refining process took place at

British sugar houses where further boiling, curing and cooling of sugar occurred before sugar loaves were produced. These arrangements were intended to protect British manufacturing interests.

Slaves were the workforce on the plantations. Governor Thomas Lynch in the 1670s had predicted accurately that the future of large plantations would be 'very much improved by Blacks'. The slave population in Jamaica and other Caribbean islands was heavily dependent on new African imports. Male captives always outnumbered female slaves. But there was always a heavy mortality rate. In some cases, this resulted from the debilitating effects of the Middle Passage. Some slaves died soon after they arrived in Jamaica from gastroenterital, respiratory and other diseases. A process of 'seasoning' took place over the next two or three years. This was a period of time during which the enslaved adapted to the new disease environment of Jamaica and to an exacting and brutal labour regime on plantations. Writing in 1740, Charles Leslie noted that 'almost half of the new imported Negroes die in the Seasoning'. Slaves on sugar plantations experienced a higher mortality rate than Africans working in any other type of staple crop production. Historians debate whether the link between sugar cultivation and heavy mortality resulted primarily from the environmental setting for growing sugar – often in low, swampy areas – or whether intensity of labour was a more critical factor.

Faced with high levels of mortality and poor fertility among their enslaved workforce, planters continually turned to the supply of fresh slaves from Africa. Problems with maintaining natural increase among the slave population were acknowledged in the 1770s by the attorney of Hope plantation, who wrote that a decrease rather than increase in slaves was 'the case with every Estate in the Island, at least with very few exceptions'. Poor reproduction rates were largely responsible for this situation. Miscarriages and stillbirths were common. Whether fetal deaths commonly occurred through deliberate abortion by pregnant slave women is unknown and little has been determined about the incidence of infanticide. Infant mortality was a particular problem, with 80 per cent of infant deaths in the eighteenth-century British Caribbean occurring in the first two weeks of life.

Slave reproduction was linked closely to the material and working lives of black captives. Slaves were fed on a diet of mainly grain or vegetables and were required to cultivate their own provisions to feed themselves rather than rely on masters' rations. Guinea corn, plantains and yams were regularly eaten by slaves. Malnutrition was common among slaves despite these sources of food. Seasonal variations in the provision of foodstuffs meant that the months from June to September were the most difficult in maintaining dietary intake levels because provision grounds were then at their least productive. During the summer, slaves often resorted to chewing rotten cane strewn across the cane fields or unripe provisions. Slave diet was monotonous and deficient in thiamine, calcium and vitamin A. An average daily plantation food allowance amounted to between 1,500 and 2,000 calories, which was less than the energy required for heavy work in the cane fields. Besides dietary deficiencies, many slaves suffered from dysentery, dropsy, fevers and diseases of the digestive and nervous systems. Yaws, a non-venereal form of syphilis, was a common complaint. This was a highly contagious and common disease that planters tried to contain by constructing a yaws house on their estates, usually placed next to slave hospitals. Dirt-eating (or geophagy) was another way in which disease entered the body, in this case through hookworm infestation.

Slave working conditions exacerbated the nutritional problem. The work performed by field slaves was arduous and exhausting in order to achieve an average sugar production per estate slave of 1,000 lbs per year. The most strenuous work involved clearing ground to prepare for sugar canes, digging cane holes, supplying, stripping, cutting, moulding and banking sugar canes, tying cane plants and carrying away field trash. This was by any standards labour-intensive work, for sugar canes often grew to a height far above the stature of a tall adult and, additionally, the diameter of the canes exceeded the span of a person's hands. Given the demands for productivity in a hot and humid climate, slave work sapped the physical energy of all who toiled at it.

Work on the sugar plantations was mainly organised in terms of gang labour before the American Revolution. A sugar estate usually had three gangs. The first gang (also known as the great gang) undertook the heaviest physical work. Hoes and bills and sheer muscle power were needed for this work. Digging cane holes, cutting the matured cane, loading it into carts and taking it to the factory works was exhausting work. The great gang could comprise more than 100 workers. Many women worked in the great gang, carrying out tough physical labour just as they did in many African societies. The second gang was responsible for lighter tasks such as clearing trash from the cane fields, chopping and heaping manure and threshing light canes. This was a mixed gang of men and women, usually aided by adolescents. Many estates also had a third (or weeding) gang comprising mothers with children. The gang system worked with military precision, with slaves working in parallel rows like cogs in a machine. The gangs were supervised by a black driver, usually a skilled and trusted slave who had risen up from the ranks. The driver was responsible for ensuring the pace, quantity and satisfactory performance of work. He was in turn supervised by a white overseer, who was often present in the cane fields. Overseers were charged with disciplining slaves. They discharged this duty by chastisement, whippings, placing slaves in stocks, or withdrawal of customary allowances. Overseers were responsible to managers or attorneys.

Slaves were given names by their masters that were partly intended to mark them out as people entirely different from the white population. The fact that slaves were usually unable to name themselves supports Trevor Burnard's contention that 'Africans' inferior positions' in Jamaica were 'indelibly shaped by European racist condescension'. Planters always referred to 'negroes' rather than 'slaves'. White Jamaicans had forenames of English derivation and their children were given one or more forenames; in both cases, a family surname was retained. Slaves, by contrast, had a forename only or, in some cases, a forename and modifier. Planters gave slaves names derived from Africa, the Bible, the classical world and English forenames. Cato, Caesar, Venus and Juno were among the names appropriated from classical sources for slaves. English forenames such as John, James, Elizabeth and Dorothy were usually changed to their informal version for slaves – Johnnie, Jemmie, Betsey and Dolly. African names commonly used for slaves included Quashie, Quamino, Cudjoe, Cuba, Phibbah and Quasheba. Freed slaves often discarded their slave names in favour of new names that aligned them onomastically with white people. This was an important way in which they relinquished the stigma of slavery.

Slaves struggled to form stable family lives. Africans were not imported to Jamaica in family groups. Many slaves had experienced a sequence of fractures in their personal lives, having been wrested often from families within Africa, sold usually as individuals on the African coast, and then resold in Jamaica without attention paid by merchants to whether they had prior or current family attachments. Nearly all slaves would have lost contact with their parents and grandparents long before they reached Jamaica, while heavy infant mortality impeded lines of descent in enslaved families. Despite these difficulties, most slaves appear to have formed nuclear family units. These appear to have been most common where slaves were living on large plantations; in that situation the family unit was a means of counteracting isolation. They also appear to have flourished where access to slave provision grounds allowed slave families to sell produce at market and enable children to contribute to family earnings. Given the isolation and fragmentation associated with the slave experience – leaving one's homeland, with no prospect of return, and kept apart from free society in the colony of disembarkation – it is unsurprising that the slave family lay at the centre of the slave community's emotional and cultural bonds.

FIGURE 3.5 A slave whipped by a settler. DEA/ICAS94/De Agostini/
Getty Images

Many slaves failed to carry out the demands of masters,
but ill-discipline, poor work and non-compliant behaviour were met by physical correction. Recalcitrant slaves
were subject to a series of physical punishments: branding
on the cheek or the shoulder, lashing on the back, place-
ment in stocks and subjection to physical abuse. Slave men
and women were both flogged on bare parts of their body.
The diary of Thomas Thistlewood, a brutal white overseer on Egypt plantation, Westmoreland parish, records
such punishments on an almost daily basis in laconic,
factual prose. An entry for 15 July 1750 states: 'this afternoon Dick (the Mulattoe) for his many Crimes &

Negligencies was bound to an Orange Tree in ye garden, and whip'd to some purpose. (Given near 300 Lashes.)' Another entry for 8 August 1755 noted that 'today Nero would not work, but threaten'd to Cutt his own throat. Had him stripped, whipp'd, gagg'd & his hands tied behind him, that ye Muskitoes and Sand Flies might torment him to some purpose.' Brutality towards slave women was manifested in frequents acts of rape by overseers and other white plantation personnel.

Planters, managers and owners exercised power through the full support of the law. English common law was silent on the status and treatment of slaves, but successive British governments allowed colonists to formulate their own laws by establishing slave codes. Laws enacted by the Jamaican Assembly established arrangements for the coercion and punishment of slaves. Large planters sat in the legislature: they were effectively making laws that suited priorities on their estates. Governor Modyford, who arrived in Jamaica from Barbados in 1664, adopted the Barbados slave code in its entirety to issue the first act for regulating slaves in Jamaica. This law gave masters virtually total authority over their slaves. They could punish slaves in any way they liked; there was no penalty for carrying punishments too far by maiming or killing slaves for misdemeanours. No rules were set down about slave food or slave working conditions. Arson, assault, rape, murder and theft of anything beyond a shilling in value were capital crimes for slaves under the Jamaican slave law of 1664. In 1696 Jamaica adopted a slave act that closely followed similar Barbados legislation of 1688. The

Jamaican slave act of 1696 expressed concern about the propensity of slaves to rebel. It was also the first legal instance of masters being urged to spread Christianity among slaves in the sugar islands. Slave court records in the eighteenth century include numerous examples of physical punishment of those convicted, including mutilation of body parts such as cutting off ears and nailing them to the gallows or authorising that a head be placed where a capital crime had been committed after an execution.

Planters had various interacting strategies that enabled them to control the numerically dominant slave population. The enslaved were heterogeneous in their African origins, and this helped the planters in safeguarding themselves, in most years, against resistance to their power from collective ethnic understandings among slaves. Planters divided the slave workforce into hierarchical groups based on status and skill. This enabled the white elite to control slaves through offering rewards and promotion to those who performed their work satisfactorily and obediently. Drivers, for example, were placed in positions of authority over other slaves and they aligned themselves with the planters' objectives. From time to time, in addition, the white elite organised public displays by military forces to remind the slaves who held the reins of power in Jamaica. Slaves undoubtedly wanted to achieve freedom but they were constrained in achieving that goal by these various control mechanisms pursued by planters.

The material lives of slaves in Jamaica have been illuminated in recent decades by archaeological investigations. One of the best-documented sites consists of New Montpelier sugar plantation in St James's parish, north-west Jamaica. Excavations here suggest that slave houses had various dimensions but commonly measured 18 by 27 feet. The layout of the houses, identified by surviving stone foundations, was similar to West African compounds such as those of the Igbo and Asante communities, with a rectangular base form. The survival of bone fragments and teeth at New Montpelier indicates that the estate had cows, pigs, chickens, horses and dogs. Hack or cut marks on many of the cattle and pig bones indicate the use of a cleaver in butchering and suggest that slaves slaughtered their own animals. Fish bones found during the excavations show that fish from the sea were a significant part of the slaves' diet at the New Montpelier works. Most of the identifiable tools found while excavating at New Montpelier were imported metal items. These included planters' bills and hoes, both used for specialised plantation work, but also cutlass blades, which had a wider use as domestic tools. The archaeological record at the site was dominated by finds of ceramics and glassware. Most ceramic remains were from vessels used for the storage or consumption of food and drink. Few traces of the textiles that comprised slave clothing have been found at New Montpelier.

Slave quarters, whether on or off plantations, were near to their place of work. They were commonly nucleated settlements in villages on Caribbean plantations. Despite their modest appearance, slave houses enabled Afro-Jamaicans to exercise control over their own domestic arrangements without too much interference from white overseers or managers. Slave quarters usually afforded little privacy between individual households because they were huddled together and often arranged around a communal yard. Yet that was probably not problematic in the plantation slave community, for personal relationships and kin were often dispersed among several contiguous households. It was unusual for planters, managers and overseers to enter slave dwellings.

Slave dwellings and their surrounding yards were the site of vibrant community and cultural life. Slave customs and cultural beliefs testify to a rich blend of African practices and adjustments to life on a new continent. Slaves enjoyed music and dance, playing a wide range of musical instruments ranging from fiddles to horns and percussion. Hans Sloane reported that Jamaican slaves played various musical instruments 'in imitation of Lutes, made of small Gourds fitted with Necks, strung with Horse hairs, or the peeled stalks of climbing Plants or Wichs'. Drums and drummers, with accompanying gourds and rattles, were an integral part of Akan culture on Africa's Gold Coast. These musical traditions were transported to Jamaica, which drew heavily on slave imports from that region in the eighteenth century. The drums often imitated speech rhythms and tones. They were used as signals to the slave community. Similarly, the West African practice of calling and shouting was widely adopted by slaves. The African dancing ring symbolised the solidarity of the slave community and the ring shout was frequently heard on the plantations, sometimes rendered as a wordless call.

Slaves also had an oral culture that provided a form of continuity between the cultural legacy brought from African societies and the New World realities of slavery. One device common among slaves was the use of proverbs, poems and fables to highlight features of the African background of those in bondage. Folk stories were told that linked with memories handed down from African traditions. Among the best-known of these folk tales are Anansi stories based on a trickster figure whose appearance and gender changed from human to animal (usually a spider, monkey or rabbit) depending on the story. Anansi in his or her various guises usually tried to deceive others and the stories associated with this figure are associated with cunning and wrongdoing. Usually, Anansi received his come-uppance as a result of wicked deeds. These stories, passed from one generation to another, served to remind slaves, especially children, of the need for good behaviour. They showed that misdemeanours would meet with punishment.

Spiritual values were an essential part of slave communities. A belief in spirits often seemed mere superstition to white observers; but it was bound up with a commonly held black belief that spirits cast spells that could harm or cure, something that was connected to medicinal treatments for ailments by herbs. African beliefs filtering through to Jamaica acknowledged the existence of a supreme being and invoked the spirits of nature and of ancestors. Magic and the supernatural formed an essential core of Afro-Jamaican beliefs. These guiding elements, it was thought, played a crucial role in promoting the essential features of life, whether it be survival or death, peace or war, plenty or famine. A belief in ancestral spirits was particularly important in providing slaves with a constant reference point to some larger purpose for their worldly existence.

Life's major staging posts – birth, marriage, death – were all steeped in spiritual significance for slaves.

Newborn babies were not recognised as fully human, and therefore not named, until the ninth day. This reflected the precariousness of survival and the notion that such babies were 'ghost-childs' until they lived beyond the eighth day after birth. Funerals were observed with a high degree of ritual and ceremony because many blacks believed that death marked a spiritual return to Africa. Slaves usually organised their own funerals without interference from whites. Rum and food were sometimes thrown into the grave and commemorative feasts held on the ninth and fortieth nights after the funeral, at which the dead were treated as guests. Jamaican slaves often had their own burial grounds where they observed their own practices to honour the dead. In 1751 the rector of St Catherine parish noted that this was taken seriously, for 'to deprive [negroes] of their funeral rites by burning their dead Bodies, [it] seems to Negroes a greater punishment than Death itself'. Edward Long observed that 'every funeral is a kind of festival; at which the greater part of the company assume an air of joy and unconcern; and, together with their singing, dancing, and musical instruments, conspire to drown all sense of affliction in the minds of the real mourners'.

Obeah men and myal men were part of the slave community. These were people who were thought to have spiritual powers to help the enslaved with prophecies, healing and communion ceremonies. They intervened in disputes to try to find a solution; they dealt with haunting and spiritual cure as part of their shaman identities; and they served as influential people over slave actions that somewhat detracted from the power of planters. The plantocracy were both wary of these ritual specialists, and regarded their powers as a form of witchcraft and as a threat to white control. Obeah practitioners were often elderly men whose wizardry was sought to assist the slaves. They were particularly consulted by slaves in relation to the souls of the dead. They carried charms that might take the form of broken glass, animal teeth, feathers, eggshells and parrots' beaks.

Slaves could resist the exploitation of the plantation world by working slowly and occasionally putting down tools; they could run away into forested parts of Jamaica; and they could organise and participate in rebellions. Work stoppages tended to occur when slaves had been mistreated by overseers or drivers; but the incidence of such practices is poorly documented before the American Revolution. Runaway slaves found it difficult to hide away from the white militia because of their obvious visibility on an island where by far the majority of black people were slaves. Slave revolts occurred from time to time but not as frequently as one might suppose. Some historians argue that slaves had a permanent spirit of rebelliousness, and were waiting for every opportunity to stage an uprising. This is unlikely to have been the case. While all slaves wanted freedom, revolts were not at all easy to stage successfully. Some slaves, especially those promoted to positions of influence on plantations, remained loyal to their white masters. The problems of organising an uprising across scattered rural plantations also mitigated the incidence of slave revolts. Nevertheless, revolts occasionally occurred that threatened to disrupt and destroy the plantation system.

The largest slave revolt in Jamaica before the American Revolution broke out on the morning of 7 April 1760 when slaves in St Mary parish rose up against their masters in a concerted uprising. This was the first major challenge to white control of Jamaica since the Maroon wars of the 1730s. The revolt had been planned in secrecy and was therefore a shock to the plantocracy. It became known as Tacky's Revolt after one of its African-born leaders. Coromantine slaves lay at the heart of the disruption. Tacky was a foreman on a plantation who organised the revolt after deciding to do so during the course of an obeah ritual. The governor of Jamaica declared martial law and drew upon militia and army regiments to quell the disturbance. Tacky and his followers initially killed twenty settlers and seized the fort at Port Maria. Serious damage occurred to plantations. Slaves from St James parish revolted but were quickly quashed by the militia.

Colonial forces suppressed the rebels with brutality, shackling ringleaders in irons, cutting off their ears and heads, and stringing their bodies up on gibbets erected in Kingston. The militia was aided by Maroons, who found Tacky, killed him and carried his head on a pole to Spanish Town. John Hamilton, a planter in St Elizabeth parish, wrote to relatives in Scotland that when British troops seized rebels 'they killed them with great Slaughter of the Prisoners they took, they hanged up without ceremony or Judge or Jury' to 'leave a Terror on the Minds of all the other Negroes for the future'. More than 500 slaves were killed in fighting or executed and a further 500 rebels were shipped to Roatán, a prison island off Honduras. 'Whether we consider the extent and secrecy of its plan, the multitude of the conspirators, and the difficulty of opposing its eruptions in such a variety of places at once', wrote Long, this uprising was 'more formidable than any hitherto known in the West Indies'. The rebellion spread to Westmoreland, Hanover and Clarendon parishes before it was suppressed by the militia aided by Maroons.

The shock of Tacky's Revolt led the Jamaican legislature to stiffen their treatment of the enslaved, with calls to scrutinise movements of slaves and to dole out harsher punishments for misdemeanours. Thus in October 1761 a new statute was passed by Jamaica's Assembly that prohibited 'irregular' gatherings of slaves and prevented them from carrying arms and ammunition. This act also forbade the folk magic practice of obeah, which was perceived by the white elite as emboldening the enslaved to rebel. The planters requested more troops from England to bolster Jamaica's internal security. In subsequent years, obeah men were brought into court and, if found guilty, executed. Punishment of shaman practitioners continued through to the end of slavery in Jamaica and beyond. Smaller slave uprisings occurred in St Mary's parish in 1765 and Westmoreland in 1766, but these were quickly stopped.

Other Economic Activities

Though increasingly dominated by sugar production as the English continued to settle in Jamaica, the island was never a monoculture. Agriculture and external trade were central economic activities. In the early years of English settlement in Jamaica, commentators underscored the island's soil fertility and its capacity to support an expanding population. It was an island 'yielding in great abundance whatsoever is necessary for mans' life', with such a quantity of cassava that Jamaica 'may be reckoned the

Granary of the rest of the Islands'. Indigo, cotton, ginger and tobacco were also cultivated on a modest scale. Many foodstuffs eaten in Jamaica before the English arrived were still consumed regularly in the late seventeenth and eighteenth centuries, including salted beef, pork and fish, plantains, potatoes and yams. Slaves grew many vegetables on their own provision grounds. This saved planters a great deal of money that would have otherwise been expended on feeding their workforce. Slaves' provision grounds produced fruit, vegetables, edible herbs and root crops. Usually situated at a distance from the slaves' huts, and often located on the hilly fringes of plantations, provision grounds were cultivated in the few hours each week when slaves were not working in the cane fields. Planters never attempted to supervise slaves working on their provision grounds: this would have involved extra costs for them, and in any case they no doubt calculated that slaves would be more content if allowed a modicum of independence in their weekly routines.

Many types of economic activity took place in Jamaica. About 350,000 acres of pasturage land was available and around 6.5 million acres capable of being manured for crop cultivation. 'The Low-lands and Plain Grounds, are where the People generally inhabit', wrote Francis Hanson in 1683, 'and in these are Level tracts of several Miles in length and bredth ... called *Savannas* (which Name they retain from the *Spaniards*) in these are bred great plenty of Cattle, Sheep, Horses, Asses and Mules, sufficient both for food and service, there is also in the Country great stocks of Hogs, Hens, Ducks, Pigeons, Rabbets, Turkeys, and diverse kinds of wild Fowl, and also sufficient stores of all sorts of Garden Herbs and Roots, Pulse and Sallads, and with excellent Fruits'.

When the English conquered Jamaica in 1655, the island had about 40,000 cattle and horses mainly roaming wild. Livestock was kept on pens overseen by small planters or penkeepers. Draught animals supplied meat for planters and were also used extensively on sugar estates, especially those lacking in wind, water or steam power. This facilitated a continuing economic exchange between sugar planters and penkeepers, and also absolved planters from having to import cattle and horses. Before the American revolutionary era, the pens exported log-wood, cotton, fustic, ginger, pimento and mahogany, but they also catered for a domestic market in provisions and livestock and for bartering commodities among proper-ties. The livestock exchanged included heifers, calves, asses, mules, horses, bulls and steers. Corn, plantains and other food provisions along with beef, fish, timber, white lime, shingles and bricks were exchanged. Pens provided labour services such as jobbing gangs, which comprised slaves hired out to plantations to assist with sugar cane holing. Pens also provided pasturage and cartage facilities, charged at monthly rates for the service.

A fully-fledged internal marketing system was a significant feature of Jamaica's economy before the American Revolution. Though crop cultivation on provi-sion grounds was mainly intended for the slaves' own consumption, surpluses were taken to local markets and exchanged for cash or other commodities. Sunday, the one day slaves did not work in the cane fields, became the established market day. Slaves were allowed to keep the crops they exchanged and the money: planters did not interfere with these activities. The great demand for provisions in Spanish Town created a very large demand for livestock, which in turn led to increased settlement in the vicinity. In 1774 about 20 per cent of the currency circulating in Jamaica lay in the hands of slaves. External trade also rose appreciably as Jamaica became quickly settled under English rule. Some of this involved commerce with other Caribbean islands; more important were shipping links between Jamaica and English colonies in North America along with legal and illegal trade with the Spanish Main, a bilateral trade across the Atlantic with England and the rise of the slave trade from Africa. By the mid-1680s about 100 ships a year were visiting Jamaica's harbours. In the seventy years after 1660, smugglers operated via Jamaica to other Caribbean markets. Lacking agents in Jamaica who could visibly assist them, smugglers ensured that no paper trail was left for their handling of illicit cargoes in case their vessels were captured and a court case resulted. By 1706–7 significant amounts of Spanish cocoa, hides, indigo and cochineal formed part of this illegal commerce conducted via Jamaica and smuggled bullion exports were worth £250,000. A small group of Sephardic Jewish merchants, based in Port Royal and Kingston, were the main organisers of this commerce. A contemporary report of 1740 estimated the value of Jamaica's entire produce at £500,000. A similar report from 1743 increased this figure to £650,000 and further stated that the goods supplied to Jamaica from Britain and Ireland were worth £1,200,000. A report of 1748 calculated the value of Jamaica's produce at £800,000. These calculations easily exceeded those for other British West Indian colonies tabulated in the same reports.

Urban Centres

The main urban centres in Jamaica were Port Royal, Kingston and Spanish Town (or St Jago de la Vega). Port Royal was a centre of maritime shipping and trade from the time of the English conquest of Jamaica until 1692, when it was suddenly destroyed by a major earthquake. Kingston, with a fine natural deep-water harbour, then superseded Port Royal as the main port for Jamaica, a position which it retained permanently. Spanish Town was the main administrative centre of Jamaica, the seat of government and the main courts. Smaller towns emerged gradually in Jamaica from the beginning of the eighteenth century, usually doubling as small ports. These included Savanna-la-Mar in the southwest and Montego Bay, Martha Brae/Falmouth and Port Antonio on the north coast.

Many changes occurred to Spanish Town during the English conquest of Jamaica. Most Spanish people living there fled the town and many buildings were destroyed. However, the English retained Spanish Town as the centre of the island's government. They preferred to keep the civil administration there for several reasons, including preserving continuity in an urban centre that had been the site of government under the Spanish and being situated in a location easily accessible to planters. Situated at one of Jamaica's main crossroads, Spanish Town served as a convenient provision centre for planters but also as a town where lawyers and other government officials could be based. Old Spanish houses survived in Spanish Town but new English private brick houses were added to them in the later seventeenth century. The earthquake of

1692, measuring 7.5 on the Richter scale, destroyed many of these new structures; many of the Spanish public and private buildings, however, remained unaffected owing to their thick roofs and deeply dug hole posts as foundations. Spanish Town was rapidly rebuilt after the earthquake. The Anglican Cathedral, which existed before 1692, was reconstructed in the early eighteenth century. A new city hall was erected in the main square and a synagogue was built as a focal point for Spanish Town's Jewish community. A grammar school was re-established with the aid of a munificent endowment from a wealthy planter, Peter Beckford, and an archives building was erected that still stands today. Residential and commercial building proceeded apace in the 1740s, including residential districts for Spanish Town's slave population. Street markets proliferated in Spanish Town, as vendors sold fruit, herbs, ground provisions, poultry, eggs and plantains. A Sunday market served as an outlet for produce grown by slaves on land assigned to them. Spanish Town served as a military as well as a commercial centre, for it housed many troops garrisoned in Jamaica. New barracks and a military hospital were built around the garrison compound in the 1770s.

Spanish Town was a relatively modest town in terms of houses and wealth. Estimates drawn up by an economic projector in 1750 suggest that it contained 400 houses worth a total of £160,000 whereas Kingston had 1,600 houses worth £960,000. Nevertheless, the people of Spanish Town adamantly insisted that their town was more suitable as a seat of government and administration than Kingston. Between 1754 and 1758, when Governor Charles Knowles tried to relocate the island's government to Kingston, petitioners from both towns vigorously defended their positions. Wide-ranging discussions took place in a highly charged political atmosphere in which the governor supported Kingston's position, taking account of its importance as an internationally important trading centre. Supporters of retaining the status quo argued that Spanish Town had a healthier environment than Kingston and was less subject to luxury and corruption. The matter was referred to the Board of Trade in London, which recommended to the Privy Council that King George II should not approve a move for the capital because Governor Knowles had not followed correct political procedures. The Board of Trade's decision was accepted and the capital of Jamaica returned to Spanish Town. After 1758 the Jamaican Assembly supported the building of splendid new buildings to house the governor, the Assembly and law courts to reinforce the importance of public affairs being based in Spanish Town.

Port Royal was situated on the Palisadoes spit, a long, thin peninsula mainly known today as the site of Kingston's international airport. Houses, a church, palisadoes, stores and a fort were constructed at Port Royal during the English conquest of the late 1650s. Fortifications were increased on the site of the town in the 1660s and 1670s to serve as a means of defence against Spanish attacks on Kingston harbour. Naval vessels were stationed at Port Royal under Admiralty instructions. Merchant ships also entered and cleared Port Royal in significant numbers. Between January 1668 and January 1670, 208 ships comprising 6,727 tons entered Port Royal harbour. Between 1686 and 1691, 40,880 tons of shipping arrived at Port Royal from England, Ireland,

Africa and North America. All sorts of manufactured goods, alcohol and textiles were carried by these ships. By the 1680s Port Royal's merchants accounted for between 20 and 25 per cent of Jamaica's commercial transactions. Plenty of contraband goods passed through Port Royal, where factors often had a considerable share in the cargo and could arrange for ships smuggling merchandise to sail on to mainland Spanish America. The items taken via Port Royal to Spanish markets consisted mainly of European manufactures, especially linens and silks, liquor and iron-ware. Profits from participation in legitimate and illegal trade enabled Port Royal's merchants and factors to become prosperous: many invested their gains in agriculture and some became Jamaican planters. By 1692, when an earthquake destroyed Port Royal, it was probably the richest merchant community in the British Caribbean.

Port Royal's population in 1673 amounted to 2,181 persons, including 714 free men, 529 free women, ninety free children and fifty slaves. According to a census of 1680, Port Royal had slightly in excess of 2,000 whites and about 850 blacks. Within a compact settlement, Port Royal housed sailors, soldiers, slaves, indentured servants, carpenters, shipwrights, fishermen, barbers, doctors and prostitutes. Taverns were prominent centres for social life. Port Royal had a reputation for bustling and boisterous activity, an abundance of alcohol, gambling, unruly behaviour and houses of ill repute. Merchants based there lived, according to Taylor, 'to the hight of splendour, in full ease and plenty, being sumptuously arrayed, and attended on and served by their Negroa slaves, which always waits on them in livereys, or otherwise as they please to cloath them'.

After establishing itself for several decades as the principal commercial centre on Jamaica, Port Royal collapsed in one fell swoop as a result of the earthquake of 7 June 1692. Buildings suddenly crashed down, the church toppled into the sea, many wharves fell into thirty or forty feet of water, houses were sunk, and many of the town's defences were destroyed. Mayhem broke out on the streets and looting occurred. Robert Renny's *An History of Jamaica* (1807) stated that 'All the wharves sunk at once, and in the space of two minutes, nine-tenths of the city was covered with water, which was raised to such a height, that it entered the uppermost rooms of the few houses which were left standing. The tops of the highest houses were visible in the water and surrounded by the masts of vessels, which had been sunk along with them.' According to a contemporary account, 'immediately upon the cessation of the extremity of the earthquake, your heart would abhorr to hear the depredations, robberies and violences that were in an instance committed upon the place by the vilest and basest of the people'. About 2,000 people died during the earthquake itself but that total doubled in its aftermath to include many injured persons and those who had caught serious fevers. A clergyman considered the earthquake 'a terrible Judgment of God' upon the 'most Ungodly Debauched People' on 'the face of the whole earth'.

The sudden demise of Port Royal led to the equally rapid rise of Kingston. Three weeks after the earthquake hit Port Royal, the Jamaica Council agreed to build a new town on a 200-acre site near the waterfront. There was a conscious decision to construct Kingston on a methodical gridiron layout, similar to the one William Penn had adopted for the streets of Philadelphia just over a decade earlier. John Goffe designed Kingston on a rectangular pattern. Thirteen equally spaced streets were designed to run from south on the waterfront to north. These were criss-crossed by eleven wider streets running from east to west. The commercial hub of Kingston was located among these streets within easy walking distance of the harbour. A large open square in the centre of these streets, surrounded by public buildings, replicated the central plaza associated with the layout of Spanish colonial cities. Kingston was therefore planned on a more uniform basis than Port Royal. Construction proceeded quickly and lots were quickly taken up by merchants and retailers. Two- and three-storey brick houses predominated. In 1764 Lord Adam Gordon noted that Kingston was 'very considerable, being large and very well Inhabited, the Streets spacious and regularly laid out'. To the north of the streets and premises in the central core of Kingston, extensive flat or gently undulating land stretched towards the Liguanea Plain. This provided plenty of additional space for the growth of the town.

By 1774 Kingston had 14,200 people, making it the third largest town in British America. Just under a third of Jamaica's white inhabitants lived there, including wealthy merchants who left estates in excess of £100,000. Forty per cent of the free black population of Jamaica also lived in Kingston. This reflected the fact that most of these people found work in retail businesses, households and around the commercial area of the harbour. Possibly, in addition, free blacks consciously distanced themselves from the slave world of the plantations. But Kingston was mainly the home to large numbers of slaves. By the mid-eighteenth century, slaves comprised 60 per cent of Kingston's population: in 1774, 9,000 slaves lived there. Until 1758 Kingston was the only port in Jamaica to which Africans were brought. These captives were transferred to urban yards or pens for retail sale by merchants, who mainly dealt with planters in need of saltwater slaves. Kingston itself had about twenty-five slaveholder residents by the mid-eighteenth century who kept thirty or more slaves in urban yards.

Kingston's economy was based on several main lines of commercial activity. First, an extensive slave trade existed, as discussed above, that included a substantial re-export of slaves to Spanish America while the *asiento* contract existed before 1740. Thereafter Kingston remained a significant entrepôt for slave re-exportation. Kingston was the main Jamaican port through which over 62,000 slave re-exports from Jamaica were processed between 1741 and 1790. Second, regular, direct transatlantic shipping to and from British ports was an important form of commerce. Ships brought out manufactured items from the mother country – textiles, metalware, glassware – and sent back primarily sugar but also coffee, ginger and other tropical produce to British ports. Third, Kingston was the central hub for the provision of credit and moneylending throughout Jamaica to planters, retailers and other businessmen. This was a vital cog for commercial transactions because credit was the most mobile factor of production in the eighteenth-century transatlantic economy.

The Maroons

Permanent runaway black communities were a significant feature of British Caribbean slave society before the American Revolution. Rugged forested areas in Jamaica's mountains were one prime location for Maroons (an Anglicised version of the French word *marronage*, meaning runaway). Maroons were at the heart of a resistance movement against the whites of Jamaica. Jamaica's government, dominated by a white elite, regarded the Maroon communities as an impediment to British control in Jamaica. The Maroons, for their part, were determined to maintain their autonomy. Two separate groups of Maroons formed settlements in Jamaica. The Western Maroons were largely based in secluded areas of the Cockpit Country, whereas the Windward Maroons lived in the mountainous parts of eastern Jamaica. The Western Maroons formed permanent communities such as Old Maroon Town, Trelawney Town, Cudjoe's Town and their headquarters at Accompong Town. The Eastern Maroons had settlements at Old and New Crawford Town, Moore Town and Nanny Town. Sympathetic newcomers were welcomed to Maroon communities.

The Maroons lived in remote, hilly, forested areas well away from most plantations. They defended their hideaway communities with disguised paths, false trails and, where possible, underwater paths. They survived economically by cultivating gardens and growing crops, by hunting and fishing, and by making utensils. They kept in secretive contact with some plantation slaves for goods and services. They were not large in numbers: a contemporary estimate suggests that there were 885

Jamaican Maroons in 1770. Nevertheless, they stood as symbols of freedom for enslaved blacks. Today remnants of these communities still exist and an annual celebration of Maroon independence takes place on 6 January, when the Accompong Maroons reunite to visit the stone-marked grave site of their late leader Cudjoe.

Maroons were already making raids on plantations in the 1680s. Sometimes they were subject to counter-raids by planters. Occasional attacks escalated into more prolonged altercations, notably during the 1720s. During the First Maroon War (1731–39), both groups resisted conquest. Though English troops tried to divide and weaken resistance, the Maroons were highly skilled at guerrilla warfare and proved difficult to capture. The whites spent £100,000 in an attempt to destroy the Maroons between 1730 and 1734, but failed to do so. The Maroons compelled the Jamaican plantocracy to seek accommodation with them, something achieved through a peace treaty of 1739 between Colonel Guthrie and the Maroon leader Cudjoe and another treaty of the same year signed on behalf of Nanny, the Ashanti-born female leader of another band of Maroons. These treaties gave the Maroons rights to hunt freely throughout unsettled areas of Jamaica, allowed them 1,500 acres of land for cultivation, but obliged them to return fugitive slaves they encountered. Most important, it pledged their support to white settlers when slave rebellions broke out.

In 1760 Maroons joined white forces in putting down the serious slave revolt in western Jamaica begun by Coromantee rebels and killed the leader, Tacky. Planters lived in fear of reprisals during the revolt. 'I praise God none of mine nor Johnson's Negroes were in the

MAROON WAR IN JAMAICA.—P. 175.

FIGURE 3.6 Maroon War in Jamaica. Universal History Archive/
Getty Images

rebellion', one planter wrote, for 'if they had we might been [*sic*] all Destroyed, as my house is so nigh to the Mountains. They often threatned to come down upon me but I praise God they never did.' After the rebellion was quashed, Maroons were sometimes engaged in seeking out runaway slaves for the settlers.

There was always suspicion by white people in Jamaica that the Maroons were a potential threat to social stability. Maroons had considerable military prowess, becoming expert in guerrilla warfare, using bows, arrows and spears. Stephen Fuller, the agent for Jamaica, noted in 1778 that the Maroons 'have never become properly incorporated with the rest of the inhabitants, nor are they interested in the defence of the Country, and their conduct in the late insurrections of the slaves sufficiently proved that they are not to be depended upon'. Despite these misgivings, peace with the Jamaican Maroons lasted until 1795 when the English commissioner assigned to Trelawny Town had two Maroons flogged for pilfering from plantations. The island's governor feared the Maroons and sent troops to capture Trelawny Town. During a Second Maroon War in 1795–6, Maroons ambushed the troops but the British army prevailed after laying siege to the Maroon towns by surrounding them with military outposts. The Maroons agreed to surrender in return for amnesty. After the 1795–6 war, Jamaica's government ordered the deportation of 600 Maroons to Nova Scotia.

The American Revolutionary War Era

During the American revolutionary era – defined here as the years following the end of the Seven Years' War in 1763 to the conclusion of the American War of Independence in 1783 – plenty of turbulence occurred in Jamaica's politics but there was little disruption in response to imperial measures. Jamaica's Assembly became embroiled in a serious internal dispute with Governor William Henry Lyttleton in the mid-1760s over constitutional matters. This concerned the relative judicial powers of the Assembly and the governor: the Assembly wanted to adhere to custom and precedent, according to its understanding of English common law, whereas the governor stood by his ability to act in an executive manner under the royal prerogative. Eventually, after a long confrontation, the Rockingham administration ordered Lyttleton to follow a conciliatory policy towards the Assembly. The governor had little option but to comply with the government request.

While this internal political dispute was in train, a major political dispute between Britain and its North American colonies had been created by parliament's passing of the Stamp Act in 1765. This famous piece of legislation imposed taxes on a variety of goods for the first time. Americans in cities such as Boston, Charleston and New York displayed their staunch opposition to what they labelled taxation without representation by writing critical letters to newspapers, petitioning parliament and staging riots. Such bitterness expressed at imperial laws was not replicated in Jamaica or throughout the British Caribbean. Certainly, the Jamaican Assembly and people living on the island disliked the Stamp Act; but they were not motivated, unlike their North American counterparts, to protest vehemently against its provisions. As Governor Lyttleton put it at the time, 'nothing has occurred here to interrupt the public tranquillity'.

Preserving the peace in Jamaica over imperial measures was aided and abetted by the fact that the Jamaican Assembly was prorogued during the period of the Stamp Act crisis, but this was not the main reason why peace was maintained. This is evident from the continued lack of protest in Jamaica at subsequent British parliamentary measures such as the Townshend Duties (1767) and the East India Act (1773), both of which provoked great opposition once again in the British North American colonies. What accounts for Jamaica's passivity in the face of parliamentary measures that were unpopular among many people living in the island? Why did

Jamaica not protest against imperial measures, and submit loyal addresses to King George III in 1775 and 1776? Why did Jamaica not revolt against British rule when the thirteen North American colonies declared their independence on 4 July 1776?

The answer to these questions lies in Jamaica's unique social and geographical structure. Jamaica was dominated demographically by black people of African descent, the vast majority of whom were slaves. The white population in Jamaica was relatively small by comparison. Thus in 1774 Jamaica's population comprised over 200,000 slaves and fewer than 13,000 whites. This racial bias was not found in any of the British North American colonies, even though in Virginia and especially South Carolina a large number of slaves could be found. Jamaica's white population felt vulnerable because it was outnumbered by black slaves. Fears of slave revolts were rife, and with justification as there were five separate slave revolts in Jamaica between 1760 and 1765. The largest of these uprisings, Tacky's Revolt (1760) described above, was the largest slave rebellion until almost the end of slavery on the island in 1834. Jamaica's vulnerability to slave disturbances led the Assembly to remain loyal to Britain, which alone could provide the troops and navy needed to defend Jamaica from internal disorders and from external attack in wartime.

A Jamaican slave revolt of July 1776 in Hanover parish resulted directly from the American War of Independence. Though swiftly put down, it was temporarily alarming for Jamaica's authorities because it involved members of the creole slave elite. Food imports from North America to Jamaica were disrupted as shipping lanes became dangerous in wartime at a time when a severe drought occurred on the island. The rebellion was triggered by these deprivations. No further significant slave revolt occurred in Jamaica during the American revolutionary war years and their immediate aftermath.

The Jamaican Assembly and leading merchants on the island strongly opposed the drive for revolutionary independence that inspired so many North Americans to take up arms against the mother country. In December 1775 Jamaica sent a declaration of loyalty to George III and requested additional troops for the island's defence. In short, Jamaica did not follow the drive towards republicanism that motivated so many North American colonists, but displayed loyalty to the Crown and the British Empire. White Jamaicans had experienced an era of general prosperity between the end of the Seven Years' War and the American Declaration of Independence. This also helped considerably in maintaining loyalty to Britain and its empire.

The Jamaican economy was badly affected by the American revolutionary war: plantation profits declined, sugar exports dwindled, shipping costs increased significantly, there was the constant possibility of enemy attack, the supply of Africans was cut back and the cessation of West Indian–American trade led to shortages in provisions and a marked increase in the prices of American foodstuffs in Jamaica. A destructive hurricane hit the island on 3 October 1780 and a smaller one occurred in August 1781, both causing significant damage to plantation properties and sugar cane cultivation.

Despite these economic problems, the political outlook of Jamaica's white elite remained unchanged throughout the American War of Independence. Though white Jamaicans regretted the inability of the British armed forces to bring the war to a swift conclusion, they remained loyal to the monarchy and the British Empire just as they had done before 1776. Governor John Dalling provoked the anger of many Jamaicans by removing troops for overseas service in 1779–80 when the island was vulnerable to attack. Thus troops were sent to the Bay of Honduras to counter Spanish attacks in that vicinity. This initiative failed, however, because troops died while fighting and from catching diseases. Worries about Jamaica's security increased after 1778, when France joined the revolutionary war on the American side and despatched naval forces to the Caribbean at a time when the British army was scattered throughout the West Indies.

After the major British military defeat at the Battle of Yorktown, Virginia, in 1781 – the decisive British loss in the revolutionary war – the French and Spanish navies prepared a large assault on the British Caribbean islands, with Jamaica as a prime target. A British fleet commanded by Admiral George Rodney gave pursuit to the French naval vessels and, aided by copper sheathing to British naval ships, was able to sail quickly enough to catch up with the French. The British and French navies engaged in a naval offensive off Dominica in April 1782 known as the Battle of the Saintes. The British navy emerged successful from this encounter with well-manned French naval ships and, by winning the battle, prevented a French invasion of Jamaica. The wealthy Jamaican planter Simon Taylor expressed his relief at the victory by hoping 'to God we and our Familys shall live and die under the British Government'. This important British naval success was commemorated by the erection of a statue erected in honour of Admiral Rodney in the main square next to the Assembly buildings in Spanish Town.

In 1781 an incident occurred, involving Jamaica, that had wide ramifications for the conduct of the slave trade and the beginnings of an abolitionist movement in Britain. This was the infamous case of the British slaving vessel *Zong*, which sought to save costs by crew throwing 122 Africans overboard to their death off the coast of southwest Jamaica in November and December 1781. This drastic action was taken to preserve the diminishing water supplies for the fractious crew. Some 208 surviving slaves were sold in Jamaica. After the end of the voyage, the owners of the *Zong* tried to claim insurance on the lost captives in a famous court case of 1783 that gained abolitionist attention and was widely publicised. The owners were initially granted compensation but this was then overturned legally in favour of the insurers. The *Zong* case demonstrated the severe human problems that could arise on an overcrowded slave ship; it helped to promote humanitarian sentiment against the slave trade into a moral campaign; and it underscored the fact that Jamaica lay at the heart of the British transatlantic sugar–slavery nexus.

4

From Slavery to Freedom, 1775–1865

~

Jamaica experienced major changes between the American Revolution and the Morant Bay rebellion of 1865. The slave trade had a new lease of life after 1783 as the return of peace after the American revolutionary war and the continuing expansion of the plantation economy required further large importations of enslaved Africans. While this occurred, Jamaica's elite were worried that the spirit of rebellion given impetus by the large successful slave uprising in Saint-Domingue in the early 1790s would spread to Jamaica. That crisis was averted, but the spectre of a successful slave uprising influenced planter behaviour in Jamaica for decades. Planters and other members of the West India Interest also contended with antislavery sentiment in Britain, which fostered the growth of an anti-slave trade movement culminating in the abolition of the British slave trade by parliamentary act in 1807. In that protracted process, the absentee Jamaica planter class, both in parliament and among the upper echelons of British society, was a strong voice among proslavery advocates.

Slavery continued for another quarter century after slave trade abolition, but antislavery advocates accelerated their campaigning after the British government in 1823 implemented amelioration as an official policy to improve slave conditions and stave off slave emancipation. The last major Jamaican slave revolt occupied the period between Christmas 1831 and Easter 1832. Occurring during a heightened atmosphere of antislavery activity, it was defeated but soon followed by the British government's enactment of slave emancipation in 1834. Four years of apprenticeship followed during which the majority of Jamaicans were neither slaves nor fully free. The first decades of freedom after 1838 witnessed a series of improvements for free people, in terms of the settlement of independent peasant villages and the growth of black participation in parish politics. On the other hand, discrimination against black people continued within a colonial context where British-style institutions preserved the status and power of the minority white elite. In 1865 tensions between Jamaicans and the white authorities led to the Morant Bay uprising, which was brutally quashed and followed by the installation of Crown Colony government in Jamaica.

The Jamaican Economy

The Jamaican economy continued to operate on similar lines to the situation before the American War of Independence. The sugar plantation sector maintained its position as the central unit of economic life, with the number of estates expanding in the late eighteenth century. Thus eighty-four new sugar plantations were established between 1792 and 1799. James Robertson's map of 1804 showed 830 sugar estates in Jamaica. In 1792–3 Jamaica despatched 142 ships carrying 52,922 casks of sugar and 15,698 casks of rum, accounting respectively for 41 per cent of total ships, 44 per cent of the sugar and 72 per cent of the rum shipped from British West Indies. Coffee plantations began to make their mark. The number of coffee estates expanded from 150 in 1774 to 686 in 1799 on hillier terrain throughout the island. Coffee contributed more than a quarter of the value of Jamaica's total exports between 1805 and 1830.

Though plantations dominated the economy, Jamaica, as before 1775, was far from being a monoculture. On the eve of slave emancipation, only around half of the slave labour force was engaged in plantation agriculture, with sugar and coffee estates absorbing most of the workers. The majority of slaves worked on estates where they lived, but before 1807 about 10 per cent of that workforce was hired out to other plantations in jobbing gangs. At least 40 per cent of the enslaved did not live and work on sugar estates, and half of these people were connected to small properties engaged in diverse lines of work including the production of pimento and mixed staples, logwood cutting, small-scale manufacturing, and the distribution, construction and transportation of other commodities. Logwood and pimento, however, played a very minor role in Jamaica's economy by the time of slave emancipation: at that time, pimento comprised only 4 per cent of Jamaica's exports and logwood accounted for 2 per cent.

Raising livestock on pens, mainly cattle but also mules, was a more significant economic activity. By 1834 there were 400 pens in Jamaica which, two years earlier, employed 40,000 slaves. Penkeepers raised livestock for the animal power needed on plantations and for milk and meat. They owned breeding cows, heifers, young cows, calves, bulls, fattening stock steers and working stock. A lively and varied internal economy entailed the marketing of produce and animals, partly carried out by white retailers but also by slaves buying and selling the surplus of their provision grounds. Planting guinea grass on pastures as fodder for livestock helped to stimulate a quicker sugar harvest through producing more manure and better-nourished livestock: heavier dunging led to better crops. Some owners of Jamaican plantations introduced specialised stock pens to raise mule and cattle for sale or use around their estates.

Internal exchange facilitating local consumption was also a central component of Jamaican economic life by the time of slave emancipation. Slaves produced foodstuffs on their provision grounds for their own consumption but sold surplus commodities at weekly markets. Plantation crops such as sugar, rum and coffee were moved around the island for internal sale. Planters and other landholders exchanged gifts and circulated commodities and labourers between plantations and livestock pens. A thriving internal livestock trade witnessed the movement of cattle, mules and horses between pens and sugar estates; they were used for hauling sugar cane and, on some properties, for cattle mills. Some animals were killed to supply butchers, who marketed the meat to plantations and towns.

As the largest British island possession in the Caribbean, Jamaica retained its important position in the commercial life of the British Empire in the late eighteenth century. Jamaica remained, in the words of P. J. Marshall, 'the most valuable of all British colonies, the one whose loss could least be afforded'. Jamaica was thus regarded as a vital colony for Britain's prosperity, strength and future prospects. In 1793 the absentee planter Bryan Edwards estimated that Jamaica contained 250,000 slaves worth £12.5 million; landed and personal property amounting to £25 million; and houses, urban property and trading vessels worth £1.5 million. Altogether, therefore, Edwards estimated Jamaica's value to Britain at £39 million. In 1814 Patrick Colquhoun suggested that the value of property in Jamaica amounted to £58.1 million, while the figure for the entire British West Indies, excluding conquered colonies, was £100 million.

Sugar plantations experienced many pressures during the long wars with revolutionary and Napoleonic France, but older studies, such as that by Lowell J. Ragatz, claiming that they experienced serious decline, have been modified by more recent investigations. Sugar estates continued to make profits in successive years of war and peace. Estimated annual profit rates for Jamaican sugar plantations amounted to 6.4 per cent for 1783–91, 13.9 per cent for 1792–8, 9.6 per cent for 1799–1819 and 5.3 per cent for 1820–34. It is a moot point whether sugar plantation owners thought a 5 per cent profit rate on their estates in the last phase of Jamaican slavery was enough to persuade them to retain their capital in Jamaica. By 1830, however, the economic prospects for Jamaican sugar estates had begun to decline because of a sharp fall in sugar prices: in 1830 the average price of sugar per hundredweight in the British market was virtually the same as the level of sugar duties.

The sugar plantation economy experienced significant decline after slave emancipation. Planters faced increased costs and no longer had access to a permanent, coerced set of workers after apprenticeship ended in 1838. The 670 sugar estates in existence in 1834 fell to 330 in 1854 and

200 in 1880. Failure to prevent plantations incurring serious indebtedness led to the abandonment of 140 sugar properties between 1832 and 1847. Parliament's removal of the sugar duties in 1846 removed a protected home market for British colonial-produced sugar, adding to Jamaican planters' woes. Coffee estates also declined after slave emancipation. In the period 1832–47, 465 coffee plantations were abandoned. Conversely, livestock pen-keeping increased after the end of apprenticeship as lands formerly under sugar cultivation were converted to pasture. The census of 1844 reported 378 breeding pens and the number increased in the second half of the nineteenth century: in 1881 there were 604 cattle pens in excess of 200 acres.

Urban Life

Kingston remained the largest Jamaican port and town between the American Revolution and the advent of Crown Colony government in 1866. In 1788 Peter Marsden described some of its main features: 'The town of Kingston is regularly built, street behind street (mostly of wood) to a considerable extent, being about a mile in length, and half a mile in breadth ... In the north part of the town is a neat church with a low spire; and nearly adjoining is a spacious parade, with barracks for soldiers. There is also a theatre, assembly-rooms, and other places of public amusement ... Except a few excellent houses which have lately been built of brick, and two or three of stone, after the English fashion, by rich merchants, the houses are in general of wood, very often mahogany, which is plentiful in this island.'

Kingston's main religious and administrative buildings surrounded the Parade, including a parish church, military barracks and, from 1800, a Theatre Royal. The Parade was the central urban location for people to stroll and meet one another. Markets and commercial premises were situated in the lower part of the town nearer the waterfront. Many homes included a 'piazza', situated in front of a house, which was both a private enclosed space and a structure that facilitated the circulation of air into the interior. Commercial premises were clustered near the waterfront, allowing easy access to the extensive harbour.

Until the British abolition of the slave trade in 1807, Kingston continued as the leading British Caribbean port for slave imports. Its significant role in sending sugar consignments to Britain continued throughout the nineteenth century. Kingston also remained the largest local market in

FIGURE 4.1 Harbour Street, Kingston. DEA/ICAS94/De Agostini/ Getty Images

Jamaica for fruit, vegetables and meat. The port's industrial sector expanded significantly in the first half of the nineteenth century. Though detailed work has not been undertaken on its nineteenth-century commerce, it appears that Kingston's merchants adapted rapidly from slave importing to acting as middlemen for the conveyance of British manufactured goods to Spanish America. It has been estimated that trade and bullion worth between £1 million and £2 million sterling passed through Kingston in the first decade of the nineteenth century. Real estate prices boomed in Kingston after the slave trade ended, pointing towards a vibrant land and construction sector in the city.

The slave, free black and white population of Kingston all grew in the later eighteenth century, but slaves were always the most numerous people found in the city before emancipation. They formed an important element in establishing the status of white inhabitants in the city. Thus it was claimed in the 1770s that in Kingston 'the wealth of a man is measured by the number of slaves he has. The one who has ten has taken a long stride toward becoming a rich man.' Households were not generally separated on racial grounds or to reflect free status. On the contrary, blacks and whites lived in close proximity in Kingston: few demarcation lines lay between their dwellings and many urban slaves lived in their masters' houses. In 1792 Anne Appleton Storrow, wife of a British army officer stationed in Jamaica, noted that Kingston had many features of an elegantly built town but 'you often see between two handsome houses, an obscene negro yard, which spoils the effect entirely'. The 'negro' yards contained slave huts, which were often impermanent, poorly constructed shacks.

Kingston contained half of Jamaica's urban slave population by 1832 whereas other port towns on the island, including Montego Bay, Savanna-la-Mar and Falmouth, individually had only between 3 and 9 per cent of the urban slaves at the same date. Those three secondary port towns contained only one-third of the total population of Kingston in both 1832 and 1861. In 1833–4, Kingston accounted for half of the import tonnage to Jamaica and for 30 per cent of the value of exports, far exceeding trade flows in and out of other Jamaican ports. Falmouth, serving the nearby town of Martha Brae, and Montego Bay increased their handling of imports and exports in the late eighteenth century, but both were far behind Kingston in population and trade levels. Other port towns, such as Old Harbour, Morant Bay and Port Maria, lagged even further behind. Collectively, these ports were the main towns on the island, containing 78 per cent of the island's urban population by 1861.

Inland towns were of minor importance by comparison. Spanish Town was the most thriving market centre and the seat of government, with nearly 5,000 inhabitants by 1807. Public offices were situated in Spanish Town, which had a new bridge built over the Rio Cobre river in 1801 to improve land communications with Kingston. Spanish Town served as the marketing centre for the agricultural districts within a twenty-mile radius. But it remained fairly static in its development: its population barely increased in the first half of the nineteenth century, reaching a total of 5,261 in 1865,

FIGURE 4.2   The Rodney Memorial, Spanish Town. Karol Kozlowski/
Robert Harding/Getty Images

and many of its wooden buildings became dilapidated.
More positively, several new churches were constructed
in Spanish Town in the 1840s and an Anglican cathedral was constructed from the existing parish church of
St Jago de la Vega.

Social Structure and Creolisation

Jamaica's social structure followed the pattern established from the early years of English settlement on
the island. Vertical divisions on a pyramidal basis, cut
through by race and class, meant that political and
economic power in Jamaica, as well as social status,
was held by a minority of white propertied males at
the top of the pyramid, supported by free white people
of more modest means. These people considered

themselves racially superior to all black and mixed-race Jamaicans. In the half century after the American Revolution, white settlers, slaves and freedmen developed a creole outlook based on living together, in unequal positions of power and status, in the Jamaican environment. Many white people in Jamaica retained the 'reluctant creole' outlook that had characterised their worldview in the eighteenth century: they were attached to Britain as home, and many wished to retire there after making their money in Jamaica.

The number of white people diminished during the final years of slavery in Jamaica from about 30,000 in 1820 to 15,000 by 1834. It continued to decline thereafter to 13,101 by 1871. This relatively small group of people, however, maintained strong control on all positions of authority, notably in the Jamaican Assembly and the island's parish vestries as well as all levels of the legal and court system. Throughout the whole period from the American Revolution to the Morant Bay rebellion, white officeholders held a sustained and unchallenged control of Jamaica's institutions, forming what appeared to be an impregnable elite that could oversee the advantages to Britain that command of Jamaica offered. White elite dominance of Jamaica's public life therefore changed very little from the era before the American Revolution.

Underneath this group lay a relatively modest number of free black people comprising mainly those who had been manumitted by slaveholders. Mixed-race people of lighter skin colour were favoured for free coloured status. In fact, each degree through which a free black person's skin colour diverged from blackness was widely recognised throughout Jamaica and the Caribbean. The categories included mulattos (the offspring of one white and one black parent); sambos (from one black and one mulatto parent); quadroons (from one mulatto and one white parent); and mustees (defined as those of one-eighth black ancestry).

Among free black women were those manumitted for providing sexual favours for white men. Such women opted more frequently for concubinage with white partners than marriage to fellow free coloureds. In 1825 there were twice as many females among the free coloured population as males. Despite their non-slave status, most free coloureds lived in difficult social and economic circumstances. A report of 1825, compiled by a free coloured person, indicated that 22,900 out of the 28,800 free people of colour in Jamaica were living in poverty. The clear gulf between whites and free coloureds remained throughout the period of slavery. Thus free people of colour were rarely welcomed in the company of white people, 'who scarce condescend to speak to them'.

Free coloureds occupied an uneasy position between the white Jamaican population, set above them by race, and slaves, the largest group in Jamaican society, located at the bottom of the social pyramid owing to their bonded racial status. Many whites believed free coloured people should not undertake field work as they were a distinct group from black slaves. Accordingly, free coloured people congregated in towns where they worked in shops and gained employment as servants and porters. They lived apart from white society but often emulated white manners and behaviour to distinguish themselves from the black population. Even after the end of British Caribbean slavery, this general attitude persisted. Thus the English novelist Anthony Trollope noted on his visit to Jamaica in 1859 that free coloureds were 'impervious to the black men, and determined on that side to exhibit and use their superiority'. Attempts by brown Jamaicans (i.e. free coloureds) to distance themselves from blacks led to a continuing mistrust between the two groups.

Bryan Edwards's contemporary estimates support this distribution of Jamaica's social structure. In 1787 he reckoned that the composition of Jamaica's population was 30,000 white people, 10,000 free blacks and 'people of colour', 1,400 Maroons and 250,000 slaves. This amounted to a total Jamaican population of 291,400. The number of free coloured people in Jamaica came to 31,000 in 1834 and to 68,529 in 1844, making them more numerous as a group than white people, whose totals in the same two years amounted to 16,600 and 15,776.

By the 1820s, the growing number of free coloureds and their importance in the militia made it more difficult for the Jamaican Assembly to ignore their desire to vote and hold public office. After civil rights legislation was passed, two brown men became assemblymen in 1831. Brown lawyers and merchants were elected to the Assembly in the 1830s to increase the political representation of free coloured people in Jamaica. They had to contend with a strong plantocracy that never regarded them as equals. Although the professional brown people aspired towards upwards status mobility, they were still easily in a minority among Jamaica's politicians by the time of Morant Bay.

Over time more creoles lived in Jamaica as direct legal slave imports ended in 1807. Edward Kamau Brathwaite characterised the half century after the American Revolution as the period when a creole society emerged as an influential force in Jamaica. This was created by the mixing of different types of people – whites, black slaves, free coloureds and free blacks. Though the white minority in Jamaica retained a strong connection with Britain, and in some cases were merely sojourners in the Caribbean, and though the enslaved were either African-born or shaped by cultural elements transferred from different African backgrounds, they were moulded in their behaviour and social outlook by living in a social setting where daily mixing occurred between the races and between the free and unfree. Such a situation led to the creation of a creole society in Jamaica, which was not based on a harmonious interplay between different races and social classes but melded out of friction, conflict and inequality as a result of the 'physical and psychological barriers between master and bondsman as had developed as a result of the nature of slavery in the New World'.

Brathwaite argued that creolisation was a process with two parts: 'ac/culturation, which is the yoking (by force and example, deriving from power/prestige) of one culture to another (in this case the slave/African to the European); and inter/culturation, which is an unplanned, unstructured but osmotic relationship proceeding from this yoke'. Brathwaite's emphasis on a hybrid society that blended African and European cultures in Jamaica – and, by implication, the broader Caribbean – was not a harbinger of greater social unity. Unbalanced power and class relations persisted in Jamaica well beyond the abolition of the British slave trade and slave emancipation.

The Maroons

Jamaica's Maroon communities lived quietly after the peace treaties of 1739 and 1740, but problems emerged towards the end of the eighteenth century. The expansion of sugar estates in western Jamaica led to boundary disputes over land between the Trelawny Town Maroons and planters. The Maroons found that this expansion of sugar cultivation impinged too much on lands they needed to support their population. In the mid-1790s the new governor of Jamaica, the Earl of Balcarres, believed that bickering between both parties would lead to conflict if the revolutionary ideas of the Saint-Domingue slave revolt spread to Jamaica. Discord led to fighting in August 1795 after a seemingly minor incident in which magistrates ordered the whipping of two Maroons who had shot two hogs of a planter whose land bordered on the Trelawny Town settlement. For three months, guerrilla fighting occurred between that group of Maroons and army regiments. Most other Maroon groups stayed neutral in the conflict but those from Accompong aided the Jamaican authorities by supporting the army regiments. It proved impossible to defeat the rebel Maroons in battle but they surrendered in January 1796 after running short of food, water and rifle ammunition. After the end of the Second Maroon War in 1796, the governor rewarded the Accompong Maroons by allowing them the sole right to hunt runaway slaves in eastern Jamaica. The Jamaican Assembly voted to deport most of the captured Trelawny Town Maroons to Nova Scotia.

During the Baptist War of 1831/2, discussed below in detail, the Accompong Maroons again helped the

Jamaican authorities by engaging in guerrilla warfare in the woods and mountains against rebel slaves. They were ruthless and effective, perhaps more so than was strictly necessary. The Methodist missionary Henry Bleby reported, with some exaggeration, that 'scores of slaves innocent of all participation in the revolt were shot by Maroons, for no other purpose than to obtain their ears for sale'. The success of the Accompong Maroons in seeking out rebels during the slave revolt of 1831/2 led the Jamaica government to make use of their services to round up runaway slaves in the aftermath of the rebellion, but in discharging this role the Maroons had less success. During the 1840s and 1850s the Jamaican authorities relied more on the West India regiments based at Kingston for military support when needed, but the Maroons were again called upon during the Morant Bay rebellion of 1865, in which they again helped to suppress the rebels. This is discussed in the section on that revolt later in the chapter.

The Age of Slave Trade Abolition

The British slave trade to Jamaica revived after the disruptions of the American revolutionary war. Heavy mortality among the existing slave population meant that, as before 1776, a large influx of Africans was needed to maintain production levels on plantations. As a contemporary put it, 'it is not practicable to keep up the labouring strength without fresh recruits of Negroes'. Jamaica's slave trade reached a new peak in the early 1790s: between 1791 and 1793 nearly 129,000 Africans disembarked in the island. This was a period when new sugar and coffee plantations were spreading throughout Jamaica and taking advantage of the precipitous decline in the sugar economy of Saint-Domingue during the massive slave revolt there. There was also a certain amount of panic buying of slaves in Jamaica during the 1790s owing to expectations of slave trade abolition. Nevertheless, Jamaica's slave imports declined in each year between 1802 and 1805 and only revived in the last two years of the legal British slave trade

In Britain a sustained abolitionist attack on the slave trade, concentrating particularly on Jamaica, continued for almost twenty years after 1788, when parliamentary committees first began to take detailed evidence on the matter. On several occasions in the 1790s abolitionist forces in the House of Commons, led by William Wilberforce, lost votes on the abolition of the slave trade even though it was a leading humanitarian cause. Pro-slave trade supporters and enthusiasts, supported by members of the West India Interest, were sufficient in number to outvote anti-slave trade supporters among members of parliament. Advocates of the slave trade could be found both in Jamaica and Britain. What was at stake economically was succinctly described in 1788 by John Grant, the chief justice of Jamaica: 'abolishing slavery would deeply wound the trade & revenue of Great Britain, ruin the white inhabitants of the West Indies, and in its consequence be an act of inhumanity to the Negroes themselves. The stopping of further supplies from Africa will in a rapid progression destroy the English sugar colonies.'

The slave trade to Jamaica and other destinations was still generally profitable by 1800 and it seemed unlikely that abolitionist pressure would make a breakthrough in transforming political opinion in parliament to support abolition. Jamaica was at the forefront of British Caribbean colonies maintaining demand for enslaved Africans by 1800, whereas other islands, including Barbados, St Kitts and Antigua, achieved natural increase among their slaves and had no pressing need for further imports. The other main destinations for slaves taken in British vessels immediately after 1800 were the colonies of rival powers, notably Cuba. This situation was changed, however, by political intervention. After pressure from the abolitionists, the British government under Prime Minister Pitt the Younger authorised an order-in-council in 1805 to stop the supply of slaves to Britain's enemies in wartime. This left Jamaica alone as the one British Caribbean colony still importing large numbers of enslaved Africans. Renewed abolitionist campaigning between 1805 and 1807 targeted Jamaica as the main bastion for slave imports in British vessels.

A change of government in Britain in 1806–7 ushered in a coalition ministry with leading figures in favour of slave trade abolition. Sugar prices plummeted in Jamaica in these years, suggesting that the plantation economy was in temporary decline. That economic situation, combined with prospects of demographic growth among Jamaica's slave population, suggested that the slave trade could be sacrificed. In 1807 the British parliament abolished the slave trade after the second reading of the bill passed in the House of Commons by an overwhelming majority of 283 to 16. This marked the ending of legal direct slave imports to Jamaica and other British colonies in the Caribbean. In future, these sugar islands would have to rely on improving rates of natural increase to maintain and extend their slave population levels.

Slavery

Between 1808 and 1834 Jamaica experienced a decline in the slave death rate, mainly as a result of the legal end of slave imports and the associated seasoning problems which had contributed significantly to slave mortality. Infant mortality remained prevalent in Jamaica, and did not decline until after slave emancipation. Inoculation against smallpox, which was common in the early nineteenth century, was the main improvement in medical care for slaves and undoubtedly helped to save lives. An ageing African proportion of the enslaved population was dying off in the last years of slavery, but by the time of emancipation creole slaves on Jamaica's sugar plantations had achieved natural increase. This occurred largely through better diet reducing mortality as a result of amelioration, a set of measures designed to improve life and work for the enslaved. Increased birth rates were more difficult to achieve, influenced by the preponderance of fertile adult women being deployed in heavy field work. Between 1807 and 1834 the Jamaican slave population fell by 43,000, a drop of 12 per cent.

The organisation of slave work on sugar estates in the half century after 1783 largely followed the pattern long established before the American Revolution. Field work was usually divided into three gangs, with the first gang carrying out the heavy lifting and muscular work involved in planting and harvesting sugar cane; the second gang undertaking lighter tasks; and the third gang being a supplementary group comprising women and children. Occasionally, on large properties, a fourth gang, consisting of younger children, would operate. Slave labour in gangs was undertaken as much by adult women as adult men. In fact, the contribution of healthy adult women to the heaviest work around the sugar estates may have increased over time. Certainly, a detailed study of Mesopotamia plantation, Westmoreland parish, found that in the 1790s there was gender equality in the field gangs but from 1802 to 1832 women easily outnumbered men in the cane fields.

The work discipline and time schedule of the work performed by the gangs was overseen and directed by slave drivers, who themselves were controlled by white overseers under the direction of other senior white personnel on plantations such as managers or attorneys. Children were incorporated into the third gangs from the ages of six or seven. After around a decade's work in that capacity, they were transferred as adolescents into the jobs they would hold for most of their working adult lives. Children in the third gang deployed cutting grass or carrying dung would become field workers from about the age of sixteen and transferred to the first gang. Field gangs worked for set hours, usually from sun-up to sun-down on six days each week. After about 1800, however, task work was introduced into slave work routines, offering an enticement of working for fewer hours in return for completing an agreed number of daily tasks. Slaves who completed their tasks by early afternoon then had time to spend on their provision grounds.

The seasonal cycle of work on sugar estates was arduous and exhausting. Deep holes needed to be cut by hand with hoes, rather than using ploughs, to plant sugar cane. The soil was often baked hard under the tropical sun and difficult to till. The holes were filled with manure, which slaves carried in baskets on their heads; the weight was often 80 lbs per basket. The harvesting of the sugar cane was carried out by hand and heavy lifting occurred as slaves dragged the cut cane to the sugar works on another part of the estate. Animal haulage was frequently unavailable to assist with this work. After the cane pieces had been rolled in the sugar mill, the remains, referred to as trash, were spread over cattle pens or stored in 'trash houses' for use as fuel. Leftover cane pieces were weeded for replanting and ratoons, the stumps of the harvested crops, needed attention so that they could produce further, though lesser, crops than newly planted cane.

Jamaican slaves worked hard in the era between the American Revolution and slave emancipation: children were assigned to field tasks from a young age, night work was regularly used during the sugar harvest, and slaves worked longer hours than their counterparts in the eastern Caribbean. These additional inputs into the work regime, along with better cultivation and cropping rates, helped to produce increases in work productivity. By 1820–34 each estate slave in Jamaica was producing 1,400 lbs of sugar, much higher than the average in Barbados and the Leeward Islands.

In addition to field workers, a minority of slaves were trained as craft workers. Carpenters, masons, sugar boilers and rum distillers, coopers, blacksmiths and carters were among them. These respected workers received a greater share of a plantation's allowances than field slaves, and also better food and medical care. Livestock on plantations was tended by stock keepers. A small proportion of slaves were domestics, employed in and around the planter or attorney or manager's house, and engaged in cooking, cleaning and waiting at table. These workers were not subject to the same labour discipline as field slaves; but even though they escaped the admonitions and pressure of monotonous work schedules, they still had to answer constantly to the demands of white personnel based on the estate.

On sugar estates, a hierarchy of status among the slave workforce existed. An elite group consisted of artisans, drivers and other head people. Attorneys and managers liaised closely with the headmen, who controlled the slave population and remained loyal to masters who had bestowed privileges upon them. Other slave workers with specialised skills were needed on sugar plantations, including domestics, craftsmen, hospital workers, boilers, watchmen, potters, stockmen, distillers and wainmen. Heavy lifting duties – hoeing and ploughing the soil, planting the sugar cane and ratoons, harvesting the crop – were carried out by field slaves who worked under the gang system. Mobility upwards among this range of occupations appears to have been relatively limited.

Though they spent a great deal of their time employed in furthering the plantation economy for the benefit of their masters, slaves also participated in an informal economy of their own through cultivation of their provision grounds. These were located on land usually situated away from the sugar cane and livestock pens, sometimes on the fringes of estates. Slaves used their limited leisure time, usually on a Saturday, cultivating their own food crops, especially fruit and vegetables, to feed themselves but also to create a surplus sold at weekend markets as part of a slave-operated internal economy. Focusing on these activities enabled slaves to self-organise activities that would benefit their own communities. This degree of choice was denied to the enslaved in their main plantation work.

Marketing goods through an informal internal economy and participation in weekly markets were the principal means through which the enslaved acquired cash. Women were significant participants in this informal economy, operating either as higglers or as purveyors of food crops, livestock and dried salted fish. The Jamaican slave code of 1788 provided for an extra day out of crop to be allowed for cultivation of provision grounds, but by the early nineteenth century, it became a common practice to permit slaves to work on their provision grounds every Saturday after the harvest. By 1816 Jamaican slaves were legally allowed twenty-six free days a year when their energies could be given over to work on provision grounds. The activities undertaken by slaves on provision grounds provided important foundations for their future by carrying over to the internal economic pursuits followed by a free peasantry after slave emancipation.

Slaves had limited leisure time but nevertheless participated in regular cultural gatherings linked to dance, music and costumes. Dancing was common among slaves at weekends or on holidays, accompanied by spontaneous vocal music with African origins. Musical performances including drumming and playing fiddles and horns have already been described in Chapter 3 along with the predilection for Anansi stories, the belief in magic and the supernatural, a concern with conducting funerals with solemnity and emotion, and the resort to myal and obeah practitioners in the slave community. Usually the planter class and their white associates would permit the enslaved to pursue these cultural practices without interference. The Baptist missionary William Knibb observed that slaves dressed up in fine waistcoats, linen trousers, ties and dresses for their communal recreations, adding that the men were 'profound dandies' and the women dressed 'in white, with an abundance of lace'.

The calendar year was punctuated by several days when the enslaved could relax together. Slaves were often allowed three or four days over the Christmas season when they would not work. During this period, masters rewarded them with allowances of rum, sugar, codfish and salt meat. Other holidays included New Year's Day, Easter, and the crop-over celebration after the sugar harvest. On these occasions a common form of cultural performance known as the John Canoe or Jonkonnu was practised. This celebration is still performed in contemporary Jamaica. The Jonkonnu is a street parade, originally derived from Africa, with folk characters dressed in elaborate colourful costumes. It includes music, dance, mime and masks and performers with a cow head and a horsehead as well as the devil, various warriors and characters such as Pitchy-Patchy, the Belly woman and the king and queen.

The Plantocracy

The Jamaican plantocracy wielded political power in the last half-century of British West Indian slavery through their dominance of the Jamaican Assembly and the courts on the island, and their access to regular lobbying in Westminster and Whitehall through the Jamaican agent of the West India Interest. Nevertheless, planters had to contend with considerable opposition in Britain. They were particularly under pressure from abolitionists during the period from the first parliamentary debates concerning the slave trade in 1788 until slave emancipation in 1834. Abolitionists made great play of the inhumanity of the slave trade and portrayed Britain's role in slavery and the slave trade as a national sin. The official antislavery position was one of gradual emancipation to be preceded by ameliorative measures for slaves.

Planters mounted a rearguard action against the speeches, printed propaganda and pressure exercised by the antislavery campaigners by emphasising that Britain's possessions in Jamaica and the rest of the Caribbean were important national economic assets, and that planters were making efforts to improve infant mortality, slave breeding and the treatment of estate workers as well as restricting legal punishments for the enslaved. A frequent line of argument made by proslavery advocates was that to free slaves would lead to social catastrophe and ruin for the plantocracy, especially if this occurred without due preparation. Slaveholding was central to the social status and capital investment made by planters; they believed in the rightness of their ability to buy and own slaves. It was therefore to be expected that they would not relinquish their human property unless forced to do so by law. The Jamaican Assembly fully supported the plantocracy, arguing that their rights were inviolable and that parliament did not have the right to abolish the slave trade or slavery because this would attack private property. Any attempt to do so without the Assembly's 'consent, or without full compensation, would be an unconstitutional assumption of power, subversive of all public faith and confidence as applied to the Colonists'.

The wealthiest Jamaican planters were usually absentees, living either in fine town houses in London, Bristol or Liverpool, the main ports where sugar was imported from the Caribbean, or on country estates with significant landholdings. A good many of these properties now operate under the auspices of English Heritage. The owners of these town and country houses fell into the reluctant creole category described in Chapter 3. They were wealthy men who kept in close contact with one another to discuss matters relating to their West Indian commercial interests. These large planters delegated the running of their Jamaican estates to attorneys and managers. Most Jamaican planters, however, continued to live in Jamaica, where they remained at the centre of social, economic and political power.

The wealth and influence of the planters was symbolised by the great houses that lay at the heart of estates. These were usually two-storied buildings. Structures such as Good Hope Great House in Trelawny parish or Rose Hall Great House in St Thomas parish were elegantly constructed mansions, with rooms decorated with expensive curtains, oil paintings hung on the walls, comfortable furnishings, sash windows and verandas. Dining tables were often made from fine mahogany and set for meals with silver cutlery and fine ceramic plates. Nothing could be further from the humble domestic slave huts than the well-appointed rooms of the Great House. More than 400 of the 700 great houses existing in Jamaica in 1838 still survive.

The oversight of plantations by attorneys operating under the instructions of absentee proprietors has been subject to different views by historians. It was often claimed that attorneys were poor plantation managers who performed ineffectively without the on-the-spot control and direction of planters, but the evidence on which these broad claims were made was fairly thin. In recent years, B. W. Higman has addressed this topic systematically, arguing that attorneys do not deserve their negative reputation; on the contrary, they carried out managerial duties skilfully and profitably. Attorneys ran estates because of absenteeism, but they also were connected to the emergence of a managerial hierarchy on Jamaican sugar plantations between 1750 and 1850. They developed efficient methods of accounting and communication; they maintained good business relations with the metropolis; and they embraced a close connection with absentee planters, which redounded to their mutual benefit. Higman argued that 'the proprietors and the attornies had entered into a pact that rewarded them for being honourable and loyal to each other for the sake of robbing other people (the enslaved and exploited free), who were not parties to the ethical contract'.

Amelioration

Jamaica's slave population was 250,000 in 1789 and 354,000 in 1808, much of the growth being supplied by importing saltwater Africans. The depletion rate averaged sixteen per annum on sugar estates in that period. Jamaica failed to increase its slave population between the abolition of the British slave trade in 1807 and slave emancipation in 1834, when the slave population amounted to 311,000 people. The absence of a regular supply of African captives was sorely missed. The total number of Jamaican slaves declined in the post-1807 period. High mortality rates rather than low fertility appear to have been the main contributory factor in the decline. Birth rates among Jamaican slaves were steady (at 23 per 1,000) between 1807 and 1834 whereas death rates fluctuated markedly. The highest mortality was association with sugar production rather than any other occupation. Thus mortality rates on early nineteenth-century Jamaican plantations were 50 per cent higher than on coffee plantations. Fetal, neonatal and infant mortality rates were especially high. Slave children aged under five often died from diseases such as yaws, worms, beri-beri, whooping cough and, especially, tetanus. Mortality gradually improved over time, however, as planters paid more attention to slave fertility and natural increase. Some of this improvement resulted from a reduction in death rates caused by the elimination of seasoning losses associated with newly imported Africans.

Realising they were on the back foot as abolitionist pressures mounted, planters, and eventually the British parliament, started to promote amelioration as a policy towards slaves. They hoped that efforts to improve the living and working condition of their slaves would accommodate anti-slavery concerns about the humanitarian treatment of the enslaved. Planters gave greater attention to the medical treatment of slaves, introducing vaccination for smallpox and lying-in wards in hospitals for women about to give birth. Task management was deployed in working arrangements to offer greater incentives for slave productivity. Reduced workloads were offered to pregnant women and rewards given in the form of cash payments, clothing or special food rations to mothers whose infants survived for up to a month after birth. Better diets offered to slaves were an important ameliorative change, helping to reduce mortality.

The progress or decline of British West Indian slave populations could be measured more precisely after 1817 when the British government implemented a triennial census of slaves on each Caribbean territory under its jurisdiction. These censuses, undertaken between 1817 and 1832, provided detailed data on the dates of births and deaths of slaves and the causes and age of deaths on a comprehensive basis for the first time. Inspired by the greater emphasis on the statistical structure of the population generated by Britain's censuses inaugurated in 1801, the material gathered could be interpreted as a proxy for the effects of amelioration on the slave population. The censuses were closely studied by government officials and by abolitionists for the evidence they produced on slave demography.

As the official policy of leading abolitionist groups in Britain remained gradual emancipation until the early 1830s, with no specified date set for freedom, the planter policy of amelioration was not so different to that of their major opponents. In Jamaica, amelioration first proceeded on a limited basis through private acts of planters on their estates. However, after renewed and reinvigorated efforts aimed towards slave emancipation by British abolitionist societies from 1823 onwards, Jamaica was expected to introduce an official policy of amelioration. This was never implemented systematically partly because

Jamaica's authorities were content to rely on planter paternalism to achieve amelioration. Whether, as the authorities wished to believe, slave owners exercised kindness and a humane disposition towards their slaves while labourers responded with cheerful compliance is far too sanguine a generalisation to be accepted.

The Baptist War (1831–2) and Slave Emancipation

The massive slave revolt in 1791 in Saint-Domingue (the western half of Hispaniola) where an upsurge of 400,000 blacks, inspired by the French Revolution's ideas of liberty, equality and fraternity, saw the overthrow of French planters and the creation of a free black republic instilled fears in Jamaica, situated only 334 miles away, that similar rebellion by slaves would be fomented there. In 1804 the English absentee Jamaican plantation owner Edward Long thought Jamaica was in 'a very perilous situation' because 'the example of successful revolt in Hispaniola [i.e. Saint-Domingue/Haiti] cannot but be known to the generality of our Negroes & some degree of intercourse between the two islands cannot be prevented'. Despite this fear, however, this turned out to be the dog that did not bark, for Jamaica remained quiescent in terms of slave revolt in the decades either side of 1800. The lack of slave disturbances on the island was largely the result of the strong British military presence in the West Indies during the wars with revolutionary and Napoleonic France. In short, British garrisons deterred Jamaican slaves from staging a rebellion during the 1790s.

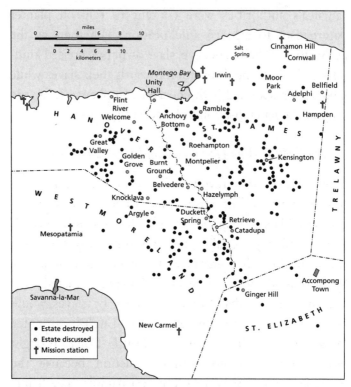

FIGURE 4.3 Area of the slave rebellion, 1831. Redrawn from Mary Turner, *Slaves and Missionaries: The Disintegration of Jamaican Slave Society, 1787–1834* (University of Illinois Press, 1982), opposite p. 1

No large slave rebellion occurred in Jamaica in the forty years after the slave revolt in Saint-Domingue, but plots occurred in 1806, 1808 and 1815. In 1823 and 1824 widespread unrest occurred among the slaves after the Jamaican Assembly refused to implement the British government's policy on amelioration. The rebels planned to devastate plantations and to kill planters, but their plans were leaked and the putative revolt was put down. It was not until the final years of slavery on Jamaica that a disruptive slave uprising broke out. The largest slave revolt in the history of Jamaica and in any British colony began suddenly on 27 December 1831, after the slaves had had time to rest and plan their activities over the Christmas holiday. Continuing until March 1832, it became known as the Baptist War because of the close involvement of Baptist missionaries in the rebellion. Beginning with a fire on Kensington estate, St James parish, it spread to five other western parishes, covering an area of 750 square miles, and involved around 60,000 slaves.

Why did this large slave revolt break out when it did, especially when considering that Jamaica had not experienced a significant slave rebellion for seven decades? Economic factors may have played some part in the revolt. Jamaica in 1831 was in the midst of a downturn in economic fortunes. A drought occurred for six months in 1831, the worst for over thirty years. Rivers had dried up. Provision grounds were badly affected by the drought. People were hungry. Heavy rain came after the drought, leading to outbreaks of smallpox and dysentery. These problems no doubt increased tensions between blacks and whites in Jamaica. Economic problems were mounting up on some plantations. Bankruptcy, sale and declining output affected St James, Hanover and Trelawny parishes. As Mary Turner has explained, 'the immediate hardships and miseries induced by drought and hunger deepened the slaves' disillusionment with a system that was increasingly unsatisfactory to black field hands and coloured artisans, supervisors and domestics'.

Higman has additionally argued that the decreasing opportunities available to skilled slaves expecting positions of higher status but unable to satisfy such aspirations were another root cause of the rebellion. Certainly, creole males assumed the main leadership positions in the revolt. An underlying factor in the background to the uprising was the fact that in December 1830 the Jamaican Assembly had bowed to pressure to grant the free black and free coloured population equal rights with whites while failing to extend those privileges to slaves, causing great resentment among the enslaved. An immediate trigger to widespread discontent lay in the Jamaican authorities refusing to allow slaves an additional day's holiday as Christmas 1831 occurred on a Sunday, when slaves who had embraced Christianity would be in church or chapel and unable to perform their customary Jonkonnu parade.

Notwithstanding these problems, there is scant evidence that the rebellion broke out specifically as a result of deteriorating relations between blacks and their white masters. On the contrary, the rebellion occurred when amelioration of slave life and work was being practised by planters. The political dimension of the revolt was important because it occurred at a time of heightened antislavery agitation in Britain. White planters in Jamaica discussed these developments openly in front of their slaves, who became well-informed about abolitionist intentions and tactics. Further details about abolitionism circulated from missionaries when addressing their congregations. The newspaper press in Jamaica was full of columns explaining the demands for emancipation. The spread of information about possibilities for freedom for slaves seems to have been an important catalyst for Jamaica's last slave revolt. David Grey, a free coloured man, stated at the Cornwall Assizes in 1832 that it was common talk among slaves for three or four months before Christmas 1831 that they were to be freed. His own slave and his relatives' slaves ceased working when this was known.

In 1831–2 Britain's Whig government pledged itself to legislate in favour of slave emancipation as soon as parliament passed the Great Reform Bill, a major reform of the parliamentary system. A campaign for slave emancipation in the British Empire was launched in the House of Commons in April 1831. Rumours concerning freedom were circulated by word of mouth and by British and Caribbean newspapers. Slaves eavesdropped on their masters' table talk. Literate creole slaves could digest newspaper accounts of improvements to slave life and possible moves towards black freedom and pass them on to their fellow slaves. Editorials in Jamaica's planter press warned about the prospects of arson, pillage and destruction to estates that would ensue if concessions were made to the slaves at this juncture, but the Assembly refused to moderate the slave system. The governor, Earl Belmore, blocked the publication of a royal proclamation issued to all British West Indian governors in order to dispel unrest, though he conceded in December 1831 and allowed the statement to be published just before the rebellion broke out.

The role of missionaries and black creole leadership also helped to stimulate the Baptist War. Baptist and other nonconformist missionaries had firmly entrenched themselves in Jamaica by 1831. Some missionary groups, such as the German Moravians, had been present in Jamaica since the American revolutionary era. But others, notably the Wesleyan Missionary Society and Baptist

Missionary Society preachers, had come to Jamaica after the end of the Napoleonic wars. These missionaries were instructed by their parent societies not to incite slaves to rebel but to teach them obedience, piety and temperance. Often, however, the work of missionaries on the spot opened their eyes to the iniquities of slavery and they experienced considerable tension between what they were instructed to preach and what they privately felt about the institution of slavery. Many planters attributed the outbreak of the Jamaican slave revolt of 1831–2 to missionary influence. As one of their number put it, the cause of the revolt was 'generally attributed to the Sectarian preachers, and you will see, from what has passed, that there are ample grounds, at least, for suspicion'. Against this viewpoint, it should be said that most missionaries were unaware of their unwitting political action.

The main leader of the 1831–2 uprising was Samuel Sharpe, a literate urban slave from Montego Bay who was also the member of a Baptist congregation. He had risen up in that group to a leadership role, and was known as 'Daddy' Sharpe. He had been holding secret meetings in the autumn of 1831 at which he expressed fears that whites were planning to block emancipation and therefore a plot against white power should be put into effect without delay. He planned a non-violent strike for the day after the Christmas holiday. This would involve a driver approaching the overseer on each plantation and telling him that the slaves would not work.

Sharpe built up an independent connection with the native Baptists. Trusted with the spiritual care of a group of black Baptist converts, he argued that slaves were entitled to freedom. He proclaimed the authority of the Bible, citing the text 'no man can serve two masters' and denying the white man the right to hold any black in bondage. Sharpe was supported by other, predominantly creole, skilled slaves who held leadership positions in the independent Baptist sects. Slaves of other denominations also took part in the rebellion. The Wesleyan missionary Henry Bleby had several conversations with Sharpe which suggested that passive resistance through work stoppages was planned rather than an armed revolt. But while it may have been intended that the majority of slaves carried out passive resistance, caches of arms were stored in slave huts on some plantations in order to undertake military action.

When news of the revolt reached the governor on 28 December 1831, martial law was declared and troops despatched to Montego Bay, situated near to the plant-ations that initially rose up in the rebellion. The slaves torched sugar estates, engaged in guerrilla warfare, and hid in the rugged terrain of the interior. The Reverend Hope Waddell, a Presbyterian missionary to the Barrett estates in St James parish, saw the fires that created destruction as 'a terrible vengeance which the patient drudges had at length taken on those sugar estates, the causes and scenes of their life-long toils and degradation, tears and blood'.

The British military garrison in Jamaica had been reduced by 30 per cent in the two years leading up to the rebellion. Rebel slaves therefore saw an opportune time to strike back at the plantocracy. But after the rebels gained control of the whole of the western interior of Jamaica in the first week of the rebellion, additional troops under Sir Willoughby Cotton were sent to

Montego Bay to fight the rebels, put down the revolt and capture those who resisted. Cotton considered that the rebellion had been 'a long time organizing, they proceed in their burnings by system & signal – and from every quarter I am given to understand the Baptist Preachers have contributed most essentially to work upon the minds of the Negroes'. Cotton gained the voluntary support of Maroons to seek out rebels in hiding and the revolt was eventually halted by these forces. The aim was to restore law and order, combining retribution against all slaves caught in a rebellious act with a free pardon to all those who returned to work. The militia took revenge on the slaves, carrying out ferocious attacks upon slave villages irrespective of whether the people there had been involved in the rebellion.

By late February 1832, 240 slaves were imprisoned, six associated with the revolt had been executed and nine flogged with between 150 and 200 lashes of the whip. Trials by court martial of rebel slaves were convened without any defence procedures or corroboration of sentences. Conclusive evidence was not sought by the courts. The court martials automatically stopped when martial law was lifted on 5 February 1832, but repression continued. The resumption of civil rule instigated slave courts with trial by jury. Planters were the main judges and jurors. Over 200 slaves were killed during the rebellion and 312 were executed after trials. Some were condemned to be shot; others were strung up on the gallows and hanged. More than 300 others were imprisoned or transported. Sharpe was captured and hanged at Montego Bay on 23 May 1832. He was the last rebel slave executed for taking part in the rebellion. While awaiting execution, he stated he was sorry for what he had caused but did not feel he had behaved wrongly in asserting his claim to freedom.

The plantocracy also turned their anger towards non-conformist missionaries, who they regarded as sectarians influencing slaves to rebel. Before martial law ended, planters and their supporters in St Ann parish formed the Colonial Church Union to harass missionaries. This was ostensibly a movement dedicated to promoting the doctrines of the Church of England in Jamaica. However, it was in reality an anti-missionary organisation that favoured the planters. In Montego Bay and Falmouth a mob following the tenets of the Colonial Church Union destroyed Methodist and Baptist chapels, tarred and feathered Bleby and arrested prominent Baptists such as the Reverend William Knibb, who feared assassination. Knibb was stirred to condemn slavery as a result of his sojourn in Jamaica's western parishes. He became intimately involved in the 1831–2 revolt, and was brought to trial for supposedly inciting the slaves to rebel.

Knibb was able to escape from Jamaica, leaving for England in April 1832. He and some fellow missionaries who also returned home informed politicians in London about the severe repression doled out by the Jamaican Assembly and by the island's planters to slaves and missionaries caught up in the rebellion. After returning to Jamaica in the early 1840s, Knibb and fellow Baptists exhumed Sam Sharpe's body from an unmarked grave and reburied him in a newly constructed Montego Bay chapel. Knibb was so respected by black freedmen that after his early death, aged forty-two in 1845, former slaves erected a memorial to his memory at the Knibb Memorial Baptist chapel in Falmouth.

Planters overreacted in their view of missionaries inciting slaves to rebel in the Baptist War of 1831–2. Nevertheless, the mission schools established by Baptist and other nonconformist preachers spread the gospels through a network of literate black deacons who liaised with the mass of black workers. Black Christian converts to the Baptist faith used an established network of mission meetings to promote political action. Large numbers of slaves were influenced in this way, for by 1831 twenty-four Baptist chapels existed in Jamaica with 10,000 members and an additional 24,000 attenders at religious services. The Native Baptists, an offshoot of the Baptist chapels, preached the message of economic and political freedom for Jamaicans. The rebellion took place in the western parishes where the missions were most numerous and independent.

The uprising caused much destruction in Jamaica and animosity towards Baptist preachers. Extensive damage was caused to property in St James and Hanover parishes. Many great houses and sugar works were destroyed. The Jamaican Assembly published a report in March 1832 claiming that losses amounted to £1.15 million sterling as a result of looting, arson, destroyed crops and lost labour. Three months after the revolt was quashed, the Baptist minister John Kingdon, while travelling from Savanna-la-Mar to Montego Bay, saw many destroyed houses, a slave's skull on a pole, and the missionary and abolitionist Thomas Burchell's Baptist chapel in ruins. 'The Baptists were charged with being most deeply connected with the late Insurrection,' he wrote in a private letter. 'While walking up to [Montego] Bay many looked at us as if we ought to be kicked out of the colony; & before the day was over, it was reported that I was to be murdered the first time I preached.' Kingdon avoided this fate, but his keen apprehension of the troubles he might face encapsulated the tension and febrile atmosphere that lingered in Jamaica after the rebellion had been quashed.

Slaves who rebelled in Jamaica in 1831–2 carried out very few attacks on white people. Only those whites who fought them were attacked by armed rebels. The rebels' targets comprised sugar properties and their buildings, where destruction, as indicated above, was widespread. The motivation behind the revolt was the desire for freedom at all costs, however it was to be delivered. Freedom was envisaged as being the creation of an independent peasantry based upon subsistence farming. Slaves had the practical knowledge of how to live in such communities by their cultivation of provision grounds on sugar estates. They believed they could consolidate and extend their extensive patterns of internal exchange in Jamaica for the future.

Encouraged by the links between the missionaries and the abolitionists, Jamaican slaves under Sharpe's leadership hoped to achieve legally sanctioned rights. After the rebellion was over, relations between planters and slaves had shifted decisively. 'It is true, rebellion was checked, nay, apparently quelled,' wrote Bernard Senior, 'but so many instances of treachery had been developed, that no one could again place the hitherto unlimited confidence in his most faithful negro, whether domestic or otherwise that he had formerly felt justified in doing. There was, besides, a kind of sullen and discontented demeanour, not to be mistaken.'

After the Baptist War ended, it was clear to the British government that the Colonial Office's policy of amelioration since 1823 had failed and that prompt action was needed to protect planters' property and estates in Jamaica. Thus parliament moved swiftly to support an emancipation bill after the Great Reform Act was passed in the summer of 1832. Pressure from radical abolitionists led to a call for immediate emancipation. The legislation drafted, however, reflected the continuing gradualism of antislavery campaigning by allowing for a period of apprenticeship to follow the end of slavery. This, it was argued, would allow Jamaica and other British West Indian islands sufficient time for the changed relationship between planters and their workers to take shape. The emancipation bill also included clauses that offered £20 million compensation to planters for the loss of their slave labour force. Some £6 million of this sum was granted via 13,240 awards to Jamaica's resident and absentee slaveholders for the loss of 311,455 slaves. No money was gifted to black workers as they moved from an enslaved status to a position of apprenticeship and then to free waged labour, but at the time hardly anyone contested this situation: it was accepted unanimously that slave owners were entitled to compensation.

At the end of the slavery era in Jamaica, a wide gulf remained between the power of the white elite and the dependency of slaves. Lord Sligo, the governor of Jamaica, was fully aware that white people continued to hold power in Jamaica but had not extended protection to black Jamaicans. Slave emancipation was not intended to create a new world of social relations whereby the economic, social, legal and political rights of the former slaves would be generously granted by the British authorities. On the contrary, white superiority over black people continued to be what one might term the main establishment mode of thinking, and there was no suggestion that the freed blacks would occupy anything other than a subordinate role in continuing British imperial control over Jamaica. The British parliament, the planter class and their associates wanted to continue the exploitation of Jamaicans to support their own economic accumulation, and to ensure that their wealth and power remained intact throughout Jamaica and the rest of the British Caribbean. There was no impetus by the plantocracy or the Jamaican Assembly to elevate free blacks to citizenship after slave emancipation.

There had been widespread predictions that emancipation day would witness disturbances and public unrest in Jamaica, but in the event it passed peaceably. Many planters distributed food rations as a gift to their black workers. Missionaries held religious services to mark the occasion. Elite whites held ceremonies and balls to register their view that emancipation was a gift to the slaves. In Kingston Jonkonnu parties occurred on the streets as blacks celebrated emancipation even though, apart from technically being free, most Jamaicans had no prospect of being materially better off. The entertainers, with their colourful masks and costumes, implicitly poked fun at white authorities, thereby offering an act of resistance to white dominance. The importance of emancipation as a demarcation line in Jamaica's history is commemorated in Laura Facey's sculpture 'Redemption Song' in Emancipation Park, Kingston, which depicts two naked black people facing skywards to celebrate emancipation on 1 August 1834.

Apprenticeship

Planters and estate workers faced two major transitions in labour relations in Jamaica and the rest of the British Caribbean during the 1830s. First, slavery officially ended with the Emancipation Bill passed by parliament in the summer of 1833. This stipulated that former slaves would become apprentices on 1 August 1834, and that full freedom would come for domestic workers, trade and skilled people (non-praedials) four years later, and for field workers (praedials) on 1 August 1840. Local legislation passed by the Jamaican Assembly in December 1833, incorporating regulations acceptable to the Crown, supplemented the imperial measure. Second, there was an early end to apprenticeship on 1 August 1838 for all apprentices in the British Caribbean, after which they were fully free. This premature conclusion to apprenticeship arose through pressure from abolitionists and through recognition by the British government and the British West Indian island assemblies that the system needed to be dismantled.

Under apprenticeship, ex-slaves worked without remuneration for between forty and forty-five hours per week for their former owners, but had the right to negotiate wages for overtime and additional labour. Apprentices continued to live on their existing plantations. All children under six were freed on 1 August 1834. The system was monitored by special magistrates, appointed in Britain and charged with being impartial and fair adjudicators of disputes between planters and workers. All British West Indian islands implemented apprenticeship apart from Antigua, which immediately made slaves free. After the early end to the system, workers had several choices to further their livelihoods: to stay on plantations and undertake waged work; to quit the estates and live independently as a 'proto-peasantry' in villages, cultivating provisions for sale at local markets; to establish their own independent places, by squatting or buying, and practise skills such as carpentry or pottery making; or to live mainly from the land without much getting involved in markets and exchange. Different negotiations and outcomes occurred on plantations as a result of the transitions to new working conditions for estate workers at the beginning and end of apprenticeship.

Planters and workers had divergent views about the operation of the apprenticeship system. Planters wanted to maintain good levels of sugar output and thereby make a profit on their agricultural investments. They expected to deploy labour as they had done under slavery but in accordance with new regulations about their coercive power over workers. Maintenance of a full labour force during the yearly sugar crop was a high priority. In order to achieve this, planters controlled the allocation of days and hours of work – up to the maximum allowed – and set wage levels for additional hired labour. They considered workers as their personal property until compensation had been paid under the Emancipation Act. Apprentices, on the other hand, had no necessary attachment to the cultivation of staple crops. They undertook tasks prescribed and allocated during the slavery era rather than freely choosing their work. Achieving high levels of sugar productivity as a result of intensive work offered them no significant monetary rewards. Apprentices considered they held customary use rights on sugar estates, especially on their provision grounds, on account of living and working on plantations for generations.

Apprentices wanted freedom and access to land, control over their lives and autonomy for their families and communities. They thought their work days and hours as apprentices should be negotiated; that they could refuse extra paid work; and that plantation land they had cultivated – allotment grounds, gardens, provision grounds – was theirs by customary right. According to one observer, the apprentices cultivated their provision grounds 'with assiduity, attention and profit'. Many apprentices wanted to continue to occupy their houses on plantations and to avoid paying rent for their houses or land.

Apprenticeship was a compromise between slavery and full freedom. Many British abolitionists and humanitarians supported the apprenticeship period as a gradual transition to freedom that would allow sufficient time for the planters and workers to adjust to a new way of operating plantations before wage labour became the norm. Lord Sligo made considerable efforts to explain the apprenticeship system to Jamaicans. Convinced that slave emancipation was the right course of action for Britain to follow, he was determined to help the apprentices as best as he could. He wanted to see apprenticeship run smoothly in a humane way. But he believed, like the planters, that former slaves needed to be civilised and settled into industrious ways of work that would prepare them for freedom. This, it was believed, was essential to avoid an abrupt and chaotic transition to freedom. As Sligo put it in an address to the apprentices, 'you will be APPRENTICES to your former owners for a few years, in order to fit you all for freedom'.

Sligo was initially optimistic about the introduction of apprenticeship in Jamaica. He noted that no bloodshed occurred when the system was introduced on 1 August 1834, and that predictions that destruction would ensue at Christmas were erroneous. He observed that the sugar crop was harvested and that wages were offered by planters where appropriate and accepted by apprentices. But the apprenticeship system turned out to be more complex and divisive than he anticipated. This was partly because he faced continued obstruction from the Jamaican Assembly, whose members were deeply opposed to slave freedom, but other difficulties with the apprenticeship system also emerged.

There was little overt opposition to apprenticeship in Jamaica, but in two parishes, St Thomas-in-the-Vale and St Ann, some workers opposed the introduction of the system. Sligo, despite his professed liberalism over the implementation of apprenticeship, acted swiftly to coordinate troops, the police and the militia to march to Ginger Hall estate, St Thomas-in-the-Vale, and arrest the leaders of the opposition to apprenticeship. They were duly apprehended and nine were punished by a public flogging. Opposition to apprenticeship was much less evident on most plantations, but black workers took a more relaxed attitude to their required labour than had been the case under slavery. Thus after a few weeks of apprenticeship being implemented in St David parish, the workers were 'acting just as they think proper, walking away from the estates there on any day, and at any time of the day they please'. Such behaviour became common in Jamaica during apprenticeship.

Apprenticeship operated in Jamaica for four years after 1 August 1834. Most plantations continued with their annual sugar production by relying on the stipulated hours of work for apprentices; but there is no doubt that many workers carried out their tasks reluctantly because they had not been granted full freedom immediately under the terms of the Emancipation Act. Planters were unwilling to offer more wage labour in the apprenticeship period for ideological rather than economic reasons. Thus planters were unwilling to finance work they had previously received for 'free' under slavery. They considered apprentices part of their compensation at emancipation and, as such, not deserving of wage levels that could be paid to free labourers. Estate workers were sometimes willing to work for extra wages, but only on their terms – they had the upper hand in bargaining with white personnel over rates to be paid, especially during the pressurised schedule of harvesting sugar. Labourers also insisted that the time worked should be less than the hours under slavery and remunerated in a way that made it worthwhile to pursue waged work.

Special magistrates did their best to alleviate disputes between planters and workers under the apprenticeship system. They were instructed to act impartially. Regarding the balance between planters and apprentices, they 'must not become the partisan of one more than the other'. Apprentices were to be protected from 'oppressive conduct' by masters but planters were to be kept safe from 'insolent and ungrateful behaviour' from apprentices. Despite these even-handed intentions, there were many ways in which apprentices were mistreated. Planters distributed hours of work according to their own needs rather than taking account of the apprentices' preferences. Customary indulgences accorded to workers in the slavery era – in food, clothing, nurseries for mothers – were reduced or stopped altogether. Special magistrates frequently lacked the power to restrain masters and managers. Planters were adept at thwarting claims for manumission. Special magistrates generally supported a liberal version of apprenticeship, attempting to ensure fair play in the treatment of black workers. However, they faced opposition from planters and the Jamaican Assembly, and were sometimes prosecuted in the courts and ordered to pay fines. Lord Sligo resigned as governor of Jamaica in 1836 after the Colonial Office overruled his dismissal of a troublesome magistrate.

Nearly thirty prisons were in operation in Jamaica during the apprenticeship. These were the locations where much of the punishment of recalcitrant black workers took place away from the plantations. Apprentices sent to workhouses and prisons were punished by instruments of torture such as chains, bilboes (iron restraints placed on a person's ankles or wrists) and treadmills. The technology of the treadmill, inflicting pain on the bodies of slaves strapped to its beams and revolving wooden slats, was copied from its deployment in contemporary English prisons to comprise a central symbol of repression and terror. Apprentices attached to treadmills stepped up continuously on the slats as the mechanism turned for hours on end as a punishment. This was not the only means of physical coercion. Thus, despite the prohibition of flogging women in Jamaica at the time of slave emancipation, the practice was common in Jamaica's prisons in the 1830s.

Elizabeth Ryan, an apprentice on Hopewell plantation, was committed to St Andrew's workhouse as a punishment for wandering away from her estate for three weeks. A special justice ordered that she perform hard labour for seven days attached to a treadmill. 'I never saw Tread Mill before and did not know how to dance it,' she testified, adding that 'after being on some time, I missed one step and tumbled off – then the Busha [i.e. the white manager] at the Workhouse took the cat from the Driver and begin flog me. I jump up the steps and begin to dance it again – and they flog me again – cut the shift from my shoulders with the cat – blood came down from my back ... they then strapped me by wrist to the Bar, keep me there for the hour that the other people rest.'

James Williams, an eighteen-year-old apprentice who was brought to England in 1837 at the behest of abolitionist Joseph Sturge, left a detailed narrative of his experience of apprenticeship. His vivid recounting of the apprenticeship period highlighted the malpractices carried out against former slaves by white personnel on plantations. Accused of being insolent in manner and failing to carry out his work properly, Williams was flogged on more than one occasion. 'I begged magistrate not to flog me again', Williams wrote, 'as the other flogging not well yet, but no use, he wouldn't hear me, but rode away from the place. Massa said he have no Cat but he would find some switches to do it with; I was flogged with lancewood switches upon the old flogging ... and I not able to lie down on my back for two or three weeks after.' Williams recorded other instances of his mistreatment by magistrates. He recounted the conflict and animosity that existed between apprentices and representatives of the British state, and argued that conditions for blacks were worse under apprenticeship than under slavery.

News of these atrocities reached Britain at a fairly early stage of the apprenticeship. In 1835 the Quaker Joseph Sturge led a series of demonstrations against apprenticeship in Birmingham and elsewhere in Britain. Sturge visited the Caribbean with three colleagues in 1836 to see the apprenticeship system in action. This resulted in the publication of a book by Sturge and Thomas Harvey entitled *The West Indies in 1837* that pointed out the injustices of apprenticeship. When this and other negative publicity was presented to the British government, it was decided to dismantle apprenticeship two years earlier than had been planned. When this change of policy was known, a special magistrate in Jamaica argued that no coercion would be justifiable to compel apprentices to work for their masters after 1 August 1838, when apprenticeship was now due to end. The magistrate referred to apprenticeship as 'modified slavery', and was fearful that, once freed, blacks would lack any voice in the formation of laws on which their political and social condition would depend; and that the legislation passed would be by those who have treated apprentices as 'mere property'.

The immediate aftermath of apprenticeship did not generally lead to troubles over the allocation of labour on estates. But it took a while for the system to settle down. 'The conduct of the negroes is neither better [n]or worse than that of others,' it was reported from a plantation in Vere parish in early 1839. It was 'uncertain to deal with, hardly appreciating the gift of freedom, farther than that it conduces to the enjoyment of their own will, and clamorous for an extent of wages which no property can stand, and no rational man will pay; and thus we get through'. For many white people connected with plantations, the emergence of full freedom for blacks was disastrous for their prospects. In April 1840, for example, the manager of Sir Henry Fitzherbert's estates in Jamaica considered that 'this splendid colony has been brought to the very brink of ruin, and many, very many, who a few years ago were in the enjoyment of affluence and comfort, are now suffering almost utter destitution'.

Many freed blacks, encouraged by Baptist missionaries, used the end of apprenticeship to make speeches, attend meetings and submit petitions about their continued restrictions in relation to access to land, to complain about the lack of equitable laws, and to argue in favour of greater political representation in Jamaica's Assembly. Physical mobility away from plantations no doubt enabled Jamaicans to discuss the need for a broader franchise and improved political representation among themselves. Freed Jamaican women played a part in this process, with their regular participation at markets providing the opportunity for discussion about a recalibration of political and economic power to better suit the condition of freedom. Black men and women gradually gained more confidence in making speeches and writing about their grievances in petitions and letters written in a creole idiom. All the requests and proposals for improvements in the social, legal and political position of black Jamaicans, however, were largely stonewalled by the authorities, as a later section of the chapter will show.

Education

Very little education was provided for slaves before the Emancipation Act of 1834. Slave infants were commonly placed in the care of elderly women so that their mothers could make a full contribution to plantation work. By the age of six, most children were already assisting in the third gang on estates. Missionaries provided religious instruction to slave children and helped with their literacy on a scattered basis. The missionaries focused most of their religious and educational work before 1834 on adult classes, especially focusing on the free black population. Some planters were keen to see the advancement of what they termed 'Negro instruction' as the apprenticeship period was introduced. Thus Richard Bright, the absentee Bristol proprietor of two Jamaican sugar plantations, favoured 'an unremitted attention to the improvement of the minds & faculties of the very young & that on every estate there should be immediate means set on foot for the establishment of an infant school to which children from 3 years old to 7 or 8 should be kept daily from early in the morning until evening'.

The British government also thought that slave emancipation was an appropriate time to promote elementary education for former West Indian slaves. Thus a public system of universal education in the British Caribbean began with the fifth resolution of the Emancipation Act. This established a Negro Education Grant that offered £30,000 per annum over five years to build schools, purchase equipment and employ teachers. Jamaica, with over 300,000 slaves in 1834, received £7,500 of this grant. The British government's intentions were to instruct blacks in the doctrines and precepts of Christianity in order to 'civilise' them as they approached freedom, to offer elementary education to improve literacy and numeracy, and to instil industrious habits in the black population.

Elementary education under the allocation of the Negro Education Grant was therefore introduced as a means of social control by which whites consolidated their superior status and blacks were subject to improvement while still contained within the power structures of colonialism.

From the end of the Napoleonic wars in 1815, when missionaries first came to Jamaica in large numbers, until the 1850s, elementary education was conducted in schools in Jamaica in which Baptist, Wesleyan and Congregational missionaries undertook much of the instruction. Day schools were widely established in Jamaica along with Sabbath schools, held after church and chapel services. Missionaries, their wives and literate blacks taught reading to the apprentices. Writing, numeracy and learning by rote of facts about Europe were the main activities undertaken in these settings. Disappointingly for the missionaries who taught in day schools, however, most of their charges did not join their chapels. It was not until the 1860s that initiatives were made to provide secondary schooling for Jamaicans.

Some teachers operated under the auspices of the British and Foreign School Society, based in London, which promoted non-denominational education in Britain and throughout its empire. The finances of this society, however, were relatively modest, and there was insufficient money available to keep up a regular supply of books, slates, pens and pencils. Another purveyor of elementary education in Jamaica after the end of slavery was the Mico charity, named after the benefactress Lady Mico. These schools were often influenced by Roman Catholicism. The Mico foundation also supported the training of volunteer teachers, mainly from a British background, from 1835 onwards. Scattered institutions in Jamaica made efforts to train teachers in the period between the end of apprenticeship and the Morant Bay rebellion. They included Mico College in Kingston, Calabar College at Rio Bueno, a Presbyterian training school at Montego Bay and a London Missionary Society training school at Ridgemount. All suffered, however, from inadequate finance and low enrolments.

Planters and apprentices differed over the purpose of education. Planters wanted to promote practical and industrial training for the creation of what would soon be a free workforce while apprentices opposed industrial training, which they equated with attempts to keep their children on plantations. The monitorial system of pupil instruction, then used widely in Britain, was adopted in Jamaica. To address the lack of qualified teachers, this system involved teachers coping with instructing large groups of children in rote learning by dividing up groups and placing them under senior pupils or monitors, who carried out the principles inculcated in them by the teachers. Rote learning in the three r's and a strong dose of Bible-reading and reflection were drilled into children.

This rudimentary form of elementary education was fairly ineffective. The government's Negro Education Grant provided funds to build school houses and to assist with teachers' salaries but inspectors of schools in Jamaica in the 1840s noted that the monitorial system was failing. Children learned to read adequately but found difficulty in understanding Christian instruction. Problems were compounded in Jamaica by sectarian rivalries among different Protestant denominations. The British government reduced the educational grant on a yearly basis after

1838, expecting that Jamaica and other Caribbean islands would appropriate money from their own resources to promote education. But Jamaica's Assembly was slow to take action and from 1844 onwards it only allocated small sums amounting to £2,000–£3,000 annually for educational purposes. In 1846 only 13 per cent of Jamaican children aged between five and fourteen attended schools. By the following year, Jamaica was spending only 3.5 per cent of its total government budget on education. In 1849 a Board of Education was established in Jamaica but funding for education from the legislature fluctuated considerably on an annual basis according to the available budget. Limited funds and too few teachers meant that by 1850 the missionary influence in the spread of elementary education in Jamaica had withered.

Freedom and Its Discontents

With full emancipation from August 1838 onwards, planters and former apprentices had to adjust to a new situation in which they became landlord employers and tenant employees. Under slavery, Jamaican rural workers had lived in huts on plantations and had a long tradition of cultivating provision grounds. They were now expected to pay rents for their huts and land if they remained on plantations, but they could claim wages for the work they provided. In the first decade after the end of apprenticeship, these major changes in labouring, housing arrangements and access to land led to many bitter disputes between planters and workers. Compulsion was no longer an option. Planters faced difficulties in paying wages for work they had received freely under slavery, while freed people had to bargain hard for acceptable wage levels and use of plantation land.

Planters tried to eject slaves who refused to continue field work on estates. This caused tension as blacks believed they should retain access to the houses they had occupied on plantations and to their kitchen gardens and provision grounds. Often their occupancy of premises and land stretched back several generations and, to all effects and purposes, these were their homes. Some planters started to charge rents immediately after the termination of apprenticeship, and sometimes high rents were charged. Within three months of gaining full freedom, the situation with regard to blacks remaining on estates changed dramatically. A survey of Westmoreland parish, for instance, found that only a quarter of the slave work-force in 1834 remained on sugar estates by the autumn of 1838.

The early end to apprenticeship created immediate problems for the Colonial Office. Over the summer of 1838 Jamaica and the other British Caribbean colonies dismantled slave codes and submitted proposals for new legislation to Westminster. But their ideas were so varied that Lord Glenelg, the colonial secretary, rejected most of the suggestions and drew up new proposals aimed at uniformity throughout the British West Indies in important areas of legislation and social policy such as workers' contracts, vagrancy, Crown land, the poor laws, the franchise and the distribution of police and the militia. The Jamaican Assembly fiercely opposed this process as an attack on its autonomy. When the government failed to secure support for its Jamaican policies in parliament, efforts were made to conciliate Jamaica's planters.

Though planters faced challenges from workers that became more difficult to resist after freedom was granted, Jamaica's first quarter century of emancipation saw planters entrench their control to ensure that colonialism persisted for many generations. Planters still dominated the Jamaican Assembly, and they intended to continue their control over political, economic, social and cultural policies that affected the newly freed workers. The Colonial Office criticised the planters' stance, with one senior government official stating that the Assembly 'was at all times inaccessible to any motives connected with even justice or humanity to the negroes, let alone their advancement in civilization and qualification for civil rights'. However, the British cabinet wished to adopt a more conciliatory attitude towards the planters. In 1839 Governor Lionel Smith was recalled to London and replaced by Sir Charles Metcalfe, whose instructions directed him to accommodate the planters' priorities.

New labour laws replaced the slave codes after 1838. They specified masters' duties and workers' rights but were concerned far more with ensuring regular labour for planters than protecting free blacks from abuse. Oral and written contracts were drawn up that included greater penalties for non-fulfilment of work by labourers than the orders of redress for planters who treated free workers improperly. Stipendiary magistrates were continued in Jamaica after 1838 to try to ensure fair play between planters and workers, but over time planters resorted to enforcing their own rules in local courts rather than abiding by magistrates' decisions. Unsatisfactory solutions were common for workers hoping to be paid fair wages. Moreover, many free blacks found it difficult to pay the rents charged by planters for continued residence on plantations. Thus in 1840 on Worthy Park plantation it proved impossible to collect much of the rent owed on provision grounds and huts: most Jamaicans on that estate had no money to pay. The seasonal nature of the work requirements of sugar estates meant that labourers found it difficult to attract good wages in the intercrop period. It was no longer the case, as under slavery, that planters were obliged to maintain their workforce throughout the year. Jamaican labourers who stayed on the plantations could be laid off from work and remuneration for many weeks of the year. However, the irregularity of estate labour also benefited enterprising workers who could sustain their lives at customary levels and market the produce from provision grounds without having to accept paid work on plantations unless the wages were attractive. By 1842 the labour situation was dire on many Jamaican estates from the planter's perspective: the Colonial Office was informed that 'the want of continuous labour is still very much felt on many estates as the labourers generally work *very irregularly* without any regard to the wants or wishes of their employers'.

In these fluctuating and turbulent circumstances, sugar output declined seriously in Jamaica, and indeed throughout the entire British Caribbean, between 1838 and 1865. Half of the sugar estates in existence in Jamaica in the early 1830s, along with three-quarters of the coffee plantations and a quarter of the cattle pens, had ceased production thirty years later. Between 1832 and 1847 information collected by the Jamaican House of Assembly indicated that 140 sugar estates were abandoned, covering over

168,000 acres and employing 22,553 slaves in 1832. Coffee estates had an even greater decline in the period 1832–47, with 465 coffee estates being relinquished along with more than half of their workers.

The British government tried to help the West Indian plantation economy by abolishing the sugar duties in 1846, thereby removing import tariffs on sugar entering British ports. This move towards free trade removed restrictive import tariffs; but the loss of fiscal privilege was detrimental to Jamaican and other British West Indian plantations because it ushered in a rapid decline in sugar prices and increased competition from Cuban and Brazilian sugar. A few years later the plight of the plantations was evident. Thus in 1852 it was observed that in Jamaica 'wherever the eye is turned, wide-spread ruin meets the view. The bustle of business is no longer perceived in our towns; shipping has almost deserted our harbours; the busy industry of the sugar-estate has given place to the stillness of desolation, and the cultivated field is lapsing into its primeval state of weeds and jungle.'

It used to be argued that Jamaica experienced a rush of workers to leave sugar plantations after freedom was granted. This is now known to be an exaggeration. Certainly, Jamaica had the advantage over smaller Caribbean islands such as St Kitts or Nevis in having relatively plentiful land and moderate population density and, therefore, opportunities existed for former slaves and apprentices to leave the plantations for a more independent life. However, in reality matters were more complex. Many labourers chose to stay on plantations rather than face the trauma of eviction from their houses. In most cases, this option was followed where workers perceived that planters treated them fairly. Others chose to leave the estates but live nearby so that they could combine some work on plantations when demand was high for their labour, either when planting crops or during the sugar harvest, with living off the produce from their provision grounds. This variegated work provided them with sufficient cash to buy meat, fish, clothes and implements such as hammers, hoes and saws. Still others, in large numbers, quit the world of the plantation altogether in order to live as free peasants.

After 1838 Jamaican planters sought to replace the dwindling black workforce in sugar cultivation with indentured workers, mainly recruited from India but with a smattering of Chinese labourers. These migrants usually had a time-specified contract, often five years for working in Jamaica; they were not mainly intending to settle on the island. Some 38,595 Indian indentured workers came to Jamaica between 1834 and 1924, a relatively modest total compared with the much larger numbers of such people who went to Trinidad and British Guiana. This inflow of labourers did not work out especially well. About a third of the Indians returned home after receiving poor treatment from planters, who were reprimanded by the Colonial Office for their breaches of faith in dealing with indentured workers. Jamaicans were also often hostile towards Indians, who they correctly identified as competitors in the labour market.

More than half of Jamaica's acreage had never been put into productive use by the time slavery ended. In addition, many plantations on the island had fallen out of cultivation. Jamaica therefore had abundant land for people to take up as squatters. By 1846 it was reported that freed

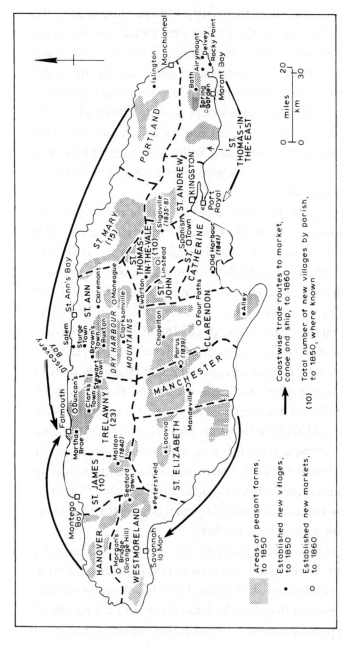

FIGURE 4.4 Major areas of peasant farming and the main peasant villages, Jamaica, to 1860. Retrieved from David Watts, *The West Indies: Patterns of Development, Culture and Environmental Change since 1492* (Cambridge: Cambridge University Press, 1987)

blacks had acquired 100,000 acres in the eight years after apprenticeship ended, and had built nearly 200 free villages. Baptist missionaries played a significant role in the establishment of these communities. One prominent example was Sligoville in St Catherine, promoted by the English Baptist missionary James Phillippo. Most free villages, however, were set up without missionary help. Knibb and Phillippo wrote admiringly about the rapid success of free blacks establishing a proud, hardworking peasantry and sustainable free villages by the early 1840s. Their view was undoubtedly seen through rose-tinted glasses, but the creation of an independent free people was an important advance for Jamaicans. Smallholders, in particular, increased their landholdings in the early years of freedom. In 1840 only 883 Jamaicans owned under ten acres of land; the number had increased to 20,724 in 1845 and to 60,000 by 1865. By that date most available small parcels of cultivable land had been taken up and many of those plots were becoming overworked.

Though missionaries helped the freed blacks in the creation of peasant villages after 1838, the spread of Christianity among Jamaicans was challenged by the rise of independent black religious expression that drew upon non-Christian sources. In particular, myalism, drawing upon African superstitions, grew rapidly as an antidote to the supposedly evil influence of obeahism. Singing, dancing and unusual rites undertaken in a feverish, emotional atmosphere were the hallmarks of myalism, which combined heathenism with some elements of Christian practice. The Presbyterian missionary Hope Waddell recalled attending a myal meeting in

1842 where a noisy gathering was 'in full force and employment, forming a ring, around which were a multitude of onlookers. Inside the circle some females performed a mystic dance, sailing round and round, and wheeling in the centre with outspread arms and wild looks and gestures. Others hummed, or whistled a low monotonous tune, to which the performers kept time, as did the people around also by hands and feet and the swaying of their bodies.'

Though the white elite could not necessarily influence the religious beliefs of Jamaicans, as the above example shows, there were many ways in which they sought to consolidate their power between 1838 and 1865. During this period, politics at the Assembly level was restricted to the male propertied classes. Fearing that newly enfranchised black voters would easily outnumber white voters, the Jamaican Assembly raised property qualifications for the franchise to exclude newly freed blacks from exercising power. Although a low financial level was set as a requirement for voting eligibility under the Franchise Act of 1840, the white elite was protected by regulations that required assemblymen to show they had an income of £180 from land or real property worth £1,800 or real and personal property amounting to £3,000. The suffrage was reduced under a hereditaments tax passed in the early 1850s. This effectively levied twelve shillings a year on the poorer freeholders, who frequently stopped registering to vote in order to avoid paying the tax. The number of voters in contested elections accordingly declined from 1,819 in 1849 to 753 in 1854. In 1859 the Assembly introduced a poll tax that effectively reduced the number of black voters.

The Jamaican Assembly largely carried out retrenchment in its spending in the 1840s and 1850s. This was effected by its control over annual revenue bills. The Duke of Newcastle argued in the House of Lords that retrenchment was the result of wasteful expenditure, the problems caused by collecting taxes through annual bills, and it was also 'occasioned by remissness in the collection of taxes'. The targets of cutbacks in spending included the Police Act of 1846, which reduced police numbers by about a half, and the building of a new General Penitentiary in Kingston, which came to a standstill in 1849 after its funding was cut. Funding for schools in Jamaica was also parsimonious in the period between the end of apprenticeship and the Morant Bay rebellion.

At the level of local government, primarily represented through the parish vestries, a somewhat different pattern emerged because, as Swithin Wilmot's research has shown, freedmen made their impact on vestry politics in Kingston after 1838 and St David parish in the 1850s. This was a significant change in political culture as the vestries, consisting of twelve elected members, had been dominated by whites from the 1670s until slave emancipation. One should not overstate the increased contribution of blacks to local government in Kingston, as whites still dominated politics in Jamaica. However, in the early 1840s the Kingston Common Council, established in 1801, witnessed a coalition of people from different ethnicities gaining seats through an alliance between free coloured shopkeepers, black artisans and Jewish retailers. By 1841 blacks held five out of twenty-four elected positions on the Kingston Common Council. This meant that the white privileged classes now had to share political power in Jamaica's largest urban setting with artisans and retailers of different ethnicities.

In the rural parish of St David, only eleven miles from Kingston, a more dramatic shift occurred in the balance of power at local level. Whereas in the early 1840s planters, penkeepers and others representative of the commercial elite held all the vestry positions, by 1857 nine of the ten vestrymen were black. Among the reasons for this change were the decline in sugar and coffee production in St David after 1838 and the rise of small black purchasers of freehold land. These economic and demographic shifts provided the impetus for greater black participation in vestry politics. Robert Jordon, a newspaper editor, and Samuel Clarke, a carpenter and small settler, were two black vestrymen in the parish who persuaded black free-holders to participate in local politics. The St David blacks remained dominant electorally until Jamaica's vestries were abolished in 1866.

Black vestrymen in St David concerned themselves with the plight of paupers, local road maintenance, tax relief, the leasing of parish land, public health and the state of local schools. In other words, they concentrated on the social and economic issues that most affected Jamaicans on a daily basis. Two issues dealt with effect-ively were convening public meetings where ordinary Jamaicans could discuss the provision of elementary education and the ability of teachers and an attempt to provide dispensaries where trained technicians could offer medical care as a substitute for the lack of trained doctors. In 1866 the attorney-general of Jamaica, con-vinced that this politicisation of freed people at local government level would follow the examples set in Kingston and St David and spread throughout Jamaica, advocated the abolition of the vestries because, in his opinion, they had become 'the training school for the demagogue'. His warning was heeded by the imperial government in 1866 when it abolished representative politics in Jamaica by closing the Assembly and the vestries, thereby pulling the rug from under the feet of small black freeholders in political office. By the time of the Morant Bay rebellion of 1865, Jamaicans had begun to make their mark in politics at the parish level but only two free blacks had ever been elected to the Jamaican Assembly.

Outbreaks against planter dominance occurred periodically after apprenticeship ended. In July 1839 a conspiracy occurred as a result of fears of re-enslavement and problems of access to land. Workers in western Jamaica bought guns and machetes as a form of protection and carried out drill exercises. Whites drifted away from the affected areas, but the conspiracy failed to break out into a riot or revolt. Another conspiracy occurred among freedmen in western Jamaican parishes in 1848. Protesters were concerned that they might be re-enslaved on 1 August, the tenth anniversary of the end of apprenticeship. There were also worries about planters cutting wages and supporting increased taxation. In the event, no general outbreak transpired, but smaller-scale protests happened in several parishes, notably confrontations between labourers and the police on Goshen estate, St Mary parish. Two riots broke out in 1859, one in several areas of Westmoreland parish and the other near Falmouth. High taxes and lack of justice for workers lay at the heart of these disturbances. Peace was restored in all these incidents but only after people were attacked and wounded.

The Morant Bay Rebellion, 1865

The most important Jamaican uprising against the authorities after slave emancipation broke out in the parish of St Thomas in the East on 11 October 1865. Occurring at a time of economic depression in Jamaica and starvation among the poor, this revolt was staged after the island's governor had circulated a report blaming Jamaicans for being lazy and contributing towards their own misery. This was a well-planned and coordinated rebellion in which peasants with machetes and sticks marched into Morant Bay, the capital of the parish, and exacted violence against sugar planters. The Native Baptist deacon, activist and small farmer Paul Bogle led the revolt. He had worked closely with George William Gordon, a wealthy mixed-race politician from St Thomas in the East, which he represented in the island's Assembly. Gordon had been ejected from the local planter-dominated vestry, and was due to attend a court case about his dismissal. He had left the Presbyterians to join the Native Baptists, which solidified his connection with Bogle, whom he urged to make the grievances of the black freedmen known to the authorities. Bogle and his associates held secret meetings, swore oaths to confirm loyalty and solidarity, and held meetings to plan the rebellion. He and his Native Baptist colleagues regarded themselves as a political as well as religious force that should resist the planter-dominated vestries and Assembly. Governor

Edward John Eyre was critical of Gordon's behaviour, while Bogle had political and religious sympathies with Gordon.

The rebellion arose from a strong sense of injustice by working class men and women. Burdened by racial and class discrimination and by high taxes and lack of voting rights, many ordinary workers in Jamaica were impoverished by unemployment or underemployment, poor wages, and the opposition of a largely white judiciary and government. The combination of an increasing black population and a declining number of sugar estates squeezed the amount of plantation layout available in Jamaica by the early 1860s. Richard Hill, the senior resident magistrate in St Catherine parish, considered that 'a great proportion of the community . . . now have no profitable occupation . . . They are from necessity idle, because they cannot get employment, and they are drifting into the vicious condition of people living how they can.'

Crop damage and a two-year drought followed by flooding had added to the woes of labourers and the unemployed. Lack of access to land was a particular source of grievance. Many planters, faced with economic problems in sugar cultivation, blamed the independent peasantry for contributing to their difficulties by working on their own lands beyond the plantation sector. Planters opposed many of the small independent farmers by bringing in regulations to make it difficult for blacks to acquire more land and by implementing strategies for ejecting them from land acquired as freehold or by gift. These problems had remained unsettled at the time of slave emancipation, and had deteriorated since from the freedmen's perspective. Groups of estate workers and the poor drew up petitions and memorials about their plight for presentation to Governor Eyre.

In January 1865 Edward Bean Underhill, secretary of the Baptist Missionary Society, had written to Edward Cardwell, secretary of state for the colonies, about the problems caused by drought, taxation and lack of political representation for Jamaican blacks. This letter was then sent to Eyre, who had it copied and printed and distributed throughout Jamaica to ask missionaries and other local officials to respond to the accusations. Eyre clearly hoped that they would reject the complaints. Instead, however, the circulated letter provoked much public debate in Jamaica about the redress needed for black people. Public meetings were held in every parish and Baptist missionaries gathered additional evidence to call for a Commission of Enquiry into the state of the island. These meetings provided impetus for Jamaicans to speak out about the plight of their condition. Their grievances were taken up by George W. Gordon's radical newspaper the *Jamaica Watchman and People's Free Press*.

Divisions between the white and black communities in Jamaica were highlighted by the conditions leading up to the Morant Bay revolt. It was reported that James McLaren, a young Native Baptist, associate of Bogle and a leader of the revolt, 'said to the people without they come together, and go down to Morant Bay in lump, to let the white people see there was plenty black in the island, it was no use at all, and cry out that they don't mean to pay any more ground rent again; and after seven years in freedom the outside land was given to them a long time, and the white people kept it to themselves'. This emotive quotation succinctly summarises the racial divide over access to land and ownership of land in Jamaica by 1865. McLaren was eventually executed under martial law for his participation in the revolt.

In the days before the rebellion, clear signs of tension were apparent in Morant Bay. On 7 October 1865, for instance, a black man named James Geoghegan interrupted a trial in which another black man was accused of trespassing on a disused plantation. This led to mayhem in the courtroom as police tried to eject Geoghegan, a scuffle broke out, and people outside the building pelted the police with sticks and stones. What appeared to be the trial of an individual for breaking the law turned into an inflammatory encounter as black freedmen's sense of injustice about their treatment with regard to access to land boiled over into a violent incident. Arrest warrants were issued by the police for those breaking order, including one for Bogle. When the police tried to arrest Bogle, he refused to go. His cries for help were supported by over 300 sugar cane workers, who came, armed with cutlasses and sticks, to his defence. It is therefore not surprising that Bogle led the protesters on 11 October in the attack on Morant Bay. Bogle had been a leader of the disgruntled freedmen for some time: earlier in 1865 he had led a delegation to Spanish Town to discuss their grievances with Eyre, but had not been granted an audience.

Over two days protesters attacked the police station and courthouse in Morant Bay and burned buildings. A hastily assembled volunteer militia confronted the rebels and fired at them. These were not professional soldiers, and their attempts to withstand the mob soon faltered. People were attacked and wounded; some vestrymen were targeted in the fracas; women in the crowd urged the rebels to seek bloodshed. Bogle led the protesters in a military line and threatened a vestryman with death if he were caught dressing white people's wounds. The rebels were carefully organised into gangs and Bogle, as their leader, was referred to as 'General Bogle'. Eighteen officials and members of the militia were killed; seven participants among the crowds also lost their lives. This was followed by freedmen taking charge of the parish of St Thomas in the East for two days. Estates were pillaged by armed rebels and shops were plundered. Local sugar workers and peasants joined the attacking crowds to protest at low wages and difficulties of access to land.

Governor Eyre declared martial law and ordered Brigadier-General Alexander Nelson to lead troops to find the rebels, including Bogle, and bring them to trial. The revolt was taken very seriously by the authorities as blacks far outnumbered other racial groups in Jamaica, and it was feared that the rebellion would spread throughout the island. Nelson's armed men marched quickly and ruthlessly throughout the parish, and soon located rebels, most of whom had no arms. Freedmen were attacked and wounded. Eyre enlisted the support of the Maroons to intercept and stop the rebels causing damage to property, placing over 200 of them under the command of Colonel Alexander Fyfe, a white man who had previously led the Maroons in helping to suppress the Jamaican slave rebellion of 1831/2.

The Maroons shot rebels and defended settlements against attack. The combined forces inflicted atrocities on the protesters. The troops and the Maroons killed 400 people across the parish of St Thomas in the East and arrested 300 people. In assisting the government forces, the Maroons remained loyal to their treaty obligations with the authorities dating from 1739. They attacked the rebels with ferocity, and were involved in acts of theft, flogging, shooting and burning buildings. The Maroons did not carry out as many killings as the troops, but their support for Eyre and his supporters belies any notion that they were freedom fighters.

The Maroons captured Bogle and delivered him to the colonial authorities. Within twenty-four hours of his arrest, Bogle was hung under martial law along with others. Gordon, one of Eyre's opponents, was arrested in Kingston, brought to Morant Bay for trial where he was convicted of conspiracy, prevented from communicating with family and friends and calling upon witnesses in his defence, and hanged on 23 October 1865, though there is little evidence that he participated in the organisation of the rebellion. He himself protested his innocence in the hours before his death, stating that he 'never advised or took part in any insurrection; all I ever did was to recommend the people who complained to seek redress in a legitimate way, and if in this I erred or have been misrepresented, I don't think I deserve this extreme sentence'. Bogle and Gordon were named in 1969 as national heroes in Jamaica.

The aftermath of the Morant Bay rebellion was conducted with severe repression by the authorities. Apart from the capture and execution of Bogle and Gordon, referred to above, hundreds of Jamaicans were flogged, many were rendered homeless, others were given prison sentences, and many homes belonging to freedmen were burned by soldiers. Troops shot suspects on sight; blind people and pregnant women were assaulted; and court martials were quickly convened and capital punishments meted out to those found guilty of participation in the uprising.

Governor Eyre firmly believed that the insurrection was part of a wider conspiracy throughout Jamaica, testifying that 'there had been an intercommunication between the negroes of the different parishes and an intention to act in concert for the destruction of the white and coloured inhabitants'. Though Eyre exaggerated the island-wide threat, other Jamaican officials had similar fears, and with good reason, for several court houses in other parts of the island were attacked during the uprising and anonymous letters were found in various places threatening to exact revenge against the authorities. The Morant Bay rebellion only lasted for a few days, but it triggered panic and paranoia among the Jamaican authorities that left a long shadow.

In Britain there was public controversy about the actions of Eyre's deployment of martial law and his use of that means to arrest Gordon and sentence him to death. The Colonial Secretary was concerned about the prolongation of martial law in Jamaica after the rebellion, and about the lack of evidence presented by Eyre concerning an island-wide conspiracy. Leading political figures took opposite sides about whether to support or denounce Eyre's conduct and actions. The writer Thomas Carlyle was a prominent supporter of Eyre while the political philosopher John Stuart Mill was a leading British opponent. Debates arose about whether Eyre had acted lawfully and whether his implementation of martial law was justified. Liberals attacked Eyre as a murderer while supporters of the existing order regarded him as a valiant and strong leader who put down a major protest in order to restore law and order.

In January 1866 a Royal Commission was set up to look into the causes and details of the Morant Bay rebellion. This was a major administrative exercise, involving interviews with over 700 people. Eyre was suspended from his position as governor, recalled to London and dismissed. A Jamaica Committee, formed in 1866, accused Eyre of mass murder but charges were never brought to court. The rebellion led to a major constitutional change. Jamaica's Assembly, which had existed for two centuries, resigned its royal charter, and voted to abolish nearly two centuries of self-rule. The main executive body on the island remained the unelected Legislative Council.

From 1866 onwards, Jamaica became a Crown Colony governed directly from Westminster and Whitehall. Many of the white elite in Jamaica thought this would be their best protection against either a further black uprising and a potential overthrow of the status quo or a takeover of the legislature for the first time by prosperous black and coloured leaders who had sufficient wealth and paid enough taxes for the right to vote. The Colonial Office, alarmed at the potential for further unrest in Jamaica, agreed to these changes. As Orlando Patterson has succinctly summarised the situation, those authorities were influenced in their decision-making by racism: 'on top of everything else was the racist conviction in England that the black and brown peoples of the empire were incapable of civilization and not fit for self-rule'.

5

The Shadow of Colonialism, 1865–1945

∼

The era of Crown Colony government in Jamaica was characterised by very slow and modest political change for the majority black population, important changes in social policies and economic affairs and continuing inequality based on class and race. Two opposing social developments underpinned Jamaican life between the Morant Bay revolt of 1865 and the end of the Second World War. On the one hand, the white elite sought to impose their social and moral values on the Jamaican masses. This involved restricting political leadership and the franchise to the minority white population who would govern the island in ways that reflected their prerogatives and their desire to exercise social control over the masses through racial discrimination, the propagation of the Christian faith and promotion of respectable moral values. On the other hand, the Jamaican people wanted to exercise self-determination even though they lacked political power, social status and wealth. The interplay between control from a small political and social hierarchy on the masses and the independent social behaviour of the Jamaican people ran in tandem throughout the era of Crown Colony government.

The racial composition of the population remained relatively stable between 1865 and 1945. The small white minority accounted for 2.6 per cent of the

Jamaican population in 1871 and 1.7 per cent in 1921. In the same years, the equivalent proportion for brown people was 19.8 per cent and 18.3 per cent, and for the large black majority – descended from slave forebears – it was 77.6 per cent and 77 per cent. Each of these three segments of Jamaica's social pyramid – the white, the brown and the black – had further gradations based on status, education, race and class. The complexity of social relations in Jamaica reflected these finely tuned distinctions within a hierarchical framework. Racial differences lay at the core of power structures in Crown Colony Jamaica. The white elite controlled most of the wealth and political positions in the island. They were indissolubly linked to whites with lower wealth and status through racial communality. Though the economic power of the sugar plantations had declined by the era of Crown Colony government, whites retained their social authority, as Patrick Bryan has succinctly put it, 'by the habit of power and by the power of habit'.

Brown Jamaicans held some bureaucratic positions, but black Jamaicans, even if they worked competently, were never given positions of status in administrative occupations. As Donal Byfield recalled, 'however efficient or good the black fellow was, the brown man or the Englishman had to be the superintendent'. Moreover, often relations between brown and black Jamaicans were unharmonious. Thus a visitor to Jamaica noted that 'a Negro as a rule will not serve a mulatto when he can serve a European or a white Creole. He thinks the mulatto to be too akin to himself to be worthy of any respect.' A hierarchy of skin colour existed whereby those with mixed-race origin, such as mustees, were regarded as of higher status because of their lighter skin than quadroons. A report dated 1930 noted that 'there is as much caste feeling and caste practice between the light-coloured negroes and the full blacks as between the white and coloured groups'. Many black Jamaicans formed personal relationships with brown or lighter-skinned people to achieve social advancement: 'each remove from the sable hue' meant 'a step higher in the social scale'. As Henrice Altink has argued, ordinary Jamaicans perpetuated these racial disparities by encouraging their children to marry someone with a lighter skin – a social attitude that persisted into the later twentieth century.

The upper echelons of the white minority included colonial bureaucrats, army officers, sugar planters, estate attorneys and managers along with bishops, archdeacons and canons in the Anglican and Roman Catholic churches. Many of these men were British expatriates. All the major political appointees in Jamaica – the governor, the colonial secretary, the postmaster general, the attorney-general, the justices – were Britons. Beneath them in the social hierarchy were middle-class professionals such as clergymen, police officers, building society proprietors, insurance company directors, school inspectors, journalists, small farmers and business owners. Lower-class whites comprised office and store clerks, plantation overseers and bookkeepers. Brown Jamaicans consisted of a growing middle-class cohort of lawyers, doctors, businessmen, civil servants, journalists, office clerks and small farmers. This group included many intelligent, educated men who mixed with the white elite but were regarded by many of those people as occupying a social niche beneath them. Smaller farmers, skilled craftspeople and policemen formed a lower middle-class group positioned between the white and brown elite and the peasants and plantation workers. Jamaica's black people included some middle-class professionals but most were poor plantation workers, peasant farmers or urban workers whose employment was intermittent. The social gulf between white and black Jamaicans remained permanent in the era of Crown Colony government.

Crown Colony Government

Crown Colony government was implemented in Jamaica immediately after the Morant Bay rebellion. Jamaica continued to be governed, by direct edict from Westminster and Whitehall, until well after the eighty years covered in this chapter. Under such government, a white minority elite held all major political appointments and the franchise for black, and many brown, Jamaicans was severely restricted. These political and constitutional arrangements meant that Jamaica was still governed under the aegis of colonialism, though, to British statesmen, the island was no longer, as in the eighteenth century, considered a thriving part of the British Empire. Quite the opposite, in fact, because Jamaica and the other British Caribbean islands were regarded by Britain's officials as colonial backwaters.

Crown Colony government brought fundamental changes to the political system on the island. Political power now resided in the hands of an appointed governor aided by a Legislative Council. The Assembly ceased to exist, which meant that there was no representative element in Jamaica's politics. The establishment of this new system from Westminster was intended to ensure there was in the future no opposition to the governor. Assisting the governor were the attorney-general, the colonial secretary and the financial secretary with up to six men nominated by the governor to sit on the Council. All the nominees came from the propertied classes. To supplement these six officials, the governor could appoint a further six unofficial members to the Council. A limited franchise operated under Crown Colony government, enabling whites to consolidate their political control, which they also solidified in local politics. Governors were usually upper-class Englishmen appointed for a few years' service in Jamaica as imperial administrators on behalf of the British Crown.

One of the unspoken but assumed stances of the political elite that ran Jamaica was to prioritise the superiority of white men as leaders. It was assumed that brown Jamaicans, let alone black people, were unfit for high office as they had received neither the training nor education for such roles. Sir John Peter Grant, the first governor after the Morant Bay rebellion, claimed that black Jamaicans were 'ill-suited' for self-government because they possessed 'not one Anglo-Saxon characteristic'. This is an example of white supremacy which Jamaicans, lacking political power, had to accept whether they liked it or not. Grant believed, as many other British governors did, that white Britons were automatically seated at the top of the hierarchy of civilization. A different explanation was provided by the Reverend Carey Berry, who argued that whites were not particularly opposed to Jamaican self-government but feared that it would 'make it too hot for any white people to remain here'. Hierarchical divisions in race and class meant that, for most Jamaicans, 'their black skins confined them to secondary roles and spaces in a society where political, social, and economic power wore white faces'.

White dominance in Jamaica preserved a hierarchical political order that reflected British norms. The electorate in Britain was still tied to property qualifications, with the urban working-class man only being granted the franchise for the first time in the Reform Act of 1867. The emphasis on property ownership in relation to the franchise was carried over to Jamaica. Thus Jamaica's white officials believed that property ownership, literacy and education underpinned the right to vote at elections and that this ruled out the majority of black Jamaicans, who were usually landless, illiterate and poorly educated. Underlying these attitudes was the view that incorporating blacks into the political process might lead to an insurrection on a scale witnessed in Saint-Domingue/Haiti in the French revolutionary era.

For their part, black Jamaicans, the majority of whom were working class, avoided overt political activity for years after the brutality of the government repression of the Morant Bay revolt. The autocratic nature of Crown Colony government also effectively eliminated brown Jamaicans from assuming significant administrative and political office. The underlying cultural assumption behind the implementation of Crown Colony government was a racialised colonialism. The imperial authorities held the view that the non-British racial composition of most Jamaicans militated against an extension of the elective principle in politics. The paternalism underpinning this viewpoint was largely accepted by Jamaica's

black population in the later nineteenth century. Thus
Kingston's blacks petitioned against a plan to reintroduce
limited male suffrage by stating that 'we are law-abiding
people, being fully conscious that without the protection
of the Government our fellow Colonists would not allow
us the breath we breathe'.

The benevolent paternalism of Crown Colony government in Jamaica attracted criticism. It was an expensive
form of government that imposed heavy tax burdens on
agriculture and commerce. Some taxpayers resented the
fact that tax revenue was mainly used to support those who
paid minimal or no taxes, but against this charge it should
be noted that many ordinary Jamaicans were paying taxes
on land and food. The government's inclination to buy
supplies from overseas rather than from local merchants
was criticised. Finally, the whole ethos of Crown Colony
government was much more comfortable for the controlling oligarchy than for the majority of Jamaicans: the
increased bureaucracy and administrative positions were
mainly reserved for whites from Britain while brown and
black Jamaicans were not given full voting rights. It was
unfeasible for the franchise to be significantly altered in
the late nineteenth century because the white elite had no
desire to surrender its hold on Jamaica's politics and
constitution.

However, the initial years of Crown Colony government had some positive outcomes. Governor Grant
avoided the draconian measures of his predecessor and,
during his eight years in office between 1866 and 1874, he
effected notable improvements in the island. An experienced, energetic colonial administrator in the Bengal
Civil Service, Grant attempted to implement the rule of

law for all; established district courts; reorganised the police service; modestly improved the provision of elementary education; brought in new taxes that were efficiently collected; improved the island's infrastructure; disestablished the Anglican Church in Jamaica; established a Government Savings Bank; and oversaw the move of the capital from Spanish Town to Kingston. He also built new hospitals and improved medical facilities.

Grant governed autocratically, but his constructive portfolio of improvements convinced many Jamaicans that he was leading the colony to advancement in a spirit of optimism. In April 1869 Grant toured Jamaica to see the effects of his improvements. A correspondent for the *Jamaica Guardian* witnessed local people in Lucea being introduced to the governor, and commented that there was 'a general feeling of confidence in Sir John Peter Grant, not only in his ability, which is undoubted, but also in his desire to obtain needful information from all quarters, and so to govern the island as to promote its true and lasting prosperity'.

No attempt to impose major changes in the governance of late nineteenth-century Jamaica came from above and no sustained agitation pressurised the status quo from below. Modest political changes occurred under Crown Colony government, however, partly as a result of agitation by the black, brown and local white people against its unrepresentative character. In 1884 a newly constituted Legislative Council came into existence, with nine elected members. Increased powers reduced the autocracy of the governor by allowing those elected, when acting together, to veto his bills and resolutions. A further increase in the number of elected seats to fourteen on the Council was introduced in 1895 as Jamaica received a new constitution. These were supplemented by ten members selected by the governor and five ex officio members.

These changes were hardly progressive. The governor had the power to veto any bills he disapproved of. A unanimous vote of the fourteen Legislative Council members after 1895 could bring down any proposal. In addition, qualifications for the franchise were implemented. Men had to pay direct taxes of ten shillings or earn a minimum annual salary of £50, and were entitled to vote from the age of twenty-one. Women had to pay taxes of £2 annually, and could vote at age twenty-five. Blacks were largely disqualified from the vote by a literacy test of 1893. Only wealthy people could stand for election to the Legislative Council, the most common requirement being an annual income of £150. This was well beyond the reach of most Jamaicans, for at that time average wages for field workers were less than six shillings per week. In 1886 around 2 per cent of Jamaicans had the franchise. By 1935 only 5.5 per cent of a Jamaican population of 1.25 million were registered voters. Planters, merchants and white professionals who dominated Jamaica's politics were content to exercise power according to a non-party political tradition in which they were the kingpins. Sir Henry Blake, the governor of Jamaica in the 1890s, staunchly defended Crown Colony government and opposed the enfranchisement of what he regarded as the dangerous black population.

At a local level, more progress was made towards political accountability. Twelve parishes were overseen by parochial boards while two – Kingston and St Andrew – were managed by a corporation. In 1865 the parochial boards were nominated bodies but twenty years later they were made elective and the franchise extended to thousands of Jamaicans. By the late 1880s successful smallholders and ordinary civil servants began to recruit blacks to improve their electoral position. They added thousands of names to electoral rolls. Whites were alarmed at this rise in black voters. The island's government decided to stem the growth of black mass participation in politics by introducing a literacy clause in a franchise act to exclude those who could not read or write from exercising the ballot. This policy appears to have been effective until the late 1880s for by then no black leader of note had emerged in Jamaica to revive the challenges to white supremacy that Paul Bogle had advanced prior to and during the Morant Bay rebellion. Black participation in the franchise was also restricted by the requirement that electors should demonstrate ownership of substantial property holdings or payment of 30 shillings in direct tax on personal property.

This situation began to change with the leadership provided by Joseph Robert Love, a black Bahamian doctor, who settled in Jamaica in 1890 and called for greater black representation in government. He founded his own weekly newspaper *The Jamaica Advocate* in 1894 and gave notable lectures in Kingston and Spanish Town promoting the franchise for black Jamaicans and the need for reforms in public institutions to provide more career opportunities for the masses. He advocated the provision of access to education for boys and girls. Love encouraged the working classes to air their political views and to protest against racial discrimination.

Love helped to found the Pan-African Association in 1901. He emphasised in his writings the oppression of Africa and Africans by European colonialism. But he was also a realist, and urged his supporters to support white politicians who advocated political advances for black people. Love's ideas were supported in Jamaica by street preachers, including Prince Shrevington, 'Warrior Higgins', and Isaac Uriah Brown. In 1906 Love won an Assembly seat for St Andrew parish and had a brief political career, halted by illness in 1910, during which he began to persuade members of the white elite that the franchise and holding of political office should not be related to skin colour. Love and his supporters favoured white politicians who were sensitive to the exclusion of Jamaican blacks from public roles and government.

The limited political skills of many white politicians in Jamaica were criticised by influential members of their own race. By the late 1930s, the governor of Jamaica, Sir Arthur Richards, was openly critical of the poor political contributions of the Legislative Council and scathing about the quality of administrative support for the colonial state. Trained civil servants were few and far between; few people working in government service had financial training; and the business of government administration proceeded slowly and inefficiently. 'In Jamaica,' he reported to his superiors in London, 'there is no district administration in the ordinary Colonial sense and ... the history of general administration in Jamaica is one of neglect ... There is little likelihood of the ordinary wants of the people receiving the personal attention and investigation which is a common place elsewhere.'

Population and Health

In the eighty years after 1865 the Jamaican population nearly tripled. Census figures record a population of 441,300 in 1861, 639,000 in 1891, 858,100 in 1921 and 1,205,000 in 1941. Most of the growth arose from natural increase in the island's people. The majority of children were born out of wedlock as common law unions predominated over marital liaisons. In some cases these unions became formal marriages, but marriage rates were low. By 1941–5 marriage rates in Kingston accounted for 8–9 per cent of the population, while in all other Jamaican areas the rates were under 5 per cent. Fertility was largely independent of nuptiality, for in the same period in Jamaica's thirteen parishes illegitimate births ranged between 61 and 80 per cent of all births. Fertility measures by family type for 1943 showed that married women aged over 45 had an average of 5.9 children compared with 4.8 for common law women.

The reasons for the low rate of marriage among the Jamaican masses and the high rate of illegitimate births were rooted in social reality. Many ordinary Jamaicans could not afford the costs of a formal marriage ceremony. In addition, it was a commonly held attitude among the working classes that being bound to one person in a monogamous relationship for one's entire adulthood was not a preferred way of life. There are indications that many Jamaican women thought that a man failing to act as a breadwinner could be discarded, which would be more problematic if they were married. Polite society frowned upon consensual relations outside of marriage and regarded illegitimacy as a moral and social evil. Yet the editor of the *Daily Gleaner* explained that whites misunderstood illegitimacy: 'In Jamaica, speaking generally, we are at a stage where permanent monogamy – that is, the life-long attachment to our wife by means of legal and religious bonds is alien to the spirit and culture of the majority, and where, therefore, it is not quite fair to apply standards of judgement that imply moral condemnation. These standards are out of place here at the present time.'

The white elite, however, regarded the extensive common law unions and illegitimacy as immoral. The Jamaican government tried to address these issues with a raft of legislation in the 1880s dealing with marriage, divorce, registration, bastardy and maintenance. These laws included a strong condemnation, sometimes implied, sometimes explicit, of much of the social behaviour of the black majority in terms of their personal and intimate relations. However, many members of the white elite kept concubines and mistresses, and they opposed compulsory registration of paternity. None of the laws passed greatly changed the existing situation in Jamaica, as the figures cited above on marriage and illegitimacy rates show.

Mortality rates in Jamaica were much improved from the late slavery era, when they averaged about 33 deaths per 1,000 of population. By the 1880s the death rate had dropped to around 24 per 1,000 and it remained around that level until the early 1920s. In periods of crisis, however, the death rate unsurprisingly increased, as was the case in years of hurricane and flooding (1903 and 1912), the Kingston earthquake (1907) and the international influenza pandemic immediately after the end of the

First World War (1918–19). Infectious and parasitical diseases were common in Jamaica and occasional outbreaks of smallpox occurred. The white population was particularly susceptible to fevers, whereas black Jamaicans were more likely to die from bowel complaints and diseases of the intestinal tract. Digestive disorders and respiratory diseases were also common among ordinary Jamaicans. Nevertheless, improved sanitation, including better sewerage for Kingston and sanitary regulations for burying the dead, had already helped to combat mortality by the 1890s.

Jamaica by the interwar period exercised good control over mortality compared with some other areas in the British West Indies, such as Barbados, which had much higher infant mortality, or British Guiana, which was susceptible to malaria outbreaks. One of Jamaica's important demographic achievements after the First World War consisted of declining infant mortality resulting from expanding medical services, improved control of diseases of the respiratory and digestive systems, and a decline in mortality from congenital debility. In the 1920s and 1930s Jamaica's health system made considerable advances in tackling whooping cough, measles, yaws and tetanus as causes of infant mortality. In the half century after 1921 Jamaica achieved a reduction of 81 per cent in infant mortality. This downward trend contributed to significant gains in life expectancy from 35.9 to 54.6 years between 1920 and 1950.

In 1867 Governor Grant oversaw the implementation of the Public Health Law. This led to the creation of island medical services under a Central Board of Health. Parochial Boards of Health were then established to forge a connection between health and Jamaica's development by overseeing safe water supplies and quarantining sufferers from diseases. Dispensaries and medical districts were also set up in the parishes along with district medical officers to provide public healthcare. In 1872 a Medical Council was established to oversee healthcare in Jamaica. There were many medical conditions that required treatment. Malarial fever was common in Jamaica, especially on coastal plantations. At Kingston Public Hospital in 1899–1900, 10 per cent of the people treated had malarial complaints. Diseases of the bowel and intestinal tract were often found among black Jamaicans. Digestive disorders, respiratory diseases, leprosy and meningitis were also among the diseases treated regularly by Jamaica's doctors.

Access to medical help was problematic for most Jamaicans in the late nineteenth century. Improvements in medical provision were distributed unevenly. A report of 1899 thus noted that 'the official medical system continues to work well within the field it covers, but that is limited, while resort is still had to the bush doctors'. Domestic sanitation remained largely unchecked and many dwellings were overcrowded. Many ordinary Jamaicans lived at a distance from hospitals and were not able to avail themselves of the medical facilities provided. Dispensaries only opened for a couple of hours in the morning. Until the 1890s Jamaicans needed a letter of recommendation from a magistrate or custos of their parish before they were admitted to hospital. Hospitals were overcrowded, and it was not until just after the First World War that new hospitals were built to ease the situation.

British and American philanthropic and investigative bodies took a close interest in healthcare and education in Jamaica. The US-based Rockefeller Foundation Commission undertook significant investigations in Jamaica between 1918 and 1932 to improve healthcare provision. Much of its attention focused on diseases such as hookworm, yaws, malaria and tuberculosis. These enquiries, and the reports emanating from them, helped to introduce a Bureau of Health Education in 1927 and new appointments in public health inspectors to monitor disease outbreaks and nurses to administer home care visits. The British-sponsored West Indies Royal Commission or Moyne Commission (1938–9) developed these improvements by advocating training facilities for healthcare workers, which were implemented in 1944, and recommending that 10 per cent of the national budget should be spent on health services.

Migration

Increasing employment difficulties for working-class people led to a rise in emigration. A net outward movement of people increased in the period 1881–1921, reaching a decadal peak of 146,000 in 1911–21. The main destinations, in descending order of numerical importance, were the United States, Panama and Cuba, but other countries were also magnets for migrants (Costa Rica, Ecuador and Nicaragua among them). Between 1881 and 1914 some 90,000 Jamaicans were recruited along with other West Indians to work on the construction of the Panama Canal connecting the Caribbean Sea with the Pacific Ocean. By 1930 over 60,000 Jamaicans were estimated to be living in Cuba, usually working on sugar estates. Many Jamaicans also moved to work in Costa Rica, Barbados and Trinidad. They also left Jamaica in substantial numbers for large cities of the United States such as New York and Washington, D.C.

The Jamaican authorities were sufficiently concerned about the exodus of people to areas dominated by American finance or indeed to the United States that they sought to restrict emigration under an Emigrants' Protection Law (1893). This required emigrants to carry a permit if they sought work outside of Jamaica. Permit officers were introduced to monitor the bureaucracy involved, but the legislation proved difficult to enforce. Emigration from Jamaica began to dry up in the world economic depression years of the 1930s. Many Jamaicans moved home in that period, notably from Cuba, where Jamaican workers were banned in 1931 at a time of heightened racial tension and contraction in the island's sugar industry.

Immigration to Jamaica did not operate on a large scale between 1865 and 1945. This reflected the paucity of employment prospects in Jamaica for the masses. Very few immigrants arrived in Jamaica from Britain and Europe and only a limited migration of Indian, East Indian and Chinese indentured contract migrants came from other parts of the world. Indian and East Indian immigrants came to Jamaica between the 1840s and 1917 under indentured servant schemes which they signed up for before leaving their country. Their contracts were usually for five years, with an additional requirement to remain thereafter in Jamaica for five continuous years. They were supposed to receive wages, a small amount of land and a funded return passage to India after the end of their term of service. Most Indian migrants were Hindus and the remainder were mainly Muslims, but the recruiting authorities paid little attention to the migrants' religious beliefs. Two-thirds of the total recruited were men while one-third were women. They usually came to Jamaica as single people, although some had been married in India and some women brought children with them. They were drawn from predominantly poor areas of India such as Uttar Pradesh and western Bihar, and many were illiterate.

The Indian indentured migrants, referred to at the time as 'coolies', worked on plantations and market gardens and later migrated to towns. They were very poorly paid, earning less on average than working-class blacks. Indian women, in particular, could earn only paltry wages. Employers assigned the Indians to various work tasks, which were often menial. Prospects for good remuneration in Jamaica after the period of indenture were poor. Integration with the Jamaican black population proved difficult owing to racial differences, though there was little overt violence. Indian contract workers usually kept themselves aloof from the black population, and were easily recognisable through their colourful, picturesque garments. But they encountered opposition from influential quarters in Jamaica who argued that they would have a negative effect on the existing Jamaican population. Thus the Baptists claimed that the religious superstitions of Indian migrants would hinder the moral and religious improvement of black Jamaicans. Governor Sydney Olivier stated to a committee dealing with Indian immigration in 1909 that Jamaican planters preferred creole labourers to Indian workers. However, the reluctance of black Jamaicans to work for the wages and in the conditions found on sugar estates meant that, in Olivier's words, it was 'expedient in the interests of the island, that estate industries should not be allowed to collapse, so long as Indian immigrants can be obtained for them on terms advantageous both to themselves and to their employers'.

Indian contract servants could be released from their indentures through physical disability or commutation. Few Indians opted for a second five-year term of indenture after receiving their certificate of freedom at the end of their first five-year stint. To persuade them to remain in Jamaica after their indentures expired, they were offered a colonization bounty of £12 in cash or ten acres of crown land. These were fairly mean inducements for them to stay. The land offered, it should be noted, was mainly mountainous, infertile or lacking a water supply. Cash grants were removed in 1879 and land grants were abolished in 1906. Repatriation was expensive for impecunious Indians and India itself did not welcome back destitute people. Though some Indians returned home, between 1879 and 1916, 53 per cent of the Indian indentured migrants settled permanently in Jamaica. In 1917 the British Colonial Office under pressure from the Indian government terminated the indentured servant scheme after serious concerns were raised about the inadequate functioning of the system and poor treatment of the labourers as well as pressure from Indian expatriate communities.

Chinese indentured servants entered Jamaica between 1854 and 1884, but in much smaller numbers than Indians. Driven by land hunger, high taxes and volatile conditions in parts of China, this small diaspora left home in search of a better life in Jamaica. The main ethnic Chinese community among the immigrants was the Hakka. They worked initially on agricultural estates under five-year contracts tied to particular planters, but later diversified into operating laundries and grocery stores. Living in shabby, often degrading conditions, and, like the Indians, ill at ease with the black community, they eked out a hand-to-mouth existence, earning derisory hourly wages. The Jamaican authorities complained that the Chinese were reluctant and indifferent workers on the plantations.

Another wave of Chinese settlers arrived in Jamaica in the early twentieth century. More entrepreneurs and small businessmen were found among this cohort. The grocery trade was their main occupational niche; they were willing to work long hours and they provided credit facilities to ordinary Jamaicans and good service. The Chinese also operated ice cream parlours and pastry shops. A minority of them took clerical jobs. But they were never a large contingent of the population in Jamaica, being less numerous than people of Indian and East Indian extraction. The 1943 census recorded 12,394 Chinese living in Jamaica, including a substantial portion of mixed African and Chinese descent. About half of that total was based in Kingston and St Andrew.

The Chinese remained closely linked together through their language and ethnicity. They formed mutual aid and freemasonry societies to protect their own interests. Better-off members of Jamaica's Chinese community sent their children back to China for their school education. Relations between the Chinese and Jamaicans, however, were often strained. Small black shopkeepers resented competition from the Chinese immigrants. The Jamaica authorities wanted to reduce interracial mixture in personal relations, an official suggesting that it was 'desirable that bona fidé wives and fiancées should be allowed to join their husbands and prospective husbands in Jamaica thereby reducing to a small extent cohabitation with native women'. This statement indicates the difficulties faced by the Chinese in coming to terms with a completely different cultural environment than their own background, but it is also true that many Chinese migrants to Jamaica did not wish to assimilate to the host culture.

The Economy

Between 1865 and 1945 Jamaica continued to rely on its agricultural resources as the backbone of the economy: industry and factory production were very limited in scope. In 1871, 68 per cent of the Jamaican population worked in agriculture; this dropped to 55.3 per cent in 1921. Most agricultural workers were small settlers who led subsistence lives: by 1890 they accounted for three-quarters of the island's agricultural output. The agricultural basis of the Jamaican economy centred around tropical produce such as sugar, rum and molasses; fruit production, notably bananas but also pineapples; and peasant production of root crops and subsistence items for domestic consumption and marketing. Yams, maize, plantains and cassava were grown by peasants for domestic consumption. In hillier areas of Jamaica, coffee was produced as a cash crop by peasant farmers. Logwood production also took place.

Cattle pens contributed to livestock production. Provisions such as breadfruit, plantains, yams, sweet potatoes and ackee provided 54 per cent of Jamaica's agricultural output in 1870 and 49 per cent in 1930. By the mid-1930s coconuts were a significant contributor to Jamaica's economy, grown on slightly more than 40,000 acres (about the same acreage as sugar cane).

Important changes occurred, however, in the distribution of agricultural activity. Sugar estates experienced great difficulties in the late nineteenth century but then recovered in the 1900–45 period, while the production of bananas and their export to foreign markets became a rising and noteworthy feature of Jamaican economic life. The influence of the United States in both the sugar and banana industries became an important aspect of the Jamaican economy by the 1880s, and this continued thereafter. Exports were much less significant for economic development by the interwar period than they had been at the end of the slavery era. Thus in 1832 exports comprised 43.5 per cent of GDP at current prices, whereas by 1930 this had fallen to 19.8 per cent. The eighty-year period after 1865 also witnessed a transition from the importance of tropical produce in export earnings to fruit becoming more prominent. In 1865 sugar, rum and coffee comprised two-thirds of Jamaica's export earnings but by 1900 fruit, notably bananas, had become the most important export product. This change was accompanied by the United States becoming for the first time the island's most important trading partner.

Between 1865 and 1900, Jamaica's sugar economy experienced hard times despite the continuing strong international demand for sugar. The island's sugar output dropped by 29 per cent in the sixty years after 1850. As sugar estates fell into bankruptcy and were either abandoned or sold, the number of sugar plantations plummeted from 316 in 1867 to 122 in 1900. A downward trend in sugar prices occurred: cane sugar prices on the international market fell from 25s. 6d. per cwt in 1873 to 11s. 3d. per cwt in 1900. International competition from German and French beet sugar, supported by bounties, were further causes of the industry's economic problems. Britain and the United States reduced their imports of Caribbean cane sugar in the late nineteenth century and began to import beet sugar as a substitute. In 1874 Britain abolished its remaining sugar duties. Britain's free trade policies ruled out a return to protectionism in the home market for imperial products via preferential duties. In these circumstances, Jamaica's cane sugar exports were channelled in larger quantities to the United States in the 1880–1900 period, though immediately afterwards Canada began to import significant amounts of Jamaican sugar.

Increased imports of beet sugar in Britain in the late 1870s and early 1880s were inextricably linked with a significant fall in sugar prices to a level that undercut the cost of production of cane sugar on many Jamaican properties. In 1896 the Germans and the French doubled their bounties on beet sugar, causing international sugar prices to drop further. These developments adversely affected Jamaican sugar production. St Andrew, St Thomas, St Mary, St Ann, Portland, St Catherine and St Elizabeth were the main parishes most affected by abandoned sugar estates. In 1897 a Royal Commission recognised the precarious state of the Jamaican sugar industry.

It led the British government to secure European agreement to curtail sugar beet bounties. This came into effect in 1903 but it failed to revive a declining Jamaican sugar industry.

A solution to Jamaica's sugar difficulties was found within a few years by the implementation of central factories on estates. These began to be constructed after 1902 when the Jamaican government passed a law to encourage their use. They were concentrated in areas where cultivation could best be undertaken on plains. Steam power replaced cattle, windmills and watermills as a motive force. The separation of molasses from sugar in rum production was improved by the deployment of centrifugal filters. The largest estates converted from private ownership to corporate control under multinational companies, notably the United Fruit Company (UFC) based in the United States. The British sugar refining company of Tate & Lyle also invested substantially in Jamaican sugar production as the large sugar mills were installed.

During the First World War, Jamaican sugar cane production increased to meet British demand. It benefited during the war years from reduced beet sugar production and from a massive increase in sugar prices. After the First World War sugar prices continued to increase and many of the remaining sugar estates in the island were concentrated on economically productive areas and combined into larger units based around central factories. The average size of these larger plantations was 660 acres. By 1930, however, though only thirty sugar estates operated in Jamaica, their output was impressive owing to the efficient use of central factories. By 1948 sugar output (at 180,318 tons) was fifteen times higher than the average output in 1911–13.

Given the declining role of sugar production in late nineteenth-century Jamaica, planters diversified into cultivating pimento and logwood and, on some properties, cattle pens were expanded or introduced. Coffee was also grown by both large and small producers. These types of productive activity were less labour intensive than sugar cultivation. Pimento and logwood earnings moved in opposite directions in the 1890s, with the former undergoing a doubling of export earnings between 1894 and 1900 and the latter experiencing a substantial decline in production and export earnings in the same period. Cattle and mules were essential for internal transportation in Jamaica and an export market for livestock in Cuba could be tapped. Pens were properties ranging in size from 200 to 2,000 acres, and the land they contained was given over to commons, woodland and guinea grass. Parts of larger pens could be leased to tenants.

Banana production was a notable contributor to the Jamaican economy after 1865. The first exports were despatched from the island in the following year. Bananas are a perennial fruit, grown by themselves or in mixed cultivation. Many late nineteenth-century lithographs and sketches depict workers in this industry carrying large bundles of bananas on their heads. Jamaica pioneered the banana trade and a substantial export market was tapped as world demand for bananas increased. The United States, which offered favourable tariffs, became a major market for Jamaican bananas; it had reasonable proximity to Jamaica and had plenty of steamships to transport bananas and other fruits.

Eastern Jamaican parishes such as Portland, St Mary and St Thomas in the East became the main centre of

FIGURE 5.1 Bananas on the way to market. DEA/ICAS94/De
Agostini/Getty Images

banana cultivation either on virgin soil or on abandoned land once used for sugar cultivation. In the
1870s and 1880s smallholders dominated banana production. Port Antonio, in Portland, became the main
port for banana exports. It grew rapidly in population
as smallholders and other working-class people flocked
there to work in this industry. Employment in
Jamaican banana production rose from nearly 4,000
people in 1891 to 23,000 in 1911. The number of
banana estates rose from 113 in 1893 to 505 in 1930.
Bananas overtook sugar as Jamaica's most valuable
commodity export by 1890 and were the most valuable
of all the island's exports by 1930. The rise of banana
production in Jamaica led to the emergence of banana

entrepreneurs, often from a mercantile background, who achieved the status of leading sugar plantation owners earlier in the nineteenth century.

By the 1890s, however, smallholders were being squeezed out by the entry of the multinational UFC into the industry. The UFC dealt mainly with larger suppliers, and soon dominated banana production in Jamaica. It developed a special fleet of ventilated steamships in the 1890s. Its dominance was not challenged until the 1920s, when the cooperative Jamaica Banana Producers' Association (JBPA) emerged as a competitor. However, the UFC had the financial resources to purchase larger supplies of bananas at lower prices than the JBPA and so its leading role in the banana export trade was not seriously challenged. In 1910 the UFC absorbed the British firm of Elders & Fyffe, which specialised in the banana trade.

Improvements in transport infrastructure aided the Jamaican economy in the later nineteenth century, but not as fully as they might have done. Building roads was difficult because of many hilly and mountainous areas: only 15 per cent of the island comprised flat areas. By 1882 there were 764 miles of main roads and around 3,000 miles of parochial roads constructed. The surface of many roads left much room for improvement, however, as the smaller roads in particular were frequently neglected. Animal-drawn carts, pack mules and donkeys were widely used to transport goods. In Kingston colourful wooden handcarts with a steering wheel were a common means for vendors to take their wares to market.

Railway development was never as extensive as Jamaica needed. A private Jamaica Railway Company opened a line covering fourteen miles between Kingston and Spanish Town in 1845. It took over three more decades for further railway track to be laid. The Jamaican government bought the Jamaica Railway Company in 1879 and extended the line in the first half of the 1880s from Porus, a village in Manchester parish, to Ewarton, a small town in St Catherine. Further planned extensions to the north coast were shelved because the governor considered that the line would not generate sufficient income. Existing railway lines were sold to a US-based company, the West India Improvement Company, which completed lines to Montego Bay and Port Antonio in 1894. These signs of improvement were short-lived, however, as Jamaican railways fell into debt and receivership by 1898. The Jamaican government assumed ownership of the railways in 1900 but added less than fifty miles of track in the first half of the twentieth century.

Land Reform and the Peasantry

Peasant farming was an important part of Jamaica's social and economic life under Crown Colony government. After 1865 most black Jamaicans worked as smallholders cultivating agricultural land. Between 1860 and 1930 there was a threefold increase in such settlers, who produced between a half and three-quarters of Jamaica's agricultural output. By 1890, 39 per cent of peasants were producing export crops. The prominence of peasant farming was an inevitable consequence of the limited opportunities available for working-class Jamaicans to make a living. It was preferable for many people to take up that option of supplying their own foodstuffs in a village setting rather than drifting away to towns in search of urban work or remaining attached to plantations. For those who chose the latter option, wages for day labourers – 1s. 6d. daily for men and 9d. for women – had barely changed by 1900 from the years immediately after apprenticeship. Small cultivators faced pressures from taxation, high rents and the incursions of the banana industry onto peasant land.

The Jamaican peasantry was composed of many people who had rejected the plantation lifestyle associated with the slavery era. Among the peasantry were tenants, day labourers, those who owned some land and could employ others and those who combined farming with other work such as masonry, blacksmithing and carpentry or manual work on railways, roads and bridge-building. Tenants sometimes leased land for a cash payment and sometimes by providing their labour. Cattle pens were a common source of leased land. Communities of black people were dominated by people who followed these different types of work, undertaking whatever work needed to be done rather than observing regular work hours by the clock and striving for productivity. Gradually between 1865 and 1900 a greater proportion of ordinary Jamaicans drifted away from working on or around plantations to sustaining themselves as peasants on small plots of land. Thus by 1900, in Gad Heuman's words, a major issue in Jamaican life and work 'was no longer the survival of the plantation but the growth of the peasantry'. Peasants were usually not just cultivating land for subsistence purposes; they also produced food surpluses for sale via Jamaica's internal marketing system, with higglers, often but not always women, taking and selling the fruit and vegetables at markets.

Jamaicans, it should be noted, tended not to refer to themselves as peasants but as large farmers, small farmers or cultivators. A contemporary report on Jamaica noted that 'it is a fact noticeable all over the island that in the sugar districts the peasantry are not so prosperous as in those taken up by small settlers, and their general condition is much poorer'. The peasantry, unlike the workers on sugar estates, acquired habits of thrift and regular hard work to support their independence. These people fell into three broad categories: squatters on Crown land; those who leased land; and those who owned title to land.

Though planters and other wealthy members of the white elite played an active role in the land market, most land transactions were carried out on a much more modest scale. By the late 1870s large tracts of land were recovered from squatters who were evicted on the governor's orders. Land seizures were often carried out suddenly and reinforced by physical coercion. Many small cultivators were largely left landless as a result. Reclaimed land reverted to the Crown and was then rented out by the government on seven-year leases. The intention was that peasants should be charged fair rents.

In 1870 Jamaica had 50,000 holdings of less than fifty acres. The growth of such holdings had stalled by the 1880s. By 1900 over half of the Jamaican population lived in peasant-sized freeholds of ten acres or less, which they acquired through purchase, rent, lease or gifts. Few public funds were distributed to help these people. The peasantry lacked the power to influence the government to provide financial support. Despite this handicap, their numbers increased significantly. Thus by 1930 some 185,000 holdings comprised less than fifty acres.

In 1895 Governor Blake introduced a government scheme to sell land to small settlers. Between 1896 and 1910 this provided for the distribution of over 30,000 acres in 211 districts. Much of this land was purchased on credit by smallholders from agricultural loan banks. Unfortunately, this enterprise was abandoned in 1910 because many plots had to be repossessed owing to non-payment during an economic depression in Jamaica during the first decade of the twentieth century – a period when the island was battered by hurricanes, an earthquake and irregular rainfall leading to drought. In addition, some land sold under the scheme lay in hilly or mountain areas where it was difficult to grow crops.

Land settlement schemes were revived by the Jamaican government from 1929 onwards. The intention was to offer derelict properties to small settlers as a means of using the land to stimulate productive labour. Land had to be purchased in interest-free instalments after a deposit of a quarter of the purchase price had been paid. Additional payments were required for surveys and title deeds. Between 1929 and 1938 nearly 34,000 acres of land were allotted under this scheme. A new version of the programme was introduced in 1938, supported by a British government loan of £650,000 to support the development. Between 1938 and 1949 nearly 121,000 acres of land was sold to small settlers. Unfortunately, insufficient attention was paid to the quality and size of the land sold, resulting in too many tiny unproductive plots of under five acres being vended. Thus the land settlement programme was a failure both for small settlers and for the colonial government, which spent an estimated £2 million pounds on the purchase and development of land in Jamaica between 1929 and 1949.

Urban Growth

Kingston, which became the capital of Jamaica in 1872, was easily the largest city on the island throughout the period of Crown Colony government. Its population reached 62,700 by 1921 and, after extensive growth in the interwar years, the Jamaican census of 1943 recorded its population as 109,000. This comprised over half of Jamaica's urban dwellers, and it meant that Kingston was ten times larger than Spanish Town. The growth of Kingston's population resulted partly from natural increase and partly from substantial in-migration, with many people leaving the agricultural workforce by 1900 to take up urban employment. The flow of people into Kingston included women taking up domestic service jobs in the first four decades of the twentieth century. Population also increased significantly in the surrounding St Andrew parish in the same period. Kingston's population was overwhelmingly black. By 1943, 31 per cent of the inhabitants of the town were brown Jamaicans, less than 3 per cent were whites and less than 3 per cent were Indians; the remainder were black town dwellers.

Kingston's physical layout changed and expanded considerably during the period of Crown Colony government. Suburbs such as Fletcher's Town, Kingston

FIGURE 5.2 Ruins of the Myrtle Bank Hotel, 1907. DEA/Biblioteca
Ambrosiana/De Agostini/Getty Images

Gardens, Franklin Town and Passmore Town grew in
the second half of the nineteenth century. However,
Kingston lacked many features of a capital city and
Jamaicans knew 'that its appearance is not calculated to
dazzle or impress the stranger'. An earthquake in 1907
destroyed buildings in the south and east parts of the city.
Hundreds of people were injured or killed. Major rebuild-
ing then took place in the main commercial section of the
city within easy reach of the harbour. It still clung to the
grid pattern that had characterised the initial layout of
Kingston centuries earlier. Public transport, electricity,
water supply and sewage facilities were extended and
improved to keep pace with urban expansion, which proceeded rapidly after the end of the First World War. In
the interwar period Kingston's suburbs extended eastwards to Long Mountain and northwards to Cross

Roads and Half-Way Tree. Central Kingston was a setting for stores, markets and cheaper housing, often little better than hovels, while an elite residential area developed in north-east Kingston. Broadly speaking, West Kingston was more impoverished than East Kingston, though slums were found in both these parts of the city by the 1930s.

Kingston's importance as an export centre declined in the last quarter of the nineteenth century as Jamaica shifted its crop production from sugar to bananas, which were largely exported from Port Antonio to the North American market. On the import side, however, Kingston remained the main Jamaican port for nearly all consumer goods. The city's economic significance largely depended on its central role as a retail marketing centre for provisions, dry goods and groceries, with a concentration of premises in and around King Street. By the 1890s Kingston was also a centre for small manufacturing units for beer, ice, bread, agricultural raw materials, cigars, bay rum (a fragrance used in soap or after-shave lotion), pharmaceutical goods and, especially, tobacco, which had the most employees. These industrial enterprises continued on a modest scale through to the Second World War, boosted by the availability of electrical power after 1924.

Other towns in Jamaica were much smaller settlements than Kingston. Most of them were coastal urban market centres, including Savanna-la-Mar in the south-west and Montego Bay, Falmouth, Ocho Rios and Port Antonio strung along the north coast in picturesque settings. According to the Jamaican census of 1861, none of these towns exceeded just over 4,500 in population and most were considerably less populous. In that year the ports contained over three-quarters of Jamaica's urban population. Of these towns, Port Antonio, as already explained, experienced the most significant growth by the turn of the twentieth century owing to its role as a hub for banana exports.

Inland towns were generally small, with the historic settlement of Spanish Town, the old capital, surviving as a dusty, higgledy-piggledy shanty town with a stagnant population in the late nineteenth century. Spanish Town gave the impression of being deserted, with little commercial activity and more dwellings than people. The central law courts and government administrative buildings were moved in 1872 from Spanish Town to Kingston, the new national capital. Between the 1880s and 1920s, working-class housing was built in Spanish Town, but the dilapidation of many buildings in the town continued. In 1930 Governor Reginald Stubbs referred to Spanish Town as 'a decaying town, too far from Kingston to share its prosperity and too near to have an independent prosperity of its own'. The census of 1943 recorded ten Jamaican towns with a population over 5,000 and five with fewer than that number. The largest urban centres in that year after Kingston, which exceeded the population of the other towns by far, were Spanish Town (14,700) and May Pen (14,100).

Education

Educational provision in Jamaica in the period 1865–1945 largely concentrated on elementary schools. The disestablishment of the Anglican Church in Jamaica under Crown Colony government after 1866 encouraged various Protestant churches to promote the opening of new elementary schools. It also enabled the Jamaican Assembly to reallocate funds previously used for the stipends of Anglican clergy for the construction of new schools. In 1867 Jamaica had 394 elementary schools; the number rose to 962 in 1894–5. Part of this growth arose through the government providing grants for trusted managers and teachers to open new schools in remote areas. Monies were also granted to increase the number of schoolmasters and their salaries. Per capita expenditure on elementary education in Jamaica tripled between 1868 and 1896. An Educational Commission for Jamaica approved regulations for the improvement of conditions for teachers by providing them with superannuation allowances and suitable housing.

Although these were welcome signs of improvement, many difficulties continued to affect elementary educational provision in the first three decades of Crown Colony government. Many schools were small, overcrowded and lacking in sufficient desks for pupils. Less than 10 per cent of these schools were government controlled. The proportion of children attending these schools never exceeded 60 per cent of the total potential intake. A good many parents preferred to keep their children at home to help with day-to-day subsistence chores, and they often took away those attending school on Fridays to accompany them to weekly markets. The fees charged at many establishments (until they were abolished in 1892 and replaced by government grants) often deterred attendance. Despite these problems, elementary schools helped to promote reading and writing reasonably effectively: by 1921 the literacy rate was nearly 80 per cent in Kingston and 64 per cent in St Andrew.

For many years, official opinion was opposed to compulsory schooling. Governor Anthony Musgrave expressed the reasons clearly in 1880: 'Compulsory education is … far too much advanced treatment for the lower strata of population which fifty years ago had not emerged from a debasing state of slavery in which any education at all was forbidden and even marriage was discouraged. What these people first need is all the help that can be afforded to them in moral training, in improving the character of their homes, and their standards of domestic and social life. When these are sufficiently raised there is ample evidence that they will be keenly alive to the advantages of secular education.' Compulsory education was not introduced in Jamaica until 1912, and even then it was only found in Kingston, Falmouth, Lucea and Port Royal.

Elementary schools taught the three r's, covering basic skills in literacy and numeracy, but, in line with Musgrave's views, they included a strong dose of Christian moral education. This was regarded by the white elite as a necessity for 'civilising' the black masses according to the precepts of moral behaviour acceptable to educated English people. Most schools were under the auspices of Christian religious bodies. Prayers and catechism began the daily routine in schools. Positive images of the empire and royalty were also projected in schools to emphasise Jamaica's imperial role and loyalty to the monarch. As was the case elsewhere in British territories, Empire Day was celebrated annually on Queen

Victoria's birthday (24 May) from 1904 onwards. This involved a holiday, parades in and around the school and children waving the Union Jack. Elementary schooling was therefore an important method of seeking to create social stability among the masses and adherence to respectable behaviour.

Secondary schooling was only offered in parts of Jamaica but additional state-funded schools were created to supplement the smaller number of private and church-run establishments. A law of 1879 led to the establishment of a national grammar school called the Jamaica High School. In 1912 this was renamed Jamaica College. Free schools operated throughout the island and in due course these were upgraded to high schools, often funded by charitable trusts. A law of 1892 helped to establish government schools with modest fees and an emphasis upon academic qualifications. These schools followed a rigorous curriculum that enabled Jamaica's middle classes to educate their children for professional jobs mainly in the civil service. Teachers for these schools were often trained at voluntary denominational training colleges. Very little tertiary education was available in Jamaica until after the Second World War. However, in 1882 the Institute for Jamaica, in central Kingston, arranged for Jamaica to become a centre for Cambridge University local examinations.

Another new educational development in late nineteenth-century Jamaica lay in the introduction of schools intended for juvenile delinquents and orphaned children. Jamaica had two privately operated and three state-run industrial schools based in the most populous district, Kingston and St Andrew. A Government

Reformatory and Industrial School was established at Stony Hill. This and similar establishments focused on vocational skills rather than reading, writing and arithmetic. A reward system was put in place to encourage good behaviour. At the end of their training, adolescents were provided with tools and equipment connected to their intended line of employment. The main intended jobs for those who attended these schools were in agricultural work, but boys could also be taught masonry, carpentry, tailoring, baking and blacksmithing.

Educational policy in Jamaica was guided by several commissions which published reports about the educational improvements needed. A report chaired by Judge Charles Lumb in 1898 recommended that an efficient system of primary schools should be established by the state throughout the island before any consideration was given to secondary schools. Underpinning this view was the belief that establishing skills in the first years of formal schooling would prepare children to grow up to achieve professional vocational skills. The Lumb report also recommended that voluntary schools should not receive further state aid; that new schools should be built in areas where there was a lack of educational provision; and that a dual system of government and voluntary schools should be followed. An act of 1912 adopted these provisions, thereby increasing state involvement in schooling. Fines were implemented for caretakers of schools if pupils failed to attend. By the 1930s there was recognition that the government should support more vocational and agricultural education. One important lacuna in Jamaican educational provision before 1945 was the lack of any university on the island to cater for those in search of professional qualifications and the paperwork accreditation for middle-class career advancement.

Spiritual Life

Two main strands dominated the spiritual life of Jamaicans in the late nineteenth and early twentieth centuries: the long-standing customs and beliefs of the black masses, emanating originally as cosmologies from west Africa, and the growing impact of Christianity, which had begun through missionary efforts during the slavery era and had continued thereafter. Both of these strands played an important role in the religious life of Jamaica in the Victorian period and beyond. Christianity did not entirely replace magical and customary beliefs, as the white minority hoped would transpire, but neither did superstitious beliefs persist to the extent that Christianity was an irrelevance.

One of the bedrocks of spiritual life among black Jamaicans was the persistence of obeahism. Obeah practitioners, who had been present in Jamaica for two centuries by 1865, used witchcraft, magic and sorcery to cast spells to control the connection between a spirit world and everyday life. Obeahism could be deployed benignly to cure illness through herbal remedies, but it could also be used as an act of revenge. Obeah practitioners, often elderly men, were revered among Jamaica's black masses but also feared because of the extent of their powers. An unusual collection of objects was corralled together for the practice of obeah, including a bottle with a turkey or cock's feathers placed inside along with parrots' beaks, blood drops, coffin nails and empty eggshells.

Besides obeahism, Afro-Creole Jamaicans often believed in duppies, the presence of an evil eye and the revivalist beliefs of myalism, a form of witchcraft similar to obeahism that involved frantic dancing. Duppies were spirits or apparitions that could assume other forms, such as an animal or a children's doll, that haunted Jamaica after nightfall. They were shadows of the dead rather than a representation of their souls. They could exercise wrath against evil-doers, and were greatly feared by the superstitious. Many ordinary Jamaicans wore charms to protect themselves against the influence of duppies. The evil eye could bring misfortune to anyone who came under its spell. An account of Jamaica from the early 1870s cited the case of a woman entering a magistrate's court with 'a piece of pink ribbon tied to one arm and piece of blue on the other to ward off its malign influence'. There were further folk beliefs connected with Anancy spiders or sudden, unexpected events that were portents of misfortune. Myalism was generally, though not exclusively, opposed to obeahism. Myal practitioners staged an elaborate ceremony in which they attempted to catch the shadow of victims; they applied herbal remedies for illness; and they tried to overturn the spells cast by obeah men.

Revival worship was an important component of Afro-Creole beliefs and practices, with an emphasis on spirit possession. People would assemble in a circle to banish spirits, chanting and murmuring in groups and behaving as if they were possessed by the spirit. These occasions combined superstitious elements from long-held folk beliefs with fragments of

FIGURE 5.3 Native religious celebration. DEA/Biblioteca
Ambrosiana/De Agostini/Getty Images

Christianity that invoked the presence of the Holy
Ghost. A witness to the frenzy of a revival ceremony
was quoted in the *Daily Gleaner* in 1904 as follows:
'They were yelling, wheeling round, and striking
against one another in a frightful manner ... One
young man was beating himself and spinning about,
till he fell down in convulsions. Afterwards, several
men and women went reeling and staggering about,
moving and striking themselves. All this they did when
possessed by "the spirit".'

Parallel to the expression of Afro-Creole beliefs in
Jamaica was the extension and consolidation of
Christianity. Many slaves had been converted to
Christianity generations before by missionaries who pros-
elytised the gospels. By the late nineteenth century, regular Christian worship had penetrated into many Jamaican
communities in Anglican and Roman Catholic churches;

in Methodist, Baptist, Presbyterian and Quaker congregations; and in new evangelical groups including the Plymouth Brethren, Seventh Day Adventists and the Church of God (or Pentecostal Church). The disestablishment of the Anglican Church in Jamaica in June 1870 led to the ordination of a handful of black Jamaican deacons, but only five black Anglican clergy were ordained in Jamaica before 1904. Equality among the races was slow to emerge in Anglican circles in Jamaica. A central objective of white officialdom in Jamaica by the later nineteenth century was to civilise the black masses. This was considered achievable by spreading Christianity in an orderly, polite, decent way to overcome supposedly barbaric Afro-Creole beliefs already described.

Spreading Christianity as a vehicle for reducing the attachment of the black masses to customary beliefs, however, was only partially achieved. Christian churches, chapels and ministers certainly played their part in seeking this goal. They operated Sunday schools for children, convened mid-week Bible meetings and emphasised a cohesive community spirit in harvest ceremonies. The Roman Catholic Church celebrated feast and saint days. The Baptists promoted adult baptism and the Methodists held regular love-feasts where hymns, prayers and readings from Scripture combined to promote a warm Christian fellowship. Enos Nuttall, the Anglican bishop of Jamaica between 1880 and his death in 1916, linked Christian worship to uplifting the educational and moral outlook of Jamaicans. A somewhat rosy picture of the effect of Christianity on Jamaicans was common in many contemporary publications. In a typical example, a Presbyterian missionary meeting in 1882 argued that 'through the labours of the missionaries sent out by other Churches as well as our own, the dark land of Jamaica has become a land of light. The island now abounds in churches and schools, the Sabbath day is ... well observed.'

Nevertheless, many superstitious beliefs persisted in Jamaica and attempts to suppress them by white official-dom were only partially successful. Obeahism was a major target for eradication. In 1898 the fine for consulting an obeahman was increased from £2 to £10 and obeahism became an offence under the vagrancy law. An Obeah and Myalism Act Amendment Law of 1892 gave magistrates the authority to bring obeah cases to court for trial. Those found guilty could be flogged as a punishment. Further laws were passed between 1898 and 1903 to rid Jamaica of obeah, but these had limited effect. Obeahmen continued to be widely consulted throughout Jamaica at the turn of the twentieth century. They were known to be crafty practitioners of their skills. Thus the Reverend Abraham Emerick noted that 'you will not be able to understand obi-ism and account for the influences of the obeahman unless you consider obi-ism as a religion and the obi-man as a priest. The real genuine obi-man is not often trapped, he is too cunning for that.'

Another significant concern for the island's authorities lay in public disturbances created by revivalist preaching. The Roman Catholic Church was particularly worried about the best-known revivalist preacher Alexander Bedward. Ordained as an elder in the Jamaica Baptist Free Church in 1876, he undertook healing ceremonies in which he presented himself as a prophet performing miracles. Though he believed in the New Testament and the power of the Holy Spirit, Bedward pursued healing practices and medical treatments that lay outside the precepts of formal church practices. The white authorities were worried about the mass following he attracted and his strange public behaviour, which stirred up strong emotions among his supporters, the Bedwardites. He spoke openly about white oppression and the evils of colonialism, arguing that the time had arrived when the black wall should knock down the white wall in Jamaica. 'Hell will be your position if you do not rise up and crush the white man,' Bedward told his followers in the 1890s.

Regarded by the white elite as someone opposed to the 'anglicisation' of Jamaican religious practice, Bedward was put on trial twice (in 1895 and 1921) and, on both occasions, he was acquitted on grounds of insanity and committed to a lunatic asylum. In between his incarcerations in the institution, he based himself near the Hope River, where he promised physical and spiritual healing to the poorest sections of Jamaicans. Bedward attracted a large following. His second term in a lunatic asylum came after he failed to ascend to Heaven and was accused of being mentally ill. Whether he was actually suffering from insanity is unknown: it was certainly convenient for the white authorities to confine him away from his followers. Bedward died in 1930.

Attempting to suppress obeahism and revivalist healers proved an impossible task. The impact of these Afro-Creole beliefs persisted into modern Jamaican life, became interwoven with aspects of Christianity and assumed a particular importance in fostering a cultural nationalism that in the 1930s began to find resonance in the political sphere. As Brian L. Moore and Michele

A. Johnson have explained, Afro-Christianity in Jamaica was 'a positive, creative expression of Afro-creole cultural self-determination that sought to establish, and in large measure succeeded in establishing, its independence of the religo-cultural power structure ... Through Revival, Afro-Jamaicans made it strikingly clear that on matters of faith they were not prepared to be dictated to; they were determined to decide for themselves what was appropriate and suitable for them.'

Jamaica and the First World War

Jamaica itself was not threatened by the First World War, which did not penetrate into the Caribbean, but it took measures to increase its defences during the conflict. The governor, Brigadier General William Manning, allocated £10,000 for the island's defence and enacted laws to establish a Jamaica Volunteer Defence Force to combine with the police, who were instructed to provide military support, in case of invasion. Three units made up the volunteer force, the largest of which was the Jamaica Reserve Regiment, which recruited 1,100 volunteers by the end of 1915. These forces remained in Jamaica and were not deployed overseas.

The outbreak of the First World War brought a prompt response from the governor, who on 1 September sent a telegram declaring that 'the people of Jamaica unanimously desire to contribute to the Imperial Government in some way towards the expenses of the war other than its own local defence'. This patriotic message of support for the mother country underscored Jamaica's continuing role in the British Empire and the

fact that Jamaicans were constitutionally British subjects. In 1915 King George V asked for contributions
to the allied war effort from the peoples of the British
Empire, and this was a successful plea. The Jamaican
government sought to assist the war effort by offering
supplies to Britain and the allied forces and by organising recruitment of men to undertake war service. The
supplies consisted of produce such as oranges and
grapefruit and over £50,000 worth of sugar. Cigarettes
were provided for troops on the front line. A law passed
in June 1917 required all British subjects in Jamaica
aged between 18 and 41 to be eligible for military
service, though no attempt was made to introduce
conscription.

A corps known as the British West Indies Regiment
(BWIR), including Jamaicans and fellow people from the
Caribbean, was formed in 1915. Significant numbers of
peasants and poor labourers volunteered to join these
units. Some recruits joined as an act of imperial solidarity
because they wanted to support the British war effort
against Germany and its allies. Attachment to the monarchy and to the symbol of the Union Jack flag was demonstrated. But there were other motives, too. Some
enlistees were worried that a British military defeat
would lead to the reintroduction of slavery in the
Caribbean. A fair amount of propaganda, found in
Jamaican newspapers during the war, propagated the
notion of Britain as the guarantor of emancipation for
Jamaicans against the barbarism of the Germans.
Jamaicans were encouraged, in line with this view, to
take an active role in safeguarding their liberty by partici-
pating in the allied military action. The Universal Negro

Improvement Association (UNIA) endorsed this support for the monarch and empire. The Jamaican press praised the recruitment of Indian troops for the British army's efforts in the war, and called for Jamaicans to follow likewise to demonstrate their support for the British Empire.

British military officialdom in Jamaica had preferences for more educated, skilled Jamaicans to enlist for the armed forces during the war. Thus Brigadier L. S. Blackden, commander of local forces in Jamaica, complained that many volunteers were an 'undersized, ragged, barefooted set of fellows, who came forward probably to get a meal'. Later he tried hard to prevent ordinary Jamaicans from volunteering for the war effort but hoped to persuade more highly skilled Jamaicans to enlist. He was influenced in his thinking by the consideration that the mental abilities of recruits would be needed in the BWIR as much as physical strength and bravery in combat.

The BWIR was an infantry regiment, but British commanders often regarded it as an inferior colonial unit that should be kept away from front-line fighting. A number of white British military officers considered that black men from the Caribbean lacked sufficient rationality and self-discipline to fight alongside British regiments. Racist views, endorsing the superiority of white troops and treating West Indian recruits as slow-witted and childlike, were expressed. An opposite point of view underlay some of these concerns; namely, that if West Indians and other non-white recruits were placed in the immediate line of fire, they might outperform regular British soldiers.

Despite these condescending views, the BWIR did participate bravely in fighting in Italy, Egypt, Palestine, Jordan and Tanganyika; and it was deployed in the liberation of the Holy Land from the Ottoman Empire, an ally of Germany. BWIR troops were not allowed to mix with British regular army personnel because it was believed in official circles that the presence of non-white soldiers would undermine the racial hierarchy of the British Empire. Besides fighting, Jamaican and other members of the BWIR were deployed as labourers supporting road and railway building, digging trenches, unloading trains and ships and carrying supplies to ammunition dumps. However, the West Indian auxiliaries in the BWIR were often subject to harsh discipline, poor pay and inferior medical facilities.

Immediately after the Armistice in November 1918 British troops were awarded a pay rise but this was not extended to the BWIR. A four-day mutiny ensued among BWIR troops stationed in Taranto, Italy. After demobilisation Jamaican members of the BWIR returned home to find themselves either jobless or in straitened economic circumstances – poor rewards for their contribution to the allied war effort. Former BWIR participants were fully aware of the racial injustices that permeated their lives as they settled down to peacetime. Disturbances occurred in Kingston where, on 18 July 1919, a riot broke out in which a crowd including ex-servicemen and seamen attacked some white sailors and civilians. Sailors and guards from the BWIR were deployed to calm down proceedings. A further outbreak of rioting by disgruntled ex-servicemen occurred in Kingston in October 1919. They claimed they had faced discrimination on class and racial grounds. The disturbances were put down, but again they had exposed the inequality of black Jamaicans in a British colony.

Marcus Garvey and Garveyism

Marcus Garvey (1887–1940) was the most notable individual to promote ideas for the advancement of ordinary Jamaicans and the most influential political thinker active in Jamaica in the quarter century after the outbreak of the First Word War. Brought up in St Ann parish, Garvey worked in the printing trade in Kingston as a young man but travelled widely in England and Central America in the years leading up to 1914. His early mentor in Jamaica was Robert Love, whose ideas and activities have been discussed above. But whereas Love's career was confined mainly to Jamaica, Garvey and his followers established an international out-reach, having a particular impact on the United States, the Caribbean, Central America and Britain. Garvey and Garveyism by the 1920s and 1930s achieved greater Jamaican and international impact than any other individual or movement concerned with the progress of the mass of black people. The influence of Garveyism on radical think-ing still resonates among African-American people today.

Garvey's upbringing in rural Jamaica and his travels in Central America enabled him to witness at first hand the subjugation and plight of working-class black workers on plantations who lacked political organisation and effective political leadership. The main problem, in his view, was that these people had failed to acknowledge the full potential of their own race; they were too embedded socially, economic-ally and politically to living under white dominance and imperial control. As Rupert Lewis has put it, most

FIGURE 5.4 Marcus Garvey. New York Daily News Archive/Getty Images

Jamaicans regarded Britain as the 'mother country' and failed to adopt 'an Afro-centric posture in a Euro-centric Jamaica'. Garvey challenged this positioning of black Jamaicans within a paternalist, hierarchical Anglosphere which privileged white people over blacks in terms of race and class. Garvey advocated via poetry, plays, extensive journalism and frequent rousing speeches the notion of black racial pride and Pan-African Nationalism, which was concerned with the exploitation of peoples of African descent by white people throughout the Americas.

Garvey's political thinking was based on the primacy of race and race discrimination. He was a black nationalist who argued for the promotion of black self-reliance and black nationhood. He promoted black women as black Madonnas and mothers of the race.

Self-educated but widely read and influenced by Biblical precepts, Garvey highlighted, more than any Jamaican before him, the plight of peoples of African descent throughout the world. In one Easter Day lay sermon he used Christ's resurrection as an example for the black person's resurrection. He hoped that eventually his influence would persuade such people to return to their African homeland, where they could agitate for an end to colonial rule. It was as though Garvey regarded blacks returning to Africa as reverting to a prelapsarian life. Garvey himself had an ambition to become president of a one-party state in a united Africa.

To organise his followers, Garvey established his UNIA in Kingston in 1914. Its motto was 'One God! One Aim! One Destiny!' Over the next two years this association was active in social welfare, with followers visiting the sick in hospital, feeding the poor and organising fund-raising events to promote assistance for working-class black Jamaicans. Though criticised about the use of the word 'Negro' in the title of the UNIA on the grounds that it was demeaning, Garvey chose it deliberately as a broad term to encompass people of African descent throughout the world. He sought financial support from educated white people in Jamaica, securing funds from the island's governor; but he had little to say to brown Jamaicans, who shied away from him as too much of a self-promoter.

Though the UNIA attracted many followers, Garvey thought it would flourish better in a larger setting so he relocated to New York in 1916 and spent the next eleven years in the United States. Based in Harlem,

New York, Garvey attracted an even greater number of followers, many of whom were given uniforms in which they paraded the streets with Garvey himself acting as a leader dressed in regimental uniform. On the larger stage of New York City, Garvey continued his speeches and organised the Black Star Line, an international steamship firm, as the courier for his message to the wider world. This steamship company was intended to convey African-American passengers to a new homeland in Liberia, west Africa. However, it was a short-lived enterprise that ended in 1922.

Garvey began publishing his weekly *Negro World* newspaper in New York in 1918. He travelled throughout the United States, giving speeches and meeting African-American political activists. Though he gained extensive publicity while living in the United States, he was never accepted by black intellectuals such as W. E. B. Du Bois, who thought Garvey the showman reeked of charlatanism. Dressing up in scarlet robes with a feathered hat and gold epaulettes in front of his 'Negro Court' in Harlem, Garvey invited ridicule for his grandiose public appearances. Despite this, however, the UNIA expanded its influence in the 1920s to embrace over 1,200 branches in forty countries. Garvey himself was quarrelsome and fell foul of the American authorities. He courted controversy by attacking Jews and holding meetings with the Ku Klux Klan, with whom he had a shared interest in racial separation. After a three-year prison sentence in the United States for fraud linked to his selling of the Black Star Line's stock, he was deported to Jamaica.

Between 1927 and 1935 Garvey was based once again in his home island, where he continued to promote his political vision. The headquarters of the UNIA followed Garvey back to Jamaica. Garvey brought racial issues to the forefront of political discourse in Jamaica at a time when other protesters avoided singling out race as a major issue for debate. He was actively involved in the Jamaica Workers and Labourers Association, initiated in 1930. This organisation laid the ground for the modern trade union movement in the Caribbean. Fully aware of the historic plight of black workers, Garvey nevertheless found there was still a low level of racial consciousness in Jamaica. 'The labouring classes of Jamaica have never had anything to be loyal about', he wrote, adding 'they have been among the most brutally oppressed peoples of the British Empire. The employer has no sympathy for the poorer classes ... The classes in the island are visibly drawn. The man with money is on the top, and the man without can easily be seen as the unfortunate human being that he is. Money and colour count for more than anything else.' Garvey looked forward to a day when people with African ancestry could proudly enjoy full recognition, status and self-direction. He continued to write regularly in newspapers but failed in his attempt to secure a seat on Jamaica's Legislative Council.

Garvey's oratorical skills easily attracted large audiences wherever and whenever he made speeches, but his outspoken demagoguery won both admirers and detractors. His emphasis on the racial unity of African-Americans and his opposition to socialism set him apart from other black radical agitators in the 1920s. Garvey was loose-tongued in his derogatory comments about black

Jamaicans being lazy, careless and backward. Articles supporting Garvey's ideals and attacking his divisive comments appeared in newspapers, notably in the *Jamaica Gleaner*. Controversy surrounded nearly every action taken by Garvey. He bickered with rivals; his private life was chaotic; and he was denounced by some fellow Jamaicans for his extreme anti-white prejudice. His pronouncements against what he believed was a corrupt judiciary led to a three-month jail sentence in a Spanish Town prison.

During the years in Jamaica between 1927 and 1935, Garvey promoted the arts and took an active interest in music, art, poetry and sculpture as they related to black people. He developed Edelweiss Park, Cross Roads, Kingston, as a major cultural centre for musical and dance performance. This became the new headquarters of the UNIA in Jamaica. Regular Sunday night meetings were held there that combined religious services, cultural activity and political speeches and debate. On occasions this was the venue for 'Gala nights' that emphasised a particular cultural activity relevant to black Jamaicans. In these activities, Garvey emphasised the theme of race pride, something he had written about explicitly many years earlier when he called upon blacks to 'take on the toga of race pride, and throw off the brand of ignominy which has kept you back for so many centuries. Dash asunder the petty prejudices within your fold; set at defiance the scornful designation of "nigger" uttered even by yourselves, and be a Negro in the light of the Pharaohs of Egypt, Simons of Cyrene, Hannibals of Carthage, L'Ouvertures and Dessalines of Haiti ... who have made and are making history for the race.'

In September 1934 a Permanent Jamaica Development
Convention was convened in Kingston. This called for
a £10 million loan to be raised for the development of the
island. Garvey made notable contributions to the discussions at the convention, and was the chairman of
a deputation that submitted a memorandum to the governor of Jamaica requesting financial and other assistance
for the black masses who 'are still backward, miserable and
unhappy, whilst just a small number of the population are
able to enjoy the benefits ... of this colony from an economic, social and higher cultural educational point of
view'. The memorandum identified the need for
a university in Jamaica to train people for the professions,
a land settlement scheme for peasants to secure cultivable
land, a national steamship line to aid producers of exports,
a central industrial bank, better hospital facilities and the
development of a tourism strategy. These constructive
ideas had no immediate effect but they gradually bore
fruit in Jamaica in later generations.

Beset by financial difficulties in the 1930s, Garvey, who
never appears to have held down a job for any length of
time, sold off Edelweiss Park and decided to leave Jamaica
permanently. He migrated to live in London in 1937 on
the eve of the most serious labour disturbances in modern
Jamaica, telling a friend he 'left Jamaica a broken man,
broken in spirit, broken in health and broken in pocket ...
and I will never, never, never go back'. A humble Jamaican
called St William Grant tried to keep Garveyism going
through frequent addresses at open-air public platforms in
Kingston, arguing that black Jamaicans should strive to
achieve equality with white people. Garvey's political exile
in Britain was fairly brief. He tried to re-establish the

UNIA in London, but its finances were stretched. In 1940 he had two strokes and died. Garvey had led a turbulent life in which he had crossed swords with many people, but his distinctive ideas and emphasis on black nationalism have had an enduring influence on Jamaica since his death. In 1964 his remains were brought back from London to Jamaica, where he was commemorated as a national hero.

Rastafarianism

The emergence of Rastafarianism as a socio-religious movement was an important development in Jamaica in the 1930s. Influenced by Garvey's Pan-African beliefs and his work for the UNIA and by religious revivalism, Rastafarianism was created in Jamaica after the coronation of the Ethiopian emperor Haile Selassie 1 in 1930. The movement was named after Selassie's original name – Ras Tafari Makonnen. Selassie was regarded by his followers as divine, a black king and human representation of the second coming of Christ. Jamaican followers of Selassie viewed him as a symbol of redemption for the black people of Africa. Rastafarians believed that following Selassie would release them from the colonial world of racial inequality, which they referred to as Babylon, to a return to Ethiopia, characterised as Zion. This was therefore a manifestation of the back-to-Africa movement favoured by Garveyism and Pan-Africanism and a challenge to the unequal social structure of Jamaican society. Rastafarianism remained largely confined to Jamaica until 1945.

Notions of Selassie as a saviour for ordinary Jamaicans were spread rapidly by preachers throughout Kingston in the 1930s. Leonard Howell, a former member of the UNIA, was the leading figure in this initial circulation of Rastafarian ideas. He promoted the idea of black racial identity and called for ordinary Jamaicans to rise up against white oppression. Believing himself to be the personal emissary in Jamaica of Selassie, he preached charismatically among Jamaica's poor. Howell believed in the psychological repatriation of Jamaicans to Ethiopia rather than in an actual movement back to Africa. His arguments supporting Selassie as the black Messiah and his message of hatred towards the Jamaican government and the colonial establishment led to his arrest and imprisonment on charges of sedition in 1934.

During the trial, attempts were made to discredit Howell as a figure of ridicule. The *Daily Gleaner* reported 'there was a good deal of mirth provoked by the fanatic utterances of a man, born in Jamaica, who from beginning to end propounded the doctrine that Ethiopia will rule the world'. Later, after Howell's release he was confined in the same lunatic asylum that had housed the revivalist Bedward and certified as insane. After being freed from incarceration, he founded the Ethiopian Salvation Society in 1939 and the first Rastafarian community in Jamaica, known as Pinnacle, on a hilltop location at Sligoville, St Catherine parish, in 1940. This operated mainly in isolation, as a reclusive Maroon-like commune, financed mainly by selling marijuana. Further Rastafarian communities were established in Jamaica in its wake. The total number of Rastafarians was relatively small – about 1,600 people according to a survey of 1958 – but they had an important impact on Jamaican life.

FIGURE 5.5   Rastafarians. Phil Clarke Hill/In Pictures/Getty Images

Rastafarianism was primarily a lifestyle that could be regarded either as a cult or as a new departure in the history of the Jamaican peasantry. Rastas, as the movement's followers were known, refused to undertake wage labour but lived either on abandoned land or in urban slums where they practised a subsistence life supported by their cultivation of marijuana and carving of artefacts. Taking cannabis in group sessions was a central practice for Rastafarians. It was thought to provide a dream-like spiritual sustenance for their beliefs as well as a challenge to the authorities. Rastafarians followed a distinctive lifestyle where they ate vegetarian (often vegan) diets, wore both head and facial hair, and held regular prayer services and all-night drumming sessions. From the early 1950s Rastafarians wore dreadlocks that visually made them appear as outcasts.

Rastafarians pursued an Afro-centric ideology, mainly among poor peasants, that set them apart from mainstream society; indeed, the drumming was seen as a connection to their African roots. Rastafarians felt an affinity with the African continent, especially with the independent nations of Ethiopia and Liberia, and many talked about migration there. They were patriarchal in their social practice: women were expected to submit to male authority. They dressed in a distinctive way, wearing hats and clothes in the colours of red, green, gold and black. Many people in Jamaica regarded Rastafarians as the flotsam and jetsam of society, living in squalid conditions, and sometimes giving the impression of being mentally unhinged.

Rastafarianism was an implicit rejection of the existing unequal social structure that had long prevailed in Jamaica. The authorities regarded it as a destabilising aberration and a challenge to law and order through its extensive use of marijuana, classified as a 'noxious weed' rather than as a herbal source of healing. Since 1924 marijuana had been an illegal substance in British colonies and its harvesting at Pinnacle provided a good excuse for the attention of the police. Howell and his followers became an outspoken nuisance for the Jamaican authorities. They emerged from their self-imposed isolation to raid the land of nearby peasants. Armed police raids took place on the Pinnacle in 1941 after complaints were made about members of the commune exercising violence against their neighbours. The police shut down the community as a communist experiment. Howell was arrested again on a charge of assault, tried for sedition and imprisoned after the raid. When he was freed in 1943, he returned to the Pinnacle and re-established it as a Rastafarian community.

Rastafarianism was limited, however, as a challenge to Jamaica's social stability in the 1930s and early 1940s even though it had a strong resonance among ordinary Jamaicans and emphasised a sense of alienation from the establishment. Rastafarianism had no economic strategy that could be followed by the island's poor. Nor did it join up with the extensive labour movement that was burgeoning in Jamaica amid the Great Depression of the 1930s. Thus Howell had no real political power beyond his commune at the Pinnacle, and he posed no particular threat to Jamaican society as a whole. However, Rastafarianism was a potential threat to Jamaica's emerging political parties and Alexander Bustamante, a leading Jamaican labour union spokesman at the time, warned the police that Howell's activities should be investigated and monitored as a threat to the island's peace.

The Great Depression and Labour Protests in the 1930s

Labour protest was a common phenomenon in Jamaica during the 1930s. The worldwide economic depression after the Wall Street crash of 1929 had an international effect on unemployment as hard times struck many countries. Falling sugar prices, declining wages and returning migrants from the United States and Central America all had a deleterious effect on ordinary Jamaicans' living standards. Economic conditions were deteriorating on an annual basis. Numerous Caribbean islands experienced unrest from 1934 onwards as ordinary people took to the streets to protest about their lack of work opportunities. Violent demonstrations occurred in Trinidad, St Kitts, Barbados and British Guiana. In Jamaica poor wages for the majority of people and high unemployment had become a perennial difficulty for ordinary people. Even those in work were miserably rewarded: in 1935, 92 per cent of employed people in Jamaica earned less than 25 shillings per week.

According to the Jamaican census of 1943, 484,300 people out of 732,675 in the workforce aged between 15 and 64 were in employment while 250,000 were not. The persisting racial divisions in Jamaican society and the lack of a universal franchise made it difficult for Jamaicans to overturn this situation. The right to vote was based on payment of taxes. Miss B recalled that 'People who pay taxes could vote. For at dem time, I know my father at the time couldn't pay taxes. For you had to pay over one pound before you could vote. That pound was a whole heap of money. For if you have land from here to ah don't know where, and your taxes was just a pound, you can't vote, no care how much land.'

Jamaica's first trade union legislation was introduced in 1919 before any other British Caribbean colonies had similar laws; but it had little immediate effect on working relations and conditions. Many Jamaicans worked in scattered small enterprises or as independent craft workers, and there was a high rate of labour turnover, making solidarity over their treatment by employers difficult to achieve. Within two decades, however, unionism began to transform political discourse on the island. Labour trade unions emerged rapidly along with charismatic, effective leaders in protests about inadequate work opportunities in

the demonstrations of 1937–8 in Jamaica. It is no exaggeration to suggest that these years witnessed the emergence
of class consciousness among Jamaicans, who combined
collectively as never before.

The two main leaders to emerge during the turbulent
political atmosphere of the late 1930s were Alexander
Bustamante and Norman Manley, brown Jamaicans and
cousins. Bustamante had lived in Spain, Cuba, Central
America, New York City and other places before
returning to Jamaica in 1934, where he worked as
a usurer for low-income people. He founded seven
trade unions in 1938. Manley was a British-educated
barrister who became involved in politics during the
labour struggles of the late 1930s. Bustamante and
Manley were charismatic speakers, effective organisers
and dedicated to the political advancement of Jamaicans
and to assisting the underprivileged. Bustamante was
initially treated with suspicion by many black
Jamaicans because of the psychological barrier between
brown and black Jamaicans. However, he overcame this
difficulty by showing compassion and concern for
impoverished Jamaicans. He became 'the only brown
man who talked the language of the exploited, down-
trodden black people of Jamaica'.

Bustamante, Manley and their supporters were keenly
aware that major improvements to the franchise were
needed in an unrepresentative political system. They
also realised that organisations and institutions to promote the welfare of Jamaicans were sorely lacking and
that there was an absence of political parties. These
would need to be developed rapidly. The social, economic and political circumstances of Jamaica were such

FIGURE 5.6 Norman Manley. Hulton Deutsch/Corbis Historical/ Getty Images

that it was inconceivable that a conservative or liberal political party would emerge because the great majority of Jamaicans had so little capital to preserve. It was also clear that, despite a modestly rising public sector, Jamaica lacked the full range of welfare policies needed to support an impoverished population. Thus it was clear that any new political parties would be left-of-centre groupings committed to state intervention.

Social and economic deprivation was the norm for most Jamaicans by the late 1930s. Ken Hill, a prominent political organiser, recalled that 'there were few jobs. There was a cesspool of unemployment. People were organizing marches in Kingston to be admitted to the prisons in order to get food. Life was intolerable. Life was a drudge, was drudgery. Women were getting 9d. per day. Domestic servants were getting 5/- per week. The country was 66 and two-thirds per cent illiterate up to 1938 ... Life wasn't worth living. Jamaica was flat on her back. She had no hope before 1938. The fact is that there was only limited suffrage, so that a majority of the people did not count.' These problems caused much uneasiness among the Jamaican working classes but there were no riots before 1938.

The disturbances in Jamaica in 1938 often began with relatively ordinary grievances such as opposition to wage reductions, false rumours of pay increases, competition from workers entering localities from other places in search of work and furloughing of workers. Attacks were made on sugar estates, burning cane and damaging property. Disturbances spread to towns where clashes with police occurred, people were injured and there was bloodshed. Shops were looted, private houses broken into in search of food and money, and estate offices robbed. Mobs roamed the streets and public order collapsed in numerous communities. Jamaica had witnessed protests and demonstrations before, but the scale of the opposition throughout the island now reached an unprecedented level of sustained ferocity against the exploitation of working-class labourers in both rural and urban settings.

Trouble started early in 1938, for on 5 January an estimated 1,400 people, armed with sticks and machetes, prevented carts and wagons entering or leaving estates in St Thomas parish after workers had been offered reduced payments for gathering the sugar cane harvest. There were 745 reported arrests in Jamaica. In April a violent strike broke out on Frome sugar estate in Westmoreland after the Tate & Lyle sugar company tried to consolidate its interests there into larger holdings. To carry out the changes, jobs had been advertised but the workers recruited found their pay was cut from the advertised level and their accommodation was inadequate. A large police contingent was despatched from Kingston to patrol the property and keep order. However, four people were killed, thirteen ended up in hospital and 105 were imprisoned. Mob action in rural areas continued into the first half of June and the police and special constables only contained it with difficulty. The ferocity of the protests was such that it was remarkable that the death rate in this phase of the protest only amounted to eight people.

The location of the strikes then shifted to Kingston, where 20 per cent of the island's population lived. In May dock workers and banana loaders began to protest, tensions rose on the street, a hostile mob of thousands gathered in public spaces, and 'disorder . . . became general and the Police were insufficient in numbers to control the situation. Persons of all classes going to business were set upon, public property was destroyed, streets blocked and tramcars attacked.' This was a revolt of the dispossessed against the seemingly unshifting divisions in the social fabric in which black workers could only register their dissatisfaction effectively through public resistance. The governor of Jamaica called in the troops to quell the disturbances.

Disorder continued in Kingston until mid-June 1938. Crowds threw sticks and stones at the police. Bustamante and his supporters tried to address a meeting but were prevented from doing so by the police, who were well aware of Bustamante's capacity to unleash incendiary rhetoric. Manley acted promptly to represent the striking dock workers in negotiations with their employers, acting as a mediator. He negotiated with the government to settle pay rates for dock workers. On 28 May Bustamante and Manley jointly addressed the protesters with details of the pay settlement, which the labourers accepted and the strike ended. This was one of the first occasions when Bustamante and Manley acted as an effective team.

The strikes and disturbances of 1938 reflected a long-simmering discontent about the lack of racial harmony that had been gathering ever since the days of slavery. They represented the first major public intervention about the systemic problems of race, class, power and employment opportunities since the emergence of Crown Colony government in 1866. O. E. Anderson, then the mayor of Kingston, acknowledged this in remarking that 'we have been behaving like the ostrich, holding our heads and pretending that there is no discrimination. We have been adopting just the attitude that those whose interests are not identical with our own would have us adopt and any attempt to break away from that will arouse universal opposition.'

The Labour Rebellion of 1938 prompted Jamaica's government to usher in a raft of labour legislation. Between 1938 and 1941 the following legislation was passed: a Minimum Wage Law; a Trade Union Law to permit peaceful picketing; a Workmen's Compensation Law; a Slum Clearance and Housing Law; a Trades Disputes Law; a Factories Law; a Master and Servants Law; a Recruiting of Workers Law; a Children and Young Persons Law; a Dock Workers (Protection against Accidents) Law; an Employment of Women Law; and a Nurses Registration Law. These statutes constituted a new labour code for Jamaicans. Many of them were long overdue. There is little doubt that the sheer force of the strikes and demonstrations throughout the island had rattled the authorities, who realised that solutions to long-standing grievances were necessary.

The British government also played a role in better social welfare provision for Jamaica. Alarmed by the violence of 1938 in Jamaica and protests elsewhere in the West Indies, Britain established the West India Royal Commission (1938), often called the Moyne Commission after its chairman 1st Baron Moyne, to investigate the problems and to propose solutions. Members of the commission visited Jamaica in late 1938, where they were appalled by the shabby, often insanitary housing conditions and poor employment prospects for the majority of the population. While the Second World War continued, the commission did not issue its full report until 1945 because the British government was worried about the neglect it would reveal; but its early findings had helped to shape the Colonial Development and Welfare Act (1940). Recommending health and education improvements, the Commission provided £1 million to support Britain's West Indian colonies over the next twenty years.

Local initiatives were vital for changes to occur. To ensure new laws were put into practice, employees needed trade union organisation and leadership. Political parties to represent the mass of the people were also required. New unions and political organisations were established rapidly in 1937–9. They included the Jamaica Workers and Tradesmen Union, the island's first modern trade union; the Jamaica Welfare League, which promoted the provision of social services and rural development; and the National Reform Association, which was devoted to political reform. Bustamante founded various trade unions, which all bore his name. The largest was the Bustamante Industrial Trade Union (BITU), founded in 1939, whose members accounted for over three-quarters of Jamaica's organised labour force by 1945. By then Jamaica had twenty-seven active trade unions, most of them small scale. Most of these organisations became permanently embedded in Jamaican social and political life, leading to increased bargaining between employers and workers over pay, work conditions and employment contracts. The autonomous action of demonstrators in Jamaica in the late 1930s, and the rise in trade unionism and political parties, meant that politics would become transformed rapidly, with no return to the previous status quo.

Manley founded the People's National Party (PNP) in September 1938. He hoped it would be the focal point for the coordination of national consciousness in Jamaica and spoke at its inauguration about the challenges it faced: 'As I see it today there is one straight choice before Jamaica. Either make up our minds to go back to crown colony government and have nothing to do with our government at all, either be shepherded people, benevolently shepherded in the interests of everybody, with at its highest ideal the contentment of the country; or have your voice and face the hard road of political organisation, facing the hard road of discipline, developing your own capacities, your own powers and leadership and your own people to the stage where they are capable of administering their own affairs. And this is not an issue that should be postponed or can be postponed into the indefinite future ...

This year coincides with the centenary of our emancipation, and there is more opportunity than there has ever been in this island for the sacrifice and thought and the working together for the benefit of the people of this country.'

Bustamante was a notable union leader in Jamaica, appearing at all of the disturbances and playing a prominent role in addressing demonstrators and articulating their grievances to the authorities. Barnstorming and spontaneous in his demeanour, speech and behaviour, Bustamante soon parted company with the more patrician Manley – a Fabian socialist – as a member of the PNP. This was partly because of the jealousy between the two cousins. The PNP held an all-day debate in 1940 in which Manley declared that it was a socialist organisation that would avoid political violence. Bustamante was an active presence in Jamaican politics, revelling in controversial union decisions and becoming a thorn in the side of the Jamaican police force. He fully supported the working person, and frequently arraigned the government over its slowness in addressing the inequities of the workplace on the island. He aired his views in his magazine *Jamaica Labour*. In September 1940 Bustamante was arrested after making an inflammatory speech in Kingston and interned for seventeen months at a military encampment on the edge of the city.

Manley spoke with Bustamante at the internment camp, and gained an agreement that he should organise the BITU as an effective body. Manley negotiated better wages for workers with sugar manufacturers but handed back the union to Bustamante on his release from internment in February 1942. This was followed by a major parting of the ways for the two men. Arguments were batted back and forth about whether Manley had wanted Bustamante's detention to continue and about who should assume control of the PNP. In late 1943 Bustamante announced that he would be forming a new Jamaica Labour Party (JLP). He did this and over the following year it gained large support from the BITU in particular.

In 1943 considerable momentum gathered apace for significant changes to Jamaica's constitution. The labour protests of the immediately preceding years had exposed large crevices in the operation of Crown Colony government: the autocratic system it had perpetuated for nearly eighty years was now withering. Manley and the PNP pushed hard to promote democratic self-government to the British authorities. A Jamaican deputation was despatched to London to discuss a new constitution. Agreement was reached with the secretary of state for the colonies for a new constitution for Jamaica and a popular government elected on a wide franchise. This was a swift move towards democracy on the island.

Under the terms of the new constitution, Jamaica was granted a new lower house of thirty-two members elected by universal adult suffrage; a legislative council of fifteen nominated members, most of whom were not to be members of the government; and an executive committee of ten. The governor was given power to act with the executive committee to implement laws not passed by both houses. Women would be eligible to vote and sit in either branch of government. Universal adult suffrage was introduced for parliamentary elections, making Jamaica the first British Caribbean colony where this was implemented. Despite the progressive changes made towards democracy, however, the new constitutional arrangements still vested most political power in Jamaica in the hands of the governor.

While these details were debated and agreed in London, political parties in Jamaica organised rapidly for an election. The new governor, Sir John Huggins, proclaimed the new constitution on 20 November 1944 and on 13 December a general election was held for a new House of Representatives. Manley and the PNP stood on a socialist programme that advocated public ownership of utilities, transportation, wharves and sugar factories. Bustamante countered this campaigning programme by his own effective rhetoric, accusing Manley and the PNP of wanting to turn Jamaica into a communist state. Bustamante had the support of his own large union, the BITU, and this proved easily strong enough for the JLP to secure a victory, gaining twenty-three out of thirty-two seats while the PNP contested only nineteen seats and won four. Manley was defeated by a JLP candidate and Bustamante, who lacked a political programme or set of policies to follow, became head of Jamaica's government. More than 349,000 Jamaicans cast their vote in the election. Despite the distribution of seats pointing to a landslide victory for the JLP, this was not the case in terms of the popular vote for the JLP received 41 per cent of the votes cast and the PNP 30 per cent.

Manley equably accepted the election result but warned that new government policies were required to aid Jamaica's masses even though many elite people feared the possibility of further public disorder. 'There is on the part of the masses, standing on one side of the dividing gulf, a deep resentment and urge to change it all,' he wrote, but 'on the other side are the privileged few. These cannot escape the fear that secretly haunts them.' One way of alleviating social tension was by providing the means for additional employment. Both Bustamante and Manley realised that this meant investment in manufacturing industry. This started with the exploitation of Jamaica's bauxite resources during the Second World War and expanded into other areas of industrialisation after the conflict ended.

Jamaica and the Second World War

War was not declared in Jamaica in 1939 but, as a colonial dependency of Britain, the island was automatically involved in the conflict. The governor of Jamaica imposed press and mail censorship. A Jamaican Home Guard was formed and blackout drills became a part of daily life. The Jamaica Infantry Volunteers offered their support. Small groups of refugees from Gibraltar were shipped to Jamaica along with Jewish refugees. British soldiers were stationed at Up Park camp, the headquarters of the British Army in Jamaica. Though the island itself was barely threatened during the Second War as it lay a considerable distance from most major theatres of war, it was used by the US armed forces in case deployment of vessels and aeroplanes was needed. In September 1940 President Franklin D. Roosevelt transferred fifty destroyers to Britain in return for access to Caribbean naval bases, including Jamaica. This was intended to defend the island against German U boats deployed in the Caribbean during the war. The United States also wanted to protect the petroleum and oil supplies it needed from the Greater Caribbean region. Under an Anglo-American agreement of 1941, the US Air Force secured a base at Vernamfield, Sandy Gully, in Clarendon parish. A US naval base, intended for submarines and destroyers, was established at Goat Island in Old Harbour Bay.

In 1942 an Anglo-American Caribbean Commission (AACC) was created as an advisory agency to discuss matters of mutual concern to the United Kingdom, its West Indian colonies and the United States. Among the areas of concern to the commission were agriculture, finance, economics, health, labour, education and welfare. The Commission was intended to strengthen and develop cooperation between Britain and the United States in relation to the Caribbean, but it was also a vehicle for greater US influence over the West Indian islands. The AACC played a role in hastening political reform in Jamaica, supporting the introduction of the new constitution there in 1944.

Jamaicans served in the British armed forces during the Second World War. Some 3,700 Jamaicans, for example, volunteered for the Royal Air Force while others were recruited into the Royal Navy. Some recruits were the sons of fathers who served in the First World War; they wanted to continue the family tradition of loyalty to Britain and its empire. In terms of armed troops, the island's main contribution was through the Caribbean Regiment, formed in 1944. Jamaicans joined this military unit alongside men from other West Indian islands. The regiment was sent to Italy and Egypt to aid the allied war effort, but it was mainly used as a way of supporting the transport and food supplies to the front line rather than as a fighting unit. The Caribbean Regiment was a fairly small group, comprising originally some 1,200 volunteers. Members returned home after the war ended and the regiment was disbanded in 1946.

6

Modern Jamaica, 1945–2022

~

Rapid changes have occurred in Jamaica since the end of the Second World War. Two fairly young political parties, the People's National Party (PNP) and the Jamaica Labour Party (JLP), continued to dominate the political scene with stable leaders until Jamaica achieved independence in 1962, and since then one or other of these two parties has been successful at general elections. Modern Jamaica is therefore largely a two-party parliamentary democracy. Third parties have failed to gather sufficient electoral support to mount a significant challenge to the PNP and the JLP. These two main parties, both left of centre in the political spectrum, have faced problems when they veered towards more extreme positions and they have both had to cope with continuing economic problems, social unrest and deprivation, but they have provided a stable framework for political decision-making. In economic life, Jamaica has faced problems with the decline of long-standing industries since 1945, notably in the agricultural export sector, but has diversified its economy to embrace industries such as bauxite mining and has seen important growth areas in financial services, information technology and tourism. Cultural vibrancy in music and the arts and international sporting prowess in cricket and athletics have presented a positive image of Jamaica to the world but the growth in the use of drugs and the gang violence prevalent in parts of Kingston and elsewhere on the island have cast a dark shadow on contemporary Jamaican life.

The Road to Independence

After universal adult suffrage was introduced in 1944, Crown Colony government ended and Jamaica advanced its political system to resemble the main features of British parliamentary politics. This marked the beginning of decolonisation in the island. A bicameral legislature on the Westminster model was established, with the lower body known as the House of Representatives and the upper body comprising an Executive Council. The House of Representatives was the democratic element in the constitution while the Executive Council consisted of five elected members of the lower house presided over by a British-appointed governor. General elections were to be held periodically at which political parties could compete in campaigns, rallies and hustings. Gradual political change was an essential part of the early period of decolonisation in Jamaica, as British officials were keen to confirm that Jamaica was proceeding along a stable political trajectory. A full ministerial system was introduced in 1953. Four years later a Council of Ministers replaced the Executive Council, cabinet government commenced and the governor retired from active internal politics.

Between the end of the Second World War and independence the JLP and the PNP dominated the island's politics, accounting for over 90 per cent of the popular vote at general elections. Smaller political parties also existed in Jamaica, but neither they nor independent candidates gained many Assembly seats. Garveyism, for example, which had flourished in the late 1920s and 1930s, still had a strong social and cultural resonance in Jamaica but that was not translated into a significant political movement or party. That was partly the result of Garvey's death and the lack of a charismatic successor but also because Garveyism was never organised along party political lines. Both the PNP and the JLP forged close relations with trade unions. They were close rivals at each general election held before full decolonisation and there was never a time after 1945 when one of these parties disintegrated. Therefore modern Jamaica never had to contend with continuous dominance by one political party.

The JLP won the 1944 election, as Chapter 5 has shown. In 1949 it was re-elected narrowly, winning seventeen seats versus the PNP's thirteen, but the latter gained slightly more popular votes. The PNP challenged the JLP persistently throughout the early 1950s and won the 1955 election by eighteen seats to fourteen for the JLP. In this election the PNP became the first Jamaican political party to achieve a popular majority. The PNP was re-elected at the 1959 general election, winning twenty-nine out of forty-five seats. In 1962 the JLP secured twenty-six of the forty-five seats and Alexander Bustamante was returned to power, leading Jamaica into independence.

Both the JLP and the PNP kept one leader throughout the period from the granting of universal adult suffrage to independence. These were, respectively, Bustamante and Norman Manley, both of whom had emerged into political prominence on the island during the turbulent protests of the late 1930s and 1940s. Both, in their different ways, were effective speakers at public rallies, an essential requirement for success as a political leader in Jamaica, where oral culture was paramount. In terms of personality, Bustamante and Manley diverged: one was a volatile authoritarian, the other a patrician rationalist with socialist leanings. Bustamante was tall, rather agitated and a highly charged public speaker in his element during political campaigns. He was very alert to the exploitation of political opportunities and to the manipulation of circumstances to his own advantage. Some would argue he was much better at drumming up support for the JLP cause than he was at administering policies when in power. Manley was more obviously intellectual and forensic in his political speeches, but he too had the ability to cut through to ordinary Jamaicans when campaigning. The dominance of these two political leaders in the first two decades of political parties has led Spencer Mawby to refer to 'the emergence of a rigid, personalist two-party system' in Jamaica.

It would be stretching the metaphor too far to suggest that one could barely place a litmus paper between the JLP and the PNP, but they had much in common. Both were closely attached to, and arose out of, trade unionism. Both relied on trusted supporters who could organise branches effectively throughout Jamaica. Both parties had headquarters in Kingston. Both appealed to white, brown and black voters across class divisions. Both had leaders who had no effective challengers for many years. Both were keen to foster Jamaica's industrial and agricultural development. If pressed to identify a difference between the two parties, one might point out that the JLP had larger support in rural impoverished parts of

Jamaica while the PNP, partly because of Manley's standing as a lawyer, appealed particularly to professionals seeking status and advancement for their families. Hugh Shearer, a Bustamante Industrial Trade Union (BITU) official who later became the third prime minister of Jamaica, noted that 'the appeal of the Bustamante people has been principally to the lower classes, rather than to the middle classes ... only demagoguery and an appeal of personality would win them to the movement'.

Bustamante's volatility came to fore on numerous occasions, notably in 1946 when nurses went on strike and violence occurred between JLP and PNP supporters. In a state of emergency – later to become almost a Jamaican speciality – Bustamante was charged with manslaughter after the death of an innocent person at a scene of protest but acquitted after a highly charged trial. Manley, for his part, shrewdly improved his political profile in several ways to challenge Bustamante after the loss of the 1944 election. First, he was elected to the House of Representatives in 1949, taking his seat as leader of the opposition. Second, he realised that Bustamante's success derived in large part from his position as leader for life of the BITU and that, for his own political prospects, it would be necessary to improve the level of trade union support for the PNP. Thus, after an exhausting tribunal, he removed four vocal left-wing unionists from the PNP, dropped socialism from his political programme and established the National Workers' Union (NWU) to gain middle-class support. He placed his journalist son Michael Manley as the head of this new body.

The growing support for the NWU played a significant role in Norman Manley achieving power as head of the

PNP in the 1955 election. By the time of the subsequent election three years later, Manley had severed his connection with the NWU but still retained power. He was keenly aware, however, that the PNP needed to justify its success at the polls. Thus Sir Hugh Foot, the governor of Jamaica, informed the Colonial Office in late 1955 that Manley was 'fighting for political survival. He knows that if he and his Party fail to seize the opportunity they now have in Jamaica his Party will be destroyed and all he hopes to achieve will be lost.'

When Jamaica achieved full self-government in 1957, the head of government was referred to as chief minister, but after the PNP won the general election of 1959 the title was changed to premier. Bolstered by the political authority that came with self-government, the PNP government of the late 1950s energetically instigated improvements to Jamaican life in relation to agriculture, tourism, business, industrialisation and education. In 1956 an Industrial Incentives Law and an Export Industries Law made arrangements to encourage inward investment in Jamaica. The PNP government established a government-owned radio station for Jamaica and a central bank. An Industrial Development Corporation helped to create fifty-eight new firms throughout the island between 1952 and 1960. A National Plan promoted the increase in the number of Jamaican children attending government and secondary schools. By 1958 grants were awarded to assist a quarter of the pupils in these schools. Manley applauded these attempts to modernise Jamaica by stating that the island 'will be as completely a self-governing unit as it is possible for any territory to be short of achieving Dominion Status'. In 1959 a new constitution was proposed for Jamaica which reduced the governor's powers and introduced an independent Civil Service Commission. By then, it was clear that the UK government would support plans proposed by Jamaica for political independence on the grounds that it could not withstand a strong desire for political autonomy from Caribbean territories.

A new political development concerning Jamaica was the formation of the West Indies Federation (WIF). The notion that the British Caribbean should be brought under a federal umbrella had been discussed at a conference in Montego Bay in September 1947, where Manley signalled his acceptance of the idea. But it was not implemented for over a decade. In an attempt in 1958 to bring together ten islands in the British Caribbean to improve their efficiency and stability before they became fully independent, Jamaica joined the WIF along with Barbados, Trinidad and some smaller islands in the Lesser Antilles. Though Jamaica had the largest number of voters in the Federation, it had not pressed a claim for Kingston to be its capital: Port-of-Spain instead was named as the headquarters of the Federation. Westminster and Whitehall had favoured federation for several years before it came into being, believing it was a sensible and pragmatic way for a series of relatively small, fairly poor territories to pool their resources to achieve political stability and economic prosperity. Two main ideas lying behind the creation of the WIF were that each territory should have a premier or chief minister and each island should be represented in a federal government. On 31 May 1962, it was envisaged that the WIF would be an independent nation comprising ten countries and their dependencies.

The WIF, however, proved to be a short-lived failure. It was idealistic to imagine that a number of disparate islands would cooperate over policies when they had previously followed their individual political trajectories, albeit all under British jurisdiction. Some members of the WIF wanted free movement of labour between individual members of the Federation; others opposed this suggestion as not being conducive to their own employment situation. Some wanted a customs union, but Jamaica disagreed. Even before the WIF was set up, Manley had advised the British government in late 1955 that the PNP was split about whether to accept a plan for federation, with many of his colleagues more interested in implementing a domestic political programme rather than pursuing political unity in the British Caribbean. And it was clear to Jamaica's governor that for Manley 'an overriding sense of obligation to Jamaica comes first in his mind and Federation is to him a comparatively secondary object'.

The ruling PNP's reservations about federation remained unresolved. One consequence was that they performed poorly in explaining to the Jamaican public exactly what federalism meant for their political life. The situation was politically complex because discussions concerning Jamaica's independence were running parallel with the discussion of a federalised British Caribbean. Bustamante and the JLP argued that federation would lead to small Caribbean islands dominating Jamaica, and that Jamaica's projected contribution to the federal budget would be too high given the urgent need to spend that money within Jamaica tackling poverty. In 1970 Michael Manley observed that federation was more popular in smaller Caribbean islands than in Jamaica because 'it was always an afterthought in the dialogue of Jamaican politics'.

Norman Manley referred to federation in a radio broadcast of 1960 as 'a dream and a hope and a promise of salvation'. But despite his commitment to a political body intended to help all British West Indian territories, the concept of federation faded away rapidly in Jamaica. On 19 September 1961 a referendum was held to determine whether Jamaica should stay within the WIF. Manley was always much more committed to the WIF than Bustamante, who, along with the JLP, was seriously worried about taxpayers in Jamaica helping the smaller territories to exist and develop. The PNP supported continued membership and campaigned for forty-five days to promote the putative advantages for Jamaica in staying within the Federation. But it struggled to gain support. A reporter for the *Sunday Gleaner* on 6 August 1961 noted that 'it is a fight against odds, against apathy, against a determined opposition and against the natural insularity of Jamaicans, grown proud in their concept of nationhood'. It was difficult to campaign for Jamaica to be part of a larger political polity before Jamaica had achieved independence. Moreover, Jamaica's economic and political development had avoided partnership with other West Indian territories. Thus a Canadian observer noted that 'because of its isolation and its nearness to the United States' Jamaica 'had tended to look northward and westward rather than eastward to a considerable degree more than do the other islands'.

Many ordinary Jamaicans were suspicious of the concept of West Indian nationhood. Tension and signs of public disorder occurred during the last weeks of the referendum campaign. The People's Political Party, formed in 1960 under the Marxist Millard Johnson, was a small third political party, but it was effective in whipping up antagonism towards the West Indian Federation among impoverished rural workers, staging meetings in provincial towns such as Savanna-la-Mar that attracted 6,000–7,000 people. Popular interest in the referendum was muted and the popular ballot rejected federalism: 54 per cent of those voting (60 per cent of the electorate) wanted withdrawal. The WIF ended a few months before Jamaican independence.

The referendum result shocked many in the West Indian political establishment. A confidential report for the Colonial Office stated that 'it is significant that of the 45 constituencies no more than 14 voted in favour and that of those 14, 7 were in the urban areas of the parishes of Kingston and St. Andrew. It was clear the rural voters had finally been swayed by lack of knowledge of the subject and by fear of the unknown.' Upper-class and middle-class Jamaicans were usually favourably disposed towards the WIF but poorer Jamaicans were generally opposed to it. The referendum result boosted Jamaican nationalism and indicated that most Jamaicans did not feel comfortable with embracing a wider West Indian identity. Possibly if Kingston had been the capital of the WIF rather than Port-of-Spain, the result in Jamaica would have been more favourable to federation. Trinidad and Tobago also voted against the WIF, which was dissolved in May 1962.

Between 1 and 9 February 1962 a Jamaican Independence Conference was held at Lancaster House, London, a venue that had been used for previous independence meetings involving Commonwealth countries. The conference approved a new written constitution for Jamaica, drafted by a bipartisan committee of its legislature. The United Kingdom agreed that Jamaica would become independent on 6 August 1962 and that the newly independent island should become a member of the Commonwealth. In Jamaica the defeat of the federal idea enabled the JLP to seize the political advantage by arguing that the referendum result was a vote of no-confidence in the ruling PNP party, a strategy that proved successful. There was a widespread belief that the PNP catered mainly for middle-class business interests and had neglected the underdog. The JLP were able to fill that void. On 10 April 1962 the JLP won the general election and the elderly Bustamante became the first prime minister of the independent nation. Jamaica adopted an aspirational motto of 'Out of Many, One People' on attaining independence and a new national flag was adopted, with black, green and gold as its colours, to replace the Union Jack.

On Independence Day, 6 August 1962, Norman Manley gave a message to the Jamaican People:

We have built up a good society where law and order are respected, where justice prevails, where men and women can respect and admire and love each other no matter what our colour may be or what race we belong to. We have laid the foundations of a decent political life and we are trying hard to build up a world of opportunity for all our people. We can be very proud of ourselves for what our forefathers in the last one hundred and twenty years and for what this generation has done in the last twenty-four years since 1938. Let us rejoice and go forward in courage and strength to make Jamaica a safe and happy home for all our people.

FIGURE 6.1 Stamp commemorating Jamaican independence. Ken
Wiedemann/Getty Images

These uplifting words included carefully judged references to the end of slavery with the demise of apprenticeship in 1838 and the political significance of the
1938 labour rebellion. They also placed the achievement of Jamaican independence within the long history
of colonialism, and offered an optimistic vision for the
future.

Independence Day was celebrated in Jamaica with
a large gathering in the National Stadium, attended by
over 20,000 people. Flags and bunting were displayed
throughout Kingston and other Jamaican towns, parades,
bonfires and Jonkonnu celebrations were widespread in
the streets, and commemorative plates and cups were
distributed. Bustamante spoke appropriate words at such
an important moment in Jamaica's history: 'Independence
means the opportunity for us to frame our own destiny
and the need for us to rely on ourselves for so doing. It
does not mean a licence to do as we would like. It means
work and law and order. Let us resolve to build a Jamaica
which will last and of which we and generations to come

will be proud, remembering that especially at this time the eyes of the world are upon us.'

Politics after Independence

Independence for Jamaica was accompanied by full dominion status within the Commonwealth under a constitution that retained the British monarch as head of state. The JLP held power for a decade after independence, with Bustamante serving as prime minister for five of those years. The PNP in opposition continued to be led by Norman Manley, but he never repeated his electoral successes of the 1950s. Manley was confident that Jamaican nationhood would prosper largely because of the respect of most Jamaicans for law and justice and their ability to endure hardships with patience. He himself never became prime minister of an independent Jamaica, and retired from politics when he reached age 75 in 1968. Looking back over his political career, he reflected that his generation 'had a distinct mission to perform. It was to create a national spirit with which we could identify ourselves as a people for the purpose of achieving political independence.' Manley realised that the future political development of Jamaica should provide economic and social reforms for the majority of the population. This would be difficult to achieve given the impoverishment, illiteracy and lack of mass mobilisation of Jamaicans for political purposes. Despite these problems, however, there was little chance that ordinary Jamaicans would resort to sustained protests to highlight their conditions because 'any rising in the near future can be coped with because of the lack of organization of the masses'.

The JLP, while in power in the 1960s, made little progress in delivering better material conditions in Jamaica. Donald Sangster became acting prime minister on two separate occasions, in 1964–5, owing to the illness of Bustamante, and was appointed prime minister on 22 February 1967 after the JLP had just won a general election. While he was forming his cabinet, Sangster fell ill and died in April 1967. Hugh Shearer, who succeeded him as leader of the JLP and prime minister, had five years in power. When elected, at the age of forty-three, he was the youngest prime minister in the Commonwealth. Under his leadership the long-standing connections between the JLP and some of the main Jamaican trade unions began to decline. Unemployment remained at a high level and corruption hovered over the political atmosphere. But these problems were counterbalanced by more positive achievements. Fifty new secondary schools were created in Jamaica while he was prime minister and three new alumina refineries and three large convention hotels were begun or constructed.

One of Shearer's most controversial decisions was to ban the Guyanese academic and black rights activist Dr Walter Rodney from re-entering Jamaica from Guyana in 1968. Students at the Mona campus of the University of the West Indies, where Rodney was a popular figure, protested against this boycott. Shearer supported the civil rights movement and the rallying calls of Dr Martin Luther King but he was concerned that Rodney's speeches extolling black pride and Pan-Africanism would stir up violence. Rodney frequently held informal meetings with ordinary Jamaicans where he spread his radical political ideas. He also visited major communist nations such as Cuba and the USSR. When the protests against Rodney's exclusion from Jamaica continued, the police used tear gas to quell the commotion. Rodney left the island for Tanzania and Guyana and later returned to Jamaica. Shearer's action against Rodney made him unpopular among many younger Jamaicans and those of all ages who occupied the middle ground in politics swung towards support for the PNP.

The British High Commissioner for Jamaica, on his first visit there in 1969, quickly recognised the economic difficulties that might spill over into political action in the island. He spoke with Shearer and upper-income groups in Jamaica and found they had an optimistic, somewhat complacent, view of Jamaica's economy and social conditions. But he noted, in a confidential document, that the sugar and banana industries were passing through troubled times and the booming bauxite industry employed relatively few Jamaicans. He noted 'the frustrations and resentments felt by the increasing number of youngsters who are unemployed, and having little hope of ever securing employment'. He witnessed the struggle between 'the haves and the have-nots' in Jamaica, and was struck by 'the extent to which though they are nearly all Jamaicans the haves seem to be mainly white and the have-nots mainly black. And the gulf between them is very wide.'

Hopes for the betterment of Jamaica now seemed to lie in the political leadership of Michael Manley. The revival of the PNP began when he took over its leadership from his father, a very different politician, in 1969. A light-skinned, articulate Jamaican with a penchant for overblown rhetoric in his public speeches, the younger

FIGURE 6.2 Michael Manley. Getty Images

Manley attracted new support to the PNP while the
JLP was struggling to improve living and working
conditions for Jamaica's masses. With a strong background of work with trade unions, Manley promised
to support policies that would enhance the economic
and social prospects of Jamaica's youth. He ran
a populist election campaign that drew upon
Rastafarian symbols. At the 1972 general election
the PNP, inspired by the younger Manley's advocacy
of progressive changes, easily won, gaining thirty-
seven seats out of fifty-three in the House of
Representatives on a high poll turnout of
78 per cent. The PNP's slogan for the election was
'better 'mus come', a phrase snaffled from Delroy
Wilson's popular reggae song.

Michael Manley decided that Jamaican politics needed
a new direction and that to distinguish the PNP from the
JLP a greater degree of ideological difference was
required. At the PNP annual conference in 1974 Manley

announced that his party had become committed to a democratic socialist programme. This was followed up with a series of state-aided programmes designed to improve socio-economic conditions for Jamaicans. An adult literacy programme in 1973–4 enabled poor Jamaicans to attend writing and reading classes. In 1975 a national minimum wage was introduced. Progressive social policies included free secondary and higher education and equal pay for women. A policy called Project Land Lease provided 23,000 small farmers with land, fertiliser and credit for 44,500 acres, but crop development on these lands was inadequately undertaken and the scheme was criticised for lacking value for money: it failed to produce a more equitable, economically sustainable use of agriculture in Jamaica.

Manley's economic policies, however, proved controversial. State penetration of the economy advanced rapidly with nationalisation of the electricity, telephone and public transport companies along with mining firms, some sugar factories and Barclays Bank. These socialist measures frightened many foreign investors, who extracted their money from Jamaica's businesses as they regarded state control as detrimental to making profits. The United States withdrew aid from Jamaica as a consequence of nationalisation: in 1971 US aid amounted to $23 million but that plummeted to $4 million in 1975. Middle-class professional Jamaicans and businessmen started to emigrate to the United Kingdom, Canada and the United States to avoid the introduction of a socialist economy. Social turbulence was rife at the time in Jamaica, where the escalation of violence alarmed many people. Manley tried to counter the violence in urban neighbourhoods by passing the Gun Court Act in 1974, giving the police and the army new powers to access such areas and implementing court sentences for firearms offences without a jury. He stated that 'there is no place for the gun in this society, now or ever'. But this failed to quell unrest and violence on his watch.

Manley visited Fidel Castro, the leader of Cuba, in 1975 and expressed admiration for Cuban improvements in public health and literacy under his communist regime. This was a controversial, high-profile visit from a democratic prime minister to the Marxist-Leninist president of a republic with strong economic and military ties to the Soviet Union. It rang alarm bells for the private sector in Jamaica, which is situated only about 240 miles across the Caribbean from Cuba. Many educated Jamaicans feared Manley would introduce quasi-communist policies; and the US government kept a watchful eye on such developments, not wishing to see the spread of Castro's influence to other Caribbean nations. Manley's support for the Cuban intervention against South Africa in Angola in 1975, intended to support communist political groups there, hardened the American diplomatic stance towards Jamaica. Alarms were raised in July 1976 when a bomb exploded while being loaded on to an Air Cubana flight at Jamaica's airport. These fears were heightened four months later when a flight to Jamaica from the same airline exploded in mid-air.

Manley's government mobilised for the 1976 general election on the basis of appealing to the working classes. This was fiercely contested and marked by a high degree of violence linked to the two main political parties. The number of murders escalated in the run-up to the election and Manley declared a state of emergency in August 1976. Edward Seaga, a disciple of Bustamante who had become leader of the JLP in 1974, attacked the PNP's economic policies for their reckless distribution of public money and accused Manley and the PNP of coming directly under the influence of communist Cuba. Manley, in an address at the PNP's annual conference in September 1976, set his cards on the table, calling upon 'comrades' to 'replace and change and remove the system of capitalism and replace it by building brick upon brick, step by step, the new system of democratic socialism'. Both Manley and Seaga tried to broaden their appeal to the masses by adopting specifically black symbols. Manley borrowed rhetoric about class struggle from the black power and civil rights movements and campaigned for black redemption from white power, while Seaga introduced African revivalist elements and Afro-Jamaican music into his campaigning.

The PNP retained power at the violent 1976 election with a landslide victory, but it was living on borrowed time. Its financial woes continued. In April 1977 Jamaica's government sought financial assistance from the International Monetary Fund (IMF), though this was later abandoned and Jamaica relied on short-term loans instead. By 1980, a worldwide oil crisis had impacted negatively on Jamaica; the island's foreign debt amounted to 90 per cent of GDP; and bankruptcy was a real possibility for the government. There were further serious problems: just over a quarter of Jamaicans of working age, for example, were unemployed by 1980. Seaga, as leader of the JLP, attributed Jamaica's problems of the late 1970s to Manley's 'failed ideological thrust . . . in which he was embattled by stronger forces of economic deterioration, social disruption and cultural confusion, which he had unwittingly unleashed'.

Meanwhile, between 1976 and 1980, the JLP under Seaga realised that it needed better political mobilisation in order to challenge the PNP. It therefore developed new organisations for young adults and for women and improved its party machinery. Seaga's characterisation of the PNP under Manley as anti-white and anti-capitalist combined with this reorganisation of the JLP to present a strong challenge at the election of 1980. This was again marked by significant political violence: at least 600 people were killed in the political conflict between February and October of that year. The PNP was defeated easily: the JLP won fifty-one out of the sixty seats in parliament in an election with high turnout at the polls. This was the largest electoral win in Jamaica since independence. There were rumours that the United States' Central Intelligence Agency (CIA) had supported the JLP's electioneering at this contest.

Seaga, the new prime minister in 1980, was determined to lead the JLP towards a more capitalist, neo-liberal political stance. He immediately established good relations with the US Republican president Ronald Reagan, and was the first foreign leader to be invited to visit the White House, in early 1981, during Reagan's incumbency. Seaga, who continued links forged in the 1970s with the CIA, supported opposition to communism and Marxism spreading throughout the Caribbean during

FIGURE 6.3 Edward Seaga. Getty Images

a tense period of the Cold War between the United States and the Soviet Union in the 1980s. Seaga expelled Cuban doctors and other personnel from Jamaica, including the Cuban ambassador, and severed diplomatic ties with Castro's Cuba. He claimed that Havana was sheltering criminals wanted for prosecution in Jamaica, a claim refuted by Cuba. Continuing his anti-communist support for the United States, Seaga supported the US invasion of Grenada in 1983, which occurred after the prime minister of that island, Maurice Bishop, appeared to be coming increasingly under Cuban influence. The evidence of public opinion polls indicated that more Jamaicans approved of this action than disapproved.

The influence of the United States on Jamaica was also important economically during the 1980s. Seaga and the JLP took office in dire economic circumstances for

Jamaica in 1980. To improve the situation, connections were revived with the IMF that the PNP had abandoned in the late 1970s. Seaga, who operated as finance minister as well as prime minister, negotiated a loan of US$698 million over three years to support Jamaica's economic development. This came with strings attached: Jamaica was given financial targets to meet and limits were placed on new external borrowing. Seaga claimed his financial policies restored the country 'to the path of prudent financial management. We have been able to restore the finances of the country to a level on the basis of which there are no more stops and starts, but a smooth functioning of the economy.' Despite these confident words, however, performance tests attached to the IMF loan were not met, leading to the suspension of the support package. The same outcome resulted from further loans negotiated between Jamaica's government and the IMF between 1983 and 1990.

By 1983, realising that the economic recovery had not yet occurred, Seaga decided to call an early general election to buy an additional five years to pursue his economic programme. This surprise move was handled in a wily way. Both main political parties were involved in continuing discussions about electoral reform and the PNP had made public statements to the effect that it would not participate in an election until the reforms had been agreed. Seaga called the election before that process had been completed; the PNP refused to field any candidates. The 1983 election, where the turnout was small, resulted in the JLP gaining all sixty seats in the legislature – a complete electoral wipeout for the PNP.

Seaga's domestic policies followed a conservative, free-market agenda. His dislike of the left-wing policies still advocated by Michael Manley and the PNP was central to his political beliefs. 'Socialism is a pulling down ideology' but 'capitalism is a pulling up ideology' were Seaga's words in his autobiography. Seaga promoted tourism and hotels in Jamaica, and encouraged private enterprise in connection with a reliance on the private sector, foreign investment and economic deregulation. Private technological and managerial skills were harnessed to make the banana and sugar export industries more efficient. A Caribbean Boom Initiative was promoted. Businesses were revitalised, including the Jamaica Mortgage Bank, the Jamaica Stock Exchange and equities markets.

The effects of the JLP's policies on ordinary Jamaicans, however, were more unsuccessful. The JLP took little interest in workplace protection for ordinary Jamaicans. After the 1983 election Seaga imposed austerity policies, with cuts to public spending. Despite the IMF loans, Jamaica's economy deteriorated. By 1985 inflation reached 30 per cent, the currency was declining on international markets, unemployment accounted for a quarter of the labour force and by 1989 poor economic performance meant that the GDP level was no better than in 1980. In addition, most of the island's social and economic structure was deteriorating. Shanty town, dilapidated conditions were common in Jamaica's small urban centres. Parts of central Kingston had worsening slums. Gang warfare was rife in a number of communities in Greater Kingston. Housing garrisons, as explained more fully later in the chapter, had become community fortresses where political enforcers with guns controlled the main social and economic activities. Riots occurred in 1987 and 1988. To add to these woes Hurricane Gilbert struck Jamaica in 1988, causing $1 billion worth of damage, and the Seaga government was slow to respond to this calamity. The time was ripe for a change in the see-saw of Jamaican politics, and the PNP was able to capitalise on the woes of Seaga's government and increase its support.

The PNP regained power at the 1989 election, winning forty-five out of the sixty seats in the lower house. Michael Manley, still popular with a broad swathe of the electorate, became prime minister for the second time. Modifying his leftist stance of the 1970s, Manley no longer wanted to nationalise Jamaican industries; instead, he privatised various state-owned enterprises and cultivated closer economic and diplomatic relations with the United States. He restored diplomatic relations with Cuba but, with the collapse of the Soviet Union in 1990, discarded his overt support for Castro's regime. Manley's domestic policies focused on support for poorer Jamaicans through state aid for training and employment, modest land reform to help small farmers, government provisions to assist with housing and dietary support for pregnant women, nursing mothers and children. Economic problems were difficult to surmount, however, and by 1991 the inflation rate in Jamaica was 80 per cent.

Manley was more subdued in his public pronouncements than in the 1970s, but retained his charismatic, populist ability to rouse an audience at public gatherings. In 1992 he retired from public life owing to ill health and was replaced as prime minister by the more measured P. J. Patterson, who had held a number of previous ministerial appointments. Patterson was the first black Jamaican

FIGURE 6.4 P. J. Patterson. Jeff Haynes/AFP/Getty Images

prime minister. He managed to win the next three general elections – in 1993, 1997 and 2002. However, the PNP's dominance of the lower house decreased at each election: it won fifty-two seats out of sixty in 1993, fifty in 1997 but only thirty-four in 2002. Patterson was the first Jamaican leader to win three successive general elections. These victories enabled the PNP to stay in power continuously for eighteen years, a record for continuous government by one party since independence.

In taking over from Manley as prime minister, Patterson was acutely aware of the political and economic challenges facing Jamaica. In his own words, 'I was under no illusion about the difficulty of the task of transforming a largely underdeveloped and fractured society into a truly democratic and people-centred nation. The challenges in the economy were truly monumental as the global economy offered limited opportunities. This was made even more so by the unpreparedness of the local private sector to take on the challenges in the global marketplace.' To prepare public policies to advance the cause of Jamaicans it was necessary, in Patterson's view, to 'find again the same type of commitment and energy with which we were infused when we struggled as a people to bring about our own independence'.

The PNP's domestic and international programmes in the 1990s were not significantly different from the JLP's, but that party experienced defections in the mid-1990s, notably to the newly formed National Democratic Movement. Some senior politicians in the JLP also expressed doubts about the record of the party in government. Thus Bruce Golding, a former chairman of the JLP and a future Jamaican prime minister, resigned from the party in 1995, stating that the island's political structures inadequately addressed economic deprivation among the Jamaican people. To accompany his resignation he stated that 'I firmly believe that without fundamental changes to our political system and constitutional arrangements we will not be able to find effective solutions to the enormous economic and social problems which plague the Jamaican people'. Golding was no doubt frustrated at the failure of the JLP to win power during the 1990s. Seaga held on for too long as leader of the JLP, suffering four successive defeats in general elections before retiring from public life in 2005.

Patterson's tenure as prime minister in the 1990s and the early years of the twenty-first century was not as successful as his longevity in power might suggest, but there were positive achievements. Looking to secure peaceful and rational solutions to a multitude of problems,

Patterson eschewed the bolder rhetoric of his predecessor. His government ended the borrowing relationship between Jamaica and the IMF, expanded the private sector of the economy especially in telecommunications, and attracted over $4.7 billion in foreign investment. Efforts were made to improve Jamaica's competitiveness in labour markets. Investment in infrastructure was followed intensively. New arterial roads were constructed and support given to public housing and land distribution.

Patterson was influential in the wider Caribbean context through his involvement with the Caribbean Free Trade Association (CARFTA) and its evolution into the Caribbean Community (CARICOM) and into a CARICOM single market by 2006. In terms of economic policy, Patterson's governments were proactive and market-oriented, ushering in significant improvements in mining, tourism, infrastructure and ICT. One important development was investment in Kingston's port infrastructure whereby one of the world's largest natural harbours was improved for large ships through the construction of the Kingston Container Terminal. This attracted $510 million from a consortium to privatise the terminal in 2015. Besides the port of Kingston, the Patterson government improved harbour and shipping facilities at Ocho Rios, Montego Bay and Port Antonio partly to improve access for large cruiser liners on Jamaica's northern shores.

Patterson's governments had mixed results, however, on other issues. Political violence, especially during election campaigning, was reduced but high criminal activity continued in Jamaica. Strikes became regular and riots occurred in 1999 after the government imposed sharp price rises for petroleum, leading to arson and the closure of the public transport system for three days. Patterson was Jamaica's longest serving prime minister. He retired from politics in 2006. Portia Simpson Miller, an experienced politician and minister, then became leader of the PNP and Jamaica's first female prime minister. In her brief period in office in 2006–7, the government abolished healthcare fees for children and provided aid for first-time home buyers, but it was beset by a financial scandal in which a Dutch-based oil trading firm transacting business with the Jamaican government transferred millions of US dollars to the PNP, a sum that had to be repaid when the donation surfaced. In addition, Miller's government was slow to provide disaster relief after Hurricane Dean devastated parts of Jamaica in August 2007.

In the general election held during the following month, the two main parties were neck-and-neck in terms of the popular vote but the JLP, now under the leadership of Bruce Golding, regained power by a margin of thirty-three to twenty-seven seats in the lower house. The JLP won the 2007 election after overcoming disunity, a leadership crisis and signs of party fragmentation. Bolstered by its dominance of municipal government in Kingston and St Andrew since 2003, enabling it to dispense patronage in terms of jobs, licences and contracts and revitalised by a competent technocratic leader in Golding, the JLP was committed to improving a weak economy, controlling spiralling living costs and dealing with high levels of crime and unemployment. This appeared to electors in 2007, albeit marginally, to offer a more progressive government programme than the PNP could muster.

Golding's JLP government proceeded to carry out improvements but some problems proved intractable and, in 2010–11, support for it plummeted as a result of prime ministerial bungling over a serious criminal matter. Golding's financial skills helped to stabilise the Jamaican economy through his negotiations over Jamaican debt exchange (JDX). Interest rates fell but by 2012 Jamaica still had a debt of £12 billion or 130 per cent of GDP. Success in providing free healthcare and education was mitigated by failure to tackle a stagnant economy, an impoverished underclass and the persistence of violence and criminal gangs. In 2007 Jamaica, with 1,574 murders in that year, had the highest homicide rate in the Caribbean. Garrison communities existed in many wards of Kingston, with gun-toting enforcers controlling the activities of those communities. In addition, abuse of police power and official acts of waste tainted the government's reputation.

Golding resigned as prime minister in late 2011 during the fall-out from his inept handling of a high-profile criminal matter. In 2009 the United States requested that Jamaica should extradite a notorious Jamaican gang leader, Christopher 'Dudus' Coke, to New York on charges of gun-running and drug smuggling. Golding refused this request. His government then sanctioned the hire of a US law firm suspected of lobbying the US authorities to drop the case, provoking a scandal when this was made public in Jamaica. Damaged by a US government report that referred to Jamaica's prime minister as a known criminal aid of Coke, Golding, in a period of public emergency, sent the police and military officers into the Tivoli Gardens garrison community in

May 2010 to arrest Coke. A heavy-handed violent struggle ensued between the police, the military and Coke's associates, leading to seventy-six deaths. Coke was eventually captured and extradited to the United States, where he pleaded guilty to the charges against him. But the incident, widely publicised throughout Jamaica and attracting world media interest, was fatally damaging to Golding's political credibility. No compensation was paid to communities harmed by the botched government incursion in Tivoli.

A JLP minister, Andrew Holness, succeeded Golding as prime minister. After a brief tenure of two months, Holness called a general election early because the JLP's competency had been compromised by Golding's disastrous handling of the Coke affair. The result, somewhat inevitably given the JLP's political difficulties, was a return to power of the PNP in 2012, with forty-two seats in the lower house out of sixty-three. Simpson Miller then began a second term as prime minister with a comfortable majority. She had clear views about the British imperial legacy of Jamaica that became manifest in two ways. One was her belief that Jamaica should move away from being tied to the British constitutional monarchy and become a republic. In her inaugural address she argued that 'as an independent nation, we now need to complete the circle of independence' and 'initiate the process for our detachment from the Monarchy to become a Republic'. Despite this aspiration, this has yet to happen. The other view was that Jamaica should be paid reparations by Britain for the misery caused by slavery. She put this view personally to British Prime Minister David Cameron when he visited Jamaica in 2015.

Jamaica's former Prime Minister P. J. Patterson also called for reparatory justice. Cameron sidestepped the issue, instead calling upon Jamaica to repatriate Jamaican-born criminals in British prisons and offering £25 million in aid to build a new Jamaican prison.

During her second term as prime minister, Miller endorsed rights for LGBT people but was later challenged about the lack of government action to bring forward legislation to overturn a sodomy law and, more broadly, to support the LGBT community in an island where homophobia and anti-gay sentiments are widespread and sexual minorities are always at risk of violence. Battling with high levels of public debt and youth employment and implementing austerity measures, however, the PNP's overall record was insufficiently good to retain power in 2016 when the JLP achieved a narrow victory at the general election, winning thirty-two out of sixty-three seats. Holness became prime minister for the second time. Since the election he has overseen a decline in unemployment and introduced a higher minimum wage but has found it difficult to weed out institutional corruption or to deal with disaffected youth and continued violence in Kingston's slums.

In 2018–19 Holness's government issued several state of emergency addresses. Popular tourist areas, such as Montego Bay and Negril, were shut down for several weeks after a spate of violent crimes and murders in southwestern parishes. When the first state of emergency action was undertaken in St James parish in 2018, it resulted in a 70 per cent reduction in murders in that location compared with the previous year. However, the incidence of crime has remained at an alarming level in other parts of Jamaica. Thus in January 2020 state of emergency action was implemented in the vicinity of Eastern Kingston, with the Jamaica Defence Force and the Jamaica Constabulary deployed after nightfall to preserve security and public order in a location where thirty-two criminal gangs were known to operate.

On 3 September 2020 Holness led the JLP to a victory in a general election. This was a substantial result in favour of his party and himself, with the JLP winning forty-nine seats and the PNP only gaining fourteen. Turnout was low at 37 per cent of the electorate. This was largely attributable to people avoiding public appearances as a result of the COVID-19 epidemic, which spread serious respiratory illness that often led to hospitalisation and, in severe cases, to death. After his landslide success, which represented large electoral gains for the JLP since the 2016 election, Holness, beginning his third term as prime minister, stated at his inauguration ceremony that his administration's priorities were to create 150,000 jobs, to take action to reduce corruption and to finance major infrastructural developments.

Population and Health

Jamaica's population has grown significantly since 1945 and improvements have been made in most demographic indicators. The island's population totalled 1.4 million in 1945, 2.1 million in 1980 and 2.9 million in 2020. This growth has been influenced more by declining mortality than by increasing fertility. The crude death rate for Jamaica was 14.9 per 1,000 of population in 1945, but this had declined to 6.9 per 1,000 in 2018. While deaths from degenerative diseases increased over this period, better public health provision, fewer deaths from infant mortality and, for adults, from respiratory and digestive diseases, malaria and tuberculosis have all contributed to declining mortality rates. The crude birth rate was 30 per 1,000 in 1945 but only 12 per 1,000 in 2018: numbers of births have consistently fallen annually during the first two decades of the twenty-first century. This trend has been affected by more secure contraceptive protection against unwanted pregnancies, but the fall in the crude birth rate has also resulted from lifestyle choices leading to adults having fewer children, a phenomenon common to many countries over the past half century. Mortality decline has helped life expectancy to increase from 58.6 years in 1950–5 to 75.5 years in 2010–15. Infant mortality rates have declined significantly from 91.9 per 1,000 births in 1950 to 11.3 per 1,000 in 2020. In children aged under five, the main causes of death are fetal growth disorder, problems associated with childbirth and respiratory distress of the newborn.

The reasons for declining deaths and increased life expectancy during many decades of population expansion can be attributed to many causes. Economic considerations have undoubtedly helped. Though Jamaica has witnessed periods of high inflation and negative economic growth, and though unemployment and poverty are common among ordinary people, living standards have not declined seriously over the past half century because of a flow of earnings in Jamaica's informal economy and the regular return of remittances from diasporic emigrants to family members. These monies have assisted Jamaicans in seeking healthcare insurance to pay fees for public health provision.

Two main positive features of Jamaica's healthcare since 1945, directly affecting the island's demographic statistics, are improvements in tackling diseases and the advance of an effective public healthcare system. In 1945 the seven leading causes of death in Jamaica were all infectious diseases. Tuberculosis was the main killer, but it had disappeared as a major cause of mortality by 1960 after an effective roll-out of a mass BCG vaccination campaign. It has not been totally eradicated from Jamaica, but is currently dormant. Owing to the development of successful vaccines, other preventable diseases have been curtailed in recent decades. Notable successes attributable to vaccines have been the eradication of poliomyelitis and measles in Jamaica in 1982 and 1992, respectively. The last case of diphtheria on the island was noted in 1994.

Rates of serious infections such as syphilis and gonorrhoea have declined in recent decades. However, the containment of these ailments has been accompanied by a rise in chronic diseases associated with lifestyle choices, which have also risen in many other parts of the world. A national survey for 2017 undertaken for adult Jamaicans aged fifteen to seventy-four shows an upward trend in obesity, hypertension and diabetes, attributable to sedentary lifestyles and poor nutritional choices. According to the survey, these health problems affected 50 per cent, 25 per cent and 10 per cent of the population, respectively. As noted above, in 2020 Jamaica had a much lower rate of infection and fewer deaths from the COVID-19 virus than many other countries.

Jamaica has developed effective public healthcare for its population since the Second World War. A private healthcare system caters for tourists and the better-off in the population. Most Jamaicans, however, receive public healthcare through hospitals, pharmacies and nursing facilities. Four regional health authorities deliver public health through a network of care facilities at primary, secondary and tertiary levels. These are coordinated through a Ministry of Health. In 1948 the University College of the West Indies Hospital was built on the Mona campus of the newly established university college and the training of doctors was improved. The hospital still serves as a major health provider in the Greater Kingston area. In the late 1960s community health aides were incorporated into health teams and dental services were improved. Hospital boards were established in 1972. Compulsory immunisation for all children was instigated in 1978 to protect against diseases such as tetanus, tuberculosis and poliomyelitis, and certificates detailing the immunisations had to be produced before children could attend school.

Programmes to advance healthcare have proliferated over the past quarter century. The National Health Services Act of 1997 implemented four semiautonomous regional health authorities to deliver public health through a network of care facilities. These four bodies rather than hospitals have assumed responsibility for healthcare decision-making. Programmes implemented include the National Health Fund (NHF), the Jamaica Drug for the Elderly Programme (JADEP) and the Programme of Advancement through Health and Education (PATH). Removal of fees for children accessing public healthcare in 2007 followed by the introduction of free healthcare for all users of the public health system in the following year have led to a surge in the number of Jamaicans accessing public health facilities. Substantial additional government funds have been allocated to regional health authorities to make up the shortfall in funds arising from the ending of charging fees for health-care services. Jamaica has private healthcare provision, but this is taken up by less than 10 per cent of the population.

In April 2020 the spread of the potentially lethal COVID-19 virus in a global pandemic led to a lockdown of the Jamaican economy, in common with many other countries worldwide. Many household and domestic work-ers lost their jobs in the lockdown, and the Jamaica govern-ment has now to decide when and how to reopen the economy while avoiding social and economic chaos. The Jamaican tourism industry has closed; foreign exchange earnings have fallen because of declining demand for baux-ite and alumina; and many Jamaicans have been left without incomes. The Jamaican government responded to the threat of the COVID-19 virus by implementing school closures, short-term curfews and work-at-home directives for many employees. Quarantine procedures and testing were established for international travellers arriving in Jamaica. State of emergency measures were introduced between April and June 2020 in several Jamaican parishes. Despite grounds for alarm in relation to public health, however, Jamaica has not witnessed anything like the spread of COVID-19 in many other countries. As of 8 July 2020, Jamaica had recorded 745 confirmed cases of COVID-19 and ten deaths. A vaccine to treat this disease was only manufactured and distributed in 2021. By late March 2022 Jamaica had suffered 2,875 COVID-related deaths.

Prime Minister Holness, in a speech dated 6 October 2020, praised Jamaica's handling of the pandemic, claiming that 'the main credit for this must go to our public health workers and front line responders' who had 'done an outstanding job in extremely difficult and trying circumstances'. He argued that containment and control measures undertaken by his government had helped to stem the spread of the virus in Jamaica and to build health system capacity through increased hospital beds, equipment and personnel. Acknowledging both an economic and a psychosocial dimension to the pandemic, he nevertheless concluded that a lockdown of Jamaica by closing borders and 'tighter and stricter limits on movement and gathering within our borders' would 'decimate the economy and further exacerbate the psychosocial issues'.

Education

Two separate reports influenced educational provision in Jamaica after the Second World War. The Kandel Report on Secondary Education (1943/4) – named after the comparative educator Isaac Kandel, a US citizen – and the Plan for Post-Primary Education addressed Jamaica's educational, economic and social conditions, pointing out the current deficiencies and looking forward to an era of post-primary education that would eliminate class and colour discrimination. The West India Royal Commission, convened in 1936 under the chairmanship of Lord Moyne, released a report in 1945 that recommended more central government control over primary schools to improve their administrative efficiency and changes in the school curriculum to reflect the realities of Jamaican life. Moyne also recommended that all newly built schools should be government controlled.

Not all of the recommendations of the two reports came to fruition, but the steer towards more state involvement in education was implemented. The Ministry of Education, founded in Jamaica in 1957, has six regional offices that monitor and manage education on the island. These are supplemented by several statutory bodies and agencies including the National Council on Education, which nominates boards of management for more than 1,000 schools, and the Early Childhood Commission, which oversees the work of elementary provision in primary schools and early childhood education providers, such as nurseries. In 1982 Jamaica established a Human Employment and Resources Training (HEART) Trust as a government agency to coordinate post-secondary vocational training at twenty training centres and institutes.

Today most Jamaican children attend nurseries between the ages of 3 and 5. Universal elementary education for children aged 7 to 11 means that nearly all Jamaican children have access to primary education. As of 2017, 90 per cent of these pupils attended state schools while the remainder were educated at fee-paying private schools. Primary schools in Jamaica follow an integrated curriculum based on learning languages, basic mathematics, academic socialisation and, in the higher years, music, physical education, religion, science and social studies. Spanish is the main non-English language taught in these schools. Academic performance in the last year of primary school was for a long time assessed by a Grade Six

Achievement Test (GSAT) but this was replaced in 2019 with a Primary Exit Profile (PEP).

Secondary school education is not compulsory in Jamaica. The share of Jamaican pupils of secondary age attending school is now between 80 and 85 per cent of the age cohort whereas by 1943 it was under 3 per cent. Almost a fifth of juvenile Jamaicans drop out of secondary school, especially among low-income households in rural areas, where the cost of uniforms, teaching materials and examination fees is financially difficult for parents to meet even though secondary education is technically free. Holness pinpointed a major problem in his country's educational provision when he noted, while education minister in 2011, that most Jamaican households were still struggling to produce one high school graduate. In an attempt to redress that situation, Holness announced a high-level Commission on Education Transformation to review and assess the structure and operation of the Jamaican education system.

British qualifications were replicated in Jamaica after the Second World War for secondary school pupils aged sixteen and eighteen. Ordinary Level examinations were the norm until the 1970s and Advanced Level examinations were taken until the 1980s. These have been replaced by exams administered by the Caribbean Examinations Council (CXC). Upper secondary school pupils prepare for the external Caribbean Secondary Education Certificate (CSEC) after five years of post-primary schooling. A successful minimum outcome would be to achieve passes in mathematics, English and three elective subjects out of a choice of six to ten subjects. Sixth formers (aged sixteen to eighteen) prepare for the

Caribbean Advanced Proficiency Examination (CAPE). Good pass grades are required at that level for students wanting to proceed to degree-level courses.

Students who enter further education and those seeking teaching certificates can take courses in community colleges and teacher training colleges, mainly founded in the 1960s and 1970s. A College of Arts, Science and Technology, now a University of Technology, was set up in 1984 to promote vocational training. For degree-level work, Jamaica has the Mona campus of the University of the West Indies (UWI). Founded in 1948, this fine, reputable institution has expanded to encompass three main campuses in the Anglophone Caribbean (the other branches are in Trinidad and Barbados). Offering a wide range of undergraduate and graduate courses, with many departments engaged in internationally recognised research, the University of the West Indies became the first home-grown institution in the English-speaking Caribbean to offer university degrees.

UWI is now the largest higher education institution in the Caribbean region, catering for 18,500 students on its Mona campus as of 2017. Until 1962 the Mona campus awarded University of London degrees, but with the coming of Jamaican independence its status was upgraded to the University of the West Indies, which grants its own degrees. Many graduates have found professional employment in Jamaica, and the school system on the island has benefited from recruiting home-grown talent. Today, however, the Mona branch of the university is facing financial pressure, for the Jamaican government cut its funding by a quarter in 2010. The University Hospital of the West Indies, based on the Mona campus, delivers patient care, teaching and research for Jamaicans. The Mona campus has seven faculties and serves as the main campus of the University of the West Indies.

A notable moment in the history of UWI was the invitation to the US civil rights campaigner the Reverend Dr Martin Luther King to speak at the valedictory service after the annual graduation ceremony in June 1965. King gave a memorable speech to a packed, appreciative audience, adapting a theme he had addressed many times before entitled 'Facing the Challenge of a New Age', in which he referred to the passing of the colonial order and to the need to face the challenges of today and the future in order to promote freedom among people and to progress to a better civil rights era for all people. King told his listeners 'the time is always right to do right' and that, in the case of Jamaica, 'whenever a new nation comes into history, it brings with it new challenges and new responsibilities. The great challenge facing all of us today is to somehow stand before the opportunities of the moment and face the challenges of the hour with creativity and with commitment and with determination.' On the day after delivering his speech, King laid a wreath at the grave of Marcus Garvey to emphasise the bonds between the Jamaican people and blacks in the United States, for Garvey during his years in North America had striven for black people everywhere to be treated with dignity and fairness.

The Jamaican Diaspora

Jamaicans had migrated overseas in search of work, notably between 1880 and 1920, when they took up job opportunities in Central America, other parts of the

Caribbean and the United States. But the interwar depression years and the Second World War had ruled out extensive out-migration. Fairly rapidly after peace came in 1945, however, numerous Jamaicans renewed an interest in seeking better livelihoods overseas, and it was natural that they would seek to move to countries in the Anglosphere. Between the end of the Second World War and the present day, emigration has always exceeded immigration in relation to Jamaica and significantly large Jamaican diasporic communities have been created overseas. One driving force behind the diaspora consists of the relatively limited work opportunities in Jamaica for skilled workers. Most of the Jamaican emigrants are therefore economic migrants in search of reliable employment and higher wages.

Emigration has involved sizeable numbers: as of 2015, 1.3 million Jamaican-born people lived abroad. Three destinations dominate the diaspora: the United States, the United Kingdom and Canada in descending numerical order. The census of 2013 indicated that 1.1 million Jamaicans were living in the United States. The figure for the United Kingdom was 800,000 Jamaicans in 2015, and for Canada, 309,000 Jamaicans in 2016. Relatively small emigration occurred from Jamaica to other Caribbean and Central American territories. Today the largest contingent of Jamaican emigrants in a non-Anglophone country is in Costa Rica. During the 1970s, Jamaica had 327,779 emigrants, but this fell to 239,207 in the 1980s and to 212,892 in the 1990s. The figures exclude Jamaicans travelling to overseas destinations on visitor visas, previously acquired work permits or residence status as well as people moving back and forwards between Jamaica and other countries on a temporary basis.

Between 1945 and the early 1960s, the main destination for Jamaican emigrants was the United Kingdom. This reflected the long historic ties between the British Isles and the Caribbean, stretching back for three centuries. The pattern changed from the early 1960s onwards in response to changing immigration laws in Anglophone countries. The United Kingdom introduced restrictive immigration policies but the United States introduced immigration regulations in 1962 that favoured the selection of immigrants on the basis of skills rather than nationality or race and, at the same time, Canada brought in immigration laws that enabled the entry of foreigners on the basis of education and occupation. These changes helped to shift Jamaica's emigrant exodus away from the United Kingdom and towards the United States and Canada during the remainder of the 1960s. This has continued as a trend in the past half century. Thus since 1970 the United States has received 80 per cent of Jamaica's emigrants, Canada has imported 17 per cent, and the United Kingdom has taken under 3 per cent.

Jamaican emigrants had arrived in Britain in small numbers for well over a century before the Second World War, mainly gravitating towards London for their residence. Some of these people had a high international profile, such as Marcus Garvey, who lived in London for the last years of his life. Ships' crew from Jamaica and other West Indian islands had entered the port of Liverpool in the 1920s and 1930s on a small scale and there had been a modestly sized black community in London since the eighteenth century, but migration on

FIGURE 6.5 *Empire Windrush*. Daily Herald Archive/SSPL/Getty
Images

a significant scale from Jamaica to Britain had never
occurred before 1945. For the subsequent three decades
this situation was transformed as Jamaicans entered the
UK workforce on an increasing scale as part of a broader
Caribbean diaspora to Britain.

The beginnings of the Jamaican diaspora to Britain
after the Second War began in earnest in 1948 with
the arrival of the British ship the *Empire Windrush*
from the Caribbean at Tilbury docks in Essex.
Among the passengers were 417 Jamaicans relocating
to Britain in search of work and better living standards. Most of them had taken this opportunity after

reading an advertisement in Jamaica's *Daily Gleaner* for ship passages costing £28 10 shillings (equivalent to over £1,000 today). Many of them had served in Britain during the Second World War in munitions factories or as ground crew for the RAF. They had returned to their Jamaican homes after the war ended, but presumably had a sufficiently positive experience of life in Britain to wish to live there in peacetime. Their arrival was a newsworthy item and many black-and-white photographs survive of smartly dressed Jamaican men, women and children walking down the ladder from the ship to set foot on British soil.

Both the Jamaican and British governments supported this diaspora. From the Jamaican government's perspective, high unemployment, poverty on the island and a strong desire to avoid a repeat of Jamaica's tumultuous labour protests of the late 1930s were encouraging elements in supporting emigration. From the British end, there was an immediate need to recruit additional overseas labour to fill employment vacancies as Britain entered an era of post-war reconstruction and the introduction of a welfare state in 1948, creating a large number of public sector jobs. But why, it might be asked, were Jamaican and other Caribbean islands regarded as prime sources of labour supply? The answer does not lie with great enthusiasm on the part of the British government, which was worried about bringing in black Jamaicans and integrating them into British life where a strong attachment to maintaining a white majority population was common. Instead, the British government allowed Jamaicans to settle in Britain after 1948 as a necessity after it proved difficult to recruit enough Irish, continental or white dominion migrants to make up the labour shortfall.

Jamaica dominated the first wave of Caribbean migrants to Britain after the Second World War. Britain's 1948 Nationality Act granted free movement to its Caribbean citizens – Jamaica, of course, not yet being an independent nation. Between 1948 and 1951, 90 per cent of the Caribbean immigrants entering Britain were from Jamaica. Thereafter the West Indian diaspora to the United Kingdom became diffused among Barbados and other small islands in the Lesser Antilles. The influx of Caribbean immigrants continued to increase until the early 1970s, and over time they were joined in Britain by people coming from other Commonwealth countries in Asia and Africa. Most Jamaicans stayed in Britain, though there were some returnees. By 2010 over 300,000 people of Jamaican descent lived in the United Kingdom, mostly in London and other large conurbations. From 1948 onwards these migrants often found work in the National Health Service, as doctors, nurses and orderlies, and in transport, becoming bus drivers, ticket collectors and general maintenance staff for the London Tube and rail systems.

Jamaican migrants to Britain brought with them their patois, dress codes, music, sport and cuisine, adding to the multiracial and multiethnic patterns of modern British life. They forged continuing networks and connections with family members back in Jamaica as part of a transnational diaspora. But it was far from plain sailing. Owing to modest levels of pay and lack of savings, many Jamaicans lived in poor, often seedy, neighbourhoods and were reliant on the provision of public sector work. Too many Jamaicans ended up in almost ghetto suburbs such as Brixton in south London or deprived areas such as Haringey in north-east London. Racial tensions in British society were common under the surface of daily life despite the British government legislating regularly in favour of better race relations. The Notting Hill race riots of 1958, the Brixton riots of 1985 and the Brighton riots of 2005 all involved West Indian residents subjected to racial abuse. Under Theresa May's Conservative government, between 2016 and 2019, Jamaicans with no official record of settled status in the United Kingdom were deported back to the Caribbean, including children of the *Windrush* generation. This was unfairly handled by the British government. Part of the problem arose from the Home Office's decision in 2010 to destroy all the landing cards of the Jamaicans who had arrived on the *Windrush* decades earlier, leaving those migrants without paper documentation of their status in the United Kingdom.

Jamaicans emigrating to the United States from the 1960s onwards included people with professional qualifications, students and economic migrants. By the late 1970s one-fifth of the Jamaicans in the United States were employed as white-collar workers. Jamaicans are now the second highest group of overseas seasonal workers in the United States apart from Mexicans. Most Jamaicans have clustered in the north-east states of New York, New Jersey, Connecticut and Maryland and in south-east states such as Georgia and Florida where Miami and its surroundings, as the largest metropolitan area in the United States with proximity to the Caribbean, has long been a magnet for Jamaicans and other West

Indian migrants. Jamaica was a pioneering Caribbean country for sending emigrants to the United States, but its dominance has declined over time. In 1980, 63 per cent of the US Caribbean population came from Jamaica; this fell modestly to 58 per cent in 1990.

US hotels and resorts recruit Jamaicans as seasonal workers because they speak English and work hard. Jamaicans permanently living in the United States have earned a reputation for a significant skilled contribution to the workforce. Jamaican men and women have migrated to the United States since the 1970s to work in service, healthcare, retail and microelectronics occupations. Many of them have become successful economic migrants as a result of their skills and industriousness. Caribbean migrants to New York City, for instance, have achieved more leadership positions and better incomes than African-Americans, for two reasons. One is that they appear to have gained more self-confidence from being raised in a predominantly black society in Jamaica and other West Indian islands rather than forging their way in the predominantly white host culture of the United States. The second is that they have worked hard, saved and taken opportunities for advancement as marginal immigrants wanting to improve their living standards.

The Jamaican government has a National Diaspora Policy, focused on international development and migration, that seeks to engage with Jamaicans living overseas in three ways: to develop the diaspora in the host country; to involve the diaspora in homeland development; and to construct partnerships and interaction between the diaspora and institutions in Jamaica. The policy is concerned to maintain the socio-cultural connections of Jamaicans with their homelands, but it also has a significant economic component as remittances from abroad to Jamaica sent via international money transfer companies amounted to US$2.3 million in 2016, which is equivalent to about 15 per cent of Jamaica's GDP. The monies remitted (which exclude informal flows) were used for food, utilities, housing, education and family support for relatives living in Jamaica.

The Economy

The pre-1939 concentration of Jamaica's economy on the agricultural production and export of sugar and bananas diversified considerably after the end of the Second World War. These commodities continued to be significant components of the Jamaican economy. Other agricultural products, such as coffee, pimento and ginger, had a high reputation for quality – especially the famous Jamaican Blue Mountain coffee – but they had limited markets. The addition of bauxite production and export became important and a number of industries were developed including food processing, oil refining, building construction, textiles and other garments, plastic goods, tourism and remittance earnings. Exports underwent a geographical shift. For centuries before 1939 Britain was the main overseas market for Jamaican products, but after 1945 this shifted quite rapidly to the United States, which took over half of Jamaica's exports by 1976.

Primary agricultural products, such as sugar and bananas, accounted for 30 per cent of Jamaica's export earnings in the 1950s, but the contribution had dropped to 9 per cent by 1970. The decline in the share of agricultural products in exports was partly the result of the increase of bauxite among Jamaica's exports but also stemmed from economic difficulties in the production and marketing of primary agricultural produce. The decline in commodity exports was mitigated to some extent by Jamaica's signing of preferential trade agreements with the European Economic Community (EEC) referred to below; but these arrangements did not fully halt the contraction in the export of primary produce.

The sugar industry fared reasonably well in Jamaica in the twenty years after the Second World War but significant decline has since occurred. The signing of the Commonwealth Sugar Agreement in 1951 provided continued access for Jamaican sugar in the British market. This attracted investment into sugar operations in the island, and production grew until a peak year in 1965, after which it declined. Tate & Lyle then decided that its sugar interests in Jamaica were becoming losing concerns, and so it sold them to the Jamaican government, which placed sugar estates under workers' cooperatives. These operated under severe financial constraints, however, and they were dissolved in 1981. Four years later Tate & Lyle returned to operate the sugar industry at the invitation of the Jamaican government; but even though Jamaica had a guaranteed price for its sugar exports to the EEC – courtesy of the Sugar Protocol of the Lomé Convention, the successor to the Commonwealth Sugar Agreement – the Jamaican sugar industry continued to decline. Jamaican sugar production fell from 290,000 tons in 1978 to 175,000 tons in 2000, when sugar accounted for 7 per cent of Jamaica's exports.

Jamaica resumed shipping bananas to Britain after 1945 under the control of the Ministry of Food. In 1966 the British banana firm Fyffes – a subsidiary of the United Fruit Company – launched a price war that badly affected Jamaica's banana growers. An agreement was made to split British imports of bananas from the Caribbean between Jamaica and the Windward Islands, but Fyffes ended the agreement in 1970. With plenty of worldwide production of bananas, Jamaica's industry suffered from sharp competition in terms of production, prices and costs. In 1999 Jamaica's banana production was 130,000 tons, amounting to only 2.4 per cent of the island's exports. In 2008 Tropical Storm Gustav destroyed 80 per cent of Jamaica's banana crop. The result was that Jamaica exported no bananas in the next six years. However, in 2015 a Banana Export Expansion programme brought infrastructural support to the industry with $53.5 million funding from the European Union.

By the late 1950s, Jamaica had made significant improvements in cattle breeding and grass pasture that proved economically beneficial. New cattle breeds suitable for local conditions were introduced, including the Jamaica Hope, a small animal that could withstand the heat, needed little oversight in herds and had demonstrated a capacity for reproduction over a period of years. These cattle were well suited to Jamaica's peasant agriculture. Other types of cattle reared in Jamaica were two cross breeds, the Jamaica Red and the Jamaica Black, and the original 'Spanish' cattle found on the island. Connected with cattle breeding was investment in pangola grass pasture. Lands mined for bauxite production had to be replaced with pangola grass, which was largely

353

immune to drought and able to feed cattle, or, alternatively, a payment had to be made to the government to fund and convert other land to pasture.

After the Second World War, Jamaica rapidly developed a lucrative new industry in bauxite. This produced ceramic material that was widely used in cutting tools, taps, appliances and spark plugs. Aluminium is produced from bauxite. Its alloys became widely used in the defence and space industries. Airplanes and automobiles were major users of aluminium. From 1952 onwards large companies were given support to establish bauxite mining at different Jamaican locations. In the same year, alumina was first made in Jamaica from bauxite. Deep mining was necessary to access the red bauxite that had the highest commercial value. The progress of this industry was rapid. In 1957 exports of alumina and bauxite were eight times the 1955 figures and made up about 44 per cent of total domestic exports.

The industry rose to become the third largest bauxite producer in the world by 1998, when Jamaica produced 10.4 per cent of worldwide output. There was a negative effect of bauxite extraction, however, on Jamaica. Between 1948 and 1968, 170,000 acres of land were acquired for bauxite mining in Jamaica. Smallholders paying rent became landless and either migrated to the towns for work or constructed shanty dwellings on scrub land. The transportation of bauxite and its stockpiling caused considerable air pollution through emissions of iron oxide as well as noise pollution. These deleterious effects of bauxite mining outweighed positive gains made through the industry's contribution to circulating capital, higher retail activity and the expansion of urban infrastructure.

Nearly all bauxite was exported as there was little domestic demand for the product. American companies invested heavily in this Jamaican resource, which was of high quality and relatively cheap to refine. Jamaica had plenty of labour to undertake the work extracting bauxite, which mainly lay between six and twelve inches beneath the earth's surface. Jamaica now supplies about half of the annual bauxite import to the United States. Bauxite played an important role in Jamaica's trade growth with the United States in the second half of the twentieth century. Before American aluminium companies arrived in Jamaica, over half of Jamaica's trade lay with Britain. However, bauxite exports from Jamaica are now mainly linked to North American markets. In the first quarter of 2019, for example, Jamaica exported 498,000 tonnes of bauxite to the United States, amounting to two-thirds of Jamaican exports of that product.

Jamaica has a variable provision of transport for the movement of freight cargo and passengers. It is well served in terms of air travel, with two large airports catering for international flights. Norman Manley International Airport, situated on the south coast, is the main air terminal for Kingston and its surrounding area, while Donald Sangster International Airport handles flights to Montego Bay and the north coast. Jamaica also has several small commuter airports. Railway provision, by contrast, is very poor in modern Jamaica. All passenger traffic on the island's railways ceased in 1992 and only short railway lines, specialising in the short-distance haulage of bauxite, still exist. Jamaica has a dense road network of arterial, secondary, tertiary, urban and parochial roads, but public resources for road improvements are scarce. The National Transport

Policy of 1993, aiming to improve road provision, was never completed and crucially omitted the issue of maintenance.

To handle overseas shipping and freight, Jamaica has three major ports: Kingston Container Terminal and the ports of Ocho Rios and Montego Bay. Before the expansion of the port area of Kingston, the wharves were crammed together with limited storage and transportation facilities. The Kingston Container Terminal transformed this situation. Covering a large area comprising 2,410 metres of berth split into three terminals and 194 hectares of cargo storage space, the terminal has provided the facilities for Kingston to handle much larger freight consignments. The management and development of the terminal, one of the largest in the Caribbean, has been operated since 2015 by Kingston Freeport Terminal Ltd. This organisation oversees the improvement of port facilities, infrastructure and operating equipment, and provides a competitive transhipment hub for shipping and freight linking Jamaica to Central, South and North America. The expansion of the Kingston Container Terminal provides sufficient water, offloading and storage space to handle the large ships using the expanded Panama Canal. Continuing dredging of sand and silt in the harbour, the deepening of several channels and the cutting of ledges will enable the largest vessels to make use of the terminal. An ambitious plan seeks to make Jamaica the world's fourth-largest logistical transport hub after Singapore, Dubai and Rotterdam.

Jamaica's government has planned for future socio-economic developments under a plan entitled Vision 2030 Jamaica. The Planning Institute for Jamaica has referred to this national development plan as a 'roadmap' to make Jamaica 'the place of choice to live, work, raise families and do business'. The plan includes four goals designed to produce positive outcomes. The first intention is to empower Jamaicans to achieve their fullest potential by supporting a healthy and stable population, by providing world-class education and training, by implementing effective social protection and by promoting an authentic and transformational culture. The second goal is to make Jamaican society secure, cohesive and just by emphasising security, safety and effective governance. A third objective is to develop a prosperous economy through emphasis on a strong macroeconomy, an enabling business environment, strong economic infrastructure, energy security and efficiency, a technology-enabled society and internationally competitive industry structures. The fourth goal is to ensure Jamaica has a healthy natural environment through sustainable management and use of environmental and natural resources, hazard risk reduction, adaptation to climate change and sustainable urban and rural development.

Urbanisation

Jamaica's urban population had risen from 500,000 people in 1960 to 1.65 million in 2021. This was the most urbanised period in the island's history. Currently, 56 per cent of Jamaica's citizens live in urban areas. Kingston has always dominated Jamaica's urban life. At the time of independence, 20 per cent of the island's population lived in Kingston; now the proportion has risen to over 30 per cent. In 2001 the population of the Kingston metropolitan region was nearly 869,000. To accommodate these people, Kingston has spread out into new suburbs on the Liguanea Plain and Portmore and scattered settlements along the main road to Spanish Town. The rise in the development of Portmore was especially striking as residential housing and shopping facilities increased its population from a few houses in 1970 to 160,000 people by 2001. Spanish Town remained a backwater, with no new government offices added to provide additional employment. In August 1951 Hurricane Charley devastated many buildings in Spanish Town, which also suffered from a yellow fever outbreak in 1955.

From the 1950s onwards, with the greater availability of motor cars, middle-class professionals working in Spanish Town chose to live elsewhere and to commute to work. Better housing was becoming available in Kingston's new suburbs, which attracted a significant number of people living and working in Spanish Town. The construction of the Twickenham Park Estate brought long overdue modernisation to the vicinity of Spanish Town, whose central core was a down-at-heel, dusty market centre full of pot-holed roads and only basic amenities. Middle-class housing at Twickenham Park along with an increase in squatter settlements and government sponsored housing estates along the Spanish Town bypass, however, helped to increased Spanish Town's population from 14,700 in 1960 to 131,000 in 2001.

The area between Kingston and Spanish Town, a distance of only eleven miles, is now full of fairly newly developed housing and it has been referred to as a spread city. Within Kingston itself the commercial centre of New Kingston, an area for banks, shops and hotels, had revitalised the uptown area by 1980. This is now the main location for international visitors to stay in hotels in Kingston. A significant building development lay in the construction of Coronation Market in the late 1980s – the largest single market in the Anglophone Caribbean. Its cast iron framed hall offers a vast food emporium for the lower classes in inner West Kingston. Vendors come from all over Jamaica to sell their produce at Coronation Market at competitive prices. In the downtown Kingston area, Duke Street has a concentration of professional business premises such as insurance agencies, real estate agencies, solicitors, barristers and dentists. Several cultural buildings, such as the Institute of Jamaica, the National Library of Jamaica and the National Gallery of Jamaica, are also located in the Kingston's downtown area.

In 1960 Kingston was dominated by rental properties, accounting for 70 per cent of households compared with 26 per cent given over to owner occupancy. Over the next three decades, owner occupiers increased in number and as a proportion of Kingston's population, clustering particularly in East Kingston and in the city's outer northern districts stretching out to Spanish Town. Some 40 per cent of Kingston's housing in 1991 was rented. In the late twentieth century, Kingston could claim considerable improvements in the availability of middle-income housing compared with the situation at independence, relatively small levels of squatting but also continuing problems with housing amenities. Thus by 1991 a quarter of Kingstonian households did not have sewerage facilities while only 60 per cent of homes had piped water. Tenements in downtown Kingston had high annual population turnovers, poor facilities and precarious tenure arrangements.

The slum population of Kingston, comprising overwhelmingly all-black households, increased from 200,000 in 1960 to 350,000 by 1991. Jamaica's authorities have periodically attempted to improve the situation. Prime Minister Seaga, for example, was proud of the efforts made under his leadership to clean up the deprived area of Tivoli Gardens in West Kingston in the early 1980s. 'What we set out to do in West Kingston', he wrote, 'was to reverse the process of decay. Where there were cemeteries, there are now playing fields; where yesterday there was crime, there is learning for tomorrow. What we have achieved is not only to take the man out of the slum, but the slum out of the man.' These stirring words, however, should not detract from the fact that corrugated iron shacks and hovels are still easily visible in downtown Kingston, with shabby, dirty alleyways interspersing many streets near the main commercial areas. One does not have to wander far away from the harbour and the government buildings of downtown Kingston to see clearly the continuing signs of housing and social deprivation.

Montego Bay is easily the largest urban area on Jamaica's north coast. With a rapidly increasing population, which reached 96,000 in 2021, Montego Bay is the second largest English-speaking city in the Caribbean, far exceeding the population levels of other north coast Jamaican towns such as Ocho Rios (9,450 people in 2021) and Port Antonio (14,450 in 2021). Most of Jamaica's tourism industry is based in and around Montego Bay, which benefits from many white sand beaches and the flagship tourist resort of Sandals Montego Bay. Major cruise ships include Montego Bay on their itinerary, bringing well-heeled international visitors to Jamaica. The central business district of Montego Bay has numerous financial institutions such as banks and credit agencies as well as auditing firms. Port Antonio's tendency to attract heavy rains has reduced its tourist potential, though it was the location of the former Titchfield Hotel, which catered to wealthy North American tourists arriving there on banana ships from the 1890s onwards.

Cultural Markers

During the era of Crown Colony government, Jamaica made few strides towards establishing distinctive cultural activity beyond the efforts of Garveyism in the arts in the 1920s and 1930s and the emergence of Rastafarianism as a unique expression of beliefs. In short, Jamaica before 1945 lacked major novelists, poets, artists, architects and sculptors. The sculptor and wood carver Edna Manley, wife of the politician Norman Manley, summed up the dearth of artistic activity in an article that appeared in the *Daily Gleaner* in September 1934: 'Who are the creative sculptors, painters, engravers and where is the work that should be the expression of its Country's existence and growth? A few anaemic imitators of European traditions, a few charming parlor tricks, and then practically silence. Nothing virile, nor original, nor in any sense creative, and nothing, above all, that is an expression of the deep-rooted, hidden pulse of the Country – that thing that gives it its unique life.'

The post-1945 cultural development of Jamaica transformed this barrenness with significant Jamaican cultural
achievements. Norman Manley believed that the awakening cultural achievements of Jamaican artists were stimu-
lated by the political changes promoted by the PNP. In
1939 he had argued that political action was giving
impetus to a nationalist consciousness in Jamaica, and
that 'this political awakening must and always goes hand
in hand with cultural growth . . . Around us and before our
very eyes are stirring the first shoots of a deeply felt
"national" artistic and intellectual life.' Though Manley
exaggerated the extent to which cultural markers in
Jamaica would be influenced by political developments,
he realised that the island's culture could only become
fully creative under its own forms of artistic expression
that moved beyond British colonial dominance.

After 1945, Jamaica's artistic expression found outlets in
the plastic arts, poetry, prose, theatrical work and music. In
the late 1940s Edna Manley convened successful art classes
in Kingston. These were instrumental in leading to the
foundation of the Jamaica School of Art and Craft in
1951, administered by the Institute of Jamaica and situated
in Kingston Gardens. This became the central school for
Jamaicans who wished to make a career of art and craft. It
still flourishes today, offering courses in painting, anima-
tion, jewellery, photography, design studies, textiles, wood
sculpture, printmaking and fashion. The forms of art produced under the aegis of this significant institution were
multifaceted, including those undertaken as part of cubism,
modernism, Afro-Caribbean cubism and installation art.

David 'Jack' Pottinger was one of the leading Jamaican
artists who emerged from Manley's tutelage. He began his

professional life as a house- and sign-painter but progressed to become an accomplished painter of scenes from downtown Kingston for more than half a century. Most of his art depicted street scenes that included higglers, market activities and hawking, penetrating the backyards and side lanes of the island's capital. The National Gallery of Jamaica contains fine examples of Pottinger's paintings such as *Backyard* (1945), *Trench Town* (1959) and *Snapper Time* (1970), with elongated figures of people set against recognisable shacks and other buildings. These are examples of nationalist paintings with urban settings. Their rural equivalents can be found in the paintings of another artist and printmaker influenced by Manley's instruction, namely Albert Huie, whose important paintings include *The Counting Lesson* (1938), a pioneer portrait of a black Jamaican girl by a black Jamaican artist, and *Crop Time* (1955), depicting the energetic activities involved in gathering the sugar harvest.

Jamaica has produced no major novelist comparable to the literary significance of fiction writers from other Caribbean islands, such as the Nobel prizewinner V. S. Naipaul of Trinidad, but prose authors have produced some notable creative writing. Lorna Goodison, partly educated at the Jamaica School of Art, has written three well-received collections of short stories – *Baby Mother and the King of Swords* (1990), *Fool-Fool Rose is Leaving Labour-In-Vain Savannah* (2005) and *By Love Possessed* (2012). Michelle Cliff wrote two novels that explore Jamaican identity in *Abeng* (1984) and *No Telephone to Heaven* (1987) as well as short stories and essays. Arguably, however, Jamaica's poets have found a larger audience for their work than prose writers.

Louise Bennett ('Miss Lou') wrote several books in Jamaican patois, hosted children's television programmes that deployed local languages, and recorded Jamaican children's songs and games. 'Dub' poetry, making use of patois, reggae and folk material, thrived from the 1970s onwards. Mikey Smith was a 'dub' poet who spoke his verse to reggae rhythms and took his poetry to the dance floor. Other notable Jamaican poets who have achieved international acclaim include the island's two most recent poet laureates, Mervyn Morris and Lorna Goodison.

Dance and theatre are other types of artistic expression that have flourished in Jamaica since the Second World War. The National Dance Theatre movement was prominent in independent Jamaica under the leadership of the choreographer and scholar Rex Nettleford and the professional dancer Eddie Thomas. Drawing on Jamaican history and contemporary life, Nettleford's important contribution to Jamaican dance highlighted the African influences that still resonated in the island's social life. His performances incorporated singing and drumming to depict Afro-Caribbean folk traditions through the medium of dance. He was responsible for training generations of Jamaican choreographers and dancers to a high professional standard with a significant international outreach. Nettleford's academic credentials led to him becoming the first graduate of the University of the West Indies to become its vice chancellor, in which role he worked tirelessly as a public intellectual and artistic champion of Jamaican independence.

The Sistren Theatre Collective (meaning 'sisterhood') was founded in Kingston in 1977. Using Jamaican performance traditions, speaking often in patois, and centred around themes connected with the patriarchal suppression of women, this collective has regularly convened workshops that alter a playscript with the testimony of local communities. This has led to revisions of the original material adjusted to appeal to community theatre groups. Improvisation is an important element in the collective's performance practice. Dance, mime and incorporation of Afro-Caribbean folklore, such as the Anancy stories, are integral parts of the group's stage work. Adults, adolescents and children throughout Jamaica have been included in the Sistren Collective's work, which has now increased its audience through its own YouTube channel. The post-colonial plays produced by the group have been expanded into community activism highlighting racial and class exploitation.

The international outreach of the Jamaican fashion industry has proliferated in recent decades. Kingston's main modelling agencies Pulse International and Saint International are responsible for some of the world's high-profile models, who feature on the cover of leading fashion magazines such as *Vogue* and secure modelling contracts with Burberry, Gucci and Prada. The marketing of models has been successfully featured through the Fashion Face of the Caribbean competition and prominent fashion events such as Style Week Jamaica. Photographs of models with a variety of Jamaican backdrop settings have helped to popularise models and the inclusion of stylists and casting directors has been important for reaching an international audience through television and online outlets.

Musical performance in Jamaica has concentrated on successive versions of different popular musical styles suitable for informal public gatherings rather than serious music written for the concert hall. In the 1940s and 1950s mento was a form of folk music (similar to calypso) that found popularity in Jamaica. It used acoustic instruments such as the guitar, hand drums, bajo and rhumba box. Mento fused European melodies with African rhythms, and was one of the first indigenous Jamaican musical forms to be recorded. Among notable Jamaican mento singers of the 1950s were Count Lasher, Lord Flea and Alerth Bedasee. Everard Williams composed most of the main mento hit songs. Harry Belafonte's rendition of 'Day-O' or 'The Banana Boat Song' on his album *Calypso*, which sold more than a million copies, was based on a Jamaican mento-style ballad. In the 1960s mento, along with calypso and American rhythm and blues, influenced ska music, which featured upbeat rhythms. Prince Buster, Duke Reid and Clement 'Coxsone' Dodd were among its leading Jamaican practitioners. Many ska songs were issued on singles (45-rpm 7-inch discs) and widely broadcast on Jamaica's radio stations. Ska music was closely associated in the 1960s with a tough rude boy culture in Kingston, comprising angry, defiant youths who railed against the status quo in Jamaica.

Both mento and ska faded in popularity by the late 1960s when they were replaced by reggae, which has had a much more significant impact on Jamaica and on the global music scene. Originating in the poor areas of West Kingston, reggae was much influenced by Rastafarianism and Pan-Africanism and by the struggle of the Jamaican masses to escape oppression. Often sung to politicised lyrics, reggae featured drums, a bass guitar, an electric guitar and a 'scraper', a corrugated stick rubbed with a plain stick, as well as a lead singer. Among the best-known Jamaican reggae performers were Desmond Dekker and the Aces, Derrick Morgan, and Sly and Robbie. Jimmy Cliff made an impact as the gun-toting star of the Jamaican-made film *The Harder They Come* (1972), which emphasised reggae's role as a voice for the poor and dispossessed. Reggae influenced British punk music of the 1970s, and is widely played today at concerts and festivals.

Reggae flourished in Kingston in the late 1960s and spread internationally thereafter. The most prominent reggae artist was the Rastafarian singer and guitarist Bob Marley, who moved from Jamaica to England in the 1970s. He was the co-leader of a group called the Wailers whose songs include 'Stir It Up', 'Get Up Stand Up' and 'One Love/People Get Ready'. Their first album together was the 'Best of the Wailers' (1970). Marley and his group had a series of hit singles in the 1970s. Marley included strong political messages in his songs, highlighting the social deprivation that existed in Jamaica. Thus in 'Redemption Song' he urged his listeners to 'Emancipate yourselves from mental slavery/None but ourselves can free our minds/ Have no fear for atomic energy/Cause none a them can stop the time./How long shall they kill our prophets/ While we stand aside and look?'

In 1979 Bob Marley and the Wailers released the album 'Survival', whose cover reproduced forty-eight African flags and an image of the abolitionists' engraving (from 1788) of the Liverpool slave ship the *Brookes*, showing slaves positioned in a cramped position

FIGURE 6.6 Bob Marley. Jewel Samad/AFP/Getty Images

beneath the vessel's deck. This was intended to highlight the injustices and inhumanity that had afflicted
black people in Jamaica during the era of the slave
trade. Marley died from cancer in the early 1980s
but his musical influence has continued as his record
sales worldwide exceed 75 million. A Bob Marley
Museum near his former home in the inner suburbs
of Kingston preserves his legacy.

The most prominent Jamaican music since the late
1970s has been dancehall. Originating in the poor suburbs of Kingston, dancehall became very popular in the
1980s and 1990s and has since become a major cultural
export. Dancehall is as far removed from genteel music-
making as one could find; it is raucous, extrovert and
spontaneous. Faster-paced and more machine-produced
than reggae, it includes the audience as part of the live
performance. Among many prominent Jamaican dancehall artists are Yellowman, Buju Banton, Shaba Ranks

and Lady Saw. Using sound systems with digital instrumentation in crowded, often outdoor, dancehall venues, this form of musical entertainment relies on active crowd participation responding to the mixing of songs through loud sound systems, with electronic programming, played at high volume and with pounding bass frequencies. Some dancehall sessions had up to eight large sound systems positioned around the venue with large speakers. Different sounds were projected through the speakers as dancehall operators clashed over the type of music to be projected in relation to an audience's response.

Jamaican dancehall features a selector, who chooses the vinyl records to play, and a DJ, who addresses the audience with a microphone, working up the crowd with rapid-fire commentary delivered in patois rather than standard English. The lyrics of dancehall songs reflect the gritty lives of poverty found throughout many Jamaican urban locations. Thus the lyrics refer to guns, ghettos, the medicinal and recreational effects of smoking marijuana, and elements of Rastafarianism, such as references to Jah (God). Dancehall lyrics have been criticised for their explicitly sexual nature, glorification of violent criminal culture, and, on occasions, their anti-homosexual words. Designed for mass consumption, dancehall has spread internationally since the millennium, and has influenced other sub-genres of popular music such as reggaeton – a mixture of Jamaican rhythms and Spanish-language hip-hop. The broad impact of Jamaican reggae and dancehall music was primarily responsible for UNESCO branding Kingston as a 'Creative City of Music' in 2015.

Sport

Sport is an important part of the leisure activities of Jamaicans. Soccer, athletics, cricket, horse racing, basketball and netball, all popular sports, were originally imported from (mainly) Britain and the United States. The climate of Jamaica is suited to outdoor sport throughout the year. Horse racing is still popular in Jamaica. The main venue is Caymanas Park, a former sugar estate in Portmore, and the sport is regulated by the Jamaica Racing Commission. Horse racing employs over 20,000 people in Jamaica, including jockeys, trainers, grooms, bookmakers and track employees. Capacity crowds often attend the twice-weekly race meetings at Caymanas Park and public interest is maintained through gambling and the operation of a sweepstakes. However, although some Jamaican jockeys have had successful careers abroad, especially in North America, few Jamaican horses compete internationally.

Soccer is a more recent sporting implantation into Jamaican society. Though football was played in Jamaica from the late nineteenth century onwards, it was mainly confined to Kingston until independence, when a Social Development Commission was tasked with spreading the game throughout Jamaica. A Jamaica Football Federation was formed to oversee the game, which spread widely among schoolchildren in the 1960s and 1970s. Jamaica started to produce professional footballers in those decades and this has proliferated in more recent times. However, Jamaican football has nothing like the international éclat achieved by its cricketers and athletics stars. The Jamaica national soccer team, nicknamed the

'Reggae Boyz', has yet to make a major mark internationally, having made only one appearance in the FIFA World Cup (in 1998). Nevertheless, high-profile Jamaican footballers have appeared in the English Premier League and various European leagues in recent years, indicating that a talent pool exists in the game in Jamaica.

Jamaica has recently made efforts to improve its sporting facilities to attract wider recognition and to promote sports tourism. The Jamaican government under Prime Minister Holness has begun legacy projects to upgrade various sporting complexes including the National Stadium Complex, the Trelawny Stadium and the Herb McKenley Stadium in Clarendon. The National Stadium, situated within Independence Park, Kingston, is mainly the home venue for football and athletics in Jamaica. A statue of Bob Marley marks the entrance to the site, which holds 35,000 people. The National Stadium has Olympic-standard swimming and diving pools, an indoor National Arena for wrestling and weightlifting and a National Indoor Sports Complex. Table tennis, volleyball, netball and basketball have administrative offices at the Institute of Sports on the site and the complex also has outdoor netball and basketball courts.

Perhaps the highest-profile sporting event held at the National Stadium was the world heavyweight boxing title fight of January 1973 in which George Foreman knocked out Joe Frazier in front of 36,000 spectators. The Trelawny Stadium, situated forty kilometres east of Montego Bay and completed in 2007, is a multi-purpose venue with a capacity of 25,000 people. However, it operates very much in the shadow of major sporting venues in Kingston. The Herb McKenley Stadium, named after a renowned Jamaican athlete who won Olympic gold and silver medals, was designed to serve the sporting needs of central Jamaica.

Cricket has traditionally been a high-profile sporting activity in Jamaica, with the national team having periods of great success. International cricket competitions come mainly in the form of test matches, played usually over five days, one-day internationals and a periodic World Cup tournament. In each of these competitions, Jamaica has not played alone but has contributed players to a West Indies team from Anglophone Caribbean countries. Cricket was a pastime of the colonial officials and administrators who comprised the elite bureaucrats in Crown Colony Jamaica, assuming a similar role among the leisure activities of expatriate middle-class Englishmen as it did in other Anglophone colonial settings such as Singapore, Australia, India, South Africa and New Zealand. The game rapidly spread down the social scale to ordinary West Indians. The West Indies played its first test match in 1928, half a century after test cricket had been inaugurated between England and Australia. It was not until the 1950s, however, that the West Indies cricket team was sufficiently capable of mounting a serious challenge to other international teams.

The heyday of West Indies cricket was between 1960 and 1990 when the team was regularly one of the best competitive sporting units in the world, renowned for its flair and for promoting the sport's entertainment value. It was during those decades that Jamaican cricketers such as Michael Holding, Jeffrey Dujon and Courtney Walsh were prominent. The West Indies won cricket's one-day knockout World Cup in 1975 and 1979. Since about 1990

FIGURE 6.7 Shelly-Ann Fraser-Pryce. RvS Media/Monika Majer/
Getty Images

the West Indies cricket team has declined, however, in its match-winning capability as other international teams – variously England, Australia, South Africa, India and Pakistan – have dominated test matches. However, Sabina Park, Kingston, the main cricket venue in Jamaica, has retained its tough reputation as a hard place for visiting sides to defeat the West Indies, as a partisan, noisy local crowd always turns out in force there to cheer its home-grown heroes.

As West Indies cricket has slipped from the highest rung of achievement, athletics has superseded it as a sport where Jamaicans excel. This is a sport where Jamaicans represent their own country rather than combining with athletes from other Caribbean nations.

The first representation of Jamaica in an international competition came in 1930 with the Central American and Caribbean Games festival held in Havana, Cuba. On 9 August 1962, three days after Jamaica became independent, the new National Stadium hosted the Ninth Central American and Caribbean Games, the first such event to be held in an English-speaking Caribbean country. Jamaican athletes won five gold, three silver and five bronze medals at the games, placing it as the third country in the rank order of medals after Cuba and Venezuela.

Jamaica has always had a very impressive record in athletics championships, including forty-two Commonwealth gold medals, fourteen World Championship gold medals and seventeen Olympic gold medals. Though they have performed well in relays and hurdles, it is in the 100 metre races that Jamaican men and women have excelled. Shelly-Ann Fraser-Pryce, a notable sprinter, won the Olympic 100 metres for women twice and seven gold medals in World Athletic championships. The Jamaican Usain Bolt has achieved world renown as probably the most famous sprinter in living history. He holds the current world record for the 100 metres sprint, having been timed at 9.58 seconds at the World Athletics Championship final in Berlin in 2009. He also holds the world record in the 200 metres sprint and the 4 × 100 metres relay, and has won eight Olympic gold medals. Bolt's record as a sprinter was phenomenal, and he has become a brand name for Jamaican athletic prowess. Jamaica's success at track athletics, with seventeen gold medals achieved at the Olympics, has become a highly visible symbol of national pride. For Jamaicans, it has the attraction of being freely available to

FIGURE 6.8 Usain Bolt. Antonin Thuillier/AFP/Getty Images

all social classes. The achievements and wealth of athletic stars have also encouraged young Jamaicans to emulate them.

A Violent Society

Jamaica's historical experience always included a violent element as the Spanish decimation of the Taino or the white elite's suppression of rebellions displayed, but in the decades since independence levels of violence have escalated, especially in Kingston but also spreading into rural areas such as Clarendon parish. Violence has been connected with politics and elections, drugs and internal turf wars between Jamaican gangs. Though Jamaica has strict gun laws, many illegal weapons, including high-grade assault rifles, are easily acquired through unlawful imports mainly from the United States, where constitutional protection for bearing arms has led to lax gun laws. The result of gun violence is that Jamaica now has one of the highest homicide rates in the world. In 1962 the murder rate in Jamaica amounted to 3.9 per 100,000 of population; by 2005 it had risen to 58 per 100,000. Jamaica now has the world's third highest national homicide rate, surpassed only by South Africa and Colombia.

In the 1960s and 1970s, impoverished parts of Kingston became the main location of crime and violence in Jamaica. Parts of West Kingston, Trenchtown and the city centre, situated near prominent national cultural landmarks, had slums and ghettos where criminal activities flourished in tenement yards. Seaga, when he was a JLP minister for development and welfare, gave a notable radio broadcast in 1966 in which he referred to West Kingston as 'home of the samfie man, the ginnal who preys on the poor, the gambler and the criminal, the men who smoke the weed and tear the flesh, men who don't eat with knives but make their living with them. These are the Cancer of West Kingston. They cluster in cells, build by attacking the healthy until they establish an area of malignant growth.'

Signs of neglect and decay were easily visible throughout downtown Kingston by the time of independence. A large corrugated iron fence, splattered with graffiti, defaced the city's central square near the bus terminus. Poverty, deprivation and social exclusion were endemic in virtually all-black communities where white people rarely strayed after dark and where middle-class brown Jamaicans only visited circumspectly outside of work hours. Tensions were increased by the overcrowding of these places as the population of Kingston's slums doubled between 1960 and 1991. It was ironic that some of the worst affected neighbourhoods in Kingston were geographically close to the yards where newly arrived African slaves had once been kept in captivity after reaching Jamaica.

The violence in these communities was inextricably linked with political realities. Both the two main political parties, the PNP and the JLP, relied on violent gangs and their leaders to enforce voting in their favour at elections – a disreputable and disgraceful state of affairs in a democratic country. Gang bosses, acting like mafia godfathers, attached themselves to these parties. Known colloquially as 'dons', 'shottas', 'rudies' and 'yardies', they divided up Kingston into different political turfs which they enforced at election time, exercising control over fearful communities on their patch. Particular sections of Kingston were so dominated by garrison communities, where solidarity behind one of the two main political parties was paramount, that inhabitants of urban communities were under great pressure to vote on a partisan basis.

Violence, in the form of knives, machetes and guns, first became significant at a political level in advance of the 1967 general election, and it has since continued. Both of the main political parties were implicated in the violence. Thus it was common in Jamaica in the late twentieth century for intimidation to occur at polling stations. Moreover, some inner suburbs in Kingston had frontier markers between the JLP and PNP in the form of logs in the road or abandoned cars or walls. It was risky to cross these boundaries, whose significance was known to all

Kingstonians. In the 1970s the JLP was connected to Claudie Massop of the Phoenix gang (later called the Shower Posse) in West Kingston, while the PNP had an attachment to Aston 'Buckie Marshall' Thompson of the Spanglers gang. Massop had close connections with the JLP leader and later prime minister, Seaga.

Organised gunmen were deployed on the city's streets under gang leaders. Arson became common. Physical intimidation was used to terrorise citizens. Contract killings proliferated as gangs disposed of enemies and people with whom there were long-standing feuds and grievances. Massop and Thompson were ruthless political enforcers who were promised control over local housing and employment contracts to consolidate their grip over specific Kingston neighbourhoods. They played their part in the electoral violence of the 1970s in Jamaica, but both had been killed by 1980. Bob Marley tried to bring together the opposing political parties at a One Love Peace Concert in Jamaica in 1978. This did produce a shaking of hands on stage between Michael Manley, leader of the PNP, and Edward Seaga, leader of the JLP, but it had no effect on the continuing use of violence for political purposes in Jamaica.

During the 1980s, gun violence in Jamaica became closely linked to international drug cartels specialising first in trafficking marijuana but rapidly concentrating on a more expensive and lethal drug, crack cocaine. The prior existence of impoverishment, gang-related crime and a narcotics culture made Jamaica susceptible to the drug cartels. Jamaica was a cog in the international illegal distribution of crack cocaine along routes from its source in Colombia to its sale mainly in the United States and

United Kingdom. Large amounts of money were made in this criminal drug trade, estimated at around 40–50 per cent of Jamaica's GDP in 2001. This proved difficult to resolve partly because many Jamaican politicians had failed to gain the support of urban garrison communities, who in turn had turned to protection from the criminal gangs. Reference has already been made to the Jamaican authorities' inept attempt to arrest the drug baron Christopher 'Dudus' Coke in Kingston in 2010, leading to over seventy deaths in a fracas between the gang leader's associates, the police and the army.

Jamaica's police force has had a murky role in dealing with this serious problem. On the one hand, there is evidence that it has protected ghetto gunmen for political reasons. On the other hand, in recent years specialist police squads have infiltrated and assassinated gang members. Organised crime and violence remains a serious problem in Jamaica today, though the attachment to the transnational trade in drugs has somewhat receded. In 2019 the island's government declared a state of emergency and sent armed soldiers into the streets to protect the public.

In addition to violence occurring in impoverished, drug-fuelled parts of Kingston, Jamaica also has a disturbing level of domestic violence. In 2012, 10 per cent of all murders in Jamaica resulted from domestic violence between men and women. Amnesty International produced a report in 2006 that documented serious levels of domestic assault against women and girls in Jamaica, and dangerous and exploitative sexual violence by criminal gang members against females. The report found that 'discrimination is entrenched and often exacerbated in the police and criminal justice system. Women and adolescent girls are rarely believed by the police, so have little confidence in reporting crimes against them.' Brutal treatment of children with physical chastisement is also common in Jamaica.

Tourism

Modern tourism to Jamaica was launched modestly after the Jamaica International Exhibition held in Kingston in 1891. This was the first notable attempt to shift Jamaica towards tourism as an industry rather than the traditional concentration on agricultural produce. Wealthy American tourists visited Jamaica on the steamships of the United Fruit Company by the turn of the century. A tourist industry to Jamaica did not develop immediately after the exhibition, however, for three main reasons: poor facilities and services in a limited number of hotels; a lack of promotion and marketing; and critical visitors' comments about the dingy, dirty setting of Kingston. A Jamaica Tourist Authority (JTA) was established in 1910 to publicise the island and provide information for prospective visitors. The JTA advertised on billboards, at railway stations, stores, shipping offices and tourist agencies, as well as producing tourist brochures.

Jamaica's tourism industry really took off after 1945. Holiday homes in the island belonging to the authors Noel Coward and Ian Fleming and to the film star Errol Flynn were well publicised, creating a glamorous allure to luxurious rural and coastal parts of Jamaica. By 1950 hotels along the north and north-west coasts and in the hills catered for tourists, as Jamaica was promoted as a tropical paradise. But it was the development of affordable international travel after jet aeroplanes began services in 1959 that brought large numbers of middle-income visitors to Jamaica, notably from North America. Jamaica attracted tourist expenditure by establishing a widespread system of 'in-bond' shops whereby anyone could purchase a wide variety of imported goods, such as clothing and perfumes, at tax-free prices, the goods being delivered at the port of export.

By the 1960s Jamaica was being marketed, along with other Caribbean destinations, as a vacation destination for sun, sea and sand. Package deals were marketed by airlines and tourist operators. The period from November to April was the height of the tourist season, months when people from Canada, the United States and Britain in particular could escape for a winter getaway. The main tourist beach resorts were situated on the north and west coasts, with a concentration on Negril, Montego Bay, Ocho Rios and Port Antonio. Luxury hotels were the mainstay of increased tourism, but more modest guest houses also tapped the tourist market.

By the late 1970s Jamaican-owned multinational companies such as Sandals and Super Clubs developed all-inclusive resorts, often located behind high walls and security gates, where tourists had privacy and all of their transport, accommodation, food and drink were included in the package cost. These resorts were promoted and packaged as centres of relaxation and leisure in a clean, regulated environment far removed from the poverty and racial inequalities prevalent outside their walls. Advertising was essential for the success of all-inclusive resorts, which were adapted skilfully to the expectations of a middle-income tourist market catering for British and

American holidaymakers, for the most part, and geared to winter vacations. The Sandals hotels were founded and owned from the 1980s onwards by the hotelier Gordon 'Butch' Stewart, who had made a fortune selling refrigerators and air-conditioning units. Stewart was widely admired for his business skills and support for philanthropic endeavours in education and entrepreneurship in Jamaica.

By the 1970s large cruise ships were calling regularly at the north coast. The all-inclusive hotels and cruise ships effectively shielded tourists from the realities of life in Jamaica, which is probably what most of the tourists wanted. Kingston, notorious for its working-class grime, drugs and violence, was largely left off the visitor's itinerary, with tourists taking coach tours through the city and (as can still be seen today) rarely leaving their seat on the coach to venture onto the street. However, the business development of Kingston, notably the construction of real estate in New Kingston, with its hotels and banks catering for international visitors, was improved from the 1960s onwards through the efforts of entrepreneurs such as Maurice Facey, who invested a great deal in Jamaica through his Pan Jamaican group and its subsidiaries.

Since the 1980s Jamaica has expanded its tourism sites to include historic buildings, such as found at Falmouth, in Trelawny parish, that have benefited from restoration. Tourists visit great houses on former sugar estates; museums and art galleries, including the Bob Marley Museum; and other properties run by the Jamaica National Heritage Trust, the institution responsible for the promotion, preservation and development of the island's material cultural heritage. One lacuna in the heritage work carried out in Jamaica is the lack of development in and around the old pirate and buccaneer haunt of Port Royal, a site well suited to the tourist market.

Visitors seeking authentic Jamaican culture can visit Rastafarian sites and purchase Rasta-themed products. Niche tourism has also now developed in Jamaica. Eco tourist sites include sustainable lodges at forest campsites and visits to the Blue Mountains, various rivers, lagoons and waterfalls. Since cannabis was declared legal on the island in 2015, marijuana tourism has begun. Medical tourism has also proven popular as international visitors pay for the high-quality care and well-qualified nurses and physicians at Jamaica's underused private hospitals. The Jamaica Tourist Board, founded in 1954, has been active in promoting the island's tourism and the government has also played its role, establishing a Ministry of Tourism in the early 1980s.

Tourist numbers to Jamaica have increased a great deal since the 1950s. The island received 191,303 visitors in 1954 and 396,347 in 1968. The number has increased exponentially over the past half century. By 2006 tourism was the island's leading economic sector and by 2017 Jamaica received 4.3 million tourists. This growth has been important economically. Since the 1980s revenues from tourism have risen upwards consistently. In 2008 tourism contributed $2 billion to the Jamaican economy, which amounted to half the island's export earnings. Tourism currently contributes over a quarter of the Jamaican government's revenues; it attracts welcome overseas investment and generates one in every four jobs on the island. Hotels and resorts are stimulated by tourism along with improved telecommunications and updated infrastructure such as ports, hospitals, banks and leisure facilities. The challenge for tourism operators is to provide evidence that small businesses, local investors and cross-sectoral linkages can flourish in Jamaica through tourism.

The growth of tourism, however, has not all been plain sailing. Between 1975 and 1977, tourist numbers to Jamaica fell by 30 per cent as Jamaica was affected by a political and economic emergency, with street violence, during two highly charged electoral campaigns. In 1987 Prime Minister Seaga drew attention to increasing evidence that tourists in Jamaica were subject to harassment by hustlers, drug dealers and n'er-do-wells, tarnishing Jamaica's image to visitors. This problem has not been eradicated beyond the high-end resorts that stretch along the north and west coasts of the island, and it is common for visitors on foot to be pestered by hustlers. Some tourist firms now cater for eco-friendly visitors to Jamaica who want to see the wildlife and remote parts of the island's interior. This is one way in which tourists can gain experience of what one might term an 'authentic' Jamaica, but the firms offering these packages are careful to control the movements of visitors to shield them from places where haggling and aggressive behaviour are common.

In March and April 2020 a severe cutback in visitors to the island occurred owing to the pandemic outbreak of the potentially lethal COVID-19 virus, which was not particularly prevalent in the Caribbean but sufficiently present to deter tourists. In the second half of June, Jamaica reopened its borders to international travellers with extra precautions established to guard against further COVID-19 infections in the absence of a vaccine to treat the disease. The new measures included regulations on social distancing, the installation of hand sanitisers in hotels, eliminating self-service buffet food from restaurants and hotels, installing physical distancing officers on public beaches and introducing into hotels and resorts a 'COVID-19 Safety Point Person' to regulate protocols. During the first phase of the pandemic, tourism was restricted to a 'COVID-19 Resilient Corridor' along the coast from Negril to Port Antonio. Tourism suffered badly during the COVID-19 outbreak in Jamaica, with tourism revenues falling by 70 per cent. Vaccinations were seen as a major way to overcome this situation. They were rolled out in Jamaica from April 2021.

The Environment

Over the past twenty years, Jamaica's environment has had a repeated negative impact from weather-related disasters that have affected the island's economic growth. Ninety per cent of Jamaica's GDP is produced within its coastal zone where tourism, industry, agriculture and fisheries are highly exposed to climate variability and change. Specific examples highlight the scale of the problem. In 2004 the category 5 Hurricane Ivan destroyed key export crops such as coffee, bananas and sugar cane, inflicting $49 million of damage. It also caused $575 million of damage to infrastructure along Jamaica's shoreline. In 2009–10 a long, severe drought led to agricultural losses and water shortages. In 2012 the category 3 Hurricane Sandy inflicted $11 million of losses to crops, livestock and irrigation systems in eastern parishes. Severe hurricanes in recent years have increased rainfall intensity.

Resultant floods have led to the spread of diseases such as dengue fever. Flourishing in humid conditions and heavy rainfall in tropical conditions, this potentially deadly virus is spread by mosquitoes.

Land erosion and deforestation are further concerns in relation to the sustainability of Jamaica's natural environment. In 1945 a report issued by the Economic Policy Commission drew attention to soil erosion in Jamaica and recommended measures to prevent it. Many causal factors led to serious soil erosion, including poor road construction and maintenance, the use of slash-and-burn agricultural methods, lack of attention to soil conservation, unauthorised sand mining and quarrying, inappropriate selection of arable lands, the unpredictable effect of tropical storms and hurricanes and deforestation arising from lumber and charcoal production. These practices have reduced water quality and quantity, increased silt in rivers and reservoirs, added to marine and coastal contamination and degradation and a growth in landslides leading to destruction of lives, properties and crops. In the past decade, Jamaica has attempted to address these problems by more sustainable management of land and water resources and by implementing measures to deal with soil erosion and soil salinisation.

Pollution is also a major problem in Jamaica. Bauxite mining has contaminated ground water with red-mud waste. Extensive use of plastic bags, one of the highest in the world in per capita terms, has degraded the island's environment. Over the past five years, the Jamaica Environment Trust has drawn attention to worsening air pollution in the Kingston Metropolitan area in relation to industrial and motor vehicle emissions, rubbish dumps, forest and bush fires and open burning by individuals and businesses. These problems are difficult to eradicate for several reasons: enforcement is insufficient even where regulations permit it to happen; the authorities frequently ignore illegal practices; and Jamaica has no motor vehicle emission standards.

The Jamaican government has responded to these challenges in various ways, and in doing so has made extensive efforts to contribute to progressive policies on climate change. A Climate Change Division is located within the Ministry of Economic Growth and Job Creation. Under the auspices of the United Nations Environment Programme, Jamaica has identified the following sectors for the transition to a green economy: fishing, agriculture, forestry, construction, energy, tourism, water and sewerage. In 2018 Prime Minister Holness announced that the renewable energy supply target for Jamaica would be half of the national energy mix by 2030. This would be a remarkable achievement if it were to be achieved, for in 2016, 90 per cent of Jamaica's energy came from imported petroleum. Holness, with the support of the parliamentary opposition, has also taken action on environmental deterioration by introducing a ban on single-use plastic bags, plastic straws and Styrofoam to reduce the environmental impact of plastic.

One area where it is hoped that Jamaica will implement environmental reform lies in water efficiency. Currently, pumping large amounts of freshwater across Jamaica's hilly interior terrain involves expensive energy costs. The aim is to reduce this expenditure by increasing water efficiency, developing local catchment facilities to increase water access and implementing waste recycling facilities. The tourism industry has been singled out as a sector to play an important part in this process by supporting medium and small businesses to enhance water efficiency and distribution. This, in turn, would benefit agricultural production to operate in a more environmentally sustainable way, thereby assisting the one-fifth of Jamaica's population working in agriculture. Vision 2030 Jamaica, the national development plan, adopts the United Nations' Millennium Development Goals, which envisage the growth of a green economy that is 'equitable, sustainable and resilient, low carbon, resource efficient and socially inclusive, and maintains current reserves of natural capital, biodiversity and environmental services'.

Conclusion

The history of Jamaica comprises a long early phase of native settlement by the Tainos, a shorter period when Spain controlled Jamaica, over two centuries of British control focused around the development of slavery, a quarter century of freedom after slave emancipation, many decades of Crown Colony government and a modern era of greater political participation and cultural awareness by black Jamaicans both before and after independence. Hierarchical divisions based on race, class and degrees of bondage and freedom, with their long-drawn-out consequences, have played an essential part in Jamaica's historical evolution with both positive and negative outcomes for Jamaicans.

The Taino era was a discrete phase in the history of Jamaica before the visits of Columbus. The Taino came to Jamaica as a migratory people from mainland South America in broad waves between AD 600 and AD 900, but virtually nothing is known about the impetus for their voyages across the sea. They organised communities throughout Jamaica, preferring defendable hilltop settlements such as Nueva Sevilla. Practising communal living under the leadership of *caciques*, who gained their positions through matrilineal descent, the Taino forged a rich culture in which they excelled at woodcarving, pottery and making stone implements. Surviving rock art in caves, in the form of pictographs and petrographs, testifies to their artistic skills. The Taino had seafaring capabilities, but there is no evidence that, once settled in Jamaica, they sought to sail to other islands. They undertook daily food gathering, picking fruits and seeds, fishing and planting root crops in *conucos*. Many crops they cultivated, including cassava, have had a lasting impact on the Jamaican diet.

The Taino were deeply religious, believing in numerous deities and the afterlife and maintaining contact with the spirit world through their possession of artefacts known as *zemis* and ritual *cohoba* ceremonies. Through these means the Taino believed they could contact their ancestors. As they left no written records and their language is extinct, knowledge of Taino culture in Jamaica is confined to our knowledge of their settlements, artisan skills, rock art and religious practices. More detailed information about the Taino will undoubtedly be available in the future through archaeological excavation, but the Taino in Jamaica will remain a mysterious people in many respects until such time as skeletal remains are located that will enable DNA attributes to be investigated.

For many centuries, the Taino influence on Jamaica's development was largely forgotten. However, a revival of interest in their foundational role in Jamaican history has recently occurred. In May 2019 the Institute of Jamaica celebrated Taino Day with a series of talks and activities. In the following month a Taino chief or *cacique* was installed in Jamaica for the first time in half a millennium. The Jamaican government is also trying, with the aid of the National Commission on Reparations, to have three wooden Taino artefacts found in a cave in Vere parish in 1792 returned to Jamaica from the British Museum – the carving of the 'birdman' spirit, a *cemi* or representation of a spirit or ancestor, and a *boiyanel* (rain giver). No reply to this request has been received in Jamaica, nor have these artefacts ever been loaned there to display in an exhibition. There is no museum in Jamaica dedicated to the Tainos; the one that existed was closed some time ago.

Spanish Jamaica was another discrete phase in the history of Jamaica, lasting for about one-and-a-half centuries. Beginning with Columbus's visits to the island, Spain established political authority in Jamaica from 1509 onwards, sending out various governors appointed by the Spanish Crown. This was part of Spanish imperial expansion in the New World west of the demarcation line established by the Treaty of Tordesillas with Portugal. Jamaica became a Spanish royal colony in 1534. The Spanish treated the Tainos harshly, forcing them into submission under the *repartimiento de Indias* labour system and removing their lands under an *encomienda* labour regime. The Taino were also affected by a range of diseases through contact with the Spanish intruders. By 1600 there were very few Taino left living in Jamaica.

Despite marginalising the Taino, Spanish settlement in Jamaica never escalated: Cuba, Hispaniola, Santo Domingo and Central and South America were always greater magnets for Spanish migration, especially those areas with gold supplies. Jamaica was regarded by Spain as a provision base for Spanish military activities on the Main. The population of Jamaica remained small and static, amounting to no more than 1,600 in the first half of the seventeenth century. Consequently, most of the island remained uncultivated. Spanish settlers supported their daily lives by growing crops and tending livestock, and they introduced numerous new foodstuffs to Jamaica, including sweet potatoes, cassava bread and cane sugar. Institutions of the Roman Catholic Church were introduced to Jamaica by the Spanish settlers and a new, albeit fairly small, leading town was established at Spanish Town.

The Spanish period in the island came to an abrupt end though an English military takeover. Cromwell's Western Design of 1655 failed to capture the intended prize of Hispaniola but instead Jamaica was invaded, captured and consolidated in English hands between 1655 and 1660. The English then set about colonising the island so that it could serve as its major possession in the western Caribbean. English legal and political institutions were rapidly transferred to Jamaica, governors were appointed from London and the island was organised according to English-style counties and parishes. Migration occurred on a substantial scale from England, with some professionals of middling rank such as doctors, teachers and lawyers, but a preponderance of indentured servants to undertake most of the manual work.

The early English settlement in Jamaica was rumbustious, with pirates and privateers using Jamaica as a base for their sea raids. Until its destruction by an earthquake in 1692, Port Royal was the most prosperous port town on the island. By then sugar plantations had been established in Jamaica as the main form of economic activity, with an increasing slave trade from West Africa supplying the bound labour force. Though English Jamaica developed a wide-ranging economy including livestock rearing, urban trades and cultivation of various types of tropical produce, it was the emergence and growth of sugar plantations that made the greatest economic and social impression on Jamaica for over a century and a half.

White merchants and planters were drawn to slavery and the slave trade in Jamaica by the opportunity to make money; and some indeed made their fortunes. Jamaica was the wealthiest colony in Britain's Atlantic Empire by the time of the American War of Independence. But economic success for some immigrants was counterbalanced by high mortality rates among the white population, notably in Kingston, during the eighteenth century. With heavy mortality and a gender imbalance in the white population, Jamaica failed to become a self-sustaining settler population. Because of the dominance of black slaves numerically, Jamaica also became less attractive as an immigrant destination for British people in 1776 compared with a century earlier.

The slave population also suffered from heavy mortality, both during and after the Middle Passage. Life for the enslaved was completely overseen by white control, sometimes exercised with humanity but sometimes also with brutality from overseers and managers. Slaves created their own family structures and practised a rich spiritual and community life in difficult circumstances. They also protested by running away and in occasional revolts, notably the rebellion led by the Coromantee leader Tacky in 1760. Maroon communities developed in more remote, inaccessible parts of Jamaica as a refuge for slaves who had permanently escaped from bondage.

During the unsettled political years of the 1760s and 1770s in British America, Jamaica was retained as a British possession though the thirteen colonies of North America were lost. The political controversy of the 1750s over where to base the island's capital was settled in favour of Spanish Town rather than Kingston. Though Jamaicans disliked the Stamp Act in 1765, they remained loyal to Britain during the American War of Independence. This arose largely from their fears of being outnumbered by a large black majority on the island from whom they needed British military forces to protect their property and livelihoods. Fortunately, Jamaica was not attacked successfully by the Americans and their allies during the war years between 1775 and 1783. After the loss of the North American colonies, Jamaica was preserved as a colony where Britain intended to continue its concentration on slavery and sugar.

Jamaica's history between the American Revolution and the Morant Bay rebellion was full of turbulent change. Sugar still dominated the island economy, though not exclusively as other marketable crops, notably coffee but also pimento, were also grown and sold. Many sugar properties fell into debt in the 1780s and 1790s, and it used to be argued that this marked a long-term decline in the Jamaican sugar economy. This view has been modified to note that many new plantations emerged in the French revolutionary and Napoleonic wars, notably on the north side of the island, and that most sugar estates were still making profits by the time of slave emancipation in 1834. The equalisation of sugar prices and British sugar import duties around 1830 spelled trouble for the sugar economy and, with the loss of compulsory labour with the end of slavery, the plantations entered a period of decline in the late 1830s. But Jamaica's economy was diversified and areas other than sugar cultivation progressed. Livestock pens supplied pigs and cattle for internal meat consumption, a complex web of internal exchange operated within Jamaica, and slaves and freedmen participated in the cultivation and marketing of crops from provision grounds.

Until 1834 slave work dominated the labour undertaken in Jamaica. Slaves became more productive, with women contributing some of the hardest field labour. Increased productivity was necessary after the ending of the British slave trade in 1807 was followed by only modest increase in the natural growth of Jamaica's slave population. Planters introduced ameliorative policies on a piecemeal basis, offering incentives to slaves through task work and improved medical care. Amelioration became the official British government policy after 1823. It was implemented partly out of a humane desire to improve living and working conditions for the enslaved, but also as an attempt to stave off the abolitionist movement, which wanted to see slavery eradicated by law. Planters were on the back foot in dealing with the movement to abolish the British slave trade, passed by parliament in 1807, and after a lull in abolitionist activity for several years, they faced greater challenges from abolitionists after 1823, culminating in a well-mobilised and strongly supported campaign for slave emancipation, which was granted by Britain in 1834.

Rumours about imminent slave freedom emboldened the enslaved to stage a major rebellion in 1831–2, known as the Baptist War, in which many sugar properties were destroyed through arson while outbreaks of unrest occurred throughout Jamaica for three months. The revolt was quashed by British military forces but it influenced public opinion in Britain to hasten the demise of slavery in the British Caribbean islands. The planters were compensated for the loss of their slaves, but the island's black population received nothing. A brief period of apprenticeship followed in which uneasy adjustments were made by planters, attorneys and managers to treating ex-slaves differently. When full freedom was granted in 1838, many former apprentices left the estates to which their families had been attached for generations and forged a new life as an independent peasantry. Freedmen started to play an active role in local politics at parish level. But despite these positive signs of progress for Jamaicans, low wage levels, poor housing, a restricted franchise and the continuance of whites in positions of power made life problematic for blacks. Difficult economic conditions and resentments spilled over into the violence of the Morant Bay rebellion, which the militia, police and armed forces put down with brutality.

Colonialism continued to dominate Jamaica between 1865 and 1945, and it was manifest particularly in politics and social conditions. Crown Colony government, implemented for the first time in Jamaica in 1865, reserved political power in the hands of a British-appointed governor and a Legislative Council, but there was no representative assembly. Ordinary Jamaicans could vote at parish level, giving them some input into local political decisions but the franchise was restricted and by the 1930s only a small minority of Jamaicans were included on electoral registers. Only towards the end of the Second World War were improvements made towards more democracy in Jamaica, with the introduction of a new constitution and a general election held in 1944. Administrative support for government was underdeveloped, with little serious train-ing for civil service appointments.

The social structure remained heavily dominated by white elite people, with an emerging brown middle class coming into professions, and a large swathe of black Jamaicans who were largely impoverished and living in shabby conditions, both in towns and country areas. Wage rates for ordinary labourers at the turn of the twentieth century had barely improved since the end of apprentice-ship. The late nineteenth century witnessed the growth of the Jamaican peasantry but land reforms implemented by the government in two periods (1896–1910 and 1929–49) often foundered on insufficient financial help for small-holders, leading to non-payment of rent and repossession.

Many Jamaicans continued to work in agriculture in the eighty years after 1865, but gradually the significance of sugar production was reduced as worldwide markets could draw upon many competing sources of supply. Within Jamaica, sugar production was largely reorganised to centre around relatively few large sugar factories. Cultivation of bananas became an important new agricul-tural activity, with bananas overtaking sugar as a valuable export by the 1920s. The Boston-based United Fruit Company (UFC) dominated the organisation of the Jamaican banana industry. Other commodities such as pimento and coffee were produced for sale, but Jamaica had limited manufacturing activity and was still to indus-trialise on a significant scale.

Elementary education improved in the late nineteenth century with a growth in the number of schools, but the development of secondary education lagged behind. Tertiary education was virtually non-existent until after the Second World War. Jamaicans remained attached to Afro-Caribbean spiritual beliefs, including obeahism and myalism, but Christianity made advances, with the spread of Roman Catholic, Anglican and nonconformist churches and chapels. Revivalist preachers, such as Alexander Bedward, gained followers. But the most important cultural changes for Jamaicans occurred in the 1920s and 1930s when Rastafarianism emerged as a new system of belief that appealed to black Jamaicans and Garvey's UNIA, with its African connections, offered hope for Jamaicans to find a future beyond colonialism. Worsening employment conditions in the 1930s led to labour protests culminating in major protests in 1938, the formation of trade unions, the emergence of Alexander Bustamante and Norman Manley as political leaders and the birth of political parties. These developments had an immediate impact on Jamaican life after the Second World War ended.

The two main political parties formed in the early 1940s, the Jamaica Labour Party (JLP) and the People's National Party (PNP), soon dominated electoral politics in Jamaica by the mid-1940s and they have continued in this position ever since. Their success has alternated at general elections without having to face a significant third party as a challenger. Garveyism and Rastafarianism exerted considerable influence on certain groups in the Jamaican population without building a large political following. The mass of the Jamaican population, even when they were dissatisfied with JLP and PNP electoral manifestos and policies, were too unorganised to rise up against mainstream political opinion. Manley and Bustamante played important political roles as founder-leaders of the two main political parties, serving for periods as prime minister. Manley was closely involved in the movement towards a West Indian Federation in the late 1950s and 1960s, but this collapsed on the eve of Jamaica achieving independence from Britain in 1962.

Jamaica's political development since independence has been beset by the seemingly intractable problems of operating a successful economy and combating deprivation, poverty, violence and drugs. Polarised political, economic and social policies in the 1970s, under the respective prime ministerial regimes of Michael Manley and Edward Seaga, saw Jamaica veering from left-wing attempts to tackle capitalism under Manley to more conservative, pro-capitalist policies under Seaga. Neither approach was fully successful. Relative political stability returned to Jamaica with the long tenure as prime minister of P. J. Patterson, the first black man to hold that position in Jamaica. More recent prime ministers have made improvements to Jamaica's healthcare and educational systems and there are ambitious plans afoot to promote a green environmental agenda by 2030, but the poverty, neglect and crime that beset swathes of the capital city, Kingston, are by no means resolved.

Jamaica has nevertheless achieved many positive and cultural objectives since the Second World War. Educational opportunities have increased rapidly with a sharp growth in the provision of primary and secondary education and with the emergence of the reputable University of the West Indies on its Mona campus. The creative arts have proliferated and made their local and international imprint in music, art, dance and literature to a far greater extent than they ever did before 1939.

Jamaica has become a notable contributor to different sports, notably to cricket, horse racing, swimming and athletics, with strong participation in sprint and relay running at Commonwealth and Olympic games. Comparing 2021 with 1945, Jamaica has assumed a greater position globally with diasporic migration creating strong networks between Jamaicans in different Anglophone countries, sustained pride in independent nationhood and as a magnet for large flows of tourists. Jamaica remains a place of landscape beauty with a welcoming people as well as a country of gritty, long-standing urban difficulties, but it has a platform to improve its economic and social opportunities for Jamaicans through the consolidation of a peaceful modern democracy.

SOURCES OF PRINCIPAL QUOTATIONS

Chapter 1 The Taino

IRVING ROUSE: Irving Rouse, *Tainos: Rise and Decline of the People Who Greeted Columbus* (Princeton, NJ: Princeton University Press, 1994), pp. 230–4.

EDWARD LONG: Edward Long, *The History of Jamaica*, 2nd vol. (London: T. Lowndes, 1774), p. 139.

JAMES KNIGHT ON WARLIKE ATTRIBUTES OF THE TAINO: Jack P. Greene, ed., *The Natural, Moral and Political History of Jamaica and the Territories Thereon Depending from the First Discovery of the Island by Christopher Columbus, to the Year 1746* (Charlottesville, VA: University of Virginia Press, 2021), p. 37.

JAMES KNIGHT ON THE CACIQUES: Jack P. Greene and James Knight ed., *The Natural, Moral, and Political History of Jamaica and the Territories Thereon Depending from the First Discovery of the Island by Christopher Columbus, to the Year 1746* (Charlottesville, VA: University of Virginia Press, 2021), p. 32.

JAMES KNIGHT ON THE APPEARANCE OF TAINOS: Jack P. Greene and James Knight, ed., *The Natural, Moral, and Political History of Jamaica and the Territories Thereon Depending from the First Discovery of the Island by Christopher Columbus, to the Year 1746* (Charlottesville, VA: University of Virginia Press, 2021), p. 32.

PETER MARTYR: David Buisseret, *Historic Jamaica from the Air* (Kingston: Ian Randle, 1996), p. 19.

Chapter 2 Spanish Jamaica, 1509–1655

BERNALDEZ ON COLUMBUS'S FIRST MEETING WITH THE TAINO: Diana Paton and Matthew J. Smith, eds., *The Jamaica Reader: History, Culture, Politics* (Durham, NC: Duke University Press, 2021), p. 23.

COLUMBUS ON JAMAICA: David Buisseret, *Historic Jamaica from the Air* (Kingston: Ian Randle, 1996), p. 26.

COLUMBUS'S SON FERDINAND ON JAMAICA: David Buisseret, *Historic Jamaica from the Air* (Kingston: Ian Randle, 1996), p. 26.

COLUMBUS ON THE TAINO: Christopher Columbus, *The Diary of Christopher Columbus* (New York: NTC Contemporary, 1997), p. 55.

COLUMBUS'S LETTER TO THE SPANISH CROWN: Columbus to Ferdinand, King of Spain, 1503, in Eric Williams, ed., *Documents of West Indian History. Vol. 1. 1492–1655: From the Spanish Discovery to the British Conquest of Jamaica* (Port-of-Spain: PNM Publishing, 1963), p. 11.

FRANCISCO DE GARAY TO KING FERDINAND: Letter of 14 January 1514, quoted in Francisco Morales Padron, *Spanish America* (Kingston: Ian Randle, 2003), p. 38.

MAZUELO ON THE TAINOS: Diana Paton and Matthew J. Smith, eds., *The Jamaica Reader: History, Culture, Politics* (Durham, NC: Duke University Press, 2021), p. 28.

HENRY BARHAM ON THE DESTRUCTION OF THE TAINOS: British Library, London, Add. MS 12,422: Henry Barham, 'The Civil History of Jamaica to the Year 1722', fol. 26.

JAMES KNIGHT ON THE DECIMATION OF THE TAINOS: Jack P. Greene and James Knight, ed., *The Natural, Moral, and Political History of Jamaica and the Territories Thereon Depending from the First Discovery of the Island by Christopher Columbus, to the Year 1746* (Charlottesville, VA: University of Virginia Press, 2021), pp. 44–5.

CROSBY ON THE COLUMBIAN EXCHANGE: Alfred W. Crosby, Jr, *The Columbian Exchange: Biological and Cultural Consequences of 1492* (Westport, CN: Greenwood, 1972).

BENEFICIARIES OF CATASTROPHE: John M. Murrin, *Beneficiaries of Catastrophe: The English Colonies in America* (Washington, DC: American Historical Association, 1997).

REPORT BY THE SPANISH GOVERNOR OF JAMAICA, 1650: National Library of Jamaica, Kingston, MS 291, Report by Governor Jacinto Sedeño Albornoz to the Admiral of the Indies [Duke of Veragua], 24 September 1650.

LETTER FROM THE ABBOT OF JAMAICA, 1583: Frank Cundall and Joseph L. Pietersz, *Jamaica under the Spaniards* (Kingston: Institute of Jamaica, 1919), p. 15.

LETTER FROM THE ABBOT OF JAMAICA, 1611: Frank Cundall and Joseph L. Pietersz, *Jamaica under the Spaniards* (Kingston: Institute of Jamaica, 1919), p. 35.

DAVID BUISSERET: David Buisseret, *Historic Jamaica from the Air* (Kingston: Ian Randle, 1996), p. 33.

WHISTLER: Eric Williams, ed., *Documents of West Indian History. Vol. 1. 1492–1655: From the Spanish Discovery to the British Conquest of Jamaica* (Port-of-Spain: PNM, 1963), p. 287.

EDWARD LONG: Edward Long, *The History of Jamaica: Reflections on Its Situation, Settlements, Inhabitants, Climate, Products, Commerce, Laws, and Government*, 1st vol. (London: T. Lowndes, 1774), pp. 19–20.

FRANCISCO MORALES PADRON: Francisco Morales Padron, *Spanish Jamaica* (Kingston: Ian Randle, 2003), p. 108.

ABBOT MARQUEZ DE VILLALOBOS: Francisco Morales Padron, *Spanish Jamaica* (Kingston: Ian Randle, 2003), p. 238.

Chapter 3   Creating an English Jamaica, 1655–1775

SPANISH SETTLERS LEAVING JAMAICA FOR CUBA: David Buisseret, ed., *Jamaica in 1687: The Taylor Manuscript at the National Library of Jamaica* (Kingston: University of the West Indies Press, 2008), p. 84.

CROMWELL'S PROCLAMATION: S. C. Lomas, ed., *The Letters and Speeches of Oliver Cromwell with Elucidations by Thomas Carlyle*, 2nd vol. (London: Methuen, 2004), p. 467.

SEDGWICKE AND GOODSON ON WEAK ENGLISH SOLDIERS: Diana Paton and Matthew J. Smith, eds., *The Jamaica Reader: History, Culture, Politics* (Durham, NC: Duke University Press, 2021), p. 46.

ENGLISH ARMY MAJOR: Robert Sedgwicke to Oliver Cromwell, 5 November 1655, in Thomas Birch, ed., *A Collection of the State Papers of John Thurloe, Esq: Secretary, First, to the Council of State, and Afterwards to the Two Protectors, Oliver and Richard Cromwell*, 4th vol. (London: Fletcher Gyles, 1742), p. 153.

JAMAICA AS A GARRISON IN 1657: National Library of Jamaica, Kingston, MS 381, Report on Jamaica, 20 June 1657.

HENRY BARHAM ON JAMAICA: British Library, London, Add. MS 12,422, Henry Barham, 'The Civil History of Jamaica to the Year 1722', fol. 80.

EDWARD LONG ON JAMAICA IN THE 1650s and 1660s: Edward Long, *The History of Jamaica: Reflections on Its Situation, Settlements, Inhabitants, Climate, Products, Commerce, Laws, and Government*, 1st vol. (London: T. Lowndes, 1774), p. 303.

SIR THOMAS LYNCH IN 1672: Sir Thomas Lynch to Joseph Williamson, 13 January 1672, in W. Noel Sainsbury, ed., *Calendar of State Papers America and West Indies: Volume 7, 1669–1674* (London: Her Majesty's Stationary Office, 1889), p. 316.

LYNCH TO THE SECRETARY OF STATE: Longleat House, Warminster, Wiltshire, Sir Thomas Lynch to Secretary Arlington, 23 September 1674, Coventry Papers, LXXIV, fol. 19.

PROCLAMATION OF OLIVER CROMWELL, 1655: Eric Williams, ed., *Documents of West Indian History, Vol.*

1. 1492–1655: From the Spanish Discovery to the English Conquest of Jamaica (Port of Spain: PNM, 1963), pp. 290–1.

CROMWELL'S PLANS FOR SETTLING JAMAICA: Oliver Cromwell, 'By the Protector: A Proclamation Giving Encouragement to Such as Shall Transplant Themselves to Jamaica (1655)', in Carla Gardina Pestana and Sharon V. Salinger, eds., *The Early English Caribbean, 1570–1700*, 2nd vol. (London: Pickering & Chatto, 2014), p. 307.

FERTILITY AND BEAUTY OF JAMAICA: Edmund Burke and William Burke, *An Account of the European Settlements in America*, 2nd vol. (London: R. and J. Dodsley, 1757), pp. 60–1.

RICHARD S. DUNN ON JAMAICAN DEMOGRAPHY: Richard S. Dunn, *Sugar and Slaves: The Rise of the Planter Class in the English West Indies, 1624–1713* (Chapel Hill: University of North Carolina Press, 1972), p. 334.

RELUCTANT CREOLES: Michael Craton, 'Reluctant Creoles: The Planters' World in the British West Indies', in Bernard Bailyn and Philip D. Morgan, eds., *Strangers within the Realm: Cultural Margins of the First British Empire* (Chapel Hill: University of North Carolina Press, 1991), pp. 314–62.

WHITE WOMEN AND SLAVERY: Christine Walker, *Jamaica Ladies: Female Slaveholders and the Creation of Britain's Atlantic Empire* (Chapel Hill: University of North Carolina Press, 2020), p. 23.

THE ROYAL AFRICAN COMPANY AND JAMAICA: David Buisseret, ed., *Jamaica in 1687: The Taylor Manuscript at the National Library of Jamaica* (Kingston: University of the West Indies Press, 2008), p. 241.

CARY HELYAR ON THE SLAVE TRADE: Somerset Archives, Norton Fitzwarren, Cary Helyar to William Helyar, 27 November 1671, Walker-Heneage MSS from Coker Court, DD/WHh 1089/3/21.

JAMAICA SUGAR WORKS IN 1675: The National Archives, Kew, CO 138/2, 'Observations on the Present State of Jamaica', 14 December 1675, Jamaica, Entry Books.

JOHN TAYLOR ON WEALTHY PLANTERS: David Buisseret, ed., *Jamaica in 1687: The Taylor Manuscript at the National Library of Jamaica* (Kingston: University of the West Indies Press, 2008), p. 266.

THE WEALTH OF JAMAICA: Edmund Burke and William Burke, *An Account of the European Settlements in America*, 2nd vol. (London: R. and J. Dodsley, 1757), p. 100.

JAMAICAN FORTUNES: Henry Bright to Francis Bright, 9 August 1754, in Kenneth Morgan, ed., *The Bright-Meyler Papers: A Bristol West-India Connection, 1732–1837* (Oxford: Oxford University Press, 2007), p. 303.

AN ELITE PLANTER CLASS: Trevor Burnard, 'Et in Arcadia ego: West Indian Planters in Glory, 1674–1784', *Atlantic Studies*, 9/1 (2012): p. 27.

GOVERNOR LYNCH ON SLAVES: British Library, London, Add. MS 11,410, Letter from Sir Thomas Lynch, 1671–2, fols. 266–7.

CHARLES LESLIE ON SEASONING: Charles Leslie, *A New and Exact Account of Jamaica ... With a Particular Account of the Sacrifices, Libations etc., at This Day, in Use among the Negroes. The Third edition. To Which Is Added an Appendix, Containing an Account of Admiral Vernon's Success at Porto Bello and Chagre* (Edinburgh: R. Fleming, 1740), p. 238.

THE ATTORNEY OF HOPE PLANTATION: National Library of Jamaica, Kingston, E. East to Roger Hope Elletson, 23 September 1778, Roger Hope Elletson letter-book (1773–80).

SLAVE NAMING: Trevor Burnard, 'Slave Naming Patterns: Onomastics and the Taxonomy of Race in Eighteenth-Century Jamaica', *Journal of Interdisciplinary History*, 31/3 (2001), p. 326.

THOMAS THISTLEWOOD DIARIES: Citations from Beinecke Rare Book and Manuscript Library, Yale University, Thomas Thistlewood Diaries, Monson MS 31, James Marshall and Marie-Louise Osborn Collection.

HANS SLOANE ON MUSICAL INSTRUMENTS: Diana Paton and Matthew J. Smith, eds., *The Jamaica Reader: History, Culture, Politics* (Durham, NC: Duke University Press, 2021), p. 68.

RECTOR OF ST CATHERINE PARISH ON FUNERAL RITES: Lambeth Palace Library, London, John Venn to Bishop Sherlock, 15 June 1751, Fulham Papers, Volume XVIII: General Correspondence, no. 47.

EDWARD LONG ON FUNERALS: Edward Long, *The History of Jamaica: Reflections on Its Situation, Settlements, Inhabitants, Climate, Products, Commerce, Laws, and Government*, 2nd vol. (London: T. Lowndes, 1774), p. 421.

JOHN HAMILTON ON TACKY'S REBELLION: South Ayrshire Archives, Ayr, John Hamilton to Rebecca Hamilton, 12 June 1760, Hamilton of Rozelle Papers, AA/DC/17/113.

EDWARD LONG ON TACKY'S REBELLION: Edward Long, *History of Jamaica: Reflections on Its Situation, Settlements, Inhabitants, Climate, Products, Commerce, Laws, and Government*, 2nd vol. (London: T. Lowndes, 1774), p. 462.

CASSAVA: Anon, 'A True Description of Jamaica, with the Fertility, Commodities, and Healthfulness of the Place (1657)', in Carla Gardina Pestana and Sharon V. Salinger, eds., *The Early English Caribbean, 1570–1700*, 3rd vol. (London: Pickering & Chatto, 2014), p. 3.

FRANCIS HANSON ON JAMAICA IN 1683: F[rancis] H[anson], 'A Short Account of the Island and Government thereof (1683)', in Carla Gardina Pestana and Sharon V. Salinger, eds., *The Early English Caribbean, 1570–1700*, 3rd vol. (London: Pickering & Chatto, 2014), p. 38.

STATISTICS ON JAMAICA'S ECONOMY IN THE 1740s: Kenneth Morgan, 'Robert Dinwiddie's Reports on the British American Colonies', *William and Mary Quarterly*, 3rd series, 65/2 (2008), pp. 305–46.

PORT ROYAL: David Buisseret, ed., *Jamaica in 1687: The Taylor Manuscript at the National Library of Jamaica* (Kingston: University of the West Indies Press, 2008), p. 238.

ROBERT RENNY ON THE PORT ROYAL EARTHQUAKE: Robert Renny, *An History of Jamaica: With Observations on the Climate, Scenery, Trade, Productions, Negroes, Slave Trade, Diseases of Europeans, Customs, Manners, and Dispositions of the Inhabitants: To Which Is Added, an Illustration of the Advantages Which Are Likely to Result from the Abolition of the Slave Trade* (London: J. Cawthorn, 1807), p. 333.

THE CESSATION OF THE EXTREMITY OF THE EARTHQUAKE: *The Truest and Largest Account of the Late Earthquake in Jamaica, June the 7th, 1692, Written by a Reverend Divine There to Is Friend in London; With Some Improvement Thereof by Another Hand* (London: Thomas Parkhurst, 1693), p. 5.

A CLERGYMAN ON THE EARTHQUAKE: E. Heath, *A Full Account of the Late Dreadful Earthquake at Port-Royal in Jamaica Written in Two Letters from the Minister of That Place, from Aboard the Granada in Port-Royal Harbour June 22 1692* (Edinburgh: John Reid, 1692), pp. 1–2.

LORD ADAM GORDON ON KINGSTON: 'Journal of an Officer in the West Indies, 1764-65', in Newton D. Mereness, ed., *Travels in the American Colonies* (Baltimore: Johns Hopkins University Press, 1916), p. 377.

PLANTERS AND THE SLAVE REVOLT OF 1760: University of California, San Diego, Mandeville Special Collections Library, MSS 220, George Ricketts to Thomas Hall, 30 August 1760, Barnett/Hall Collection, flat box 25.

STEPHEN FULLER ON THE MAROONS: Boston College, Memorial from Stephen Fuller to Lord George Germain, 23 December 1778, Stephen Fuller letterbook (1776–84), Nicholas M. Williams Ethnological Collection.

GOVERNOR LYTTLETON ON THE STAMP ACT: The National Archives, Kew, CO 137/34, William Lyttleton to

the Lords of Trade, 24 December 1765, fols. 48–9, Jamaica, Original Correspondence.
SIMON TAYLOR ON JAMAICA IN THE AMERICAN REVOLUTION: Cambridge University Library, Taylor to Chaloner Arcedeckne, 8 May 1782, Vanneck MSS, 2/10.

Chapter 4 From the Slavery to Freedom, 1775–1865

P.J. MARSHALL ON JAMAICA: P. J. Marshall, 'Britain without America: A Second Empire?' in P. J. Marshall, ed., *The Oxford History of the British Empire. Volume 2. The Eighteenth Century* (Oxford: Oxford University Press, 1998), p. 584.
BRYAN EDWARDS'S VALUATION OF JAMAICA: Bryan Edwards, *The History, Civil and Commercial, of the British Colonies in the West Indies*, 1st vol. (London: J. Stockdale, 1793), p. 248.
PATRICK COLQUHOUN'S VALUATION OF JAMAICA: Patrick Colquhoun, *A Treatise on the Wealth, Power, and Resources of the British Empire in Every Quarter of the World, Including the East Indies* ... (London: Joseph Mawman, 1814), p. 59.
LOWELL JOSEPH RAGATZ ON THE DECLINE OF THE WEST INDIES: Lowell Joseph Ragatz, *The Fall of the Planter Class in the British Caribbean, 1763–1833* (New York: Century, 1928).
PROFITS ON JAMAICA'S SUGAR PLANTATIONS: J. R. Ward, 'The Profitability of Sugar Planting in the British West Indies, 1650–1834', *Economic History Review*, 2nd series, 31/2 (1978), pp. 197–213.
PETER MARSDEN ON KINGSTON: Peter Marsden, *An Account of the Island of Jamaica with Reflections on the Treatment, Occupation and Provisions of the Slaves to Which Is Added a Description of the Animal and Vegetable Productions of the Island* (Newcastle: S. Hodgson, 1788), pp. 6–8.

WEALTH AND SLAVES: National Library of Jamaica, Kingston, MS 2006, Johann Waldeck, Hessian Accounts of America, fol. 123.

ANNE APPLETON STORROW ON KINGSTON: Massachusetts Historical Society, Boston, Anne Appleton Storrow to Miss Butler, 23 September 1792, folder for 1790–92, Anne Appleton Storrow Papers.

FREE PEOPLE OF COLOUR AND WHITE PEOPLE: Peter Marsden, *An Account of the Island of Jamaica with Reflections on the Treatment, Occupation and Provisions of the Slaves to Which Is Added a Description of the Animal and Vegetable Productions of the Island* (Newcastle: S. Hodgson, 1788), p. 8.

ANTHONY TROLLOPE ON JAMAICA: Anthony Trollope, *The West Indies and the Spanish Main*, 2nd ed. (London: Chapman and Hall, 1860), pp. 81–2.

BRYAN EDWARDS ON JAMAICA'S POPULATION IN 1787: Bryan Edwards, *The History, Civil and Commercial, of the British Colonies in the West Indies*, 1st vol. (London: J. Stockdale, 1793), p. 230.

EDWARD BRATHWAITE ON CREOLE SOCIETY: Edward (Kamau) Brathwaite, 'Creole Society', in Diana Paton and Matthew J. Smith, eds., *The Jamaica Reader: History, Culture, Politics* (Durham, NC: Duke University Press, 2021), p. 113.

EDWARD BRATHWAITE ON CREOLISATION: Edward Kamau Brathwaite, *Contradictory Omens: Cultural Diversity and Integration in the Caribbean* (Mona: Savacou, 1974), p. 6.

HENRY BLEBY ON THE JAMAICAN SLAVE REBELLION, 1831/2: Henry Bleby, *Death Struggles of Slavery: Being a Narrative of Facts and Incidents Which Occurred in a British Colony, during the Two Years Immediately Preceding Negro Emancipation* (London: Hamilton, Adams, 1853), p. 21.

LABOUR RECRUITS VIA THE SLAVE TRADE FOR THE PLANTATIONS: 'Minutes of Evidence Taken at the Bar of the House of Lords, upon the Order Made for Taking into Consideration the Present State of the Trade to Africa, and Particularly the Trade in Slaves ..., Session 1792', in F. William Torrington, ed., *House of Lords Sessional Papers* (Dobbs Ferry, NY, Oceana Publications 1975), pp. 384–5.

JOHN GRANT ON JAMAICA, 1788: The National Archives, Kew, CO 137/87, John Grant to Stephen Fuller, 25 April 1788, Jamaica, Original Correspondence.

WILLIAM KNIBB ON SLAVE RECREATIONS: Angus Library and Archive, Regent's Park College, Oxford, William Knibb to Mrs S. Nichols, March 1826, William Knibb Papers, Baptist Missionary Society Papers.

THE JAMAICA ASSEMBLY ON THE PLANTOCRACY: The National Archives, Kew, CO 137/88, 'Remonstrance of His Majesty's Dutiful and Loyal Subjects', 20 October 1789, fols. 300–10, Jamaica, Original Correspondence.

B. W. HIGMAN ON PROPRIETORS AND ATTORNEYS: B. W. Higman, *Plantation Jamaica, 1750–1850: Capital and Control in a Colonial Economy* (Kingston: University of the West Indies Press, 2005), p. 281.

EDWARD LONG ON THE IMPACT OF THE SAINT-DOMINGUE SLAVE REVOLT ON JAMAICA: William Salt Library, Stafford, Edward Long to Madam [Mary Jervis], 6 June 1804, Ricketts Papers.

MARY TURNER ON THE JAMAICAN SLAVE REVOLT OF 1831/2: Mary Turner, *Slaves and Missionaries: The Disintegration of Jamaican Slave Society, 1787–1834* (Urbana-Champaign: University of Illinois Press, 1982), p. 149.

B. W. HIGMAN ON SKILLED SLAVES IN THE JAMAICAN REVOLT OF 1831/2: B. W. Higman, *Slave Population and Economy in Jamaica, 1807–1834* (Cambridge: Cambridge University Press, 1976), p. 230.

A PLANTER ON SECTARIAN PREACHERS: Surrey History Centre, Woking, Alexander Bayley to Henry Goulburn, 16 January 1832, Goulburn Collection, 304/J/21/152.

HOPE WADDELL ON DESTRUCTION DURING THE JAMAICAN SLAVE REVOLT, 1831/2: Hope Masterson

Waddell, *Twenty Nine Years in the West Indies and Central Africa: A Review of Missionary Work and Adventure, 1829–1858* (London: Thomas Nelson, 1863), p. 52.

SIR WILLOUGHBY COTTON ON THE JAMAICAN SLAVE REVOLT OF 1831/2: Public Record Office of Northern Ireland, Belfast, Willoughby Cotton to William Bullock, 2 January 1832, Belmore Papers, D/3007/G/1/17.

JOHN KINGDON ON THE BAPTISTS: Angus Library and Archive, Regent's Park College, Oxford, John Kingdon to Edward Steane, 28 July 1832, Original Correspondence with the Reverend Edward Steane (1794–1844).

BERNARD SENIOR ON THE AFTERMATH OF THE JAMAICAN REBELLION OF 1831/2: Bernard Senior, *Jamaica As It Was, As It is, and As It May Be: Comprising Interesting Topics for absent Proprietors, Merchants &c. and Valuable Hints to Persons Intending to Emigrate to the Island: Also an Authentic Narrative of the Negro Insurrection in 1831 ...* (London: T. Hurst, 1835), p. 277.

APPRENTICES AND PROVISION GROUNDS: British Library, London, Add. MS 51,818, E. Dawes Baynes to Lord Holland, 20 July 1835, Holland House Papers.

LORD SLIGO ON APPRENTICESHIP: The National Archives, Kew, CO 137/192, Lord Sligo to Edward Stanley, 27 May 1834, no. 19, Jamaica, Original Correspondence.

APPRENTICESHIP IN ST DAVID PARISH: *Commercial Advertiser* (Jamaica), 9 September 1834.

INSOLENT AND UNGRATEFUL BEHAVIOUR OF APPRENTICES: Staffordshire Record Office, Stafford, Commission given to Dr J. R. Hulme as Special Justice of the Peace for Jamaica, 12 August 1834, J. R. Hulme, Diary of a Special Magistrate in Jamaica, D538/C/16/1.

ELIZABETH RYAN AND THE TREADMILL: National Library of Jamaica, Kingston, MS 321, Copy of Affidavits of Aggrieved Apprentices in Jamaica submitted to Mr [Joseph] Beldam.

JAMES WILLIAMS AND APPRENTICESHIP: Diana Paton, ed., *James Williams, A Narrative of Events, since the First of August, 1834, by James Williams, an Apprenticed Labourer in Jamaica* (Durham, NC: Duke University Press, 2001), p. 8. Lancewood tree branches were commonly used for whipping slaves.

A SPECIAL MAGISTRATE ON APPRENTICESHIP: British Library, London, Add. MS 51,818, E. Dawes Baynes to Lord Holland, 24 November 1837, Holland House Papers.

THE IMMEDIATE AFTERMATH OF APPRENTICESHIP: Historical Society of Pennsylvania, Philadelphia, Charles Scobie to Mrs Bowen, 15 January 1839, box 52, Bowen Papers, Edward Carey Gardiner Collection.

SIR HENRY FITZHERBERT ON JAMAICA: Derbyshire Record Office, Matlock, Andrew Cooke to Sir Henry Fitzherbert, 26 April 1840, Fitzherbert Papers, D 239 M/E 21167.

RICHARD BRIGHT ON EDUCATION FOR BLACK JAMAICANS: Richard Bright to Edward Smith, 4 November 1834, in Kenneth Morgan, ed., *The Bright-Meyler Papers: A Bristol-West India Connection, 1732–1837* (Oxford: Oxford University Press, 2007), p. 649.

THE COLONIAL OFFICE ON THE JAMAICA ASSEMBLY: The National Archives, Kew, 30/48/7/44, Henry Taylor's memorandum, 19 January 1839, Edward Cardwell Papers.

THE WANT OF CONTINUOUS LABOUR: The National Archives, Kew, CO 137/263, no. 6, T. McCornock, March 1842, enclosed in Lord Elgin to Lord Stanley, 6 June 1842, Jamaica, Original Correspondence.

THE CONDITION OF JAMAICA IN 1852: Memorial of the Jamaica College of Physicians and Surgeons, April 1852, *Parliamentary Papers*, 1852–3, lxvii (76), p. 142.

HOPE WADDELL ON MYALISM: Hope Waddell, *Twenty-Nine Years in the West Indies and Central Africa: A Review of Missionary Work and Adventure, 1829–1858* (London: Thomas Nelson, 1863), p. 189.

THE DUKE OF NEWCASTLE ON JAMAICA: Statement by the Duke of Newcastle, 30 June 1853, House of Lords Papers, *Hansard*, vol. 128, pp. 950–2 (quotation on p. 950).

RICHARD HILL ON EMPLOYMENT: The National Archives, Kew, CO 137/390, Richard Hill to Hugh Williams Austin, 15 March 1865, Jamaica, Original Correspondence.

JAMES MCLAREN AND THE MORANT BAY REBELLION: Evidence of William Anderson (5 February 1866) on a public speech by James McLaren. *Royal Commission on the Origin, Nature and Circumstances of Disturbances in the Island of Jamaica. Part II. Minutes of Evidence.* Command Papers. 19th century House of Commons Sessional Papers. *UK Parliamentary Papers*, xxxi (1866), p. 165.

GEORGE WILLIAM GORDON AND THE MORANT BAY REBELLION: Evidence of Mrs M. J. Gordon (6 March 1866). *Royal Commission on the Origin, Nature and Circumstances of Disturbances in the Island of Jamaica. Part II. Minutes of Evidence.* Command Papers. 19th century House of Commons Sessional Papers. *UK Parliamentary Papers*, xxxi (1866), p. 722.

GOVERNOR EYRE AND THE MORANT BAY REBELLION: Despatch of Edward Eyre (2 November 1865) in *Royal Commission on the Origin, Nature and Circumstances of Disturbances in the Island of Jamaica. Part II. Minutes of Evidence.* Command Papers. 19th century House of Commons Sessional Papers. *UK Parliamentary Papers*, xxxi (1866), p. 1006.

ORLANDO PATTERSON ON JAMAICA BECOMING A CROWN COLONY: Orlando Patterson, *The Confounding Island: Jamaica and the Postcolonial Predicament* (Cambridge, MA: Harvard University Press, 2018), p. 55.

Chapter 5 The Shadow of Colonialism, 1865–1945

PATRICK BRYAN: Patrick Bryan, *The Jamaican People 1880–1902: Race, Class and Social Control* (London: Macmillan Caribbean, 1991), p. 69.

DONAL BYFIELD: Recollections of Donald Byfield in Patrick E. Bryan and Karl Watson, eds., *Not for Wages Alone: Eyewitness Summaries of the 1938 Labour Rebellion in Jamaica* (Mona: University of the West Indies, 2003), p. 109.

VISITOR TO JAMAICA: Colin G. Clarke, *Kingston, Jamaica: Urban Development and Social Change, 1692–1962* (Berkeley and Los Angeles: University of California Press, 1975), p. 48.

CASTE FEELING AND CASTE PRACTICE: Colin G. Clarke, *Kingston, Jamaica: Urban Development and Social Change, 1692–1962* (Berkeley and Los Angeles: University of California Press, 1975), p. 49.

HENRICE ALTINK ON RACIAL DISPARITIES: Henrice Altink, *Public Secrets: Race and Colour in Colonial and Independent Jamaica* (Liverpool: Liverpool University Press, 2019), p. 2.

SOCIAL ADVANCEMENT: W. P. Livingstone, *Black Jamaica: A Study in Evolution* (London: Sampson Low, Marston, 1899), p. 217.

SIR JOHN PETER GRANT ON BLACK JAMAICANS: The National Archives, Kew, CO 137/441, Sir John Peter Grant to the Dissenting ministers of Falmouth, 19 April 1869.

REVEREND CAREY BERRY: Rev. Carey B. Berry to the Editor, 17 August 1895, *Jamaica Advocate*.

CROWN COLONY GOVERNMENT AND BLACK SKINS: Colin A. Palmer, *Freedom's Children: The 1938 Labor Rebellion and the Birth of Modern Jamaica* (Chapel Hill, NC: University of North Carolina Press, 2014), p. 23.

KINGSTON BLACKS ON GOVERNMENT PROTECTION: Sydney H. Olivier, *Jamaica, the Blessed Island* (London: Faber & Faber, 1936), p. 233.

A CORRESPONDENT FOR THE *JAMAICA GUARDIAN*: *Jamaica Guardian*, 24 April 1869.

ARTHUR RICHARDS ON JAMAICA: Colin A. Palmer, *Freedom's Children: the 1938 Labor Rebellion and the Birth of Modern Jamaica* (Chapel Hill, NC: University of North Carolina Press, 2014), p. 6.

EDITOR OF THE *DAILY GLEANER* ON ILLEGITIMACY: Editorial, *Daily Gleaner*, 21 May 1908.

A REPORT OF 1899 ON THE MEDICAL SYSTEM: W.P. Livingstone, *Black Jamaica: A Study in Evolution* (London: Sampson Low, Marston, 1899), p. 188.

GOVERNOR SYDNEY OLIVIER ON INDIAN IMMIGRATION: Sydney Olivier to the Secretary of State, 6 April 1909, *Report of the Committee on Emigration from India to the Crown Colonies and Protectorates. Part III. Papers laid before the Committee* (1910). Command Paper 5194, *UK Parliamentary Papers* (1910), xxvii, p. 84.

INTERRACIAL MIXTURE: Jamaica Archives, Spanish Town, Chinese Aliens: Conditions governing entry into Jamaica Colonial Secretariat (Colonial Secretary's Office 1B/5/77/1/116 [1926]).

GAD HEUMAN: Gad Heuman, 'Victorian Jamaica: The View from the Colonial Office', in Tim Barringer and Wayne Modest, eds., *Victorian Jamaica* (Durham, NC: Duke University Press, 2018), p. 153.

KINGSTON LACKING THE ATTRIBUTES OF A CAPITAL CITY: Herbert Lisser, 'Travelling from Kingston to Montego Bay (1913)', in Diana Paton and Matthew J. Smith, eds., *The Jamaica Reader: History, Culture, Politics* (Durham, NC: Duke University Press, 2021), p. 203.

CONTEMPORARY REPORT ON THE PEASANTRY: Brian L. Moore and Michele A. Johnson, eds., *The Land We Live In: Jamaica in 1890* (Kingston: University of the West Indies, 2000), p. 121.

GOVERNOR STUBBS ON SPANISH TOWN: The National Archives, Kew, CO 137/790/2, item 6, Sir Reginald Stubbs to Lord Passfield, 7 June 1930.
GOVERNOR ANTHONY MUSGRAVE ON EDUCATION: The National Archives, Kew, CO 137/496, Anthony Musgrave to the Earl of Kimberley, 10 October 1880.
INFLUENCE OF THE EVIL EYE: Charles Rampini, *Letters from Jamaica: The Land of Streams and Woods* (Edinburgh: Edmonston and Douglas, 1873), p. 84.
THE *DAILY GLEANER* ON REVIVAL WORSHIP: *Daily Gleaner*, 18 October 1904.
PRESBYTERIAN MISSIONARY MEETING, 1882: National Library of Jamaica, Kingston, MST 51, Excerpt from *Jamaica Witness*, 3 January 1882, Church of England Scrapbook No. 1.
REVEREND ABRAHAM EMERICK ON OBEAHISM: Abraham J. Emerick, SJ, *Jamaica Superstitions: Obeah and Duppyism in Jamaica* (Woodstock, MD: Woodstock Letters, 1915–16), p. 37.
ALEXANDER BEDWARD: Colin A. Palmer, *Inward Yearnings: Jamaica's Journey to Nationhood* (Kingston: University of the West Indies Press, 2016), p. 13.
BRIAN L. MOORE AND MICHELE A. JOHNSON: Brian L. Moore and Michele A. Johnson, *Neither Led nor Driven: Contesting British Cultural Imperialism in Jamaica, 1865–1920* (Kingston: University of the West Indies Press, 2004), p. 95.
TELEGRAM OF THE GOVERNOR OF JAMAICA: The National Archives, Kew, CO 137/704/58, Gift from Jamaica to Britain towards the expenses of war, 1 September 1914.
BRIGADIER L. S. BLACKDEN: *Daily Gleaner*, 20 October 1915, p. 4.
RUPERT LEWIS: Rupert Lewis, 'Garvey's Perspective on Jamaica', in Rupert Lewis and Patrick Bryan, eds., *Garvey: His Work and Impact* (Trenton, NJ: Africa World Press, 1991), p. 232.
MARCUS GARVEY ON JAMAICA'S LABOURING CLASSES: *The Black Man*, July-August 1938, n.p.

MARCUS GARVEY ON RACE PRIDE: Marcus Garvey, 'A Talk with Afro-West Indians (1916)', in John Henrik Clarke, ed., *Marcus Garvey and the Vision of Africa* (New York: Random House, 1974), p. 85.

PERMANENT JAMAICA DEVELOPMENT CONVENTION: The National Archives, Kew, CO 137/183/18, Memorandum from Marcus Garvey and the Permanent Jamaica Development Convention to Sir Edward Denham, 8 November 1934.

MARCUS GARVEY ON LEAVING JAMAICA: Colin Grant, *Negro with a Hat: The Rise and Fall of Marcus Garvey* (London: Jonathan Cape, 2008), pp. 434–5.

THE *DAILY GLEANER* ON LEONARD HOWELL: *Daily Gleaner*, 16 March 1934.

MISS B: Recollections of Miss B in Patrick E. Bryan and Karl Watson, eds., *Not for Wages Alone: Eyewitness Summaries of the 1938 Labour Rebellion in Jamaica* (Mona: University of the West Indies, 2003), p. 18.

BUSTAMANTE AND IMPOVERISHED JAMAICANS: Recollections of Vivian Durham in Patrick E. Bryan and Karl Watson, eds., *Not for Wages Alone: Eyewitness Summaries of the 1938 Labour Rebellion in Jamaica* (Mona: University of the West Indies, 2003), pp. 33–4.

KEN HILL ON ECONOMIC DEPRIVATION: Recollections of Ken Hill in Patrick E. Bryan and Karl Watson, eds., *Not for Wages Alone: Eyewitness Summaries of the 1938 Labour Rebellion in Jamaica* (Mona: University of the West Indies, 2003), p. 52.

DISORDER IN KINGSTON: *Report (with appendices) of the Commission Appointed to Enquire into the Disturbances which Occurred in Jamaica between the 23rd May, and the 8th June, 1938* (Kingston: Government Printing Office, 1938), p. 4.

O. E. ANDERSON: Colin A. Palmer, *Inward Yearnings: Jamaica's Journey to Nationhood* (Kingston: University of the West Indies Press, 2016), p. 14.

NORMAN MANLEY ON NATIONAL CONSCIOUSNESS IN JAMAICA: Speech in the *Daily Gleaner*, 18 September 1938.

NORMAN MANLEY ON THE MASSES AND THE PRIVILEGED: Philip Sherlock and Hazel Bennett, *The Story of the Jamaican People* (Kingston: University of the West Indies Press, 1998), p. 379.

Chapter 6 Modern Jamaica, 1945–2022

SPENCER MAWBY ON POLITICAL PARTIES: Spencer Mawby, *Ordering Independence: The End of Empire in the Anglophone Caribbean, 1947–69* (Basingstoke: Palgrave Macmillan, 2012), p. 43.

HUGH SHEARER: Robert J. Alexander, ed., *Presidents, Prime Ministers and Governors of the English-Speaking Caribbean and Puerto Rico: Conversations and Correspondence* (Westport, CT: Praeger, 1997), p. 17.

SIR HUGH FOOT: Sir Hugh Foot to Lord Lloyd, 25 November 1955, in S. R. Ashton and David Killingray, eds., *West Indies: Documents on the End of Empire* (London: HMSO, 1999), p. 110.

NORMAN MANLEY ON SELF-GOVERNMENT: Speech, 17 June 1958, *Jamaica Hansard*, 2 May-17 June 1958.

GOVERNOR OF JAMAICA AND NORMAN MANLEY: Sir Hugh Foot to Lord Lloyd, 25 November 1955, in S. R. Ashton and David Killingray, eds., *West Indies: Documents on the End of Empire* (London: HMSO, 1999) p. 111.

MICHAEL MANLEY ON FEDERATION: Michael Manley, 'Overcoming Insularity in Jamaica', *Weekly Gleaner*, 11 November 1970.

NORMAN MANLEY RADIO BROADCAST: Radio broadcast of 9 June 1960 in Rex Nettleford, ed., *Norman Washington Manley and the New Jamaica: Selected Writings and Speeches, 1938–1968* (Kingston: Longman Caribbean, 1971), p. 175.

THE REFERENDUM AND WEST INDIAN FEDERATION: 'Referendum a Fight for Life', *Sunday Gleaner* (Kingston), 6 August 1961.

A CANADIAN OBSERVER: 'Some observations on the Jamaican economy': despatch no. 403 from R.G.C. Smith to the Canadian Ministry of External Affairs, Ottawa, 23 December 1958, in S. R. Ashton and David Killingray, eds., *West Indies: Documents on the End of Empire* (London: HMSO, 1999), p. 238.

CONFIDENTIAL REPORT FOR THE COLONIAL OFFICE: [Jamaica referendum]: Jamaica intelligence report analysing the result, September 1961, in S. R. Ashton and David Killingray, eds., *West Indies: Documents on the End of Empire* (London: HMSO, 1999), p. 449.

NORMAN MANLEY'S MESSAGE ON INDEPENDENCE DAY, 1962: Rex Nettleford, ed., *Norman Washington Manley and the New Jamaica: Selected Writings and Speeches, 1938–1968* (Kingston: Longman Caribbean, 1971), p. 296.

BUSTAMANTE ON INDEPENDENCE: 'A Special Gleaner Feature on Pieces of the Past', *Jamaica Gleaner*, 20 November 2001.

NORMAN MANLEY ON HIS GENERATION: Franklin W. Knight, *The Caribbean: The Genesis of a Fragmented Nationalism* (New York: Oxford University Press, 1978), p. 225.

LACK OF ORGANISATION OF THE MASSES: Colin Clarke, *Race, Class, and the Politics of Decolonization: Jamaica Journals, 1961 and 1968* (London, Palgrave Macmillan, 2016), p. 59.

THE HAVES AND THE HAVE-NOTS: The National Archives, Kew, FCO 63/494, E. N. Larmour, British High Commission, Kingston, Jamaica, to T.R.M. Sewell, Caribbean Department, Foreign and Commonwealth Office, London, 29 May 1970, Foreign and Commonwealth Office Papers.

PEOPLE'S NATIONAL PARTY SLOGAN FOR THE 1972 ELECTION: Colin G. Clarke, *Kingston, Jamaica: Urban*

Development and Social Change, 1692–1962 (Berkeley and Los Angeles: University of California Press, 1975), p. 46.

MICHAEL MANLEY ON GUNS: 'Stalag in Kingston', *Time Magazine*, 23 September 1974.

MICHAEL MANLEY ON DEMOCRATIC SOCIALISM: Diana Paton and Matthew J. Smith, eds., *The Jamaica Reader: History, Culture, Politics* (Durham, NC: Duke University Press, 2021), p. 345.

EDWARD SEAGA ON JAMAICA'S PROBLEMS: Edward Seaga, *My Life and Leadership. Volume 1. Clash of Ideologies, 1930–1980* (London: Macmillan Education, 2010), p. 235.

SEAGA'S FINANCIAL POLICIES: 'Edward Seaga: Man Who Turned Jamaica Around', *The Bajan*, January 1982, p. 5.

EDWARD SEAGA ON SOCIALISM: Edward Seaga, *My Life and Leadership. Volume 2. Hard Road to Travel, 1980–2008* (London: Macmillan Education, 2010), p. 19.

P. J. PATTERSON ON THE CHALLENGES FACING JAMAICA: P. J. Patterson, *My Political Journey: Jamaica's Sixth Prime Minister* (Kingston: University of the West Indies Press, 2018), pp. 179–80.

P. J. PATTERSON ON PUBLIC POLICIES: 'Fourteen Years of P. J. Patterson', *The Gleaner*, 30 March 2006, p. E2.

BRUCE GOLDING: 'Golding Officially Resigns', *The Jamaica Herald*, 3 October 1995, p. 3.

PORTIA SIMPSON MILLER INAUGURAL ADDRESS: 'National Library of Jamaica, Kingston, Inaugural Address by the Most Hon. Portia Simpson Miller', King's House, 5 January 2012.

ANDREW HOLNESS ON THE COVID-19 PANDEMIC: 'Parliamentary Statement on the COVID-19 Pandemic Delivered by the Most Honourable Andrew Holness, ON, MP, Prime Minister, Tuesday, October 6, 2020', p. 7 (https://jis.gov.jm/media/2020/10/PMs-Statement-in-Parliament-Covid-October-6-2-20-draft-v4.pdf).

ANDREW HOLNESS ON LOCKDOWN IN JAMAICA: 'Parliamentary Statement on the COVID-19 Pandemic

Delivered by the Most Honourable Andrew Holness, ON, MP, Prime Minister, Tuesday, 6 October 2020', pp. 11–12 (https://jis.gov.jm/media/2020/10/PMs-Statement-in-Parli ament-Covid-October-6-2-20-draft-v4.pdf).

MARTIN LUTHER KING SPEECH: 'This Day in Jamaican History: Dr. Martin Luther King Jr' (https://jamaicans.com).

VISION 2030 JAMAICA: 'Green Economy in the Context of Vision 2030 Jamaica', p. 19, www.vision2030.gov.jm.

EDWARD SEAGA ON WEST KINGSTON: 'Edward Seaga: Man Who Turned Jamaica Around', *The Bajan*, January 1982, p. 5.

EDNA MANLEY ON THE DEARTH OF ARTISTIC ACTIVITY: Edna Manley in the *Daily Gleaner*, 13 September 1934.

NORMAN MANLEY ON POLITICAL ACTION: Rex Nettleford, ed., *Norman Washington Manley and the New Jamaica: Selected Writings and Speeches, 1938–1968* (Kingston: Longman Caribbean, 1971), p. 109.

BOB MARLEY 'REDEMPTION SONG': Carolyn Cooper, *Noises in the Blood: Orality, Gender and the 'Vulgar' Body of Jamaican Popular Culture* (London: Macmillan, 1993), p. 124.

EDWARD SEAGA RADIO BROADCAST ON WEST KINGSTON: Diana Paton and Matthew J. Smith, eds., *The Jamaica Reader: History, Culture, Politics* (Durham, NC: Duke University Press, 2021), p. 313. A samfie man was a swindler. A ginnal was a trickster.

AMNESTY INTERNATIONAL REPORT: Orlando Patterson, *The Confounding Island: Jamaica and the Postcolonial Predicament* (Cambridge, MA: Harvard University Press, 2018), pp. 158–9.

GREEN ECONOMY: 'Green Economy in the Context of Vision 2030 Jamaica', p. 7, *www.vision2030.gov.jm*.

SELECT BIBLIOGRAPHY

≈

This is a select list of the main published secondary works dealing with the history of Jamaica. I have given monographs and textbooks priority over research journal articles. A useful resource for those wanting to read further comprises copies of the *Jamaica Journal*, freely available on the internet as part of the Digital Library of the Caribbean (www.dloc.com). The best single source for reviews of new publications on Jamaica's history is the venerable *New West Indian Guide/Nieuwe West-Indische Gids* (https://brill.com/view/journals/nwig/).

General Books

Black, Clinton V., *A New History of Jamaica* (Kingston: William Collins Sangster Jamaica, 1973).

Higman, B. W., *A Concise History of the Caribbean*, 2nd ed. (Kingston, Cambridge: Cambridge University Press, 2021).

Paton, Diana and Matthew J. Smith, eds., *The Jamaica Reader: History, Culture, Politics* (Durham, NC: Duke University Press, 2021).

Sherlock, Philip and Bennett Hazel, *The Story of the Jamaican People* (Kingston: Ian Randle, 1998).

Watts, David, *The West Indies: Patterns of Development, Culture and Environmental Change since 1492* (Cambridge: Cambridge University Press, 1987).

Chapter 1 The Taino

Aarons, George A., 'The Jamaican Taino: The Aboukir Zemis, Symbols of Taino Philosophy, Mysticism and Religion', *Jamaica Journal*, 25/2 (1994): 11–17.

Allsworth-Jones, Philip, *Pre-Columbian Jamaica* (Tuscaloosa: University of Alabama Press, 2008).

Allsworth-Jones, Philip and Wesler, Kit W., *The Taino Settlement at Guayguata: Excavations in St Mary Parish, Jamaica* (Oxford: BAR International Series, 2012).

Atkinson, Lesley-Gail, 'Sacred Landscapes: Imagery, Iconography, and Ideology in Jamaican Rock Art', in Michele H. Hayward, Lesley-Gail Atkinson and Michael Conquino, eds., *Rock Art of the Caribbean* (Tuscaloosa: University of Alabama Press, 2009).

Atkinson, Lesley-Gail, ed., *The Earliest Inhabitants: The Dynamics of the Jamaican Taino* (Kingston: University of the West Indies Press, 2006).

Bercht, F., Brodsky, E., Farmer, J. A. and Taylor, D., *Taino: Pre-Columbian Art and Culture from the Caribbean* (New York: The Monacelli Press, 1997).

Burley, David V., Woodward, Robyn P., Henry, Shea and Conolley, Ivor C., 'Jamaican Taino Settlement Configuration at the Time of Christopher Columbus', *Latin American Antiquity*, 28/3 (2017): 337–52.

Conolley, Ivor, 'Jamaican Taino Symbols: Implications for Regional Chiefdoms and Their Chronology', in Jeannette A. Bastian, John Aarons and Stanley Griffin, eds., *Decolonizing the Caribbean Record: An Archives Reader* (Sacramento, CA: Litwin Books, 2018).

Golding-Frankson, Dianne, 'Jamaican Taino "Shellsmithing" Techniques Explored: A Study in Method', *Caribbean Quarterly*, 55/2 (2009): 42–63.

Handler, Jerome S., 'The "Bird Man"; A Jamaican Arawak Wooden "idol"', *Jamaica Journal*, 11/3–4 (1977): 25–9.

Henry, Shea and Woodward, Robyn, 'Contact and Colonial Impact in Jamaica: Comparative Material Culture and Diet at Sevilla Nueva and the Taino Village of Maima', in Corinne L. Hofman and Floris W. M. Keehnen, eds., *Material Encounters and Indigenous Transformations in the Early Colonial Americas: Archaeological Case Studies* (Leiden: Brill, 2019).

Higman, B. W., *A Concise History of the Caribbean*, 2nd ed. (Cambridge: Cambridge University Press, 2021).

Higman, B. W., *Jamaican Food: History, Biology, Culture* (Kingston: University of the West Indies Press, 2008).

Keegan, William F. and Hofman, Corinne L., *The Caribbean before Columbus* (Oxford: Oxford University Press, 2017).

Lamarche, Sebastián Robiou, *Tainos and Caribs: The Aboriginal Cultures of the Antilles* (San Juan: Editorial Punto y Coma, 2019).

Lyew-Ayee, Parris and Conolley, Ivor, 'The Use of Imagery to Locate Taino Sites in Jamaica in a GIS Environment', in Basil A. Reid ed., *Archaeology and Geoinformatics: Case Studies from the Caribbean* (Tuscaloosa: University of Alabama Press, 2008).

Mickleburgh, Hayley L., Laffoon, Jason E., Pagán Jiménez, Jaime R. et al., 'Precolonial/Early Colonial Human Burials from the Site of White Marl, Jamaica: New Findings from Recent Rescue Excavations', *International Journal of Osteoarchaeology*, 29 (2019): 155–6.

Ostapkowicz, Joanna, 'The Sculptural Legacy of the Jamaican Taino: Part 1: The Carpenter's Mountain Carvings', *Jamaica Journal*, 35/3 (2015): 52–9.

Rouse, Irving, *The Tainos: Rise and Decline of the People Who Greeted Columbus* (Princeton, NJ: Princeton University Press, 1994).

Saunders, Nicholas J. and Gray, Dorrick, 'Zemis, Trees and Symbolic Landscapes: Three Taino Carvings from Jamaica', *Antiquity*, 70/270 (1996): 801–12.

Watson, Karl, 'Amerindian Cave Art in Jamaica: The Mountain River Cave', *Jamaica Journal*, 21/1 (1988): 13–20.

Wesler, Kit, 'Jamaica', in William F. Keegan, Corinne L. Hofman and R. Rodríguez Ramos, eds., *The Oxford Handbook of Caribbean Archaeology* (Oxford: Oxford University Press, 2013).

Chapter 2 Spanish Jamaica, 1509–1655

Aarons, G. A., 'Sevilla la Nueva: Microcosm of Spain in Jamaica. Part 1: The Historical Background', *Jamaica Journal*, 16/4 (1983): 37–46.

Altman, Ida, *Life and Society in the Early Spanish Caribbean: The Greater Antilles, 1493–1550* (Baton Rouge: Louisiana State University Press, 2021).

Bryan, Patrick, 'Spanish Jamaica', *Caribbean Quarterly*, 38/2–3 (1992): 21–31.

Buisseret, David, *Historic Jamaica from the Air* (Kingston: Ian Randle, 1996).

Crosby, Alfred W., *Ecological Imperialism: The Biological Expansion of Europe, 900–1900* (Cambridge: Cambridge University Press, 1986).

Cundall, Frank and Pietersz, Joseph, *Jamaica under the Spaniards* (Kingston: Institute of Jamaica, 1919).

Emmer, Pieter C., ed., *General History of the Caribbean. Volume II. New Societies: The Caribbean in the Long Sixteenth Century* (London and Basingstoke:UNESCO, 1999).

Padron, Francisco Morales, translated Patrick E. Bryan, *Spanish Jamaica* (Kingston: Ian Randle, 2003).

Robertson, James, *Gone Is the Ancient Glory: Spanish Town, Jamaica, 1534–2000* (Kingston: Ian Randle, 2005).

Schmitt, Casey, 'Centering Spanish Jamaica: Regional Competition, Informal Trade, and the English Invasion, 1620–1662', *William and Mary Quarterly*, 76/4 (2019): 697–726.

Snyder, Amanda J., 'Reassessing Jamayca Española: Spanish Fortifications and English Designs in Jamaica', in L. H. Roper, ed., *The Torrid Zone: Caribbean Colonization and Cultural Interaction in the Long Seventeenth Century* (Columbia, SC: University of South Carolina Press, 2018).

Woodward, Robyn P., 'Feudalism or Agrarian Capitalism? The Archaeology of the Early Sixteenth-Century Spanish Sugar Industry', in James A. Delle, Mark Hauser and Douglas V. Armstrong eds., *Out of Many, One People: The Historical*

Archaeology of Colonial Jamaica (Tuscaloosa: University of Alabama Press, 2011).

Wright, Irene, 'The Early History of Jamaica, 1511–1536', *English Historical Review*, 36 (1921): 76–95.

Wynter, S., *Report on Archival Materials Relating to Spanish Jamaica in Spain* (Kingston: Jamaica National Heritage Trust, 1983).

Chapter 3 Creating an English Jamaica, 1655–1775

Brown, Vincent, *Tacky's Revolt: The Story of an Atlantic Slave War* (Cambridge, MA: Harvard University Press, 2019).

Buisseret, David, *Historic Jamaica from the Air* (Kingston: Ian Randle, 1996).

Burnard, Trevor, *Jamaica in the Age of Revolution* (Philadelphia: University of Pennsylvania Press, 2020).

Burnard, Trevor, *Mastery, Tyranny and Desire: Thomas Thistlewood and his Slaves in the Anglo-Jamaican World* (Chapel Hill, NC: University of North Carolina Press, 2004).

Burnard, Trevor, 'Passengers Only: The Extent and Significance of Absenteeism in Eighteenth Century Jamaica', *Atlantic Studies*, 1/2 (2004): 178–95.

Burnard, Trevor, '"Prodigious Riches": The Wealth of Jamaica before the American Revolution', *Economic History Review*, LIV (2001): 506–24.

Burnard, Trevor, 'A Failed Settler Society: Marriage and Demographic Failure in Jamaica', *Journal of Social History*, 28/1 (1994): 63–82.

Burnard, Trevor and Garrigus, John, *The Plantation Machine: Atlantic Capitalism in French Saint-Domingue and British Jamaica* (Philadelphia: University of Pennsylvania Press, 2016).

Dunn, Richard S., *Sugar and Slaves: The Rise of the Planter Class in the English Caribbean, 1624–1713* (Chapel Hill: University of North Carolina Press, 1972).

Eltis, David, *The Rise of African Slavery in the Americas* (Cambridge: Cambridge University Press, 2002).

Fuller, Harcourt and Jada Benn Torres, 'Investigating the "Taino" Ancestry of the Jamaican Maroons: A New Genetic (DNA), Historical, and Multidisciplinary Analysis and Case Study of the Accompong Town Maroons', *Canadian Journal of Latin American and Caribbean Studies/ Revue Canadienne des Etudes Latino-Américaine et Caraïbes*, 43/1 (2018): 47–78.

Graham, Aaron, 'Jamaican Legislation and the Transatlantic Constitution, 1660–1839', *The Historical Journal*, 61/2 (2018): 327–55.

Greene, Jack P., *Settler Jamaica in the 1750s: A Social Portrait* (Charlottesville: University of Virginia Press, 2016).

Latimer, Jon, *Buccaneers of the Caribbean: How Piracy Forged an Empire* (Cambridge, MA: Harvard University Press, 2009).

Metcalf, George, *Royal Government and Political Conflict in Jamaica, 1729–1783* (London: Longmans, 1965).

Morgan, Kenneth (ed.), *The Bright-Meyler Papers: A Bristol-West India Connection, 1732–1837* (Oxford: Oxford University Press, 2007).

O'Shaughnessy, Andrew J., *An Empire Divided: The American Revolution and the British Caribbean* (Philadelphia: University of Pennsylvania Press, 2000).

Patterson, Orlando, *The Sociology of Slavery: An Analysis of the Origins, Development and Structure of Negro Slave Society in Jamaica* (London: MacGibbon & Kee, 1967).

Pawson, Michael and David Buisseret, *Port Royal, Jamaica* (Oxford: Oxford University Press, 1975).

Pestana, Carla Gardina, *The English Conquest of Jamaica: Oliver Cromwell's Bid for Empire* (Cambridge, MA: Harvard University Press, 2017).

Pestana, Carla Gardina, 'Early English Jamaica without Pirates', *William and Mary Quarterly*, 71/3 (2014): 321–60.

Robertson, James, 'Making Jamaica English: Priorities and Processes', in L. H. Roper, ed., *The Torrid Zone: Caribbean*

Colonization and Cultural Interaction in the Long Seventeenth Century (Columbia, SC: University of South Carolina Press, 2018).

Robertson, James, *Gone is the Ancient Glory: Spanish Town, Jamaica, 1534–2000* (Kingston: Ian Randle, 2005).

Robertson, James, 'Re-writing the English Conquest of Jamaica in the late Seventeenth Century', *English Historical Review*, 117 (2002): 813–39.

Sheridan, Richard B., *Sugar and Slavery: An Economic History of the British West Indies, 1623–1775* (Bridgetown: Caribbean Universities Press, 1974).

Thornton, A. P., *West-India Policy under the Restoration* (Oxford: Oxford University Press, 1956).

Walker, Christine, *Jamaica Ladies: Female Slaveholders and the Creation of Britain's Atlantic Empire* (Chapel Hill: University of North Carolina Press, 2020).

Whitson, Agnes M., *The Constitutional Development of Jamaica, 1660–1729* (Manchester: Manchester University Press, 1929).

Wilson, Kathleen, 'The Performance of Freedom: Maroons in the Colonial Order in Eighteenth-Century Jamaica and the Atlantic Sound', *William and Mary Quarterly*, 66/1 (2009): 43–86.

Wright, Irene, 'The Spanish Resistance to the English Occupation of Jamaica, 1655–1660', *Transactions of the Royal Historical Society*, 13 (1930): 117–47.

Zahedieh, Nuala, '"A Frugal, Prudential and Hopeful Trade": Privateering in Jamaica, 1655–89', *Journal of Imperial and Commonwealth History*, 18/2 (1990): 145–68.

Zahedieh, Nuala, 'The Merchants of Port Royal, Jamaica, and the Spanish Contraband Trade, 1655–1692', *William and Mary Quarterly*, 3rd Series, 43/4 (1986): 570–93.

Zahedieh, Nuala, 'Trade, Plunder, and Economic Development in Early English Jamaica, 1655–1689', *Economic History Review*, 2nd Series, 39/2 (1986): 205–22.

Select Bibliography

Chapter 4 From Slavery to Freedom, 1775–1865

Brathwaite, Edward, *The Development of Creole Society in Jamaica 1770–1820* (Oxford: Clarendon Press, 1971).

Brown, Vincent, *Tacky's Revolt: The Story of an Atlantic Slave War* (Cambridge, MA: Harvard University Press, 2020).

Brown, Vincent, *The Reaper's Garden: Death and Power in the World of Atlantic Slavery* (Cambridge, MA: Harvard University Press, 2008).

Craton, Michael and James Walvin, *A Jamaican Plantation: The History of Worthy Park, 1670–1970* (London: W. H. Allen, 1970).

Green, William A., *British Slave Emancipation: The Sugar Colonies and the Great Experiment, 1830–1865* (Oxford: Oxford University Press, 1976).

Hall, Douglas, *Free Jamaica: An Economic History, 1838–1865* (New Haven, CT: Yale University Press, 1959).

Heuman, Gad, *'The Killing Time': The Morant Bay Rebellion in Jamaica* (Knoxville, TN: University of Tennessee Press, 1994).

Heuman, Gad, *Between Black and White: Race, Politics and the Free Coloureds in Jamaica, 1792–1865* (Westport, CT: Greenwood Press, 1981).

Higman, B. W., *Plantation Jamaica, 1750–1850: Capital and Control in a Colonial Economy* (Mona: University of the West Indies Press, 2005).

Higman, B. W., *Slave Populations of the British Caribbean, 1807–1834* (Baltimore: Johns Hopkins University Press, 1984).

Higman, B. W., *Slave Population and Economy in Jamaica, 1807–1834* (Cambridge: Cambridge University Press, 1976).

Holt, Thomas C., *The Problem of Freedom: Race, Labor, and Politics in Jamaica and Britain, 1832–1938* (Baltimore: The Johns Hopkins University Press, 1992).

McDonald, Roderick, *The Economy and Material Culture of Slaves: Goods and Chattels on the Sugar Plantations of Jamaica and Louisiana* (Baton Rouge: Louisiana State University Press, 1993).

Paton, Diana, *No Bond but the Law: Punishment, Race, and Gender in Jamaican State Formation, 1780–1870* (Durham, NC: Duke University Press, 2004).

Petley, Christer, *White Fury: A Jamaican Slaveholder and the Age of Revolution* (Oxford: Oxford University Press, 2018).

Petley, Christer, *Slaveholders in Jamaica: Colonial Society and Culture during the Era of Abolition* (London: Pickering and Chatto, 2009).

Robotham, Don, *'The Notorious Riot': The Socio-Economic and Political Bases of Paul Bogle's Revolt* (Kingston: Institute of Social and Economic Research, 1981).

Ryden, David Beck, *West Indian Slavery and British Abolition, 1783–1807* (Cambridge: Cambridge University Press, 2009).

Shepherd, Verene, *Livestock, Sugar and Slavery: Contested Terrain in Colonial Jamaica* (Kingston: Ian Randle, 2009).

Sivapragasam, Michael, *After the Treaties: A Social, Economic and Demographic History of Maroon Society in Jamaica, 1739–1842* (PhD thesis, University of Southampton, 2018).

Smith, Matthew J., *Liberty, Fraternity, Exile: Jamaica and Haiti after Emancipation* (Chapel Hill: University of North Carolina Press, 2014).

Turner, Mary, *Slaves and Missionaries: The Disintegration of Jamaican Slave Society, 1787–1834* (Urbana: University of Illinois Press, 1982).

Turner, Sasha, *Contested Bodies: Pregnancy, Childrearing, and Slavery in Jamaica, 1770–1834* (Philadelphia: University of Pennsylvania Press, 2017).

Ward, J. R., *British West Indian Slavery: The Process of Amelioration, 1750–1834* (Oxford: Oxford University Press, 1984).

Williams, Eric, *Capitalism and Slavery* (Chapel Hill: University of North Carolina Press, 1944).

Wilmot, Swithin R., *Freedom in Jamaica: Challenges and Opportunities, 1838–1865* (Kingston: Jamaica Information Service, 1997)

Chapter 5 The Shadow of Colonialism, 1865–1945

Altink, Henrice, *Public Secrets: Race and Colour in Colonial and Independent Jamaica* (Liverpool: Liverpool University Press, 2019).

Altink, Henrice, *Destined for a Life of Service: Defining African-Jamaican Womanhood, 1865–1938* (Manchester: Manchester University Press, 2011).

Barringer, Tim and Modest, Wayne, eds., *Victorian Jamaica* (Durham, NC: Duke University Press, 2018).

Brereton, Bridget ed., *UNESCO General History of the Caribbean, Vol. 5: The Twentieth Century* (London: Macmillan, 2003).

Bryan, Patrick, 'The Settlement of the Chinese in Jamaica: 1854-c. 1970', *Caribbean Quarterly*, 50/2 (2004): 15–25.

Bryan, Patrick, 'The White Minority in Jamaica at the End of the Nineteenth Century', in Howard Johnson and Karl Watson, eds., *The White Minority in the Caribbean* (Kingston: Ian Randle, 1998).

Bryan, Patrick, *The Jamaican People, 1880–1902* (London: Macmillan, 1991).

Bryan, Patrick and Rupert Lewis, eds., *Marcus Garvey: His Work and Impact*, rev. ed. (Trenton, NJ: Africa World Press, 1995).

Eisner, Gisela, *Jamaica 1830–1930: A Study in Economic Growth* (Westport, CN: Greenwood Press, 1961).

Ewing, Adam, *Age of Garvey: How a Jamaican Activist Created a Mass Movement and Changed Global Black Politics* (Princeton, NJ: Princeton University Press, 2014).

Grant, Colin, *Negro with a Hat: The Rise and Fall of Marcus Garvey* (London: Jonathan Cape, 2008).

Hart, Richard, *Rise and Organise: The Birth of the Workers and National Movements in Jamaica (1936–1939)* (London: Karia Press, 1987).

Holt, Thomas C., *The Problem of Freedom: Race, Labor, and Politics in Jamaica and Britain, 1832–1938* (Baltimore, MD: Johns Hopkins University Press, 1992).

Howe, Glenford, *Race, War and Nationalism: A Social History of West Indians in the First World War* (Kingston: Ian Randle, 2000).

Jones, Margaret, *Public Health in Jamaica 1850–1940: Neglect, Philanthropy and Development* (Kingston: University of the West Indies Press, 2013).

Laurence, K. O., ed., *UNESCO General History of the Caribbean, Vol. 4: The Long Nineteenth Century: Nineteenth-Century Transformations* (London: Macmillan, 1997).

Lewis, Rupert, *Marcus Garvey: Anti-Colonial Champion* (London: Karia Press, 1987).

Moore, Brian L. and Michele A. Johnson, *'They Do as They Please': The Jamaican Struggle for Cultural Freedom after Morant Bay* (Kingston: University of the West Indies Press, 2011).

Moore, Brian L. and Michele A. Johnson, *Neither Led nor Driven: Contesting British Cultural Imperialism in Jamaica* (Kingston: University of the West Indies Press, 2004).

Moore, Brian L. and Michele A. Johnson, eds., *The Land We Live in: Jamaica in 1890* (Kingston: Social History Project, University of the West Indies, 2000).

Moore, Brian L. Moore and Michele A. Johnson, eds., *'Squalid Kingston' 1890–1920* (Kingston: Social History Project, University of the West Indies, 2000).

Palmer, Colin A., *Freedom's Children: The 1938 Labor Rebellion and the Birth of Modern Jamaica* (Chapel Hill: University of North Carolina Press, 2014).

Phelps, O. W., 'Rise of the Labour Movement in Jamaica', *Social and Economic Studies*, 9/4 (1960): 417–68.

Riley, James C., *Poverty and Life Expectancy: The Jamaica Paradox* (Cambridge: Cambridge University Press, 2005).

Roberts, G. W., *The Population of Jamaica* (Cambridge: Cambridge University Press, 1957).

Satchell, Veront M., *From Plots to Plantations: Land Transactions in Jamaica, 1866–1900* (Mona: Institute of Social and Economic Research, University of the West Indies, 1990).

Sheller, Mimi, *Democracy after Slavery: Black Publics and Peasant Radicalism in Haiti and Jamaica* (Gainesville: University Press of Florida, 2000).

Shepherd, Verene, *Transients to Settlers: The Experience of Indians in Jamaica, 1845–1950* (Leeds: Peepal Tree Press, 1994).

Smith, Richard, *Jamaica Volunteers in the First World War: Race, Masculinity and the Development of National Consciousness* (Manchester: Manchester University Press, 2004).

Stolberg, Claus and Wilmot, Swithin, eds., *Plantation Economy, Land Reform and the Peasantry in Historical Perspective: Jamaica, 1838–1980* (Kingston: Friedrich Ebert Siftung, 1992).

Will, H. A., *Constitutional Change in the British West Indies, 1880–1903: with Special Reference to Jamaica, British Guiana, and Trinidad* (Oxford: Oxford University Press, 1970).

Chapter 6 Modern Jamaica, 1945–2022

Altink, Henrice, *Public Secrets: Race and Colour in Colonial and Independent Jamaica* (Liverpool: Liverpool University Press, 2019).

Arnold, Bertram, *N. W. Manley and the Making of Modern Jamaica* (Kingston: Arawak, 2016).

Barrett, Leonard E., *The Rastafarians* (Boston: Beacon, 1997).

Brereton, Bridget, ed., *General History of the Caribbean. Volume V: The Caribbean in the Twentieth Century* (London: Macmillan, 2003).

Bryan, Patrick, *Edward Seaga and the Challenges of Modern Jamaica* (Kingston: University of the West Indies Press, 2011).

Bryan, Patrick, *Inside Out & Outside In: Factors in the Creation of Contemporary Jamaica* (Kingston: Grace Kennedy Foundation, 2000).

Chevannes, Barrington, *Rastafari: Roots and Ideology* (Kingston: University of the West Indies Press, 1995).

Clarke, Colin, 'From Slum to Ghetto: Multiple Deprivation in Kingston, Jamaica', in D. McGregor, D. Dodman and D. Barker, eds., *Global Change and Caribbean Vulnerability: Environment, Economy and Society at Risk* (Kingston: University of the West Indies Press, 2010).

Clarke, Colin, *Decolonizing the Colonial City: Urbanization and Stratification in Kingston, Jamaica* (Oxford: Oxford University Press, 2006).

Clarke, Colin, 'Politics, Violence and Drugs in Kingston, Jamaica', *Bulletin of Latin American Research*, 25/3 (2006): 420–40.

Cooper, Carolyn, *Soundclash: Jamaican Dancehall Culture at Large* (New York: Palgrave Macmillan, 2004).

Duval, David Timothy, ed., *Tourism in the Caribbean: Trends, Development, Prospects* (London: Routledge, 2004).

Eaton, George, *Alexander Bustamante and Modern Jamaica* (Kingston: Kingston, 1975).

Johnson, Hume and Kamille Gentles-Peart, eds., *Brand Jamaica: Reimagining a National Image and Identity* (Lincoln: University of Nebraska Press, 2019).

Mawby, Spencer, *Ordering Independence: The End of Empire in the Anglophone Caribbean, 1947–1969* (Basingstoke: Palgrave Macmillan, 2012).

Nettleford, Rex, ed., *Jamaica in Independence: Essays on the Early Years* (Kingston: Heinemann, 1989).

Nettleford, Rex, *Caribbean Cultural Identity: The Case of Jamaica* (Kingston: Institute of Jamaica, 1979).

Palmer, Colin A., *Inward Yearnings: Jamaica's Journey to Nationhood* (Kingston: University of the West Indies Press, 2016).

Patterson, Orlando, *The Confounding Island: Jamaica and the Postcolonial Predicament* (Cambridge, MA: The Belknap Press of Harvard University Press, 2019).

Riley, James C., *Poverty and Life Expectancy: The Jamaica Paradox* (Cambridge: Cambridge University Press, 2005).

Smith, Godfrey, *Michael Manley: The Biography* (Kingston: Ian Randle, 2016).

Smith, M. G., Roy Augier and Rex Nettleford, *The Rastafari Movement in Kingston, Jamaica* (Mona: University of the West Indies Press, 1960).

Stolzoff, Norman C., *Wake the Town and Tell the People: Dancehall Culture in Jamaica* (Durham, NC: Duke University Press, 2000).

Taylor, F., *To Hell with Paradise: A History of the Jamaican Tourist Industry* (Pittsburgh: University of Pittsburgh Press, 1993).

Thomas, Deborah A., *Modern Blackness: Nationalism, Globalization, and the Politics of Culture in Jamaica* (Durham, NC: Duke University Press, 2004).

Wiley, James, ed., *The Banana: Empire, Trade Wars and Globalization* (Lincoln: University of Nebraska Press, 2008).

INDEX

abolitionists, 178
Aboukir, 34
absenteeism, 180
Accompong Town, 81, 145,
    168-9
Aguacadiba, 14
Albemarle, Governor, 93
Alligator Pond, Manchester
    parish, 14
Altink, Henrice, 230
Amazon Basin, 13
amelioration, 172, 194
American War of Independence,
    148, 152
Ameyro, 14, 48
Anancy, 268, 365
Anancy spiders, 176
Anderson, O. E., 294
Anglo-American Caribbean
    Commission (AACC), 301
Anglo-Dutch war of 1665-7, 87
Angola, 320
Antigua, 171
Antonelli, Juan Bautista, 75
apprentices, 196, 198, 200-1, 208
apprenticeship, 194, 197-9, 203
Arawaks, 13
Archaic Age, 12
areytos, 26
asiento, 62, 108, 144
Atabey, 34
attorneys, 123
Avila, Don Gil Gonzales de, 54
axes, 32

Bahamas, 45
Balcarres, Earl of, 168
bammie, 31
bananas, 253
Banton, Buju, 369
Baptist, 192, 204, 245, 270
Baptist Free Church, 271
Baptist Missionary Society,
    188, 222
Baptist War, 168, 185, 187, 193
Barbados, 78, 103, 110, 171, 174,
    241, 289, 309
barbakoa (barbecue), 17
Barclays Bank, 319
Barham, Henry, 56, 84
Barrett estates, 189
batata (potato), 17
batey, 27
bateye, 35
Battle of Yorktown, 152
bauxite, 354-5, 386
Bay of Campeche, 84
Bay of Honduras, 84
Bayly, Zachary, 116
Beckford, Thomas, 116
Bedasee, Alerth, 366
Bedward, Alexander, 271-2, 285
Beeston, Sir William, 93
behique, 33, 36-8
Belafonte, Harry, 366
Belize, 13
Bellevue, 15
Belmore, Earl, 187
Bennett, Louise, 364

Index

Goodison, Lorna, 363
Goodson, William, 79
Gordon, Adam, 143, 225
Gordon, George W., 220, 222
Goshen estate, 219
Grant, Sir John Peter, 170, 232, 234, 241
great house, 179
Great Reform Act, 194
Great River, 20
Greater Antilles, 12
Grenada, 323
Grey, David, 186
Griddles, 30
Guabanex, 33
Guaca, 33
Guanaboa, 14
guinea grass, 119, 157
Gun Court Act, 320
Guyana, 317

Haiti, 17, 183
Half-Way Tree, 261
hamaka (hammock, 17
Hamilton, John, 133
Hanover parish, 134, 150, 185, 192
Harlem, 280
Harvey, Thomas, 203
Havana, 67, 323
health authorities, 337
healthcare, 336
Helyar, Cary, 107
Herb McKenley Stadium, 371
Heuman, Gad, 256
Higgins, Warrior, 238
higglers, 257
Higman, B. W., 180, 185
Hill, Richard, 221
Hispaniola, 10–13, 15, 17, 28, 45, 47–50, 53–4, 56, 58, 61, 64, 76–8, 80, 86
Holding, Michael, 372

Holland Hill, 15
Holness, Andrew, 332–4, 339, 341, 371, 387
Hope plantation, 121
Hope Tavern, 15
Hopewell plantation, 201
hospitals, 337
House of Commons, 171, 187
Howell, Leonard, 285, 287
Huggins, Sir John, 299
Huie, Albert, 363
Human Employment and Resources Training (HEART) Trust, 340
Hume, Benjamin, 116
hurricanes, 17, 22, 151, 240, 358

immediate emancipation, 194
indentured contracts, 98
indentured servants, 98, 244
Independence Park, 371
Indian indentured workers, 213
Indian migrants, 245–7
Industrial Incentives Law, 308
infant mortality, 172, 181, 241
influenza pandemic, 240
Institute for Jamaica, 265, 359
internal exchange, 157

Jacks Hill, 15
Jackson, Captain William, 75
Jamaica
  agriculture, 29, 64, 249, 352
  archaeological remains, 14–15, 40, 43, 128
  Assembly, 91–2, 140, 166, 191
  census, 159, 239, 247
  climate, 21–2
  diseases, 101, 109, 121, 241, 243
  English invasion of, 78–81
  food resources, 29–30, 65, 68, 121, 135

441

Index